TERPSICHORE

CODE OF TERPSICHORE:

A

PRACTICAL AND HISTORICAL TREATISE,

ON

THE BALLET,

DANCING, AND PANTOMIME;

WITH

A COMPLETE THEORY

OF

THE ART OF DANCING:

INTENDED AS WELL FOR THE INSTRUCTION OF AMATEURS AS THE USE OF PROFESSIONAL PERSONS.

BY C. BLASIS,

PRINCIPAL DANCER AT THE KING'S THEATRE, AND COMPOSER OF BALLETS.

TRANSLATED UNDER THE AUTHOR'S IMMEDIATE INSPECTION,

BY R. BARTON.

" Terpsichore affectus citharis movet, imperat, auget."—VIRGIL.

LONDON:

PRINTED FOR JAMES BULCOCK, 163, STRAND.

1828.

One of a series of republications by Dance Horizons, 1801 East 26th Street, Brooklyn, N.Y. 11229

This is an unabridged republication of the first edition published for James Bulcock, London, in 1928.

International Standard Book Number 0-87127-055-2

Library of Congress Catalog Card Number 75-9166

Printed in the United States of America

The copy from which this facsimile edition was reproduced contained the title pages for the first and second editions of this work and both are reprinted here. Originally titled *The Code of Terpsichore*, the second edition changed the title to *The Art of Dancing*.

THE

ART OF DANCING.

COMPRISING ITS

THEORY AND PRACTICE,

AND A

HISTORY OF ITS RISE AND PROGRESS,

FROM THE EARLIEST TIMES.

INTENDED AS WELL FOR

THE INSTRUCTION OF AMATEURS

AS THE

USE OF PROFESSIONAL PERSONS.

BY C. BLASIS,

PRINCIPAL DANCER AT THE KING'S THEATRE, AND COMPOSER OF BALLETS.

TRANSLATED, UNDER THE AUTHOR'S IMMEDIATE INSPECTION,

BY R. BARTON.

THE SECOND EDITION.

LONDON:

PRINTED FOR EDWARD BULL, HOLLES STREET.

1831.

PREFACE.

THE works hitherto published on the Art of Dancing, the composition and performance of Ballets and Pantomimes, are few in number, and, in the opinion of those who are best qualified to judge, deficient in sterling merit and general utility. The subject has certainly been treated by Noverre in a masterly manner, considering the time when he wrote, and the apparent intention of his labours; he threw many new and brilliant lights upon the art, but his letters were more adapted to instruct the Professor than to improve the pupil, even at the time of their publication; and the art has since advanced with such rapidity, that his works are now of little use to either. The greater part of those who have written on this subject seem to have been persons of taste, talent and learning; but they, evidently, were not dancers: so that, however attractive their productions may be to the general reader, the lounger, or the literary man, they are of little practical utility to the Mime, the Dancer or the Ballet-master. They contain a string of theoretic and unconnected ideas, but do not develope the powers and practice of the art, in all its various branches. In fact, a practical work adapted to the present day, and calculated at once to assist the professor, to enlighten and amuse the amateur, and to instruct the student, appeared to have been a desideratum. Impressed with the truth of these remarks, after several years of study, research, and practical experience, encouraged by many, whose opinions he values most highly, emboldened by the flattering reception which several of his papers already published on different portions of the subject met with on the Continent, the Author resolved on undertaking the composition of a work on the origin and progress,—the theory and practice of dancing, and the composition and performance of the Pantomime and Ballet. He has proposed ameliorations as he advanced, and offered a new method of instruction, which is more certain, as well as shorter, than those at present followed: he has endeavoured to give a greater latitude to Pantomime than the art has hitherto been allowed; to apply the rules and various styles of the regular drama to the composition of Pantomime; to show that Ballets should not be mere *divertissements* or dancing *spectacles;* that the art not only aspires to, but can even give evidence of, her rightful claim to a higher rank among her sisters, than many persons, judging only from what they have seen, may be induced to imagine; that all the passions of the human heart,—the comic and the serious, the terrible and the ludicrous, have been, and still may be, perfectly expressed by a skilful Ballet-master and an accomplished Mime. He has attempted to treat the subject in such a manner as to enlighten and instruct those who profess or study the art, without becoming dull or uninteresting to the general reader of taste and education. Such have been the Author's objects; enamoured of his art, and zealous for its advancement in a great, a learned, and a polished nation, his most ardent desire is, that the present work, which has been conceived and executed in the heart of England, may meet with a favourable, or rather an indulgent, reception from its people, and be in some measure conducive to their pleasures, by tending to ameliorate one of their most elegant and rational amusements.

London, August, 1828.

PART THE FIRST.

RISE AND PROGRESS

OF

DANCING.

THE study of the Fine Arts is the most pleasing occupation to which the human mind can be dedicated. It entertains us; and the clouds which the labours and cares of life often cast over our spirits are, for a while, agreeably dispersed :—nor is amusement the only advantage attending this study; its utility is also very conspicuous. The knowledge of one branch or other of the fine arts has immortalized many men; and some nations, by moral superiority, which their cultivation has given them over others, have been rendered for ever illustrious and celebrated.

The countries where a Newton calculated infinity; where a Shakspeare and a Milton wrote; where a Bramante and a Michael Angelo built; where Raphael painted, and where *Cinna, Athalie, &c.*, were composed, are the first countries in the world. The rest, with regard to the fine arts, are but mere barbarians or children, notwithstanding their antiquity, and all that nature has done for them.

I have, in these preliminary remarks, perhaps, departed from my subject ; but let the motive plead my excuse. The arts are linked together in one and the same chain ; poetry, music, painting and dancing bear a strong affinity to each other, and the enjoyments we derive from them merit an equal gratitude and homage ; and most enviable are they whose souls are susceptible of the pleasures which they inspire.

> " Le véritable esprit sait se plier à tout ;
> On ne vit qu' à demi quand on n'a qu'un seul goût."
>
> VOLTAIRE.

Singing, no less delightful than natural to man, must, in its progress have inspired him with certain gestures relative to the various sounds which he uttered. His breast became agitated ; his arms opened or approached each other ; his feet began to form certain steps, more or less rapid ; his features participated in these movements ; in short, his whole body was soon responsive to the sounds that vibrated in his ears. And thus singing, which was the expression of one pleasure, gave rise to another, innate, but till then unknown ; to which we have given the name of dancing. Such were unquestionably, the primitive causes of the origin of this art.

Music and dancing have a very strong ascendancy over our intellectual faculties. " La musique," says d'Alembert, " tantôt douce et insinuante, tantôt folâtre et gaie, tantôt simple et naîve, tantôt enfin sublime et pathetique, tour à tour nous charme, nous éleve et nous dechîre."

The powers of this enchanting art are well known to every one. The learned Saverio Mattei relates, that the republic of Rome had expressly established a college of

Tibicini, whose device was composed of the five following letters: Q.S.P.P.S. " *qui sacris publicis præsto sunt.*" They were held in high estimation, and treated in an honourable manner; they might even aspire to the first dignities in the commonwealth. Sometimes they were priests of Jupiter and augurs; at others, admirals of fleets, captains of legions, commanders of the cavalry, &c., and History speaks of them in many places[1].

The name of the Muse, Terpsichore, who presides over the dance, is composed of two Greek words, τερπω, to delight, and χοεος the dance; and the name of the Muse Euterpe, who presides over music, is derived from two words, ευ well, and τερπω to delight.

The former appears to have been created for climates that are under the influence of a torrid sun. It is a pleasure everywhere—there it is a passion; warmed by an incessant heat, the glowing constitution of the native of the South, contains the seed of every pleasure; each moment of his rapid existence seems to him made only for enjoyment. The inhabitant of the North, forced by nature to maintain a constant combat with the rigours of the seasons, seldom aspires to delight. His whole care is engrossed in securing himself from snows and frosts. The roughness of his manners almost extinguishes his sensibility; and the delicate sentiments that voluptuousness imparts are to him wholly unknown.

How could dancing, that amiable offspring of pleasure, display her gracefulness and attractions amid perpetual ice and never melting snows?

Music and dancing are nearly coeval with the world. The Egyptians, the Persians, the Indians, the Jews, and the Arcadians, the most ancient of nations; Amphion, Orpheus, Chiron, Thamyris, the prophetess Miriam, David, and others, together with the dances that the

Israelites performed in honour of the golden calf, proclaim its antiquity. These two arts were in the sequel reduced to certain rules and limits by ingenious and inventive artists.

We are informed by Moses that the inventor of music was Jubal, who was of the family of Cain; and that his brother, Tubalcain, was a worker in brass and iron [3]. It is, therefore, to be supposed that he conceived the idea from the reiterated blows of his brother's hammers on the anvil, the sounds of which induced him to compose musical tones, and regulate their time and cadence. But Macrobius and Boetius give the honour of the discovery to Pythagoras, which he made in a similar manner. They say, that as the philosopher passed by a forge, he remarked the sounds that issued from the anvil as the hammers struck on it in rotation; and the variety of notes thus produced, gave him the first hint towards laying down rules for the art of melody.

With respect to the origin of dancing, Burette has gathered the following information from ancient writers:—Opinions do not agree as to the names and country of those from whom the Greeks received the first lessons of such an exercise (dancing). Some pretend, and amongst the number Theophrastus, that a certain flute player, named Andron, a native of Catania, in Sicily, was the first who accompanied the notes of his flute with various movements of the body, which fell in harmony with his music; and that it was for this reason that the ancient Greeks expressed the verb to dance by σιχετίζεω, wishing it thereby to be understood, that they originally derived dancing from Sicily.

Lucian attributes its invention to Rhea, who taught it to her priests in Phrygia, and the Island of Crete [3]. Others suppose that it is owing to the Tomans, or, at least, that it was they who brought it to perfection. These last seemed more than any other people destined by nature to practise it. They excelled in voluptuous dances.

Dancing and music were more particularly cultivated by the Greeks than by the rest of the ancients. The Athenians were fond of the former in the extreme. Plato and Socrates approved of it; the Thessalians and Lacedemonians deemed it equal in rank, with any other of the fine arts [4].

Cliophantes, of Thebes, and Eschylus greatly advanced the progress of dancing. The latter introduced it in his pieces, and, by uniting together all the imitative arts, gave the first models of theatrical representations. Painting had a great share in adding to their charm, and the pencil of Agatharcus, under the directions of that celebrated dramatist, traced the first ornaments of a stage. This Agatharcus wrote a work upon Scenic Architecture, which must have then been very valuable and useful.

A few centuries afterwards, when the Romans exhibited magnificent and ravishing spectacles in the same style as the Greeks, dancing obtained the praises of Lucian, Apuleius, Martial, Seneca, &c., and was especially practised in pantomimes, a sort of performance wholly unknown to the Greeks. These pieces were composed of comic or heroic subjects, expressed by gesture and dances. The names of Pyladus, and Bathyllus, the original authors of the pantomimic art, remain celebrated on the pages of history, as famous performers of these kind of ballets, then called *Italic dances.*

> "La Pantomime est dûe à l'antique Italie,
> Où même elle eclipsa Melpoméne et Thalie."

CHENIER.

The Romans were all enraptured with these pantomimes and blessed the tyrant (Augustus), whose policy well knew how advantageous it was to him to afford them amusement. The primitive Romans called dancing *Saltatio*, and the Greeks, *Orchesis*. Salius, an Arcadian, was the first who taught the former the *Ars Saltationis*. With them, therefore, the original dance was the Salian, which consisted in the imitation of all the gestures and motions that man can possibly make. In this class of gymnastics, the mimicks and buffoons usually exercised themselves.

According to the information we derive from such authors as have treated of the dances of their times, I am of opinion that this *Saltation*, properly so called, must have been something very similar to the grotesque kind of performance so prevalent in Italy, a few years ago, but which seems at present almost banished from the theatres of that country. The Italian grotesque is nothing but leaps, tumbling, feats of strength, &c. and cannot be endured except in ballets of the burlesque and extravagant kind. Marino describes a grotesque actor in the following manner:—

"One who ventures on prodigious exertions, so extraordinary, and so dangerous, that they inspire at once both horror and admiration [5]."

The corruption that had crept into the theatrical exhibitions of ancient Rome, induced Trajan to forbid them entirely; in consequence of which they were for awhile abandoned. Some time after that emperor's death, they again made their appearance, but still accompanied with the same obscenities, to which they owed their decline. The christian pontiffs, therefore, followed the example of Trajan by prohibiting them again.

At length, after a lapse of some ages, modern Italy brought forth Bergonzo di Botta, the reviver of dancing, music, and histrionic diversions. He signalized himself in the fête which he prepared for Galeazzo, Duke of Milan, on the marriage of that prince, with Isabella of Arragon[6]. The taste and magnificence displayed in this superb festival at Tortona, was imitated by all the principal towns of Italy, who seemed eager to concur in the regeneration of those agreeable arts.

Italy has, at different times been the garden of every art and science. It was there that Dante, Columbus, Galileo, and Machiavel were born; and there also was the enchanting Terpsichore honoured under a more pleasing and elegant form, than antiquity had bestowed upon her.

> "D'ogni bell' Arte non sei madre, o Italia?
>
>   SILVIO PELLICO.

We may, therefore, say that the Italians were the first to subject the arms, legs, and body to certain rules; which regulation took place in the sixteenth century. Before that time they danced, in my opinion, much in the same manner as the Greeks and Romans had done before them, which was, by giving high leaps, making extravagant contortions, uncouth and indelicate motions, and resting in the most unbecoming attitudes. A common-place practice was the only instruction such dancers received[7]. The greater or less pleasure they enjoyed in their performance, occasioned them more or less to excel. Dancing (as an art) was then only in its infancy.

Taste and experience having, at length, established precepts whereby the steps, attitudes, and motions, were systematically arranged, all was done afterwards, according to method, and in strict harmony with the time and cadence of the accompanying music. The works of the best sculptors and painters must have served as models towards the attainment of grace and elegance, in the various positions adopted in dancing, as they did to the

Greeks and Romans in their dumb shews, &c. Dancing thus made rapid strides towards being perfected and rendered a more pleasing and imitative art; especially when united with pantomime.

Dancing, pantomime, and histrionic splendour have, in our days, been carried to the highest point of perfection. With respect to magnificence, truth of imitation in costume and scenery, nothing can be compared to the theatres of the principal towns of Italy—none can be admitted to dispute with them the palm of excellence, but the opera of Paris, and the theatres of Drury Lane, and Covent Garden, of London. One reason that may be urged for Italian superiority in theatricals, is, that the inhabitants of that country greatly resemble their ancestors, the Romans, when the universal cry was " Panem et Circenses !" The taste and style of the present decoration, the powers of our machinery, and the talent now displayed by performers, far surpass the infantine attempts of the ancients.

Notwithstanding the vicious taste, and even ignorance, with which our forefathers are reproached by modern innovators, we have not extended much beyond them the principles of the art. Our execution is ·unquestionably more graceful, complicated, and bold than that of our old masters; but, is it not to them that we are indebted for our pre-eminence? They afforded us the means of surpassing them; they showed us the paths that led to perfection; they pointed out the goal to us, and we attained it.

I will prove this by quoting a few stanzas from Marino's celebrated poem of *Adonis*, which will also serve as an authority for what I have said concerning the origin of modern dancing, and Italian dancers. The amateur will find in them many interesting details, and the professor much useful knowledge of his art. I have never seen any thing so truly descriptive and pleasing.

The poet exaggerates at times, but that is a prerogative of his muse; all he says is, however, in the order of possibilities. He enables us to judge of the state in which dancing was, two centuries ago; and the parallel that I shall draw, by means of notes, between the steps and attitudes of those times, and such as we now practise, may be of some interest to the reader.

Marino displays much taste and knowledge in the art, which he here treats of. What he tells us of Terpsichore, fully explains to us the improvement of which dancing was susceptible at its origin. This modern Ovid, in the twentieth canto of his poem, makes Venus institute games to celebrate the obsequies of Adonis. All the divinities assemble to dispute the different prizes. The muse of dancing bounds into the lists, and pompously exhibits her skill. The following is the animated description which the enthusiasm of the poet has produced:—

" ——— Soletta a ballar resta in disparte
     Tersicore, che diva è di quell' arte.

Si ritragge da capo, innanzi fassi,
     Piega il ginocchio, e move il piè spedito,
     E studia ben come dispensi i passi [8],
     Mentre del dotto suon segue l'invito [9].
     Circonda il campo, e raggirando vassi
     Pria che proceda a carolar più trito,
     Sí lieve, che porria, benchè profonde,
     Premer senz' offender le vie dell' onde [10].

Sul vago pié si libra, e il vago piede
     Movendo a passo misurato e lento,
     Con maestria, con leggiadria si vede
     Portar la vita in cento guise e cento [11].

Or si scosta, or si accosta, or fugge, or riede,
Or, a manca, or, a destra in un momento [12],
Scorrendo il suol, siccome suol baleno
Dell' aria estiva il limpido sereno [13].

E con sì destri, e ben composti moti
  Radendo in prima il pian si avvolge ed erra,
Che non si sa qual piede in aria roti,
  E qual fermo de' due tocchi la terra.
  Fa suoi corsi, e suoi giri or pieni, or voti,
  Quando l'orbe distorna, e quando il serra,
  Con partimenti sì minuti, e spessi,
  Che il Meandro non ha tanti reflessi [14].

Divide il tempo, e la misura eguale,
  Ed osserva in ogni atto ordine e norma,
Secondo che ode il sonatore, e quale
  O grave il suono, o concitato ei forma,
  Tal col piede atteggiando o scende, sale,
  E va tarda, o veloce a stampar l'orma [15].
  Fiamma ed onda somiglia, e turbo, e biscia,
  Se poggia, o cala, o si rivolge, o striscia [16].

Fan bel concerto l'un e l'altro fianco
  Per le parti di mezzo, e per l'estreme,
Moto il destro non fa che subit' anco
  Non l'accompagni il suo compagno in sieme [17].
  Concordi i piè, mentre si vibra il manco,
  L'altro ancor con la punta il terren preme.
  Tempo non batte mai scarso, o soverchio,
  Nè tira a caso mai linea, nè cerchio [18].

Tien ne' passaggi suoi modo diverso,
  Come diverso è de' concenti il tuono.
Tanti nè fa per dritto, per traverso,
  Quante le pause, e le periodi sone.
  E tutta pronta ad ubbidire al verso,
  Che il cenno insegna del maestro suono,
  Or si avanza, or si arretra, or smonta, or balza,
  E sempre con ragion si abbassa ed alza [19].

Talor le fughe arresta, il corso posa,
    Indi muta tenore in un istante,
    E con geometria maravigliosa
    Apre il compasso delle vague piante,
    Onde viene a stampar sfera ingegnosa,
    E rota a quella del pavon sembiante,
    Tengono i piè la periferia e il centro,
    Quel volteggia di fuor, questo sta dentro [20].

Sul sinistro sostiensi, in forme nove
    L'agil corpo sì ratto aggira intorno,
    Che con fretta minor si volge e move
    Il volubil paleo, l'agevol torno.
    Con grazia poi non più veduta altrove
    Fá gentilmente, onde partì ritorno.
    Si erge, e sospende, e ribalzando inalo
    Rompe l'aria per mezzo, e trincia il saltro [21].

Il capo inchina pria che in alto saglia,
    E gamba, a gamba intreccia, ed incrocicchia,
    Dalle braccia ajutato il corpo scaglia,
    La persona ritira, e si rannicchia.
    Poi spicca il lancio, e mentre l'aria taglia,
    Due volte con l'un piè l'altro, si picchia,
    E fá battendo, e ribattendo entrambe
    Sollevata dal pian, guizzar le gambe [22].

Poiché ella è giunta in su quanto più pote,
    La vedi in giù diminuir cadente,
    E nel cader si lieve il suol percote,
    Che scossa, o calpestio non se ne sente,
    E bel veder con che mirabil rote
    Sullo spazio primier piombi repente,
    Come più snella, alfin che strale, o lampo,
    Discorra a salti, e cavriole il campo [23].

      [See Translation at the end of the Notes.]

Setting aside poetical exaggeration this gives us a tolerably good idea of the estimation in which dancing was held in the 16th century, and of the manner in which it was executed. Connoisseurs will best appreciate its merit.

Italian dancing was universally applauded, and excited the admiration and imitation of foreigners ; among whom the Spanish were the first to follow it. They at first partially succeeded ; the use of the castagnettes, which they added, produced a pleasing effect ; but having in the sequel incorporated with it a multiplicity of leaps, capers, uncouth postures, and, in short, the most graceless and extravagant motions ; the art of dancing in Spain became a degradation and a vice, whilst in Italy it preserved a certain dignity and decency. This corruption in style and taste among the Spaniards, must be chiefly attributed to the *Chica*, a dance of a very immoral nature, which the Moors had brought with them from Africa [24]. The native of the Peninsula, under the influence of the climate where he is born, and with the natural heat and vivacity of his constitution, eagerly received the *Chica*, which soon became one of his chief delights. To this dance I therefore ascribe the indelicacy, and sometimes even the lasciviousness so common in Spanish dancing. The *Chica* afterwards changed its name to that of *Fandango*, of which Dr. Yriarte speaks in the following terms:— " The melodious *Fandango* that spreads a joy through the souls of natives and foreigners, of sages and old men."—*(Abridgement of the History of Spain.)*

I cannot here omit the charming description which Marino, in the above quoted poem, gives of this dance. The poet records the true manner in which it was performed in his time ; and his time was nearly that of its origin.

" Due castagnette di sonoro bosso,
 Tien nelle man la Giovinetta ardita.
 Che accompagnando il piè con grazia mosso
 Fan forte ad or ad or scroccar le dita.

Regge con timpano l'altro il qual percosso
Con sonaglietti ad atteggiar l'invita ;
Ed alternando un bel concerto doppio
Al suono a tempo accordono lo scoppio.

Quanti moti a lascivia, e quanti gesti
Provocar ponno i più pudici affetti,
Quanto corromper può gli animi onesti,
Rappresentano agli occhi in vivi oggetti.
Cenni, e baci disegna or quella, or questi,
Fanno i fianchi ondeggiar, scontronsi i petti,
Socchiudon gli occhi e quasi infrá se stessi
Vengon danzando agli ultimi complessi."

[See Translation at the end of the Notes.]

The Fandango cannot be described in a more exact
and lively manner. The mode of its execution at present
is much the same. Marino declaims against its immorality and the abuse that was made of it in Spain and
afterwards in Italy. He calls it

———— oscena danza.
Pera il sozzo inventor, che trà noi questa
Introdusse primier barbara usanza.
Chiama questo suo gioco empio e profano
Saravanda [25], e Ciaccona [26], il novo Ispano*.

The Fandango, we thus perceive, again changed its
name, but suffered little variation in its character. It was
introduced into Italy but performed with more restraint.
Almost every Spanish dance, such as the *Bolero*, the
Cachucha, the *Seguidillas*, of Moorish origin, are imitations
of the African *Fandango* or *Chica*. They are therefore
all marked with that voluptuousness, I might even say
obscenity, which characterised their model.

* In English—" Perish the man who first introduced this obscene
and shocking dance among us !" The inhabitants of New Castile called
this profane exhibition by the name of Saravanda and Ciaccona.

Dancing, far from being, as among other nations, an innocent amusement is, with the Spanish an excitement to vice and immorality. Compare the national dances of the former with those of the latter, we shall see that the *Chica*, the *Fandango*, the *Sarao*[27], and a few others, bear the stamp of the strongest, deepest, and most immoderate passion, whilst the *Tarantella*, the *Fourlane*[28], the *Contredanse*[29], the *Provençale*, the *Mazourque*, commonly called *la Russe*[30], *l'Ecossaise*, *l'Allemande*, *la Hongroise*, &c., all well known popular dances, are kept within certain limits and forms, far more creditable to society.

The Neapolitan *Tarantella* is, of all modern dances, the liveliest and most diversified, but like the *Sicilienne*, it possesses much similitude to the Fandango.   Both are, I believe (but particularly the former), a mixture of Spanish and Italian dancing, and must have had their rise on the introduction of the Spanish style into Italy.

The *Tarantella*[31] is the national dance of the Neapolitans. It is gay and voluptuous ; its steps, attitudes and music, still exhibit the character of those who invented it.

This dance is generally supposed to have derived its name from the *Tarantella*, a venomous spider of Sicily. Those who have the misfortune to be bitten by it cannot escape dissolution but by a violent perspiration, which forces the poison out of the body through the pores. As exercise is the principal and surest method to effect this perspiration, it was discovered, by repeated experiments, that music was the only incentive to motion on the unhappy sufferers. It possessed the power of making them leap about, until extreme fatigue put an end to their exertions. They then fell, and the sweating thus occasioned, seldom failed of effecting a radical cure.

The music best adapted to the performance of this kind of miracle, is excessively lively; its notes and cadences strongly marked and of the $\frac{6}{8}$ measure. The reiterated strains of these *triolets*, together with the vivacity of the movement, are capable of electrifying frames, whose total derangement appears on the point of depriving them of animation [32].

Whether the Tarantella dance was first used as a remedy for the bite of the spider, or whether the attitudes and gestures with which the music inspired the sufferers, gave the first idea of forming them into a dance, it is impossible to determine ; but it owes its origin unquestionably to that complaint.

Love and pleasure are conspicuous throughout this dance. Each motion, each gesture is made with the most voluptuous gracefulness. Animated by the accompanying mandolines, tambourines and castagnettes, the woman tries, by her rapidity and liveliness, to excite the love of her partner, who, in his turn, endeavours to charm her with his agility, elegance and demonstrations of tenderness. The two dancers unite, separate, return, fly into each other's arms, again bound away, and in their different gestures alternately exhibit love, coquetry and inconstancy. The eye of the spectator is incessantly diverted with the variety of sentiments which they express; nor can any thing be more pleasing than their picturesque groups and evolutions. Sometimes they hold each other's hands, the man kneels down whilst the woman dances round him; then again he rises; again she starts from him, and he eagerly pursues. Thus their whole dance is but assault and defence, and defeat or victory appear equally their object.

The fall of certain powers in Italy, occasioned a decline in dancing and ballets. The Italians lost their taste for these amusements, and seemed to transfer them to the French. Catherine de Medicis made them the chief ornaments of her court. Baltaravim, a very successful director and composer, greatly advanced their progress, and did with respect to ballets, what Jodelle had already done with regard to tragedy. To Triffino, and to these two ingenious men, we are indebted for our theatres, tragedies, and ballets.

The encouragement which histrionic diversions received from Louis XIV., contributed in a powerful manner to their cultivation. This gay and liberal monarch ruling a nation ever devoted to pleasure, was particularly partial to ballets: he introduced them in all his fêtes, and the gardens of Versailles have been the scene of many a spectacle of this kind, exhibited in a style of unprecedented splendour and magnificence. The Chevalier Servandoni, a famous architect and perspective painter, offered to the public, on various theatres, a multiplicity of pieces, wherein music, pantomime and machinery were agreeably combined. This Florentine must be considered as one of the chief promoters of theatrical ballets,

" Oú tous les arts enchantent tous les sens*."

BERNARD.

Hence arose that scenic grandeur which the talents of successive artists, and especially those of the present age, have at length brought to so high a point of perfection.

The Parisian dancers established the real method of attaining a graceful and dignified execution; and the French school of dancing acquired a pre-eminence over all Europe, equal to that of the Italian school of music. A pre-eminence which both nations have ever since preserved.

* Where every art enchanteth every sense.

Lany, who has obtained some reputation as a dancer of the *demi-caractère*, ranks first among the ballet-masters of the opera of Paris. Beauchamps, the director of the ballets of Louis XIV.[33], Sodi, a famous pantomimic performer, De Hesse and Malter, were regarded as the best composers of their period. Pitrot succeeded them, and feeling in himself a capacity for heroic compositions, he brought forth his ballet of *Telemachus,* which met with considerable applause. His cotemporaries, Picq, an excellent dancer of the serious kind, Gaspard Angiolini and Canziani, distinguished themselves in the tragic line. Noverre came next, and carried stage-dancing many degrees towards perfection. Duprè, G. Vestris, Pitrot, and Gardel, the elder, were reckoned among the best of their time. Dumoulin surpassed them but little ; he excelled in *pas de deux*, and in his style of accompanying his partner in the different groups and attitudes. Fossan disputed the palm with him in the comic and pastoral.—Of the other sex, the most celebrated dancers were the Melles Sallé, Lany and Camargo, who followed and surpassed the Melles Guyot and Favier ; the first was a very graceful dancer of the graver sort, the second of the *demi-caractère,* and the third principally excelled in cross capering, and in dancing to the liveliest tunes. Prévot was her equal. Beauchamps, Pécour, Blondi, Ballon, Laval, Javilliers, Lépi, Melles Heinel, Pélin, &c., hold also an honourable rank among the disciples of Terpsichore. Melles Guimard and Allard, their successors, eclipsed many a name by the gracefulness and brilliancy of their steps.

Dauberval shone in the comic line, and that of the *demi-caractère ;* P. Gardel in the serious, and A. Vestris in a combination of both. These three, together with Laborie, Deshayes, Duport; Mesdames Chameroy, Gardel, Gosselin, the elder; Melles Léon, Fanni Bias, and Bigottini, all estimable supporters of the honours of Terpsichore, gave the finishing touches to this delightful art.

Messrs. Dauberval and Gardel stand pre-eminent as composers. The *Télémaque* and the *Fille mal gardée* of the former are justly regarded as perfect models of serious and of comic ballets; whilst the *Psyché, Achille á Scyros, Páris* and *La Dansomanie* of the latter, are proofs of his excellence in the mythological and anacreontic branch. He was also a fertile inventor of steps and dances. Didelot, the pupil of Dauberval obtained a brilliant success by his *Flore et Zephyre, Psyché* and *Cendrillon;* Coindé, author of the *Amours de Venus Pygmalion,* and *la Double Féle,* acquired an equal share of applause, and *Clary of* Milon, by his *Nina* and his *Ulysse;* Blache by his *Almaviva et Rosine,* and his *Filets de Vulcain;* and, finally, Aumer, by his *Antoine et Cleopatre* and his *Somnambule,* merit recording, as ingenious improvers in the composition of ballets.

Whilst dancing was making these rapid strides towards perfection in France, the degenerate taste of Italy was turned wholly on uncouth and graceless pantomimes. But the introduction of French composers and dancers, who were received there with applause and much encouraged, contributed in no small degree to ameliorate the style of performance in that country.

Noverre composed many of his ballets at Milan, from whence his method and taste began gradually to spread through the principal towns of Italy. He had a number of Italian pupils, among whom D. Rossi, F. Clerico, P. Franchi, Mazzarelli, P. Angiolini, and J. B. Giannini deserve to be mentioned, as artists who raised dancing from the abject state in which it was then languishing; but it is to Viganó and Gioia that dancing is indebted for its principal improvements.

As the Italians, in general, prefer strong emotions of terror in their theatrical amusements, their ballet-masters have chiefly succeeded in historical and tragical subjects. The French, on the contrary, are fond of the soft sentiments of refined love and tenderness; their composers dedicate themselves, therefore, almost exclusively to the anacreontic kind [34].

From all that I have hitherto said, we perceive that poetry, music and dancing, have agreeably occupied every nation. These arts, which are innate in man, could not, from the pleasure they afforded, fail of being cultivated. They were duly appreciated and esteemed. The orientals, from whom we received our first instructions in every thing, speak constantly in their favour. We all know how much music, and dancing in particular, are valued and practised among the Chinese, and cannot but own that these three arts have possessed an absolute sway over all those nations that enjoy a clear atmosphere and a beautiful sky.

The Iroquois, and even the Hurons, have their dances, their pantomimes and their music. The Italian comedians (in 1725) gave a very curious novelty at their theatre, in Paris, which occurs to me as a proof of my argument in the foregoing paragraph:—" Two savages, about twenty-five years of age, tall and well made, (says the author of the *Mercure de France*, Vol. II.) who lately came from Louisiana, performed three different sorts of dances, together and separately, and that in such a manner as not to leave the least doubt of their having learnt their steps and leaps at an immense distance from Paris. Their gestures are, undoubtedly, very easily understood in their country, but here nothing can be more difficult to make out. The first dancer represented a chief of his nation, rather more modestly dressed than the Louisianians generally are, but not so much as wholly to conceal his nakedness. He wore on his head a kind of crown, of considerable size, adorned with feathers of different colours. The other had nothing to distinguish him from a common warrior. The former, by his manner of dancing, and his various attitudes, expressed to the latter, that he came with a proposal of peace, and therefore, presented to him his *calumet,* or standard. After this they performed together the dance of peace. The second dance, which was warlike, exhibited an assembly of savages, who appeared to be deliberating as to a war against some other nation or tribe. They represented in their different gestures all the horrors of a combat. Those whose opinions were in favour of war joined in the dance, and thus expressed their votes. The third dance was performed in the following manner :—the warrior, armed with a bow and quiver full of arrows, pretended to go in quest of the enemy, whilst the other sat down and beat a kind of drum or tymbal, not larger than a common hat. Having discovered the enemy, the warrior returns and informs his chief of it. He then imitates a fight, wherein he pretends to have defeated the enemy ; after which both perform the dance of victory." A little episode of love introduced in this pantomime would almost turn it into a good modern ballet.

The pleasures of dancing are universally known, at least to those who practice it : such as do not, cannot be deemed competent judges. Let us, therefore, now examine its utility. This is not the slightest of its advantages, nor that which must excite the smallest interest.

Dancing was upheld, no less than music, as an object of much importance by the ancients. Religion claimed it as one of her chief ornaments on all solemn occsaions, and no festivals were given without uniting it to the other

ceremonies or diversions. The holy writings mention it
in many places. It was not only reckoned in a high
degree honourable, but, as Pariset and Villeneuve observe,
it was the object of a number of laws, made by various
ancient legislators, who introduced it into education, as a
means of strengthening the muscles and sinews, of preserving the agility, and developing the gracefulness of the
human frame.

Plato, the gravest philosopher of antiquity, did not
consider music and dancing as mere amusements, but as
essential parts of religious ceremonies, and military exercises [36]. In his books of laws he prudently prescribed
such limits to music and dancing as were most likely, in his
judgment, to keep them within the bounds of utility and
decency. The Greeks frequently amused themselves
with dancing, and carefully practised it, on account of its
immediate tendency to the improvement of gesticulation,
from whence it derived the name of Chironomia [37]. Theseus, Achilles, Pyrrhus, and even Socrates [38], as also
many other illustrious men, often diverted themselves by
means of this art. In short, from the remotest ages a
multiplicty of high authorities have successively proved
that dancing tends equally to our amusement and to our
instruction.

The whole body moves with more freedom, and acquires an easy and agreeable appearance. The shoulders
and arms are thrown back, the inferior limbs attain
greater strength and elasticity, the muscular masses of
the hips, thighs and legs, are symmetrically displayed, the
feet are constantly turned outwards, and in the gait there
is something peculiar, by which we immediately discover
a person that has cultivated dancing. Dancing is of
signal service to young people, at that time of life when

motion is almost a natural want, and the exerting of their strength is the surest means of increasing it.

All persons, whatever may be their condition in society, wish for strength and activity ; all, I may next venture to say, are, or would be, glad to possess physical beauty. It is a natural desire. And among those whose rank or fortune enables them to frequent good company, there are very few who do not wish to unite to those three qualities, elegance of carriage and deportment. Now nothing can render the frame more robust and graceful than dancing and pantomimic exercises. Every other kind of gymnastics strengthen or beautify particular parts, whilst they weaken others, and make them in a manner *difform*. Fencing invigorates the arms and legs, but renders the rest of the frame somewhat unshapely. Horsemanship increases the thickness of the loins [39], but debilitates the thighs. In short, all other exercises leave something disagreeable about those who practice them ; neither singly nor conjointly, can they bestow that becoming aspect and those agreeable manners which dancing, when well taught, never fails to impart. By it the head, arms, the hands, legs, feet, in short all parts of the body are rendered symmetrical, pliant and graceful.

Dancing is extremely useful to women, whose delicate constitutions require to be strengthened by frequent exercise, and must be very serviceable in relieving them from that unhealthy inaction, to which so many of them are usually condemned.

Captain Cook wisely thought that dancing was of special use to sailors. This famous navigator, wishing to counteract disease on board his vessels as much as possible, took particular care, in calm weather, to make his sailors and marines dance to the sound of a violin, and it was to this practice that he mainly ascribed the sound health which his crew enjoyed during voyages of several years continuance [40]. The dance they generally indulged in is called the *Hornpipe;* is of a most exhilarating character, perhaps more vivid than the *Tarantella* dance.

Bodily exercise, says an English writer, is conducive to health, vigour, liveliness, a good appetite, and sound sleep; but a sedentary occupation occasions many derangements in the nervous system, which sadden, and often shorten existence, disturbs repose, produces a certain disrelish for every thing, and brings on a continual languor and listlessness, of which it is sometimes difficult to dicover the cause.

The most celebrated disciples of Hippocrates concur in recommending dancing as an excellent remedy for a number of diseases [41]. Tissot absolutely orders it to be practised in all schools, for the minds of young persons, burthened with continual study, require some amusement above the trivial kind, on which it may fix with pleasure. Phædrus gives us a hint on this subject.

> " Cito rumpes arcum, semper tensum habueris
> At si laxaris, quum volès, erit utilis.
> Sic ludus animo debet aliquando dari,
> Ad cogitandum melior ut redeat tibi."

Anaxarchus, the Scythian, used also to say that it was often necessary to amuse ourselves by games or other diversions, so that the mind, after tasting a little useful repose, might return with increased vigour to the exercise of its delicate functions.

A laborious and painful life are a capital regimen for melancholy and sadness.

Dancing ought to form a part of the physical education of children, not only for their better health, but also to counteract the many vicious attitudes and habits which they too often contract.

The art of dancing is not only necessary, but almost indispensible to those who are fond of society. The manner of presenting one's self, and of receiving others, in company, with a graceful propriety, and the easy and polite demeanour which is so becoming in society, is acquired most effectually by those who have studied the art of dancing.

I shall now conclude by remarking that dancing, besides the amusement it affords, serves to improve our physical, and even to animate our moral powers; gives relief in certain diseases, affords a cure in others, promotes the harmony of society, and is a most requisite accomplishment for all who have the happiness to possess a good education.

" — Quacunque potes dote placere, place."—OVID.

NATIONAL DANCES.

THE CHICA.

The *Chica* was brought to us from Africa, where every tribe dances it, particularly the Congos. The Negroes carried it with them to the Antilles, where it soon became naturalized.

This dance was so universal throughout South America and the West Indies, that at the commencement of the present century it was still danced in all religious ceremonies and processions. The nuns during the night of Christmas eve showed themselves to the public through the gratings of their convents, expressing, in the voluptuous agitations of the Chica, the joy they felt for the birth of the Son of God, who came to take away, by his death, the sins of the world. This dance is passionately admired among the Creoles, who enthusiastically adopted it on its introduction among them.

America is not the only country that has been influenced by Africa in dancing; for, from the Moors it was that Spain first received that dance now so peculiar to it, the Fandango, which is nothing else than the Chica, under a more decent form, the climate and other circumstances not permitting the performance of this latter with all its native concomitants.

The origin of this dance it is very difficult to discover; but every thing in it seems to be the effect of a burning climate, and ardent constitutions.

The Chica is danced to the sound of any instrument whatever, but to one certain kind of tune, which is in a manner consecrated to it, and of which the movement is extremely rapid. The woman holds one end of a handkerchief, or the two sides of her apron, and the chief art on her part consists in agitating the lower part of the loins, whilst the rest of the body remains almost motionless. A dancer now approaches her with a rapid bound, flies to her, retires, darts forward a-fresh, and appears to conjure her to yield to the emotions which she seems so forcibly to feel.

When the Chica is danced in its most expressive character, there is in the gestures and movements of the two dancers, a certain appearance more easily understood than described. The scene offers to the eye, all that is lascivious, all that is voluptuous. It is a kind of contest, wherein every trick of love, and every means of its triumph, are set in action. Fear, hope, disdain, tenderness, caprice, pleasure, refusals, flight, delirium, despair, all is there expressed, and the inhabitants of Paphos, would have honoured the inventor of it as a divinity.

I will not attempt to say what impressions the sight of this dance must occasion, when executed with all the voluptuousness of which it is susceptible. It animates every feature, it awakens every sensibility, and would even fire the imagination of old age.

The Chica is now banished from the balls of the white women of South America, being far too offensive to decency; and is only sometimes performed in a few circles, where the small number of spectators encourage the dancer.

At Cairo, where there are no theatres, there are a sort of actors, or leapers, who go about to private houses, and represent various scenic performances, wherein the most licentious and obscene attitudes bear a strong resemblance to the Chica, and the ancient mimics. Many of the Greek and Roman dances may be compared to the Chica and Fandango, and especially those practised at the time of the decline of dancing in both nations, when this art naturally became an object of contempt among men of taste and morality.

I am almost inclined to believe that the Chica owes its origin to some of the ancient dances. Greece, so fertile in productions of every kind, and which gave birth to Socrates and Diogenes, Phocion, and Alcibiades, Homer, and Aristophanes, Agoracrites [43], Cleophanes [44], Callipides [45], all of most extraordinary, but opposite, talents, Greece, I think the most likely nation to have created this voluptuous dance. The dance of the Angrismene, usually performed at festivals in honour of Venus, and still very common among the modern Greeks, may bear me out in my opinion.

THE ANGRISMENE.

The *Angrismene,* or *la Fachèe* (the angry maiden), is performed by two persons of different sexes. A young girl first appears dancing (the music plays a languid andantino); after she has gone round in a *glissade* kind of step, a young man presents himself, also dancing; he plays about her with a handkerchief he holds in his hand, and attempts to approach her, but she, by her countenance and motions, expresses her scorn and contempt, and runs away. The lover exhibits much grief on seeing himself thus rejected, and accuses fate for his ill fortune. He however, again advances towards the object of his love, and seeks to move her compassion, but the young girl, proud of her advantages, again drives him from her, and forbids him to mention his love. In the mean time the steps and motions of both dancers are in perfect concert with the music, and express with precision the sentiments of anger and love. At length, the young man seeing himself so inhumanly treated, trembles with fury, and knows not on what to resolve; after a short time, however, he decides on adopting violence. She then darts a severe and threatening look at him. He becomes motionless, sighs, and gradually seems to give himself up to despair. He turns his fervid eyes upwards, and conjures heaven to put an end to his existence, then tying his handkerchief round his throat, pulls it very tight, and appears on the point of falling. The maiden immediately runs to support him, and deplores her unnecessary rigour. She unties the handkerchief, calls her lover, and endeavours, by every means, to reanimate him; he gradually revives; the languishing voice of his mistress strikes his ear, he looks around him, finds himself in her arms, and his happiness is complete. Joy then unites the hearts of the two lovers, and they swear to each other eternal fidelity. Their dance then regains its former liveliness, and becomes the interpreter of their reciprocal sentiments.

THE SPANISH DANCES.

The Spanish dances, both from their character and variety, always excite the curiosity of men of taste, and more especially of the lovers of the art of dancing.

That pretty little performance, *The Progress of the Fandango*, a highly boasted dance, is one of the proofs which, backed by the decision of the Spaniards, establishes the Fandango as the leading dance of Spain, and as the one which stands in the highest estimation. Their other dances are scarcely any thing more than imitations of it, and are looked upon but as second-rate.

The attitudes, and the graceful and voluptuous groupings of the Fandango, the cadences and thrillings of the music, have a most potent effect upon every spectator, and the Spaniards give a loose to ecstatic feeling whenever they witness the above-mentioned dance.

As an investigation and minute description of these dances seem requisite with the nature and subject of the present work, I feel myself called upon to present them to my readers. They will behold in these pastimes—these imitative exercises of the Spaniards—depicted a transcript of their character and their taste.

In their steps it is the lightness, the grace, the elasticity, the balance, which are remarkable ; and the majestic movements express those feelings which determine the national character ; namely, hauteur, pride, love, and arrogance.

In the execution of the Spanish dances, the arms are always expanded, and their movements, let them be in what direction they may, always undulating. They at times represent the generous sentiment of an absolute protection of the object beloved, at other times they describe with vivacity the tender feeling it inspires, and the sincerity of the avowal. The eyes, oftentimes directed towards the feet, glance over every part of the body, and testify the pleasure which symmetry of form inspires them with.

The agitations of the body, the footing, the postures,

the attitudes, the waverings, whether they be lively or dull, are the representatives of desire, of gallantry, of impatience, of uncertainty, of tenderness, of chagrin, of confusion, of despair, of revival, of satisfaction, and, finally, of happiness.

It is from these different gradations of the passions that the description and nature of the Spanish dances are characterized, in which the minds and manners of those who invented them are so faithfully pourtrayed. Thus we see an enamoured Roderic at the feet of a Chimène, and a Bohemian heroine of Cervantes, or the respectful gallantries of the ancient Spanish heroes of romance. We have already observed that some of the Spanish dances trace their origin from the American dances ; we must also observe that the Moors, from having inhabited Spain, and introduced their customs there, may lay claim to some part of the honour attributed to the Americans.

THE FANDANGO.

The Fandango is danced by two persons, and accompanied by the castanets, an instrument made of walnut wood, or of ebony. The music is in the time of $\frac{3}{8}$, and is a rapid movement. The sound of the castanets, and the movements of the feet, arms, and body, keep time to it to the greatest nicety. It is all life and action in the Fandango.

It was formerly danced much more generally by persons of quality, after the regulations enacted for the theatre, which introduced more dignity, more formality, and unaccompanied by the slightest movement that could give offence to modesty, or shock good taste.

The lower orders, amongst whom this dance is in high request, accompany it with attitudes which savour of the vulgarity of the principal performers, and their extravagant movements never slacken, never cease, till they are airly tired out.

THE BOLERO.

The Bolero is a dance far more noble, modest, and re-strained, than the Fandango; it is executed by two persons. It is composed of five parts, namely—the *paseo*, or promenade, which is a kind of introduction; the *traversias*, or crossing, to alter the position of the places, which is done both before and after the *differencias*, a measure in which a change of steps take place; then follows the *finales*, which is succeeded by the *bien parado*, a graceful attitude, or grouping of the couple who are dancing. The air of the Bolero is set to the time of $\frac{2}{4}$; there are some, however, in the time of $\frac{3}{4}$. The music is extremely varied, and full of cadences. The air or melody of this dance may be changed, but its peculiar rythmus must be preserved, together with its time, and its flourishes, which latter are called also *false pauses*. The steps of the Bolero are performed *terre à terre;* they are either sliding, beaten, or retreating, being always, as it were, clearly struck out.

THE SEGUIDILLAS BOLERAS.

When the *Boleros* are sung, and accompanied by a guitar, they are called *Seguidillas Boleras*. The great difficulty of this dance consists in resuming the part called the *paseo*, which is immediately after the first part of the tune in the prelude of the accompaniment, which precedes the *estribillo*. The *estribillo* is that part of the couplet, not indeed where the moral is found, but which contains the epigrammatic point or turn.

THE SEGUIDILLAS MANCHEGAS.

These *Seguidillas*, which are danced by four, six, eight, or nine persons, are far more rapid in their movements, beginning without the *paseo*. The *traversias* of it is shorter, and its *bien parado* is without gesture. This dance is very sprightly in its motions, and a great favourite with the lower orders, who give themselves up to it with a peculiar zest. It is of Moriscan origin.

THE CACHUCHA.

The name of this dance is a word applied to caps, fans, and an infinite number of articles, which are thus promiscuously termed, by way of abreviation.

The *Cachucha Solo*, danced either by a man or a woman alone, though better suited to the latter, is admirably calculated to accompany the medley of music peculiar to this dance; which is sometimes gracefully calm, sometimes sprightly, and sometimes impassioned.

THE SEGUIDILLAS TALEADAS.

This dance is a species of the Bolero, mingled with some measures of the *Cachucha*.

THE MENUET AFANDANGADO.

A Minuet partly composed of the Fandango.

THE MENUET ALLMANDADO.

A Minuet intermixed with steps from the Allemand.

THE GUARACHA.

This dance, the music of which is in $\frac{3}{8}$, is danced by one person, accompanied by the guitar. Its movement, which should grow progressively quick, renders it rather difficult. It is now but seldom danced, and never except at the Theatres.

EL ZAPATEADO.

This is the same sort of movement as the *Guaracha*, and is in the time of $\frac{3}{8}$. There is in this dance a considerable noise made by the feet. Its steps are struck, as it were, similar to the *Anglais* and the *Sabottière*.

EL ZORONGO.

This dance has given name to a head-dress for women, which in Spain is composed of ribands, mingled with the hair. Its steps are simple, following a very sprightly movement, and are practised backwards and forwards; while sometimes the hands are clapped to the time.

EL TRIPILI TRAPOLA.

This dance is nearly similar to the Zorongo, excepting that it finishes with three *demi-tours* or half-turns.

The original character of these dances, their pleasing and varied figure, exciting, as they do, tender and agreeable feelings, have always obtained for them a marked preference. With respect to these peculiar qualities, there are few dances of other nations, worthy of being compared with them.

The music that accompanies them, or rather that inspires them, is so harmonious, and of a melody so sweet and original, that it finds an instantaneous welcome into the heart, which it delights; and extremely insensible must that person be who does not feel those emotions which it is calculated to inspire. The great Musician of the age corroborates my assertion, by the introduction which he has composed to these charming airs, in several of his fine performances. The exquisite taste, in short, of Rossini is my guide.

Another circumstance, which renders this dancing still more seducing, is the picturesque costume of the dancers; than which nothing can be handsomer in design, or more beautiful in its ornaments and variety of colours. The striking features of the Spanish girls also, their expressive looks, their light figure, which seems formed for the dance, and adorned with their elegant apparel, their fancifully laced sandals, all conspire to raise delight in the spectator. We can imagine, while these *Bayadères* are dancing, that some picture of Titian or Veronese has become animated.

Many of our readers will remark that we have omitted those dances called the *Follies d'Espagne*, the Follies of Spain. It is generally believed that this is a dance very much practised and admired in Spain; but we must observe that the air was originally composed by Corelli, and so universally practised by the Spaniards, that they became crazed with it. It was first sung, then played on instruments, and finally danced. Any kind of step was adapted to it, every one forming for himself a measure, according to his own peculiar taste and style.

It may not, perhaps, be found unacceptable if we add some etymological explanation of those characteristic words by which the Spanish dances are designated. We have, therefore, undertaken the attempt, notwithstanding the great difficulty with which it is attended, owing principally to the total deficiency of the Spanish Dictionary in this respect. Its definitions are never sufficiently precise to allow of a determinate conclusion being drawn from them.

The word *Bolero*—*Saltationis Hispaniæ genus*, is derived from the verb *volar*, or from the Spanish noun *volero*, which is the same as *volador*, the sense of which has probably been applied to the *Bolero*, from the lightness with which it ought to be executed.

Seguidillas means no more than *continuation*, and indeed the air of the *Seguidillas* is the same as the *Bolero*, continued by the voice, and followed with a flourish of the accompanying instrument.

The adjective *Taleadas* is taken from the word *taleo*, which signifies a *noisy amusement*.

The adjective *Manchegas* signifies of *La Mancha*, a southern province of Spain, between Andalusia and New Castile.

Cachucha; this word is not to be found in any dictionary of the Spanish language. It is customary to apply this word to a fair, a bird, a little cap, and, in short, to any thing that is graceful or pretty. In the language of the Andalusian Gittanos, the word *cachucha* signifies gold. In a still more elevated style, *cachucha* means that part of the quiver in which Cupid puts his darts. *Sagitta capsula in pharetra.* The following verses may give an idea of the general sense in which this word is applied by the Spaniards.

" Mi Cachucha por la mar
A todos vientos camina,
Pero nunca va mejor
Que cuando va de bolina."

IMITATED.

My Cachucha, haste o'er the seas,
When gentle gales are blowing ;
But when the winds of winter roar,
Ah ! do not think of going."

The word *Fandango* means *go dance.*

Afandangado is any thing belonging to the Fandango.

Guaracha is an expression of the Negroes, signifying liveliness.

Zapateado, means performed by the motion of the feet.

Tripili trapala, are only expressions used to signify a certain modulation of the voice amongst the Gittanos, or Andalusian gipsies.

NOTES.

1.

Vide Reinesius, Gruter, Gudio, &c.

2.

Genesis Ch. IV. v. 21 and 22.

3.

Read Lucian's *Dialogue upon Dancing*.

4.

The ancients gave a proof of their taste and judgment in making the distinctions that subsist between the various styles of theatrical dancing ; of this *Lucian* has informed us. They saw that it was requisite to have different kinds, and they accordingly divided them in the following manner :—the *Cordax*, the *Sicinnis*, and the *Emmeleïa*.

The *Emmeleïa* was a sort of tragic movement or ballet, of which the elegance and majesty were greatly celebrated by Plato, and other eminent men who make mention of its use.

The *Sicinnis* was a dance so called from the peculiar shaking of the body, and violent motion of the limbs, practised in it. (*Vide Athenœus.*) This dance must be considered of the grotesque style.

The *Cordax* was a loose kind of dance introduced into comedies, performed by persons elevated with wine. (*Vide Ath.*) This dance was void of all dignity and decorum ; its movements were gross and ridiculous ; those who executed it made the most indecent motions with their backs, hips, and loins. This exhibition, therefore, I suppose, may be compared to the *Dythyrambic* dance of the Bacchanals. In short, certain songs of a violent and infuriated character were sung in honour of Bacchus, and, at the same time, accompanied by dances of the above description.

Besides these three sorts of dances, there was also another, called the *Pyrrhic* or *warrior* dance. (*Vide Meursius Antiq. Graec. de Salt. verbo.* ΠΙΡΡΙΧΗ.*)

This dance imitated those movements and positions of the body, by the aid of which the wounds or darts of any enemy were avoided, that is, by bending

---

* " *Pyrrhicam.* Ea Saltationis species est, nomen ab inventore sortita, quem alii Pyrrhum Achillis filium, alii Pyrrhum quemdam Cretensem, vel etiam à ratione Saltandi quod Pyrrichii pedis modulo soleret agitari, de quo pede, *Quint. Lib.* IX. *Cap.* 14. Háec fuit Saltatio, ut plures existimanto armat, pro juvenibus ad militarem disciplinam exercendis : varii enim illius motus et flexus, vitandu vel in ferendáe plagae reddebant idoneos."—CASAUB.

flying away, leaping, and stooping. The attitudes also of the party attacking were described ; the hurling of the javelin, and the postures when aiming a blow with the sword. Plato says that dancing, with all its varied corporeal exercises, draws its origin from an imitation of speech, described by the movements and gesticulations of every limb. *(Vide Plat. de Leg.)*

5.

This kind of performance, bad as it is, has nevertheless, in our days, met with a zealous supporter, who has had the boldness to insert, in a newspaper of Turin, an article where he speaks of the theatre Carignan, and much in favour of his beloved Grotesques. This singular amateur, after lavishing a thousand praises on dancers far beneath the middle order, adds :—" The grotesques, B. A. S. &c., must also be mentioned with praise, as performers who do their utmost to dignify this style of dancing, which, I know not why, was for some time almost generally proscribed in Italy, Its native country. It often serves to give a relief to that tedious sameness of grave steps, which serious dancers have introduced." To the reader who is acquainted with the grotesque style, I will leave the task of commenting on these extraordinary words. Were the arts to possess no other connoisseurs and amateurs than such as are of this stamp, we should very soon fall back, I think, to the thirteenth century. Let us conclude with Boileau, that

" *Un sot trouve toujours un plus sot qui l'admire.*"

It is, however, nearly the same style as that of the English clowns.

6.

See *Encyclopédie Française*, ART. BAL.

7.

Those who are desirous of knowing in detail what dancing was among the ancients, will gather much information from Lucian, Meursius, Scaliger, Cahusac, Ménètrier, Bonnet, Burette, Brown, Baron and some others.

8.

The dancer prepares for the performance of his step. He studies to adopt the most becoming way of holding his arms, body, &c., and of moving his legs, so as always to preserve a perfect harmony with each other. We now do precisely the same when on the point of beginning to dance, that every thing may be graceful and systematical.

9.

The steps must keep exact time to the music, and responsively mark each bar, each cadence, &c. This unity is indispensable, and produces a very agreeable effect. Madame Léon excels in this part of her profession.

10.

The dancer gradually introduces all that his art comprises. His execution must be progressive, and managed so as to give a kind of light and shade to the performance. Vivacity and nimbleness are essential requisites to a good dancer : the spectator delights to see in him an appearance of something more than *earthly*. This is what is so much admired in Madame Léon, the wife of a distinguished Ballet-Master, and occasioned the celebrated poet, Count Paradisi, to say in one of his finest odes, which he may not be displeased with my quoting —

> " —————————— l'agile
> Pié d' Egle (Madame Léon), la decente
> Mollezza, e la pieghevole
> Salma, che in alto lieve
> Par che qual piuma o neve,
> Perda al vento di scendere il vigor."

11.

Uprightness and equilibrium are essential requisites. The *grands tems* must be made with elegance and correctness. The dancer must endeavour always to display his person in a graceful manner, and minutely vary his attitude at every rest.

12.

No monotony in the steps and *entrechats*. Let the charms of novelty adorn the performance throughout. Our best masters do not speak otherwise than the poet.

13.

Rapidity gives a brilliancy to the steps, which renders their effect more delightful.

14.

The modern Ovid, in this stanza, alludes to *tems vigoureux*, to *tems enlevés*, to *entrechats*, steps in turning round, pirouettes, &c. His description is a faithful painting of his thoughts, and nothing could be said with more precision on the performance of the first dancers of our age.

15.

Marino points out the harmony that must exist between the music and the dance, and how necessary it is for the artist to render his legs, arms, and whole body responsive to the sound. This, together with the skill of appropriating the steps to the time, cadence and character of the music, are essential qualities in our art, and indeed the very life of it.

16.

Pliability, agility, and a kind of graceful negligence are the most pleasing things in a dancer. I remember on one occasion dancing with Madame Léon a *pas de deux*, which I composed myself, and wherein we each held one end of a scarf, that contributed much to the variety and novelty of our attitudes and groups. This excellent artist displayed, with the utmost gracefulness, all the qualities I have above enumerated, all the charms that dancing possesses. The performer must move with taste and decency, let nothing be unnatural, nor in the least lascivious ; all must contribute, as the poet says, to

" ——. —— —————— la decente
Mollezza ———— ———." "

And this is precisely what the spectator should admire in artists of our class. Ease, elasticity, gracefulness and decency, must be always preferred to the extravagant movements, contortions, and grimaces of dancing Phrynes.

Among the ancients there were two kinds of dancing : one for respectable and well bred people, the other for debauchees and the vulgar. This dis- tinction even existed in the time of Homer.—*(Vide Iliad, Book* 13*th.)*

Many of our modern dancers might learn something from those of the age of Alcinous.

17.

Every part of the body must, in its motions, be in harmony one with the other. It is the acme of perfection.

18.

These last verses unquestionably describe what we now call *petits batte- ments* on the instep, or *ronds de jambe.* The poet will have every thing done according to rules, and not as an effect of mere chance.

19.

The author of the *Adonis* again reminds us of the concord between dancing and music. All must be studied and duly performed according to precept. You must, nevertheless, endeavour to conceal, by ease and variety, this systematical difficulty.

20.

The poet here presents us with an ingenious description of the *pirouette.* Its execution and effect are painted in the truest manner. The dancer begins by turning *à la seconde*, and then continues the pirouette with *petits battements* or *ronds de jambe.*

" E'l corpo non leggiero e non gravoso
D'intorno al centro si raggiri e volga."—TASSO

21.

The first four lines of this stanza show what rapidity pirouetting admits of, and what elegance may be displayed in turning. The last lines speak of the preparation for, and effect of, the *cabriole.*

22.

It is impossible to explain more minutely, or in a more poetical manner, the time of the *entrechats*. These eight lines are admirable, and may serve as a lesson to dancers. Marino describes with exactness the principal action, and every movement accompanying the spring from the ground. But our dancers would not be much encouraged in those violent efforts, which, although natural, are far from being graceful. The *entrechat* must be performed in an easy manner. The strength of the instep and tension of the calves and loins give a sufficient impulse to the body. But facility and elegance in doing this can be acquired only by dint of study, and constant practice.

23.

We have already observed that lightness, elevation, vivacity, vigour and elasticity, are essential qualities to form a good dancer. The poet again introduces them to our notice, and makes a proud display of them in the Goddess of dancing.

24.

Vide the Chica.

25.

This dance, in the course of time, changed its character into one of a nobler kind. The philosopher of Geneva says, with regard to its music : *Sarabande* " Air d'une danse grave, portant le même nom, laquelle paraît nous être venue d'Espagne, et se dansait autrefois avec des castagnettes. Cette danse n'est plus en usage, si ce n'est dans quelques vieux operas Francais. L'air de la sarabande est à trois tems lents."

26.

The *Chaccone*, also degenerated in the days of our forefathers. The above quoted author speaks of its music in the following terms :—" Chaccone, sorte de pièce de musique faite pour la danse, dont la mesure est bien marquèe et le mouvement modéré. La chaccone est née en Italie, et elle y était autrefois fort en usage, de même qu'en Espagne. On ne la connaît plus en France, que dans les vieilles partitions*." We thus see that the Italians and Spanish now and then made a mutual exchange of their national dances.

The *Minuet* is, of all ancient dances, that which has continued longest in vogue. But it has undergone various modifications and changes. It originated in Poitou, and after having acquired a little dignity, became a particular favourite at all French and Italian balls.

27.

The *Sarao* is a proof of that abundance of national dances which the Spaniard possesses. The *Sarao* is an assembly held at private houses

---

* Jean Jacques wrote this about sixty years ago. Since that time fresh Chaccones have been composed, and are still danced in Paris.

during the carnival, and composed of young persons of both sexes, in disguise, but unmasked. A woman, with a small basket full of silk sashes, of different colours, stands at the door of the room where the *Sarao* is held, and presents a sash to each lady that enters. Another woman distributes the same kinds of sashes to the gentlemen, and each immediately sees, by the colour of his sash, the person who is to be his lady for the evening. He approaches and salutes her, and remains at her feet during the whole time that the *Sarao* lasts. He is even permitted to speak to her with all the love and tenderness he chooses, without her taking the least offence. This is a custom that gives rise to numberless intrigues. The evening terminates with dances, analogous to the character of the party.

We observe in these balls and diversions, the Spanish disposition in its full extent. The passion of love constantly transports the Spaniard, and appears conspicuous in every action of his life. In France and in Italy, a public street, crowd, and disguise, often occasion many things which they at the same time conceal; but in Spain there is no restraint, or at least there was not when the Sarao was most in vogue. The inhabitants there gave full scope to their desires, and did every thing publicly. The most select assemblies never restrain them. The only people to whom, in my opinion, they may be compared are the Venetians, or rather the Venetians as they were fifty years ago.

28.

Fourlane, a dance well known at Venice, and much in vogue among the Gondoliers. It is very lively, and its music is $\frac{6}{8}$ time, played in a *molto allegretto* style. It is called Fourlane on account of its having been first danced in the Frioul. This dance is very similar to the Tarantella, but not quite so diversified.

29.

Contredanse, a dance generally performed by eight persons, four men and four women. It is of modern invention, and comprises a variety of steps, according to the nature of the music. Liveliness is the characteristic of this dance, which has prevailed over all others.* It may be varied *ad infinitum*, from the surprising number of evolutions which it admits of, and among which the principal ones are the circle O, the half circle C, the cross †, the cross of four ✳, the chain ✕✕✕. Contredanses, quadrilles,

---

* Spain, and the German provinces, abound in dances of different kinds. France, on the contrary, possesses a very small number of national dances, but can boast of an immense variety of tunes well suited to their composition. Italy, of all nations the most musical, is, perhaps, the poorest in national airs and songs. This remark relates only to civilized countries.

and waltzes, the last of which took their rise in Switzerland, are the most fashionable dances of the day. The performance of these should be easy, and the steps executed elegantly; and brilliant gavottes are also now and then danced in genteel society, but they require much more study and practice than the other three.

30.

This dance is graceful but affected. *L'Ecossaise* is all gaiety. *L'Anglaise* lively and whimsical.

31.

The description of this dance was translated into Italian, and inserted in the *Aurora*, a literary periodical paper published in London, and edited by Mr. F. C. Albites, professor of Italian literature; but at present discontinued.

32.

Claritio and Serrao, two Neapolitan physicians, have proved by various experiments, that all that has been said with regard to the bite of the Tarantella spider, is false. The terrible accounts given of it arise from ignorance and prejudice, and are propagated by quackery.

33.

This artist had the honour of giving lessons to his sovereign. Lully associated himself with him, and their united efforts brought forth those works which have since served as models to the grand modern operas, whose greatest charms consist in music and dancing. Every one knows how passionately fond Louis the XIVth was of theatrical representations. He often performed in them himself. He danced with part of his court in the opera of the *Temple de la Paix*, which was represented at his palace in 1685. The Princess of Conti, the Duchess of Bourbon, Mademoiselle de Blois, Count Brionne, the Marquis of Mony, and other distinguished personages performed the principal parts in the ballet.

34.

I shall speak in another place (*Composition of Ballets*) of these dancers, and of the different sorts of ballets.

35.

In music, similar advantages were perceived. Architas, Aristoxenes, Eupolis, Aristophanes, Cicero, G. Gracchus, Theophrastus, Micomachus Theodore, Pythagoras, and all his sect; Ptolomy, Plato, Lycurgus, Boetius, all men of never-fading celebrity, whose wisdom and knowledge do honour to philosophy and the sciences, eulogized the art of music, approved of its practice, and made it form a part of the education of youth. Cimon, Epaminondas, Appius Claudius, M. Cecilius, L. Crassus, D. Sylla, and Cato, thought it not beneath their rank and glory to sing or play on some musical instrument. Music was almost universally cultivated in Greece. Those who had no knowledge of this art were in some measure despised and regarded as barbarians.

The Arcadians, says Polybius, having despised the laws of harmony, fell from civilization and humanity into a ferocious barbarism, and thenceforward were continually troubled with dissentions. The natives of Gaul, on the contrary, who had formerly been savage and untractable, became, by a different education, gentle and docile.

Doctor Zulatti has also copiously treated of this matter, and with much good sense, as may be seen in his dialogues.

36.

Rollin, Histoire Ancienne, Tom IV. livre 10, chap. 1 § 10, pp. 578 and 579.

37.

Fab. Quintil. Instit. Orat. lib. 1 cap. xi.

38.

Scaliger, Tom. III. page 13.
Athenæus, lib. 4. cap. 6. et lib. 1. cap. 19.

39.

Vide *Dictionnaire des Sciences Médicales.*

40.

Vide—idem.

41.

Music also has, at times, operated wonderful cures. Democritus and Theophrastus have transmitted some of its miracles to posterity. Plutarch and Boetius have recorded the names of Terpandre, Thales of Creta, Isménie, Xenocrates, Hyerophilus, and a few others, who made a valuable use of music to the same purpose. The modern Italian music is deserving of a similar commendation.

42.

I shall demonstrate, in the part on *Theatrical Dancing*, by what means physical defects in dancers may be in some measure concealed.

43.

The first Greek sculptor.

44.

The first Greek painter.

45.

An actor, dancer, and a famous mimic.

FROM THE ITALIAN.

Terspichore, the Goddess of Dancing, finding herself alone, betakes herself to the pleasures of graceful movements : first, she retires, then advances, displaying, as she lightly trips along, a beauteous knee. Her attention is fixed, on the harmonious sounds, while she arranges her steps in prelude [9]. She flies around her new theatre ; her motion quickens, and her steps increase ; so bouyant she appears, that waves might well sustain her tread [10]. On her small foot she pauses skilfully, and gives to every limb some graceful attitude [11]. Now, she seems to haste away, and now again returns ; now she vanishes, and now she re-appears. Darting from side to side, she glances over the ground [12], as shoots the lightning suddenly through the serenity of a night in summer [13].

By such well-studied motion, and so light, the Goddess scarcely deigns to touch the earth. She wantons gaily, and springs aloft with such velocity, that her winged feet deceive the sight, and seldom can we detect which foot it is that prints the soil. Shooting along in airy bounds, she traces circles with her limber feet ; then, with step exact, retraces them, enlarging and diminishing ; as the dipping waves that dance along the bright Meander [14], so are the motions of her twinkling feet, whether on earth, or quivering in the air ; whether she lightly trips, or firmly treads the ground [15].

When she springs aloft she seems the spiry flame ; and like the undulating wave, she skims along ; but her more stately turns assume the whirlwind's power, or seem like eddying billows by the tempest stirred [16]. Harmonious symmetry prevails throughout her person. The attitude of one limb induces corresponding motions in the rest. Each foot moves, but by mutual consent it answers to the other in fraternal motion [17]. The strictest ties unite her to the measure, never is a line mistaken, or a step misplaced [18]. The linked, and entwined figures of her dance are varied to the change of melody ; marking each note, and minding every pause, promptly she obeys each phrase of music, which she respects as mistress of every motion. Now she advances, stops, rises, leaps on high, or reverently bends, and then regains the upright attitude [19].

Suddenly she pauses in mid-dance, assumes another attitude, and on the instant, her whole style is changed ; her feet separating, form a figure, unmatched in mathematics for precision ; she turns, and seems a moving sphere, resembling most perhaps the peacock's airy plumes. One foot in the centre stays, while the other swiftly marks the outer round [20]. On her left foot her figure rests, and adopting a new posture, she swiftly whirls around ; with less rapidity the darted *Paleum* flies. With grace inimitable she now regains the spot from whence she parted, there stops, then leaps aloft, and hangs her feet on nothing, quivering in the air [21]. Again she springs, and in that spring she strikes her feet twice together, and strongly agitates every lower limb [22]. From her greatest elevation she descends, but slowly; and so lightly she regains the ground, that no one can distinguish when her noiseless foot alights. Around she flies! how admirable! and with what truth she finds again her first position! The darting lightning, or the winged arrow, goes not a swifter course than she, while flying o'er the soil with agile springs and airy bounds [23].

THE FANDANGO.

A young girl, of bold character, places in her hand two *castagnettes* of sonorous wood. By the aid of her fingers she produces a clattering noise, and to that she keeps time with the graceful motions of her feet. The young man holds a tamboureen (or a *tambour de basque*, which, however, is now out of use), this he strikes with little bells, seeming, as it were, to invite his companion to accompany him in gesticulation. While dancing, both alternately playing the same air, both keep time to its measure.

Every description of lascivious motion, every gesture that is offensive to modesty, and whatever can corrupt innocence and honesty is represented by these dancers, to the life. Alternately do they salute, exchanging amorous looks; they give to their hips a certain immodest motion, then they meet and press their breasts together; their eyes appear half closed, and they seem, even while dancing, to be approaching the final embrace.

PART THE SECOND.

THEORY OF THEATRICAL DANCING[1].

" Que la danse toujours, ou gaie ou sérieuse,
Soit de nos sentimens l'image ingénieuse ;
Que tous ses mouvemens du cœur soient les échos,
Ses gestes un langage, et ses pas des tableaux!"

DELILLE.

CHAPTER I.

GENERAL INSTRUCTIONS TO PUPILS.

You who devote yourselves to the enchanting Terpsichore, and aspire to an honourable rank amongst her votaries; who are gifted by nature with every quality necessary to obtain admission into her temples, and are predetermined to leave nothing undone that may aid in the accomplishment of perfection, attentively observe the following instructions :—

Success or failure in all studies, chiefly depends on the manner in which they are commenced. Your first attention must be therefore directed to the choice of a master, with whom you may run no hazard of being led astray. All professors have not issued from good schools, and few have distinguished themselves in the art which they pretend to teach. Many there are of ordinary abilities, who, far from increasing the number of good dancers, are daily diminishing it, and whose defective mode of instruction imparts a variety of vicious habits, which the pupil afterwards finds extremely difficult, nay sometimes, impossible to eradicate. Neither follow the precepts of simple unpractised theorists, utterly incapable of demonstrating clearly the true principles of the art: nor be guided by the imaginary schemes of innovating speculators, who, whilst they think themselves contributing to ameliorate the elementary rules of dancing, are gradually working its destruction.

Carefully shun the baneful lessons of such preceptors; and seek to place yourself under the direction of an experienced master, whose knowledge and talent will serve as true guides to perfection, and point out the path that leads to pre-eminence.

I shall in the next place recommend you seriously to consider your personal qualifications and mental dispositions, for the art you attempt to learn. Can you be passionately fond of it? Can your chief delight be concentrated in its study and practice? Are you in most respects adapted to it? If in yourself you meet with a negative to these questions never expect to excel, nor even to attain the order of *tolerables* and *passables*.

Be not discouraged at difficulties. Every obstacle is surmounted by perseverance and reiterated exercise. Remember the painter's advice to his pupils: *Nulla dies sine linea.* Nothing is of greater importance in dancing than frequent practice; to masters even it is necessary, to students indispensible. No other art demands a stricter attention in this particular; without it, he that has made himself perfect cannot long remain so; he soon loses part of what has cost him so much labour to acquire, his equilibrium becomes less steady, his springs less elastic, and he at length finds, that through a remission of diligence, he has much to do over again. This is not the case with music and singing; a good ear, a fine voice, are usually sufficient, with a few years of moderate study, to conquer all difficulties. Nor does painting require such intense application, both from learners and professors, as dancing, which, like all other bodily exercises, cannot be acquired and retained without the utmost study and assiduity. Remain not, therefore, twenty-four hours without practising. The pupil that frequently interrupts his studies, opposes a considerable impediment to his progress. All the lessons that he takes, when widely separated one from the other, can be of no service towards making him a good dancer; and are little else than a loss of so much time, which I would advise him to spend in a more profitable manner. Avoid, however, running into opposite extremes, for too much practice is often as prejudicial as too little. Excess in every thing is a fault; let me remind you of the philosopher's maxim: *La moderation est le trésor du sage.*

Be temperate and sober if you desire to become a finished dancer. To render yourself capable of sacrificing before the shrine of Terpsichore, partially renounce every pleasure but that which the goddess affords. Let no other exercise be intermingled with dancing: horsemanship, fencing, running, &c. are all powerful enemies to the learner's advancement.

Do not rely on your own natural qualities, and therefore neglect to study or practise so much as those to whom nature has been less liberal; for were you to possess the symmetry of an *Apollo Belvedere*, or an *Antinous*[2], together with the happiest endowments, you would have but little reason to expect to attain excellence in your profession without study, industry, and perseverance.

" Non giova che tu sia bello e leggiadro :
Sotto quel bello son bruttezze ascose."

RICCOBONI.

Particularly attend to the carriage of your body and arms. Let their motions be easy, graceful, and always in accordance with those of the legs. Display your form with taste and elegance; but beware of affectation. In the *leçon*[3] and *exercices* pay an equal regard to both legs, lest the execution of the one surpass that of the other. I have seen many dance with one leg only; these I compare to painters that can draw figures but on one side. Dancers and painters of such limited talent are certainly not to be considered as good artists.

Take especial care to acquire perpendicularity and an exact equilibrium. In your performance be correct, and very precise; in your steps, brilliant and light; in every attitude, natural and elegant. A good dancer ought always to serve for a model to the sculptor and painter. This is perhaps the acme of perfection and the goal that all should endeavour to reach[4]. Throw a sort of *aban_don* into your positions, groups and *arabesques*[5]; let your countenance be animated and expressive; *siano le attitudini degli uomini con le loro membra in tal modo disposte, che con quelle si dimostri l'intenzione del loro animo*[6]. These words of the great Leonard should be as deeply engraved in the memory of the mimic and dancer as in that of the painter.

" Les gestes et les pas d'un mutuel accord
Peignent *(de l'âme)* la même ivresse et le même transport."

DORAT.

Be vigorous, but avoid stiffness; seek to acquire a facility of spring, that your entrechats may be easy, precise, and well crossed. Rapidity is also very pleasing in a dancer; lightness, still more so; the one imparts a brilliancy to his performance, the other has in it something of an aerial appearance that charms the eye of the spectator. Observe the *ballon;* nothing can be more delightful than to see you bounding with graceful elasticity in your steps, scarcely touching the ground, and seeming at every moment on the point of flying into the air.

Preserve a perfect equilibrium in the execution of your pirouettes, and be careful how you begin and end them. Tread with assurance and uprightness, holding your body and limbs as the following chapters will direct. Use your utmost endeavour to twirl delicately round on the point of your toes; this is the most finished and agreeable style of execution; for what can be more unpleasing to the sight than a heavy, clumsy, dancer, who twists about alternately on his heels and toes, and uncouthly jerking his body at each revolution of his pirouette.

Attentively study the invention of steps; try to vary incessantly your *enchaínemens,* figures, attitudes, and groups. " Variety is one of the great charms of nature; nor can you please the beholder for any length of time, but in changing often your compositions."—*Dauberval.*

Enchaínemens in dancing are very numerous. Every good dancer has his peculiar mode of combining his periods, steps, &c. Form, therefore, a style of your own, as originality is the chief means to procure yourself distinction. By copying others you may, perhaps, sometimes excel; but the absence of novelty will, unquestionably, deprive you of attraction.

" Il en est de la danse comme de la musique, et des danseurs comme des musiciens; nôtre art n'est pas plus riche en pas fondamentaux que la musique l'est en notes; mais nous avons des octaves, des rondes, des blanches, des noires, des croches, des temps à compter, et une mesure à suivre ; ce mélange d'un petit nombre de pas et d'une petite quantité de notes offre une multitude d'enchaînemens et de traits variés ; le goût et le génie trouvent toujours une source de nouveautés en arrangeant, et en retournant, cette petite portion de notes et de pas de mille sens et de mille manières différentes ; ce sont donc ces pas lents et soutenus, ces pas vifs, précipités, et ces tems plus ou moins ouverts, qui forment cette diversité continuelle[7]."

Imitate a painter in your manner of combining and arranging ; let all the objects of your picture be in strict harmony one with another, the principal effect spirited, every tint (if the expression be allowed as relating to the modulations of steps, attitudes, &c.) flowing into each other, and the whole polished off with softness and taste. Keep a vigilant ear to the movements, rests and cadences of the music, that your dancing may be in exact concert with its accompaniment. Every thing depends on this melodious union, and, when really perfect, it is charming in the extreme. Not an eye can follow the performer without delight, not an ear, however unsusceptible of the impressions which music conveys, can listen without being worked upon by an assemblage so ravishing and harmonious.

Observe with attention, and judiciously examine all that concerns your art. Maturely weigh every advice that is offered to you, and afterwards make use of it as your judgment best directs. Disdain not to learn from an inferior. A bad dancer may, at times, have in his style of dancing something good that had previously escaped your notice. A middling figurant, or even a man utterly devoid of taste, shall now and then give you salutary counsel.

Do not fear rendering yourself importunate to your teacher by questions ; reason freely with him upon the art you are acquiring : if you fall into an error, blush not to

confess your mistake in consulting him, but in every respect profit by his opinions, follow his directions and put
his precepts into immediate practice, that they may be
thereby more firmly rooted in your memory.

Never depart from true principles, nor cease to follow
the best guides.   Above all, do not permit yourself to be
led astray by the example of some miserable performers,
who enjoy for awhile the applause of an ill-discerning
public, by feats of strength, gambols and ridiculous pirouettes.   Be assured that the laurels of such pitiful dancers
are seldom lasting.

> "———————— che non è assai
> Piacere a sciocchi o a qualche donnicciuola.
>
> Riccoboni.

The approbation of men of distinction in the art, the
only judges to be esteemed and consulted, is ever a sufficient stimulus to the man of talent, who cannot but entertain a profound contempt for that praise which fools lavish
on every mountebank they behold.

Ease and softness in the execution of your dance, I repeat, ought always to be aimed at.   In this acquirement
you show that the exercise is natural to you, and that you
have overcome the greatest difficulty, namely, the concealment of art.

When once possessed of this great quality, which I
may term the highest step on the ladder of perfection,
you may claim every suffrage, and justly merit the name of
a finished dancer.

Examine well the style of dancing best suited to yourself.   Nothing exhibits a greater want of taste in a dancer
than the choice of a style not at all adapted to his powers.
Can any thing be more ridiculous than the appearance
of a tall majestic performer, fit, in every respect, to pursue the serious branch, dancing a *pas villageois* in a little

comic ballet? And, on the other side, can any thing be more ludicrous than to see a thick-set dancer, of a diminutive stature, come forward, robed in a heroic garment, and gravely figure off in a slow and mournful *adagio?* The ancients have, by the purity of their taste in this respect, set us an example of severity towards performers of this stamp, and of which the following anecdote is an illustration:—" A certain mimic, very short in person, was representing Hector, in a play performed at Antioch. The people, beholding the hero thus transformed into a dwarf, simultaneously exclaimed,—*Astyanatem videmus, ubi Hector est?* We see Astyanatus before us; but where is Hector?" Both the dancer and actor should consider their form and physical powers, before they adopt any particular style of dancing or performance, that they may only assume the character which they are framed by nature to represent.

The union of several branches in one person is blameable only in certain dancers of the middle order, who, by their endeavours to ape the highest favourites of Terpsichore, seem bent on bringing her enchanting art to degradation. But those who are neither very tall nor very short, and are endowed with the requisite abilities, may exert themselves in every kind: by diligent study and practice they may even shine in whatever part they take. Not so with a dancer of high stature: let him exclusively adopt the serious and heroic kind. Nor with one below the middle size ; let his be the pastoral and *demi-caractère.* You must always vary your style of dancing with your dress; it would be a vicious taste to make it the same in an ancient Greek or Roman costume, as in a modern villager's spencer. Men of the most illustrious genius, whether poets, painters, or musicians, have ever carefully avoided confounding the character and expres-

sion of their different personages and styles.   Distinction
has always been their study.   Follow their example:
such an imitation, on your part, will show a sound judgment, and powerfully assist you in your progress to perfection.

The music of a dance or ballet must be livelier, and of a
stronger accent and cadence, than vocal music ; and as it is
required to signify a greater variety of things, it ought
also to be much more diversified.   It is music alone that
can inspire the dancer and mimic with that warmth of
expression which a singer derives from his words.   Music
supplies, in the language of the soul, all that dancing, by
its attitudes and gestures, cannot make known to the
spectators.

An anonymous author, speaking of these two delightful
sciences, says : " Ces deux arts sont frères, et se tiennent
par la main ; les accens tendres et harmonieux de l'un ex-
citent les mouvemens agréables et expressifs de l'autre ;
leurs effets reunis offrent aux yeux et aux oreilles des tableaux animés ; ces sons portent au cœur les images intéres-
santes qui les ont affectés ; le cœur les communique à l'âme ;
et le plaisir qui résulte de l'harmonie et de l'intelligence de
ces deux arts enchaîne le spectateur, et lui fait éprouver
ce que la volupté a de plus séduisant."

Pantomime, unquestionably, expresses a great deal ; but
without melodious sentimental accents of musical sounds,
it never can entirely move our minds.

I shall conclude this chapter by recommending to your
attention the study of drawing and music, as almost indispensable to make a perfect dancer.   By drawing you acquire better ideas of symmetry, elegance, and gracefulness;
especially if you pursue the *beau ideal,* which this art
possesses.   Music enables you to be more precise in your
performance, your ears are more awake to the real time

and cadence[8] of the accompaniment; and all your movements are made in strict accord with the rythmus of the
tune[9].   Music and drawing will afford you much facility
in composition also, as whatever be your genius and creative powers of imagination, one thing is certain, your productions cannot easily fail of being correct.

CHAPTER II.

STUDY OF THE LEGS.

In the management of your legs, endeavour chiefly to acquire a facility of turning them completely.   To this end
make yourself easy about your hips, that your thighs may
move with freedom, and your knees turn well outwards.
All the openings of your legs are thus rendered easy and
graceful.   By dint of practice and attention, you will be
able to accomplish this without any painful efforts.

A dancer whose hips are much contracted, and whose
legs cannot turn entirely out, is never esteemed; as by
these defects his performance is deprived of its greatest
charm.   But one that is gifted with freedom and pliancy,
that exhibits a foot well attached to the instep, and the
points of which are strong, elastic, and low, has a very delightful appearance.

Some young people are framed by nature with their limbs turning outwards; they possess, therefore, more facility, and succeed to greater advantage than those whose legs turn towards each other: a person of the latter kind indeed can cherish no hopes of becoming a good dancer, how diligent soever his labour and study may be. Practice will do no more than turn his feet, and bend his soles a little downwards, but his thighs and knees must remain always in their natural state.

Here we perceive how requisite it is that all who intend devoting themselves to the study of dancing, should scrupulously examine the make and faculties of their body, before they begin to learn an art in which it is impossible to succeed without several gifts of nature.

Be attentive, in practising, to the movements and position of your insteps; do not let them relax in strength and elasticity, nor suffer one of your ankles to be higher than the other; these would be two very serious defects. Render your insteps as pliable and graceful as possible, and give them sufficient strength for the execution of rapid, vigorous, and elevated movements. The action of the instep principally consists in raising and letting down the heel. Study above all things to make it easy and strong, as the equilibrium of the whole body depends on it. When you spring upwards it catches your weight on coming down, and, by a strong rapid movement, makes you fall on your toes.

The movement of the knee is inseparable from that of the instep, and differs from it but in being perfect only when the leg is extended and the point of the foot low. The movement of the hip is a sort of guide to that of the knee and instep, as it is impossible for these last to move unless the hip acts first. In some steps the hips alone are set in motion, as in *entrechats, battements tendus, &c.*

Dancers who have not a natural elasticity, or whose calves are weak in muscle, are compelled to have recourse to their insteps, which make amends in a great measure for the debility of other parts, but not without an immense deal of practice. Daily exercise gives them also vigour and rapidity; but let them beware of interrupting their endeavours, as they would then be of no avail.

Let your openings be easy, precise, and elegant. Many dancers imagine that nothing further is required to be *liant et moëlleux* than to bend their knee very low; but this is a great error, as too low a bend makes the dance appear dry and insipid. You may be very easy and yet jerk your body at every movement, no less by bending too much, than by not bending at all. The reason is obvious, if we consider how subordinate every motion in dancing is to music. For when the bend is too low, and therefore longer in performing than the time of the tune allows, you are obliged to make a sudden spring, or rather jerk, to regain the air which you have for a few instants lost, and this rapid transition from flexion to tension is extremely harsh, and produces an effect equally as disagreeable to the spectator, as that which results from stiffness.

" The *moëlleux* depends in a great degree on a proportionate flexion of the knees, but the instep must contribute, by its elasticity, to the gracefulness of the movement, and the loins serve as a kind of counterpoise to the frame, which the spring of the instep raises or lets down, with softness and elegance, the whole being in perfect accord and harmony."

Let all your openings be consistent with established precept, and in their design strictly uniform with the position of your body and arms.

If your bust is very long, try to raise your legs higher than common rules prescribe; if very short, keep them lower than the usual height. By this means you conceal the defect that exists in the construction of your body.

In your steps and *tems* of vigour be energetic and strong, but, at the same time, beware lest these qualities degenerate into faults, by stiffness and a painful tension of the nerves.

As there are many persons so formed that their legs are closely joined to each other, and, on the contrary, a great number naturally bow-legged, I shall here point out the means of remedying, or, at least, of hiding those two defects.

A man is close-legged when his hips and thighs are firmly contracted, his knees thick, and apparently joined together, and the lower part of his legs, that is to say, from the bottom of the calf to the heels, forming a triangle, of which the ground is the base; the inside ankles very large, the instep high, and the *tendo Achillis* thin, long, and but faintly distinguished. (See plate III, fig. 5.)

The bow-legged person is he in whom the opposite defect is conspicuous. His thighs are too much divided, his knees very distant from each other, his calves do not join, and the light that should be perceived only in certain parts, is seen throughout the whole length of his legs, which are, therefore, in appearance very similar to two bows, whose extremities are turned to each other. Persons of this description have a long flat foot, their exterior ankles stick out, and the *tendo Achillis* is thick and too close to the joints. (See plate III, fig. 4.)

These two natural defects, so diametrically opposite, prove how much the rules of instruction must vary according to the peculiar make of a pupil, as those that are fit for the one to pursue, are prejudicial in the extreme to the other: the studies, therefore, of two dancers so different in point of shape, cannot, in any manner, be the same.

The close-legged dancer must endeavour, as much as possible, to separate the parts that are too nearly united. To succeed in these attempts, let him, in the first place, turn his thighs outwards, and move them in this position, which he is enabled to do by the freedom of the rotatory movement of the *os femoris* in the *cotyloid* cavity of the hip bones. The knees, assisted by this movement, will follow the same direction, and at length get into their right place. The *rotula*, which hinders the knee from bending backwards, will then fall perpendicularly on the point of the foot ; and the thighs and legs at last become perfectly straight, and firmly maintain the stability of the trunk. In the second place, he ought to keep a continual flexion in the articulation of his knees, and make his legs appear much extended, without being so in reality. This is the work of time and practice. Having once acquired the habit, it will be almost impossible to make the legs return to their primitive vicious situation, without the most painful and insufferable efforts.

The bow-legged dancer must also try to diminish the vacuum between his legs, by drawing them as close as possible to each other. It is as requisite to him as to the close-legged one, to practise moving his thighs outwards. He should, moreover, keep his knees in constant extension, that they may thereby acquire pliancy and softness, and thus conceal his natural stiffness ; yet a dancer of this kind can never succeed in the serious or heroic branch; he should, therefore, devote himself to the *demi-caractère,* or I would advise him rather to embrace the pastoral, and study its characteristic steps.

The close-legged dancer is tolerably well adapted to the serious and *demi-caractère;* and is, in general, far more skilful than the preceding ; his execution is easier, his movements more delicate, natural and graceful ; but as he seldom possesses the same strength as the former, he is often compelled to have recourse to the assistance of his instep. In the performance of *entrechats* he may not be brilliant, yet always correct and elegant. Such a dancer may even sometimes aspire to perfection in every branch, provided the height of his stature throw no impediment in the way.

A close-legged dancer should preserve a slight flexibility in his execution, and never extend his knees, excepting at the termination of openings, steps, attitudes, &c. ; by this means he conceals his natural closeness. A bow-legged dancer must, on the contrary, be stretched out as stiff as possible ; always avoiding harshness, to which such a mode of performance necessarily tends, and cross his legs very closely, so that their union may decrease, in a great measure, the interval that would otherwise exist between them. But, notwithstanding all his efforts, he has not the same chance of success as the close-legged performer ; he is usually very strong and vigorous, his muscles are therefore less pliable, and his articulations cannot act with much freedom and ease. Let it be also remembered, that if this defect of *bow-leggedness* proceeds from the natural construction of the bones, every attempt to remedy or amend it must prove fruitless. Art is then of no avail.

SIMPLE POSITION OF THE LEGS, FIG 1. PLATE I.

First Positions of Dancing.

First position, fig. 1, plate I.

Second position, fig. 2, plate II.

Second position on the toes, fig. 3, plate II.

Third position, fig. 3, plate I.

Fourth position, (side view) fig. 1, plate II.

Fifth position, fig. 4, plate I.

Fifth position on the toes, fig. 5, plate I.

N.B. In the second position the distance between the two

heels is the length of the foot. In the third position the feet must be only half crossed.

Bending in the first position, fig. 4, plate II.

N.B. The positions on the toes of the first, third and fourth positions, and the bendings in the four others, are omitted not for the sake of increasing the number of plates ; these positions are very easily understood, and executed without the assistance of plates.

Method of holding one's self in practising, fig. 5, plate II.

Physical construction of the close-legged pupil, fig. 5, plate III.

Physical construction of the bow-legged pupil, fig. 4, plate III.

N.B. The delineator has somewhat exaggerated in the lines of these figures, for the purpose of better exhibiting to the pupil those defective constructions.

A dancer at the second position, in the air and on the heel, fig. 5, plate II.

A dancer at the second position, in the air and on the toes, fig. 1, plate VI.

A dancer at the second position in the air, forwards on the toes (side view), fig. 1, plate IV.

A dancer at the fourth position in the air, forwards on the toes (front view), fig. 2, plate IV.

A dancer at the fourth position in the air, backwards (side view), fig. 3, plate IV.

Positions of the legs in *poses,* and in different attitudes, plates V, VI, VII, VIII, and IX.

Positions of the legs in arabesques, plates X, XI, and XII.

N.B. In arabesques, and several other attitudes, the feet must not be entirely turned ; if they were, these positions would lose their gracefulness.

CHAPTER III.

STUDY OF THE BODY.

LET your body be, in general, erect and perpendicular on your legs, except in certain attitudes, and especially in *arabesques*, when it must lean forwards or backwards according to the position you adopt. Keep it always equally poised upon your thighs. Throw your breast out and hold your waist in as much as you can. In your performance preserve continually a slight bend, and much firmness about your loins. Let your shoulders be low, your head high, and your countenance animated and expressive.

A dancer who wishes to charm the beholder's eye must display all the elegance that his fancy can inspire him with, in the carriage of his body, the easy development of his limbs, and the gracefulness of every attitude into which he throws himself. But let no affectation intermingle with his dancing ; that would mar every thing. By due attention to these particulars, he will make each of his accomplishments shine forth to their greatest advantage, and feel always rewarded for the labour he has taken.

The elegance of the upper part of the body is chiefly to be attended to by a dancer, as in that, one of his principal merits consists. Carry your bust[10] gracefully, impart to its motions and oppositions a certain *abandon*, and by no means let it lose the beauty of its *pose* nor the purity of its design.

Your head, shoulders, and bust, ought to be supported and adorned by your arms, and so precisely follow their motions, that they may present altogether a graceful *ensemble;* and, as we have already remarked, the legs must, of course, participate in the harmony of their movements.

In the performance of your steps let your body be quiet, firm, and unshaken, yet easy and pliant, according to the play of the legs and arms. But in this beware of stiffness. He who, whilst dancing, moves his body by jerks—raises his shoulders at each movement of his legs—bends or relaxes his loins to facilitate the execution of his *tems,* and who shows, by the distortion of his features, how much pain his performance occasions him, is, unquestionably, an object of ridicule, and the name of a *grotesque* would suit him much better than that of a dancer.

I have repeatedly seen examples of this defective mode of dancing; and cannot but attribute it principally to the negligence of masters, who, over-anxious to see their pupils exhibit on a public stage, leave them to themselves before they have completed their studies.

The public, also, by their too indulgent applause, or their want of taste, considerably increase the number of this class of dancers, or, more properly speaking, leapers, who, finding themselves so much encouraged, immediately imagine that they have attained the summit of perfection in their art.

> " ———— le vulgaire s'extasie
> Aux tours de force aux entrechats."
>
> L'Hospital.

Such miserable dancers ought to be banished from the boards of every threatre, as actors devoid of merit, and tending only to the preservation of bad taste.

Simple position of the body, fig. 1, plate I.

Epaulement, opposition of the body, fig. 3 and 4, plate I.

Positions of the body in *poses* and in different attitudes, plates V, VI, VII, VIII, and IX.

Position of the body in arabesques, plates X, XI, and XII.

N.B. In arabesques the body goes out of a perpendicular line, and inclines forwards or backwards in a pleasing *abandon.*

CHAPTER IV.

STUDY OF THE ARMS.

THE position, opposition, and carriage of the arms, are, perhaps, the three most difficult things in dancing, and, therefore, demand particular study and attention.

Noverre, speaking of opposition, says, that " of all the movements executed in dancing, the opposition or contrast of the arms to the feet is the most natural, and, at the same time, the least attended to."

" Observe, for instance, a number of persons walking; you will see that when they place the right foot before, the left arm naturally falls before also, and is thus in opposition with it." This appears to me a general rule, and from thence it is that skilful dancers have acquired the true manner of carrying their arms, and forming a constant opposition of them with their feet; that is to say, that when the left arm is behind, the left leg must be before."

Noverre does not, in my opinion, treat of the opposition with that clearness and exactness which the subject requires ; indeed, few writers have done so. The obscurity, therefore, that has existed on this important particular in dancing, has occasioned it to be an object of continual controversy among professional dancers.

Let us endeavour to elucidate it a little. The opposition of one part of a moving solid to another part is a law of equilibrium by which the gravitating powers are divided. This is precisely what Noverre wishes to demonstrate in his example of the gait of a man ; and when he further says that opposition takes place each time that the man or dancer puts one leg forward, he means to point out that if such foot so placed before be the right, the left arm must naturally be carried forward at the same instant, whilst the opposite limbs remain behind ; the whole counterpoising the deviation of the body from the central line of gravity. This opposition gives the dancer a very graceful appearance, as he thereby avoids that uniformity of lines in his person so unbecoming a true favourite of Terpsichore. (See examples of opposition, fig. 3, plate I, fig. 4, plate IV, and all the figures of plate VIII.)

There are two methods of moving the wrists—upwards and downwards. When the movement is to be made downwards, the wrist must be bent inwards, moving the hand demi-circularly, by which movement the hand returns to its first position ; but care must be taken not to bend the wrist too violently, for it would then appear as if broken. With respect to the second movement, which is upwards, the wrist must be bent in a rounded position, allowing the hand to turn upwards, making a *demi-tour* or half-turn, and by this movement the hand will be found in the first position for the arms.

The elbow, as well as the wrist, has its movement downwards and upwards, with this difference, that when you bend the elbows, the wrists are bent also, which prevents the arms from appearing stiff, imparting to them much grace. Still it is not necessary to bend the wrist much, as it would produce an extravagant effect; the same thing may be observed of the legs when the knee is bent; it is then the instep that completes the movement, by raising the foot, in the same manner as the wrist and elbow.

Thus, in order to move them downwards, the arms being prepared, the elbow and wrist must be bent, and when the arms are bent also, extend them, to complete the movement. They will then return to the first position in which they were. When you perform a movement with the wrists, they should be bent and straightened in the same manner as when accompanied by the movement of the elbows.

As to the second movement, which is upwards, the hands being down, the wrists and elbows must be bent, forming a circle, observing that both arms form at the same time a motion exactly similar ; and then return to their first attitude.

A dancer that holds and moves his arms in a graceful manner, and according to the true rules of art, shows that he has studied at a good school, and his performance is invariably correct. Few artists distinguish themselves by a good style of action in their arms, which deficiency generally proceeds either from the mediocrity of principles they receive from bad instructions, or else it originates in their own negligence, believing, as I have known many do, that if they possess a brilliant mode of execution in their legs, they can do very well without the fine additional ornament of the arms ; and thus exempt themselves from the labour which so important a study requires.

When the arms accompany each movement of the body with exactitude, they may be compared to the frame that sets off a picture. But if the frame is so constructed as not to suit the painting, however well done this last may be, its whole effect is unquestionably taken away. Even so is it with a dancer : for what gracefulness soever he may display in the performance of his steps, unless his arms be lithsome, and in strict harmony with his legs, his dance can have no spirit nor liveliness; and he presents the same insipid appearance as a painting out of its frame, or in one not at all adapted to it.

Should you not be favoured with well made rounding arms, you cannot bestow too much attention on them ; and endeavour to supply by art what nature has left you defective in. Diligent study and exercise often render a thin, long angular arm, tolerably round and elegant.

Learn also to hold them as best accords with your physical construction. If you are short in stature let them be higher than the general rule prescribes, and if tall let them be lower.

A good dancer should omit nothing that may tend to remedy or conceal his personal defects. It is one of those necessary accomplishments to which the mind of every one who desires to become a skilful artist ought to be directed. Take care to make your arms so encircling that the points of your elbows may be imperceptible. From a want of proper attention in this respect, they are deprived of all softness and elegance ; and instead of presenting to the eye, fine oblique or circular lines, (see fig. 1, 4, 5, plate I.) they exhibit nothing but a series of angles, destitute of taste and gracefulness, (see plate III, fig. 1, 2, 3), unpleasing to the spectator, and by imparting to all your attitudes a grotesque and caricature-like appearance, make you only an object of ridicule to the painter.

Let the *Saignée*[11] be level with the palm of your hand, your shoulders low, and always motionless, your elbows round and well supported, and your fingers gracefully grouped together. The position and carriage of your arms must be soft and easy. Let them make no extravagant movement, nor permit the least stiffness to creep into their motions. Beware lest they be jerked by the action and reaction of your legs : this is a great fault, and sufficient to degrade a dancer, what perfection soever he may possess in the exercise of his legs.

> Simple position of the arms, fig. 1, plate I.
> Position of the wrist and fingers, fig. 1, plate I.
> Arms in the second position, fig. 1, plate I.
> Arms in the opposition, fig. 4, plate I.
> Arms encircling above the head, fig. 5, plate I.
> Half-arm, or *demi-bras*, fig. 2, plate II.
> Oppositions of the *demi-bras*, fig. 3, plate I.

Position of the arms in various attitudes, plates V, VI, VII, VIII, and IX.

Position of the arms in arabesques, plates X, XI, and XII.

N.B. It must be observed that in arabesques the position of the arms deviates from the general rule ; it is, therefore, the good taste of the dancer that must arrange them as gracefully as possible.

Position of the hand in different attitudes and arabesques, fig. 5, plate V.

Defective positions of the arms, fig. 1, 2, 3, plate III.

CHAPTER V.

ALWAYS draw your body well up, and especially your head, even in your minutest *poses,* (See plate V, &c.) if not, your performance will be void of expression, and your position or attitude become insipid. In some of the first positions of dancing the head is placed fronting; those are *poses* of attitude.

Action of the Head.

" Never let your head rest perpendicularly upon your shoulders, but incline it a little to the right or to the left, whether your eyes are cast up or downwards or straight forwards; as it is essential that it should have a pleasing yet natural vivacity of motion, and not appear inactive and heavy."

Endeavour to hold your body in a perfect equilibrium; to which end never let it depart from the perpendicular line that should fall from the centre of the collar bone down through the ankles of both feet. (See fig. 4 and 5, plate I; fig. 5, plate II; fig. 1, plate IV; fig. 1, 2, 3, and 4, plate V; fig. 4, plate VII. See Chap. III.)

Attitude.

The pit of the neck must correspond perpendicularly with the feet; if you move one leg forwards the pit then goes back out of its perpendicularity on the foot; if backwards it is thrown before, and thus changes its place with every variation of position.

Besides a graceful carriage, let the dancer acquire uprightness, by forming an exact counterpoise with every part of his frame, and thus enable himself to support his body on one leg only, as, also, to obtain an elegant style of attitude upon both.   (See plate VIII, X, XI, XII, &c.)

Of the Centre of Gravity in a Dancer.

The weight of a man standing upon one leg is divided in an equal manner on the point that sustains the whole, (see fig. 1, plate X.) and as he moves, the central line of gravity passes exactly through the middle of the leg that rests wholly on the ground.   (See fig. 1, plate VIII, &c.)

Counterpoise.

A person that carries a burthen placed out of the central line of his body, must necessarily add, from his own weight, a balance sufficient to counterpoise it on the opposite side, and thus form a true equilibrium round the perpendicular of gravity. (See fig. 2, plate VIII, &c.) But in certain attitudes which the dancer throws himself into as he springs from the ground, as also in inclined arabesques, such as that presented by fig. 3, plate XI, the central line of gravity is not to be attended to in the same manner as it is in the figures of the plates I, II, III, IV, &c. (See fig. 1, plate IX, fig. 1, plate X, as relating also to this remark.)

Of the Figure that moves against the Wind.

A dancer that goes against the wind, in whatever direction it may be, cannot preserve with exactitude the centre of gravity on the line that supports him.   (See fig. 2, 4, and 3, turned on opposite sides, plate XIII.   See also fig. 1, 2, 3, plate XIV, and fig. 4, same plate, which represents a Bacchanalian group, which I composed, during the first year that I was engaged at the Theatre of La Scala, at Milan; a theatre much celebrated for its magnificence, and the combination of talent which it usually displays.)

That particular position technically termed attitude is the most elegant, but at the same time the most difficult which dancing comprises. It is, in my opinion, a kind of imitation of the attitude so much admired in the Mercury of J. Bologne. (See fig. 1, plate VIII, and fig. 2. id., which exhibit two side views of it; see also fig. 1, plate IX, representing the statue of Mercury.) A dancer that studies this attitude, and performs it in a chaste manner, cannot but be remarked as one who has acquired the best notions of his art.

Nothing can be more agreeable to the eye than those charming positions which we call *arabesques*, and which we have derived from antique basso relievos, from a few fragments of Greek paintings, and from the paintings in fresco at the Vatican, executed after the beautiful designs of Raphael.

Arabica ornamenta, as a term in painting, mean those ornaments, composed of plants, shrubs, light branches and flowers, with which the artist adorns pictures, compartments, frises, panels, &c. As a term of architecture, they signify various fanciful foliages, stalks, &c. with which pediments and entablatures are often embellished. The taste for this sort of ornaments was brought to us by the Moors and Arabs, from whom they have taken their name.

Our dancing-masters have also introduced this term into their art, as expressive of the picturesque groups which they have formed of male and female dancers, interlaced in a thousand different manners, one with another, by means of garlands, crowns, hoops entwined with flowers, and sometimes ancient pastoral instruments, which they hold in their hands. These attitudes, so diversified and enchanting, remind us of the beautiful Bacchantes that we see on antique basso relievos, and by their aerial lightness, their variety, their liveliness, and the numberless contrasts they successively present, have, in a manner, rendered the word *arabesque* natural and proper to the art of dancing. I may flatter myself in being the first to give the precise meaning of this expression, as applied to our art; without which explanation it might afford a motive of derision to painters and architects, to whom it originally and exclusively belonged.

Dancers should learn from those chaste pieces of sculpture and painting, the real mode of displaying themselves with taste and gracefulness. They are a fount of beauty, whereto all who aspire to distinction must resort for purity and correctness of design. In the Bacchanalian group above-mentioned, I introduced, with some success, various attitudes, arabesques, and groups, the ideas of which I had conceived on seeing the paintings, bronzes, and marbles excavated from the ruins of Herculaneum, and by these additional images, rendered its appearance more picturesque, characteristic, and animated. (See fig. 4, plate XIV, the principal group.) Those precious monuments of ancient skill have been repeatedly pronounced the best models for the painter and sculptor: in my opinion they are of equal service to the dancer.

Poses, preparations, and endings of steps and *temps*, fig. 4, plate IV, fig. 1, 2, 3, and 4, plate V.

N. B. Enchaînemens and steps may be also finished in attitudes and arabesques.

Different attitudes, plates VI and VII.

Attitude, (as technically so denominated), fig. 1, plate VIII.

The same, side view, fig. 2, plate VIII.

Different manners of resting in attitudes, fig. 3 and 4, plate VIII.

Derivatives of the attitude, fig. 2 and 3, plate IX.

Example of the attitude of the Mercury of J. Bologne, fig. 1, plate IX.

Arabesques, plates X, XI, XII.

Arabesques, on both legs, fig. 4, plate VII.

Arabesques, back view, fig. 3 and 4, plate XI, fig. 4, plate VII.

Groups, attitudes *de genre*, plate XIV.

N.B. I have left out several attitudes and arabesques upon one foot resting flat on the ground, and the same arabesques upon two feet, which are done by merely putting down the leg that is in the air, as represented in figure 4, plate VII, which is derived from the arabesque shown in fig. 4, plate XI.

Attitudes, poses, and arabesques, may be varied *ad infinitum ;* for the slightest change in the situation of the body, in the oppositions of the arms, or the motions of the legs, when all is happily combined, must produce an immense diversity. It is the good taste of the dancer that must decide on the best manner of combining and changing them, taking especial care to appropriate them to the style and character of his dancing. These modified attitudes are much practised in the enchaînements of groups, similar to those presented in figures 1, 2, 3, and 4, of plate XIV.

CHAPTER VI.

OF *TEMPS*, STEPS, *ENCHAINEMENT*, AND OF THE *ENTRECHAT*.

LET your *grands temps* be wide, mellow, and bold; perform them with preciseness, and in ending them, be upright and firm on your legs. In all your *terre-à-terre* steps you cannot be too active about your instep, nor bend your feet too much downwards; as the former gives your execution considerable brilliancy, and the latter renders it light and graceful.

A truly good dancer ought to throw a sort of light and shade into his steps, and by great exactness of performance, distinctly mark each variation he makes in them, In all your high caperings, develope a manly vigour, and let your *steps of elevation* be agreeably contrasted, by the rapidity of your *terre-à-terre* steps. Do not, however, forget to regulate your choice of steps, on the kind of dancing you have adopted, as also, on your physical construction.

In *enchaînemens*, let variety and novelty be your constant aim; carefully study their composition, and do all that your taste points out, to make yourself agreeable. Never intermingle with them any high capers or steps that require much strength to perform, nor relax into coolness by pauses or long openings; as this would, unavoidably, destroy all the effect which *enchaînmens* produce, when correctly executed to a quick and lively music.

The *entrechat* is a light brilliant step, during the performance of which, the dancer's legs rapidly cross each other, and then come down either in the fifth position, or in an attitude upon one leg, as in the *entrechat à cinq, à sept, à neuf,* the *cabriole, brisés* and the *rond-de-jambe en l'air;* all these, ending thus on one leg, may also finish in any of the attitudes and arabesques pointed out in the plates referred to at the close of the foregoing chapter. *Entrechats* are generally begun with an *assemblé, coupé,* or *jetté;* the body then springs into the air, and the legs pass to the fifth position, to cross and cut. In *entrechats,* you may cut four, six, eight, ten, and even twelve times, if you possess the requisite strength. Some can go as far as fourteen, but such efforts have a disagreeable effect, and occasion nothing more, in the beholder, than wonder at the extraordinary muscular powers of the leaper. When a dancer endeavours to make too great a number of cuts, he cannot finish his *entrechat* in time, and his body, shaken by such rapid movements, writhes in a variety of contortions, that offend the eye of the spectator. The most elegant *entrechats* are the *entrechat à six,* and the *entrechat à six ouvert,* done by opening at the third cut, (see plate XII, fig. 4.,) and the *entrechat à huit.*

The following different entrechats, viz:—*entrechat à cinq dessus; entrechat à cinq dessous; brisé de côté, dessus et dessous; en arrière et en avant; entrechat à cinq de côté et en arrière; sissonne battue en avant et sissonne battue derrière; entrechat à quatre sur une jambe; entrechat à sept en avant et en arrière; la cabriole à un et à deux temps; la cabriole Italienne en avant et en arrière; les deux ronds-de-jambes en dehors et en dedans, &c.* may be done in turning, excepting the *entrechat à cinq de côté et en arrière,* the *entrechat à sept en avant* and the *cabriole. L'entrechat à six, se fait en tournant.*

OBSERVATIONS ON *ENTRECHAT*, AND ON THE MANNER OF BEATING AND CROSSING IN CLOSE-LEGGED AND BOW-LEGGED DANCERS.

Close-legged dancers.

The contraction of the muscles, occasioned by the efforts of leaping, stiffens each articulation, and forces every part back into its natural place. The knees, thus compelled to turn inwards, regain their primitive thickness, which greatly opposes the beatings of the *entrechat*. The more united are the legs at their upper part, and divided at their extremities, the more incapable are they of beating or crossing; they remain, therefore, nearly motionless during the action of the knees, which, in consequence, appear to roll uncouthly one upon the other; and thus the *entrechat*, being neither cut, beaten, nor crossed at the feet, cannot have that rapidity and brilliancy which constitute its principal merit. A good method of studying, diligent practice and time, as I have already intimated (Chap. II, *Study of the Legs*,) are the only means of remedying this defect.

Bow-legged dancers.

These are nervous, rapid, and brilliant, in all things that require more strength than agility. Nervous and light, on account of the direction of their muscular *faisceaux*, and the thickness and resistance of their articular ligaments; rapid, because they cross more at bottom than at top, their feet having but a very small distance to perform the beating steps in; and brilliant, by reason of the light being so very conspicuous through their legs as they cut or uncut. This light is precisely what we may term the *clair-obscur* of dancing: for if the *temps* of the *entrechat* be neither cut nor beaten, but, on the contrary, rub_ bed or rolled one upon the other, there is no light to relieve the shade, and the legs, through being too closely joined, present an indistinct mass, void of brilliancy and effect. Bow-legged dancers are, usually, not very skilful, as they chiefly reckon on their bodily strength. This very strength it is, that opposes the greatest obstacle to their acquiring ease and pliancy.

Observations on a person in the act of leaping.

" Nature instructs and acts of itself, without any assistance from reason. When a person wishes to leap, he rapidly elevates his arms and shoulders, which are thus simultaneously set in motion, together with part of the body, and remain elevated so long as they are supported by the movement of the body (the loins of which are bent), and by the impulse of the joints or springs of the thighs, knees, and feet. This extension is made in two directions, upwards and forwards ; the motion intended to send the body forward, places it so at the moment of the leap, and that destined to carry it up, makes it describe a large segment of a circle, rendering the leap yet more rapid."—*Tratt. di Pittura*.

Leonard gives us a true definition of the actions of a man in leaping, and the means he employs to spring from the ground. He explains the strength and impetuosity of the arms and shoulders in their movements, and the manner in which they raise the body up after them. He points out the position of the body, bent and resting gracefully on the hips and knees, which, by folding, prepare to give the impulse and facilitate the spring of the instep. Much study is required to make these movements in a graceful manner, for if done carelessly nothing can be more uncouth. (See Chap. III.)

In *entrechats*, and steps of elevation, a dancer can display every attitude and arabesque. According to my opinion, the finest positions are such as are shown by fig. 1, 2, 3, and 4, of plate XIII, and by fig, 4, plate XII.

Entrechat and step of elevation, wherein the body is inclining forwards, fig, 2 and 4, plate XIII. *Entrechat* and steps of elevation, in which the body is inclining backwards, fig. 3, same plate. Ordinary elevation of a dancer, two feet, fig. 4 and 5, plate XII.

PHYSICAL REMARKS ON A MAN IN THE ACT OF SPRINGING FROM THE GROUND.

In what manner a man makes three movements in leaping.

" When he springs upwards, his head is three times more active than his heels, before his toes leave the ground, and twice more so than his hips. This happens by reason of the three angles that are made in the act of leaping; the first of which is, where the trunk is joined in front of the thighs; the second, where the thighs on the side of the hams are united to the legs; and the third is formed before, at the joints of the legs and insteps."—*Léonard.*

Attitudes of the dancer in *tems* of elevation and *entrechats*, fig. 4, plate XII.; fig. 1, 2, 3, and 4, plate XIII.

Elevation of two feet, fig. 5, plate XII.

CHAPTER VII.

PIROUETTES.

OF THE MANNER IN WHICH A DANCER MUST PREPARE FOR
THE EXECUTION OF HIS PIROUETTES; OF THE VARIOUS
POSITIONS HE MAY TAKE IN TURNING, AND OF THE DIF-
FERENT WAYS OF STOPPING AND ENDING THEM.

THE art of dancing has been carried to so eminent a
degree of perfection by Dauberval, Gardel, Vestris, and
other famous artists, that Noverre, who died during the
finest period known in the annals of Terpsichore, must have
felt surprised at the rapidity of its progress. The dancers
of the last century were inferior to those who flourished
towards the latter end of it, and still more so to those of
the beginning of the present age. We cannot but admire
the perfection to which modern dancers have brought their
art. They have a much more refined taste than their
predecessors, and their performance is full of gracefulness
and charms. Among our ancient artists those beautiful
tems of perpendicularity and equilibrium, those elegant
attitudes and enchanting arabesques were unknown. That
energetic execution, that multiplicity of steps, that variety
of *enchaînemens,* and pirouettes were not then in practice ;
and the rising art, unadorned with those complicated embellishments, encircled the performer in the narrow limits
of simplicity*.

---

* See in the Encyclopediæ, those articles written by Noverre, on ancient
dancers.

We must, however, grant, in favour of our old masters, that they very much excelled us in the serious and grave kind, and that Duprè, and Vestris the elder, were the most perfect models in this boasted branch of dancing, in which they have been equalled by very few of their followers. It is true, they possessed not that diversified execution, that abundance of steps, and variety of movements, now in vogue, but they were always extremely correct in what little they did. At present, the art of dancing is become so complicated, and each dancer devotes himself so much to every branch, that it is somewhat difficult to meet with one truly perfect.

"Qui trop embrasse, mal étreint*."

Pirouettes owe their origin to the surprising advancement made of late years in dancing ; they were unknown to Noverre and all our old masters, who thought it impossible to go beyond the three turns on the instep. The best dancers of the day prove the contrary, as, by their steady uprightness, and the unshaken equilibrium which they preserve as they revolve round, we may say that the present execution of *pirouettes* is really extraordinary. All beginners, I am confident, will acknowledge this to be true. They are aware how much labour it costs to hold one's self on one leg, and how much greater to do so on his toes. Imagine, therefore, what difficulty there must be in turning in such a position, without the slightest jerk in any part of the body.

We may reasonably consider Messrs. Gardel and Vestris as the inventors of *pirouettes :* the latter, by perfecting and diversifying them, brought them most into vogue. Succeeding dancers improved on these, and performed some of all kinds in the most wonderful manner.

---

* Who aims at much, completes but little.

A pirouette of three or four turns, in the second posi-sition, and stopped in the same, or in an attitude, offers the greatest proof of a dancer's uprightness. Nothing is more difficult in dancing than the performance of this pirouette.

Pirouettes require considerable exercise and study. He whom nature hath favoured with pliancy and agility, is always able to perform them gracefully ; but he that is tight about the hips, whose legs are not sufficiently lith-some as to open with ease, and who, therefore, cannot turn well but on his instep, never meets with more than a partial success. Such a dancer should abandon all thoughts of distinguishing himself in the higher kind of pirouettes. It is the same with respect to bow-legged dancers, and those who are of too vigorous a construction : the strength of their muscles deprives them of flexibility and softness, and their bodies are ever wavering as it turns round. Slender and close-legged dancers, are far better adapted to it than the last mentioned ; their limbs are softer, more pliant, and, in general, turned more outwards ; three essential qualities to perform a good pirouette.

The sole of the foot is the true basis on which our whole machine is supported. A sculptor would be work-ing in vain, were he to rest his statue on a round and moveable foundation ; it would, undoubtedly, fall and be broken to pieces. A dancer, for the same reason, must not be seen vacillating on the point of support, but by making use of all his toes as so many branches or roots, the expansion of which, increasing the space of ground he rests upon, maintains his body in a steady equilibrium, he must fasten himself, in a manner to the board, and hold himself with firmness and uprightness. If he neglects to do this, his pirouette will be far from pleasing ; his foot must lose its natural shape, and rolls backwards and forwards, from the great to the little toe ; this sort of wavering motion, caused by the convexity of the toes, when in that position, impedes all stability, and by the vacillation of the instep the equilibrium is entirely lost.

Let your body be steadily fixed on your legs before you begin to do your pirouettes, (see fig. 3, plate VII), and place your arms in such a position as to give additional force to the impulse that sends you round, as also to act as a balance to counterpoise every part of your body as it revolves on your toes.

Previous to the commencement of a pirouette, either from the inside or outside, the dancer may pause in any sort of attitude or arabesque in which he pleases to end his enchaînement. But the positions best suited to its preparation, and that are generally chosen, on account of the body being already upright on the legs, are the positions represented in fig. 3, 4, and 5, plate I; fig. 4, plate IV ; fig. 1, and 4, plate V ; fig. 1, plate VI ; and fig. 1, plate VIII.

The usual attitudes adopted in the performance of pirouettes are that of the second position, (see fig. 1, plate VI), that of the attitude of fig. 1, plate VIII, and on the instep (fig. 4, plate IX). But why should dancers be so limited as that in the position of the body during the performance of their pirouettes ? When an artist has once acquired an easy method of revolving on his toes, a little exercise will soon enable him to turn in an arabesque, or any other different attitude. I was one of the first to go out of the common track in this respect, and possessing much facility in the performance of pirouettes, I obtained some success in the new kind that I invented, one of which is done in the following manner :—turn three times round in the second position, then place the leg

and the arms in the arabesque attitude shown by fig. 4,
plate X, and give three or four more turns in that attitude,
ending it in the same. When this pirouette is correctly
performed it has a very graceful effect.

Another very beautiful pirouette, which I also invented,
is this :—having turned a few times in the second position,
change it into that of the arabesque represented in fig.
3, plate XI ; stretch out your body, and incline it forwards
as much as possible, whilst your head and arms gracefully
follow its motion. This pirouette has something in it of a
magical appearance, for as the body leans so much over, and
seems on the point of falling at each turn of the pirouette,
one might think there was an invisible power that supported the dancer, who counterbalances his eccentricity
from the line of gravity by the positions of his arms and
leg, and the great rapidity of his motions. I believe this
pirouette to be the most difficult that can be performed.
I have sometimes turned in the attitude of fig. 4, plate
VIII, which is a pirouette of much gracefulness, and produces a good effect ; the angular positions of the right
arm giving it a peculiar brilliancy. It may be made much
use of in a *pas de caractère.*

On one occasion, performing the part of Mercury, I
took, as I turned in my pirouette, the attitude of the statue
of Mercury by J. Bologne. (See fig. 1, plate IX.) This
fine position is very difficult to stand in. Unless a dancer
is naturally arched he never can do it well, and the pirouette
loses all its effect. The body must lean forward, and the right
arm develope itself almost entirely. The leg that is in
attitude must be bent, and by its motion accompany the
rounding contour of the position of the body. To render
this attitude yet more graceful, let the dancer stretch out
his left arm, in which the *caduceus* is held ; this takes off
the angle at his elbows that it would otherwise present,

and gives the pirouette much more elegance.   In the gesture expressive of the action, this position is replete with
truth, and therefore should not be modified.

I shall conclude by telling the pupil that he may revolve
in any kind of attitude or arabesque, provided that the
design of the body, arms and legs be graceful, and every
movement natural, and free from affectation.

Pirouettes may be ended in any position, attitude or
arabesque whatever.   The following are various different
sorts of pirouettes : *pirouette à petits battemens* on the
instep, pirouettes *à rond-de-jambe ; à la seconde avec
grand rond-de-jambe ; avec fouetté, pirouette en attitude,
en arabesque; pirouette sur le coude-pied ; pirouette en
dedans à la seconde sur le coude-pied et en attitude ;
pirouette renversée ; pirouettes composées, &c.*

Position of the dancer in beginning his pirouette from the
outside, fig. 3, plate VII.

N.B. The feet must herein be placed between the second and
fourth position.

Position of the dancer in beginning his pirouette from the
inside, fig. 4, plate VII.

CHAPTER VIII.

OF THE SERIOUS DANCER, THE DEMI-CARACTERE, AND THE
COMIC DANCER.

IT is in vain that a dancer devotes himself to the serious
or heroic branch, unless he is gifted with symmetry of
form, and elevation of stature ; indispensable qualities to
excel in this kind of dancing. Those whose persons approach nearest in height and shape to the statues of
Apollo, or of Antinous, and of the Troadian Venus, or of
Diana, are perfectly adapted to serious dancing ; but they
would never do for the *demi-caractère* and the *pastoral.*
They are too majestic. (See fig. 1, plate XIV.)

All who wish to signalize themselves in this sort of performance must be of a noble, elegant, and elevated carriage, replete with dignity and gracefulness, but void of
the least affectation.   The serious is the most difficult
branch of dancing, it requires a close study, and cannot be duly appreciated but by connoisseurs and men of
a refined taste. He who excels in it, deserves the highest
applause. A correct execution of an *adagio* is the *nec
plus ultra* of our art ; and I look on it as the touch-stone
of the dancer.

It is truly to be lamented that the finest style of dancing is now so much neglected, I might perhaps say completely laid by. The causes of this sad abandonment are

chiefly attributable to that confusion of branches which at present tarnishes the art of dancing ; to that want of perseverance and study in most dancers, and to that vicious taste, so conspicuous among those who frequent the greatest part of our theatres. Our masters, as I have before observed, were perfect in this style ; but they have had very few followers. I know only one dancer capable of executing it to advantage ; but let him not, by an ill-placed complaisance, endeavour to please a crowd of ignorant spectators. It is, nevertheless, in some measure, the province of a perfect artist to bring back public taste to what is really good and beautiful, by persisting in performing according to the true rules of art. It was said in one of the Parisian papers, speaking of my *début*, in the serious style, at the Royal Academy of Music, that " for some length of time past the noble and serious kind of dancing has been treated with a singular contempt. It is, indeed, difficult to imagine how any one can dance without being lively. Serious dancing, however, possesses its peculiar attractions. Beautiful positions, majestic movements, dignity of step, &c., give a certain character of importance to dancing, which, with respect to imitation, assimilate it in a manner to the art of sculpture. The ancients were very partial to this sort of recreation, and cultivated it with great success. We despise and neglect it because we are far beneath that perfection which the Greeks, and especially the Romans, once obtained. Their mimic plays bore some analogy to our grave style, which is a reason why we should encourage the small number of dancers who devote themselves to these performances. At some future time they may, perhaps, afford enjoyments hitherto unknown to us."

This last sentence proves how great is the decay of the beautiful serious style of dancing ; since the enjoyments which it promises are unknown to the public of the present day.

A serious dancer should be perfectly shaped in his legs, have a well formed instep, and be extremely flexible and easy about his hips ; without which essential qualities he cannot succeed in the line that he has taken. In all other kinds of dancing it is not so requisite to possess those peculiar qualities in the same perfection, as in this. That preciseness and correctness, which we always expect to see in the heroic artist, are not exacted from a *demi-caractère* or comic dancer. The heroic dancer must pre-eminently distinguish himself by the dignity of the upper part of his body, by the most harmonious combination of movement in his arms, and by the finest polish which the best rules of art can impart to his performance.

This kind of dancing comprises the most beautiful developments, all the *grands temps,* and the noblest steps. The performer must attract the beholder's attention by the elegance of his design, the correctness of his *poses,* and the gracefulness of his attitudes and arabesques. The finest pirouettes in the second position, in attitude or on the instep, *entrechats,* and all other *tems d'élèvation,* are required in the serious branch. We thus perceive that the performance of the heroic dancer in our days is much more complicated than that of our predecessors, and that such an artist must now possess a great number of accomplishments.

The *demi-caractère* dancer ought to be of the middle stature, and of a slender and elegant shape. Those who are gifted with the proportions of Canova's Mercury [12], or of his Hebe, are well suited to this charming kind of dancing.

This *demi-caractère* is a mixture of every style. Those who devote themselves to it may make use of all the *tems*

and steps which the art of dancing possesses. Their performance, however, must be noble and elegant, their *tems
d'abandon* executed with some little restraint, and
a certain amiable dignity ought to accompany their dance
throughout. The *demi-caractère* does not admit those
grands tems of the serious kind. A dancer of the
demi-caractère class is chiefly adapted to perform in the
characters of Mercury, Paris, Zephyrus, or of a Faun, and
to represent the elegant and graceful manners of a Troubadour, &c.

The comic and pastoral must be the department of
those whose persons, of the middle stature, are thick set
and vigorously constructed ; and if a dancer, together
with these almost athletic proportions, possesses a stature
a little above the ordinary size, he is perfectly framed for
the performance of characteristic steps, the greater part
of which are united to the comic branch. In my opinion,
the very type of this branch consists in the imitation of all
those natural motions which have been denominated
dances in every age, and amongst every people. To offer
a true picture of pastoral life, the dancer, in his performance, must copy and mimic the steps, attitudes, simplicity
of manner, and sometimes even those frolicsome and rude
motions of the villager, who, inspired by the sound of his
rustic instruments, and animated by the society and liveliness of his cherished companion, or beloved mistress, gives
his whole soul up, without restraint, to the pleasures of
dancing. The pupil that aspires to excellence in these
imitations should study nature, and the best painters who
have enlivened their canvass with these interesting images.

All other dancers of the comic cast may study characteristic steps, and render themselves servile imitators of
every kind of dancing, peculiar to different countries,
giving their attitudes and movements the true national

stamp of the dances they are performing. That correctness, which artists of the *demi-caractère* kind must possess, is not so rigorously exacted from dancers of the
comic and pastoral branches.

The following are the characteristic dances most practised: *la Provençale, le Bolero, la Tarantelle, la Russe,
l'Ecossaise, l'Allemande, la Tyrolienne, la Cosaque, la
Fourlane,* &c. The *pas Chinois,* the pas *de Sabotiers,
l'Anglaise,* steps of caricature, &c. appertain to the lower
comic style.

> Serious kind, fig. 1, plate XIV.
>
> The demi-caractère, fig. 2, plate XIV.
>
> Comic kind, fig. 3, plate XIV.
>
> Example of the composition of groups, attitudes de genre,
> and principal picture of a Bacchanalian dance, fig. 4, plate XIV.
>
> N.B. The explanation of the plates in their order is given at
> the end of the treatise.

CHAPTER IX.

THE PRECEPTOR.

New Method of Instruction.

A dancer, after having been educated at the best schools, must trust to his execution for the attainment of the first rank. He that knows the theory only of the art, can never be a perfect guide. A man should be a first rate dancer before he pretends to the title of a master [13]; otherwise he cannot teach but in a common-place and mechanical manner; nothing will be positive in his lessons, and his demonstrations must be always uncertain and without force. Incapable of imparting the true principles of a good execution, he affords his pupil no means of gaining success and distinction. A dancer coming from the misguiding hands of such a professor, cannot possibly be perfect, he has not imbibed the true spirit of the art, and his performance is invariably cool, inexpressive, and devoid of grace. He presents the spectator with a picture incorrectly drawn, feebly coloured, without any gradations of light and shade, and, therefore, wanting effect. If then he does not possess those qualities, no less essential in dancing than in painting, it is in vain for him to hope to please and interest the beholder.

I have, however, seen instances of dancers bred up at a good school, who, from some circumstance or other, not being able to attain pre-eminence on the stage, have set themselves to teaching, and furnished our theatres with excellent dancers. But the number of such professors is very small, as nearly all those who are not distinguished by their practice are incapable of producing a finished dancer.

A master, to whom long exercise and experience have given views beyond the common track of custom, before he commences teaching a young pupil, will always examine whether his construction is suited to the attitudes and motions of dancing ; and, whether, as he increases in growth, he will possess an elegant shape, a graceful mien, and perfect pliancy in his limbs ; for, without these natural gifts and dispositions towards making a rapid progress in the study, the scholar will neither acquire skill nor reputation.

> " —————————— Se adeguata
> Non avrà la figura, non imprenda
> Un' arte sì gentile e delicata."
>
> RICCOBONI.

A famous actor used to say that it was impossible to excel on the stage, without the assistance of nature. These words, which experience itself dictated, are replete with truth.

The age of eight years is the best time of life for commencing the first rudiments of dancing ; the young learner soon comprehends the demonstrations of his preceptor, who, being then perfectly enabled to judge of his physical powers, instructs him to much greater advantage.

As soon as the master has prepared his pupil by the first exercises, he should immediately make him study the *lesson*[14]; then perfect him in the *tems d Ecole* in the principal steps of dancing, and afterwards point out, and make him practise the kind of performance best adapted to his disposition, physical construction, and sex.

Men must dance in a manner very different from women; the *tems de vigueur*, and bold majestic execution of the former, would have a disagreeable effect in the latter,

who must shine and delight by lithsome and graceful
motions, by neat and pretty *terre-à-terre* steps, and by
a decent voluptuousness and *abandon* in all their attitudes[15].

All who are of an elevated stature, of either sex, the
master must set apart for the serious and more noble kind
of dancing. Those of a middle height, and of a slender
and delicate form, let him appoint to the *demi-caractère*,
or mixed kind. And those who are beneath that height,
and of a thick-set, vigorous construction, let him devote
to the comic branch and to steps of character. The master should finish his instructions, by instilling into his
pupil's mind, to make him truly accomplished, the real
spirit and charm of his art. He must carefully point out
the difference that exists between one kind of dancing and
another, fix with preciseness the manner of its performance, and, finally, render his pupil familiar with all the
diversified modes of dancing, which the variety of costumes he will have to assume requires.

If the pupil is endowed with a genius for composition,
and a creative imagination, the master, skilful in his art,
should let him exercise his powers of invention and combination of steps, and make him acquainted with the finest
designs of choreography.

At the age of twenty-three or twenty-four years, a dancer
ought to have acquired the whole mechanism of his art,
and possess the most brilliant execution he is susceptible
of attaining. In dancing, merit is not to be estimated by
the number of years the performer has devoted to its practice. Nor is it to be under-rated as he advances in life.
A dancer at the age of forty, if he be of a good school,
and has been diligent in the preservation of what he has
learned, may still shine as an artist of the first order.
Of this we have many instances.

New Method of Instruction.

In order to deserve success in the art of forming a good dancer, I have added to the rules contained in this part, figures, which I have had drawn from nature; these represent the positions of the body, the arms, and the legs; the different postures, the attitudes, and *arabesques*. The learners having these examples before their eyes, will easily understand the theoretical principles which I make known to them. The poet of Tibur judiciously observes,

" Segnius irritant animos demissa per aurem.

Quam quæ sunt oculis subjecta fidelibus . . ."

And, in order that their execution may be correct, I have drawn lines for them over the principal positions of these figures, which will give them an idea of the exact form they are to place themselves in, and to figure in the different attitudes of dancing. It will remain for the learners to study well these geometrical lines, paying strict attention to their diversity. As soon as they have rendered this labour, (which I may venture to term mathematical by reason of its precision,) familiar to them, they will be sure to place themselves properly, giving proofs that they have been well taught, and have acquired a correct taste. I have preferred this novel method, which is undoubtedly a more sure and efficacious one, to that of a long and wearying description of the movements in dancing, which oftentimes do but perplex and confound the learner.

Were I to form a dancing school, I should immediately put into practice amongst my pupils the following method, which I believe would prove very useful, and which all masters might adopt without having any knowledge of drawing. I should compose a sort of alphabet of straight lines, comprising all the positions of the limbs in dancing, giving these lines and their respective combinations, their proper geometrical appellations, viz : perpendiculars, hori-

zontals, obliques, right, acute, and obtuse angles, &c., a
language which I deem almost indispensable in our lessons.
These lines and figures, drawn upon a large slate and exposed to the view of a number of scholars, would be soon
understood and imitated by them, and the master would
not then be compelled to hold a long demonstrative
discourse to each of them separately.   The most diligent
might take copies of those figures on small slates, and
carry them with them to study at home, in the same manner
as a child, when he begins to spell, studies in his horn-book
in the absence of the master.   Let the reader compare
the two following delineations with fig. 1 and 3, of plate VI,
and he will conceive a clearer idea of this new system.

Fig. 1, plate VI.   Fig. 3, plate VI.

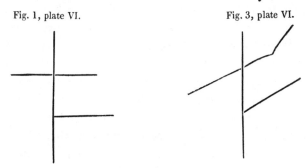

It is necessary that the pupil should study these geometrical lines and all their derivatives.   If he subjects
himself to this task, which I may venture to call mathematical, on account of its laboriousness, he is certain of
holding himself correctly afterwards, and will show that
he received notions of a pure taste in the school at which
he was educated.

A teacher cannot too strongly recommend his scholars
to have incessantly before them those master-pieces of
painting and sculpture, which have been saved from the
wreck of antiquity.   Those immortal offsprings of genius,

those enrapturing examples of the *beau idéal* of the fine arts, will considerably assist the cultivation of their taste. A dancer who knows not how to develope himself, who is deficient in gracefulness, and void of good taste, can never afford the smallest delight to the connoisseur and cultivated spectator.

Of the Composition of Steps.

I shall conclude with an admonitory remark, that may perhaps be of service to young artists, who, having successfully combatted all the first difficulties of their art, wish to betake themselves to the composition of steps.

Why should they not follow the example of Dupré, in order to hasten their progress in this branch of study? That celebrated dancer used to dance extempore to familiar airs; by which means he rendered his imagination more creative in the forming of steps and *enchaînement* and accustomed his ear to catch the measure and rythmus of the music with greater rapidity.

This exercise would prove extremely useful to develope the genius of a youthful dancer. His first attempts might probably be incorrect, sometimes even ungraceful, but when he has once laid the foundation of the step, if I may use the term, he can afterwards correct it and make all the changes suitable to its perfection. I have very often practised this extemporizing, and had the good fortune, at times, of producing some things that were tolerable. I have frequently, by this exercise, been enabled to compose with facility a variety of steps which I had to execute in public, and particularly when I allowed myself a little time to perfect their combinations. M. Gardel, speaking once of our old dancers, mentioned, with approbation, this practice of Dupré, who, whilst he was making himself an excellent dancer, gave a higher flight to his genius.

His remark struck me, and I immediately set about imitating that distinguished performer. I made my first essays under the eye of my father. Whilst he extemporized on the piano-forte, I endeavoured to follow his *musical intentions,* and to form *pas de deux, de trois,* which I afterwards performed in his operas of *Omphale, Achille, Dibutade, &c.* These essays were so fortunate as to meet with general approbation.

APPENDIX.

FIRST EXERCISES.

First Positions.

In the first position the legs are much extended, the two heels close to each other, the feet turned completely outwards in a straight line. (See fig. 1, plate I.) In the second, the legs are more apart, but only by the length of the foot. (See fig. 2, plate II.) In the third, the feet half cross each other and are close together. (See fig. 3, plate I.) The fourth is very similar to the third, with this difference, that the feet half cross each other without touching. (See fig. 1, plate II.) In the fifth, the feet cross each other entirely. (See fig. 4, plate I.) In all these positions the knees must be bent without raising the heels in the least from the ground ; but to give flexibility and strength to the instep they should be often practised on the toes. (See fig. 5, plate I, and fig. 3, plate II.)

Battements.

Battements consist of the motions of one leg in the air, whilst the other supports the body. They are of three kinds, viz., *grands battements, petits battements,* and *battements* on the instep.

The first are done by detaching one leg from the other and raising it to the height of the hip, extending it to the utmost. (See fig. 5, plate II, which shows also the manner in which a beginner must hold himself.) After the performance of the *battements* the leg falls again into the fifth position. They may be crossed either behind or before. *Grands battements* enable a dancer to turn his legs completely outwards, and give much facility to the motions of his thighs, for high developments, and the execution of the *grands tems ; grands battements* are made both forwards and backwards. When they are done forwards the leg must be in the positions shown in fig. 1 and 2 of plate IV. When backwards its positions must be that of fig. 3, same plate.

Petits battements are performed after the same way, but instead of raising the leg into the air you only detach it a little from the other leg, without letting your toes leave the ground. These *battements* make the legs very lithsome, because the pupil is obliged to redouble his motions.

Petits battements on the instep. It is the hip and knee that prepare and form these movements ; the hip guides the thigh in its openings, and the knee by its flexion performs the *battemens*, making the lower part of the leg cross either before or behind the other leg, which rests on the ground. Suppose that you are standing on your left foot, with your right leg in the second position, and the right

foot just touching the ground at the toe, cross before the
left, by bending your knee and opening again sideways'
then bend the knee again, crossing your foot behind, opening also sideways ; and so continue to do several of these
battemens one after the other.   Gradually increase in
quickness, till you can perform them so rapidly, that the eye
cannot count them.   These *battemens* have a very pretty
effect, and give much brilliancy to the motions of the legs.
They should also be practised a great deal with both legs
resting on the toes.

Ronds-de-Jambes.

To begin your *ronds-de-jambes* from the outside, take
the same position as that in which you commence your
petits battemens.   Suppose it is the left leg that stands on
the ground whilst the right, in the second position, is prepared for the movement, make it describe a semicircle backwards, which brings your legs to the first position, and
then continue on the sweep till it completes the whole
circle, ending at the place from whence it started.   This
is what we technically term *ronds-de-jambe*.

The *ronds-de-jambes* from the inside are begun in the
same position, but the right leg, instead of commencing the
circle backwards, must do so forward.   After the pupil has
practised the *ronds-de-jambe* on the ground, he should
exercise himself in performing them in the air, holding the
leg that supports his body, on the toes.

The pupil must at first practise in resting his hand on
something, that he may keep himself upright, and exercise
each leg alternately.   When he has acquired some facility
in this, let him practise without holding, which gives him
uprightness and equilibrium, essential qualities in a good
dancer.   He will also thereby gain strength, and means
of executing, with ease, every kind of step.   He must
repeat his practice daily to establish his execution ;

for were he gifted with the rarest talent he can never become perfect, but by incessant application and study.

OF THE TEMS.

We call *tems* a movement of the leg.

Of the Pas.

The *pas* denotes the various manners of arranging one's steps in walking or in leaping, either as he moves in front or turns round. It generally means a combination of steps arranged to some musical air: thus we say such a one made a beautiful *pas* on such a *chaccone*, such a *gigue*. *Pas* are often combined for the performance of two or more persons; *pas de deux, pas de trois, quatre, cinq, &c.*

OF THE LESSON.

The combination of elementary exercises, and of the principal steps of dancing is what is usually termed the *lesson*.

The learner first exercises himself in bending his knees in all the positions, in the practice of *grands et petits battemens*, the *rond-de-jambes* on the ground and in the air, the *petits battemens* on the instep, &c. Afterwards come the *tems de courante simples et composès*, the *coupés à la premiére, à la seconde, et composès*, the attitudes, the *grands rond-de-jambes, tems de chaccone*, the *grands fouettés*, facing and revolving, the *quart-de-tour*, the *pas de Bourrée* and the various movements of different kinds of pirouettes. These exercises tend to form a good dancer, and afford him means of obtaining success. The *lesson* concludes by the practice of pirouettes, of *tems terra-à-terre*, and *tems de vigueur*.

But after the pupil is enabled to perform all the exercises which the lesson comprehends, he does not yet attain that end which he in the beginning hoped to reach. To become a finished dancer he must divest himself of that school-boy appearance which necessarily hangs about him, and by his boldness and ease of execution, at length show that he is master of his art. Let his whole attention be then directed to delight his beholders, by the elegance of his positions, the gracefulness of his movements, the expressive animation of his features, and by a pleasing *abandon* diffused throughout his whole performance. These qualities constitute a truly finished dancer, and, with them, he is certain of enrapturing all who behold him.

GAIT.

A graceful manner of walking on the stage is of much importance to a dancer, although a number of our artists neglect it, both in moments of repose and in presenting themselves to the public for the execution of a *pas,* which is a serious defect, as it, in the first place, offends the eye, and, secondly, deprives the performance of its pleasing illusion.

A good style of walking is very useful, for in that consists one of the first qualities that dancing imparts, which is a graceful carriage. Let your legs be well extended in their movements or steps, and your thighs turned perfectly outwards, all the lower parts of your legs will then be turned in the same manner. Your steps should be no longer than the length of one of your feet. Avoid stiffness in their motions, which must be neither too slow nor too quick ; as both extremes are equally unpleasing. Do not separate your legs from each other sideways. Carry your head upright and your waist steadily ; by which means your body is kept in an elegant position. Let your breast project a little and your arms fall naturally on each side. (See Chapter IV.)

EXPLANATION OF THE PLATES.

PLATE I.

Fig. 1. First position, arms in the second.

2. Position of the wrist and fingers.

3. Opposition, *épaulement du corps*; half-arm in opposition and legs in the third position.

4. Arms extended in opposition; legs in the fifth position.

5. Arms encircling over the head, and legs in the fifth position on the toes.

PLATE II.

Fig. 1. Position of the body, *demi-bras*, and legs in the fourth position (side view).

2. Second position, feet flat on the ground, and position of the *demi-bras*.

3. Second position on the toes.

4. Bend in the second position.

5. Manner in which a dancer should hold himself in practising; leg in the second position.

PLATE III.

Fig. 1, 2, and 3. Defective positions of the arms.

4. Defects of the physical construction of the bow-legged dancer.

5. Defects of the physical construction of the close-legged dancer.

PLATE IV.

Fig. 1. Fourth position forwards and in the air. Arms in the second position (side view).

2. Same position on the toes. Arms in opposition (front view).

3. Fourth position, leg in the air behind (side view).

4. *Poses*, preparation, and termination of *tems* and steps.

NOTES

TO PART THE SECOND.

1.

This Second Part was commenced at Paris, and completed and published at Milan, in the month of April, 1820. It is styled an *Elementary, Theoretic, and Practical Treatise on the Art of Dancing, containing all those discoveries and demonstrations of general and individual principles which ought to guide a dancer.* Two translations were made of this work into Italian, the first by Mr. Grini, the second by the Chevalier Valmarana.

The French edition of this work is dedicated to Mr. F. A. Blasis, late Member of the *Conservatoire de Naples,* and Governor of the *Section Philharmonique du Museum d' Instruction Publique,* at Bordeaux.

The First Part, *Origin and Progress of Dancing,* has also been translated into Italian by Mr. Velli, and, together with the above mentioned Treatise, placed in the Gallery of celebrated artists.—*(Galleria Degli Art. celebri.)*

2.

The Apollo Belvidere, the Laocoon, the Medicean Venus, the Mercury, usually called the Antinous, and a few other masterpieces of Grecian sculpture, are the most sublime models of perfection, in human forms, and the most perfect in natural expression.

" Spesso vinta da lor cedè natura."—Metastasio.

3.

Vide Appendix after the end of Chap. IX.

4.

At the conclusion of a long and learned discourse, which I once had with M. Gardel, on dancing, that celebrated artist told me, that to judge of the merit of a dancer, one should take him as he places himself in attitude, or at the moment of his elevation in the execution of some difficult movement. If in his position and performance, he is found to display the true principles of art ; if his body, arms and legs offer an harmonious assemblage, if, in short his whole figure be deemed worthy of attracting a painter's attention, that dancer is perfect and deserves the palm. Mr. Gardel shows, by this observation, how extensive his knowledge is in dancing, as also how difficult it is to obtain perfection in that art. Every artist cannot say with equal truth *anch' io son pittore.*

5.

Vide Chap. V.

6.

Trattato della Pittura. This is perhaps the best work in existence on this sublime art. Leonardo da Vinci, its author, was one of those extraordinary beings on whom nature sometimes pleases to lavish her highest gifts. He was a musician, a poet, a mechanician, a geometrician, an architect, an engineer, an excellent modeller, and one of the greatest painters that Italy ever produced. His picture of the Lord's supper is considered a masterpiece of painting.

7.

All the fragments marked with commas, and to which no author's name is subjoined, are extracted from the French Encyclopedia. The article that furnished them is the only one in the work that treats of dancing in such a manner as to be useful to our present dancers. Those observations concerning the mechanism of certain branches of the art, and especially those which relate to the physical constructions of many individuals, are full of judgment and sound reasoning.

8.

Cadence * is that movement which, in good music, affords the performer a quick comprehension of its measure, so that he feels it gradually fall, and marks its decline without thinking, as if directed by a kind of instinct.

Cadence is particularly required in tunes for dancing. We commonly say " that *minuet marks a good cadence,* that *chaccone* has no cadence." Cadence moreover denotes the accord of the dancer's steps, with the time of the accompanying music. But it must be observed that the cadence is not always marked precisely as the time is beaten. The music-master beats the time of the minuet by striking at the beginning of each bar ; the dancing-master only beats at the commencement of every other bar, as it requires that time to perform the four steps of the minuet. (J. J. Rousseau, *Dict. de Musique.*)

This applies only to Minuets.

9.

Rythmus, in its general definition, means the proportions between the several parts of the same whole. In music it is that difference of movement which results from the slowness or vivacity of the time, and from the length or shortness of the bars. This is Plato's definition of it.—(J. J. Rousseau, *Dict. de Musique.*)

Rythmus is a Greek word, signifying *number;* which number is applied in ennumerating and measuring equal and unequal distance.

Rythmus serves to mark musical composition more sensibly ; for the varied and infinite combination of bars that music freely borrows of Rythmus, constitutes the difference of one air with another ; and that difference also which subsists between the meaning, thoughts, and ideas, of the same subject. This caused Virgil to say, " That he could recollect an air, if the words were present to his mind." By the assistance of this number, or Rythmus (which is regulated by measured time), dancers can, without any other accompani-

---

* We also call cadence that warbling in the throat, which the Italians term *trillo.* The terminations of musical phrases are also denominated cadences

ment of melody or harmony of voice and instrument, perform their parts. On this account it is that Ovid gives to the arms of a dancer, the epithet of *numerous* instead of *harmonious.*

" This dancer, delighting in gesture, gently moves her *numerous* arms, gracefully inclines or turns with ease her beauteous body."—METASTASIO.

10.

Statuaries, painters, and antiquaries, give the upper part of the body the name of *torse;* but we are here obliged to make use of such terms as are generally employed in our dancing schools.

11.

We ought rather to say, the point of junction of the *humerus* or *shoulder-bone* with the *radius* or lower bone of the arm ; but our scholars will better understand it by the name of *saignée.*

12.

I cannot refrain from paying, in this place, due homage to that great sculptor, the Praxiteles and perhaps the Phidias, of our age. His talents have placed him on a level with Michael Angelo, Fiamingo, Algardi, and other sublime geniuses, that Italy can boast of having produced. Canova alone holds the sceptre of modern sculpture*. His numerous works, dispersed through all Europe, are known by that softness of contour, that infinite expression, that enchanting simplicity, that natural grace and rare suavity, which have been so much admired and extolled by all who have had the pleasure of seeing his Hebé, Madeleine, Paris, Venus, Cupid and Psyché, Dædalus, Dancer, Muse, &c.

Il ne manque rien à ces charmantes sculptures,

. . . .

Ni le mélange exquis des plus aimables choses,
Ni ce charme secret, dont l'œil est enchanté,
Ni la grace plus belle encor que la beauté.

LA FONTAINE.

Let the beholder, after he has been charmed with the ease, purity, delicacy, and lightness that reign so conspicuously in these delightful statues, turn to the contemplation of the grand sublimity which this immortal sculptor has displayed in his *Hercules defeating Lychas;* in his *Theseus, conqueror of the Centaurs,* and in many other of his productions of the same class. The statue of M. Letizia is remarkable for that noble simplicity by which the Greek chisel is so easily distinguished.

13.

I myself have had a convincing proof of this. After receiving the first rudiments of dancing and studying sometime at the school of a *coryphaeus,* my

---

* When this work first appeared, this artist was still living.

parents, thinking I possessed some natural disposition for the art, and wishing to accelerate my progress, placed me in the hands of M. Dutarque, a ballet-
master.   No sooner did I begin studying under the directions of that artist,
who had been educated in the best schools, and had already distinguished himself as a first-rate dancer, than I was obliged to learn all over again, and forget what I had previously acquired.   I found in him a very different method
of demonstrating, and the art of dancing appeared to me altogether in a new
light.   I discovered in its cultivation a seductive charm, accompanied, however, by increasing difficulties ; but the manner in which he instructed me to
surmount every obstacle, encouraged me to proceed with redoubled ardour,
and strengthened me in the hope that my endeavours would not prove entirely fruitless.   Several tours, which I afterwards made through some of
the principal cities, such as Marseilles, Bordeaux, &c.* afforded me further
acquirements and a more extended knowledge of my profession.   It was at
the Opera of Paris, that I first saw to what degree of perfection the art of
dancing was carried†. M. Gardel, the first among modern *orchesographers*,
showed me, in his various productions, the richest beauties of the art.
Encouraged and assisted by his advice it was, that I danced at the Royal
Academy of Music.

14.

Vide—Appendix.

15.

I am acquainted with a master of great repute in Paris, who has the
defect of teaching men and women to dance after the same manner, so that
all his pupils have a certain air of affectation, by no means pleasing to the
eye of a person of taste.

---

* Bordeaux is the next town in France, after Paris, for the performance of
grand theatrical ballets. Its superb theatre has always possessed good composers, and has even supplied the Opera of Paris with many an excellent
dancer. In the last few years, this theatre has produced three or four dancers who have held, and still hold the first rank at the Royal Academy of
Music.

It was said in a newspaper, relating to my *débuts* at the Opera, "The
theatre of Bordeaux seems destined to furnish our boards with dancers."

A provincial paper said about the same time, " Our grand Theatre of Bordeaux appears henceforth to be the last step to that Olympus (the Opera)."
I mention this in honour of the Bordeaux Theatre, which at this present
time reckons on its stage several capital dancers, under the direction of
M. Blache, one of our best ballet-masters.

† It is very requisite for a young dancer to spend a little time at the schools
of Paris ; it is there, if any where, that he will be able to make himself
perfect.

PART THE THIRD.

ON PANTOMIME,

AND THE STUDIES NECESSARY FOR A PANTOMIMIC PERFORMER.

" ————atto degli occhi e delle membra."

LE TASSE.

" ——————————— art ingénieux
De peindre la parole et de parler aux yeux."

BREBŒUF.

HAVING frequently reflected on Ballets, and the usual method of composing them, it has as frequently occurred to me, that their prevailing defects might be separated from them; and that, by enlarging the pantomimic department of them, and by improving the incidental dancing, they might be advanced to something like perfection.

Pantomime is, undoubtedly, the very soul and support of the Ballet. The art of gesture possesses powers capable of raising an interest, unknown to the generality of artists; and it is to the slight attention paid to this department, and to a want of useful information in composers, that must be attributed the glaring imperfections that prevail throughout the greater part of those pieces improperly styled

Ballets, which, however, are continually performed at theatres of the first rank.

Gesture is the earliest sort of language which man acquires from nature. Children and savages make use of it, for the purpose of supplying their wants. It is a means of communicating the ideas and the sentiments of those who talk different languages, and is, in fact, a resource for such unfortunate beings as are deprived of the faculties of hearing and speaking. What a subject then, for exciting an interest in this imitative art, and for its cultivation! " Pantomime," says a great master of the fine arts, " expresses with rapidity the movements of the soul—it is the language of all nations—of all ages—and of all occasions : it portrays, more perfectly even than speech itself, extreme grief, or excessive joy." The ardent mind of Diderot knew how to appreciate this natural expression, and he lavished upon it all due eulogium.

The following beautiful lines will perhaps convey a still clearer idea of the importance of our subject :—

" Negli occhi, ove il sembiante più si ficca."

DANTE.

" E ciò che lingua esprimer ben non puote,
Muta eloquenza ne' suoi gesti espresse."

LE TASSE.

" Words (when the poet would your soul engage)
Are the mere garnish of an idle stage.
When passion rages, eloquence is mean;
Gestures and *looks* best speak the moving scene."

Prologue to Busiris.—YOUNG.

" His rude *expression* and untutor'd *airs,*
Beyond the pow'r of language, will unfold
The form of beauty, smiling at his heart;
How lovely ! how commanding !

AKENSIDE.

Independently of the natural gestures, it is known that the figurative and symbolical language of motions, com-

posed of regulated signs, or signs of intelligence, is some_
times more striking than the slower and systematic language of words. It derives its origin from Pantomime.
The Oriental nations have adopted it, and are greatly attached to it. Their imagination ardently availed itself of
this mode of expression, that is, by an imagery of things;
and hence arises, also, their partiality for a picturesque
style. It was from reflections like these, so favourable to
the art of Pantomime, that I studied the science of composing Ballets, and establishing more precise and exact rules
for conducting them, consulting on such a subject the rules
both of art and of taste. " Art furnishes rules, and taste
exceptions; taste discovers to us on what occasions art
ought to be subservient, and when, in turn, the latter should
submit."—MONTESQUIEU.

" Man has three means of expressing his ideas and feelings:—by speech, tone of voice, and gesture. By gestures we
understand, those exterior movements and attitudes of the
body which relate to the inward operations of the mind.
' *Gestus,*' says Cicero, ' *est conformatio quædam et figura
totius oris et corporis.*'

" I name speech first because we generally pay more attention to it than to the two others; which latter, however,
possess many advantages over the former. Our tone of
voice and gesture are of a more natural and extensive
use; for by them we supply every deficiency in speech.
By gesture we present to the eyes all that we cannot express to the ears; it is a universal interpreter that follows
us to the very extremities of the globe, and makes us intelligible to the most uncivilized hords. It is understood even by
animals. Speech is the language of reason: it convinces our
minds; tones and gestures form a sentimental discourse that
moves the heart. Speech can only give utterance to
our passions, by means of reflection through their relative

ideas.   Voice and gesture convey them to those we address, in an immediate and direct manner.   In short,
speech, or rather the words which compose it, is an artificial institution, formed and agreed upon between men,
for a more distinct reciprocal communication of their ideas ;
whilst gestures and the tone of voice are, I may say, the
dictionary of simple nature; they are a language innate in
us, and serve to exhibit all that concerns our wants and
the preservation of our existence; for which reason
they are rapid, expressive, and energetic.   Such a language, of which the terms are rather those of nature
than of cultivation, cannot but be an inexhaustible source
to an art whose object is to move the deepest sensations of the soul !"—LE BATTEUR.   These lines speak
sufficiently in favour of Pantomime, and may serve for an
introduction to the lessons of the performer.

Gestures are of two kinds, *natural* and *artificial.*   The
first are in our nature—we are born with them, they are
the outward signs of all that passes within us.   The latter
we derive from art; they express, by imitation, all objects
that are independent of ourselves.   *Natural* gestures are
the physical signs of our sentiments ; *artificial* ones the
emblems of all that is without the moral world.   Those of
the former kind exhibit the emotions of love, sadness, anger,
hatred, joy, fear, pleasure, despair, &c., and are what we
may call the mechanical effects of our intellectual over our
physical being.   Those of the latter sort serve to represent
objects, as a warrior old age, a child, a temple, a ship, arms,
robes, &c., they can also describe a storm, a fallen edifice,
a fight, a death, &c.   There is another class of gestures,
termed, in Pantomime, gestures of *convention,* which are
often necessary to cast a light on some obscure parts of
its performance.   These gestures of *convention,* which
art has created and custom established, paint those things

that we cannot perfectly understand but with the assistance of our imagination; and all events, of which the extent and multiplicity cannot be represented by one person only. Such are, for instance, a festival, a wedding, a coronation, the imitation of a father, a husband, a son, the indication of power, slavery, revolt, &c. All of which cannot be clearly understood but by gestures of *convention*. The spectator soon learns their meaning from theatrical habit; besides, they always bear some kind of analogy to the things they represent, which makes them sufficiently intelligible; they are, indeed, a sort of symbolic signs. From what we read of ancient Pantomimes, it seems evident that they had a great variety of gestures, both of art and of *convention* or agreement, since we are told that they could express past and future time, and even abstract ideas. An ancient writer [1] speaks of a trial of skill between Roscius and Cicero, in which these two celebrated men were to express the same things by different means—the orator by his speech, the player by his gestures. It does not appear that Roscius gained the victory over his rival, neither is he to be considered as vanquished, for he conceived so high an idea of his own art from this trial, shat he immediately wrote a work on gesticulation, which he therein placed on a level with eloquence itself. A greater proof cannot be brought forward, in favour of the perfection of ancient mimicry.

Among the ancients, the name of *mimes* was originally given to those dialogues, which were founded upon their habits and morals. These dialogues were spoken by men, and, when necessary, by women also. The best compositions of the kind were those of Sophron, who lived before Plato, those of Xenarchus, and those of Publius Sirus, a Roman. Laberius, Philistion, Lentulus and Marulus shone also in this class of comedy, which was very similar to the *Atellanes* formerly represented at Averso. These authors were termed *mimographers*, from the Greek words *mimos* an imitator, and *grapho* I write. The name of *mime* was afterwards given to those performers who imitated, by their gestures only, what was spoken by the *histriones*, or comedians and singers, or declaimers, both in tragedy and comedy*. These performers in the sequel, degenerating into frivolity, bombast and indecency, were merely regarded as buffoons and jugglers. The men were treated with the utmost contempt[2], and the women regarded only as concubines and prostitutes.

Some time afterwards, two celebrated actors, in the reign of Augustus, gave the art of mimicry a new birth, which they brought to much perfection and distinction. It was under these skilful hands that it acquired a splendour and importance unknown even to the brilliant ages of Greece. Their dexterity, in representing sentiment by gesture, became at length astonishing[3].

The Romans gave the name of *pantomimes* (from the Greek *pantos*, all, and *miméomai*, to counterfeit) to those performers who expressed all kinds of things by means of gestures. The arts of Pantomime and dancing were afterwards called *saltatio*. The word *Tripudium* was also used to signify dancing. The Greeks termed both, when united, *Orchestica*[4].

Lucian, in his celebrated dialogue upon dancing, raised that art to much dignity, by presenting it in its true light. He pointed out its utility; the many advantages derived from it; presented all the charms with which it abounds, and confirmed the judgment of those who decreed it an equal rank with tragedy and comedy.

Scipion Maffei very erroneously believed that Lucian

---

* Anciently, declamation was a species of recitative.

was merely railing, according to his usual way, when he in his work gave a certain character of importance to dancing, and set a high value on the talent of the performer. His motive for writing on pantomimic representations cannot in any way be suspected; his ideas of it seem the same throughout; he no where contradicts himself; besides, he is not the only author that speaks with enthusiasm on these ancient spectacles. The illustrious Veronese, it is true, does not appear to have bestowed much thought upon this subject; but, it is no less true that dancing, Pantomime, and Ballets were, in his time, very far from that degree of perfection to which they have since been carried, both in France and Italy. What we are told of the ancients surprises us, but we have discovered many things that might have astonished them.

Let us only require that which is reasonable and natural to make a Pantomime truly interesting and agreeable. Let us go no further; if we exceed those limits which art and good sense appoint, our efforts will unquestionably be fruitless.

The outward motions of the body are effected by the influence of the inward operations of the mind.

All gestures that indicate, in a clear and striking manner, the objects to which they refer, never fail of meeting with applause at a theatre. Beware, therefore, of making use of any that are trivial or ignoble ; copy the best models, but improve, if possible, on them in your imitation.

M. Gioia, among other philosophers, observes, " I sentimenti da communicarsi o riguardan oggetti esterni presenti o lontani," &c. (*See Note 5.*)

The actor points out with his hands every part of his body, as also all objects at a distance from him, by stretching them towards the same. His eyes should accompany each motion, and, by adding to the general expression, serve to point out more clearly the object to which he directs his thought.

Symbolic gestures, and gestures of *convention* and of art, are employed to signify every thing that cannot be exactly imitated or counterfeited by means of simply *natural* gestures alone. They point out to the imagination of the spectators all that cannot be seen by them on the stage. They in general bear as much analogy as possible to the things they endeavour to describe. This is their chief object.

Study to make yourself understood by imitating the form of the objects you wish to signify ; and, when that is not possible, point out, as clearly as you can, their use, &c., so that your beholders may conceive your meaning without ambiguity. Let all your expressions be precise and distinct. One of Lucian's commentators has said, that Pantomime is capable, by gestures of *convention*, to express past and future times, with every abstract action which bears no relation to the passing moment : this is precisely what was done by the ancient Pantomimes. I am aware that many persons would be ignorant of the meaning of those artificial gestures not immediately founded on passion and nature ; but in that case, to raise a desire to learn their signification, the Ballet-master, and those who represent his compositions, should exhibit pieces both easy and accurate, thus would such be obliged to relish their excellence by applying themselves to the *grammar*, if we may so call it, of this new language [6].

This is, in some measure, reasonable enough, and might be done with no great difficulty in Italy, where the people are naturally inclined to Pantomimes, and where the mimes already make use of gestures of *convention*. In France, some length of time, and a course of deep study, would be required to attain the same degree of perfection.

The French Pantomimes have adopted only a small number of gestures, of which the greater part is destitute of correct expression. Thus circumscribed in their means, their art cannot accomplish its due end, which is to represent to the eye a picturesque imitation of all things.

In certain theatres, where Ballets have been intended as much to please the intellect as the sight, this art has made considerable progress; and the number of gestures of art has much increased. The want of them was felt, their advantages were discovered, and success seems to have crowned the innovation.

It is natural to the Italian to gesticulate; it is not surprising, therefore, if the mimes of Italy are superior to those of other countries; or if Pantomime is there carried to so great a degree of perfection as to be capable of expressing perfectly all the passions, with every object sensible to the sight. They are, however, most materially assisted by the gestures acquired by art, which have greatly enlarged the sphere of their performances.

Pantomime being incapable of producing any very striking effect, but when employed in expressing strong emotions, and objects easy of perception, the Italians have selected the most celebrated deeds of both history and fiction, the more deeply to fix the attention of the spectators; their magnificent pictures are represented always vigorous, and sometimes sublime. This system excites great interest for the Ballet, and renders the pantomimic department important; at the same time augmenting and varying the pleasure of the public.

The Italian, endowed by nature with deep sensibility and a vivid imagination, is attached to powerful impressions, and prefers the stately and pathetic style to the comic or even the pleasing. He is willing to be amused by theatrical representation, but he had rather be affected;

and hence arises the interest taken by him in the performance of Ballets. It may be observed here that the Ballet has been more essentially assisted by the art of painting in Italy than in France; nor has the art itself lost any thing by it, but, on the contrary, gained infinitely.

In France, however, lately, several of my friends have distinguished themselves as mimes, and have attained the same perfection in expressing the passions as I have witnessed in Italy. This need not appear extraordinary, if it be considered that man is every where nearly the same. The only defect in these performers was a want of sufficient gesture to express perfectly every circumstance; but this was less their fault than that of their art. Notwithstanding this, their description of sentiment was true; their features spoke, and their attitudes were gracefully conceived.

I remarked that the best of these pantomimic performers were from provincial theatres; they are more industrious, and their stock of pieces is greater than at the capital. In Paris, about a dozen pieces form their round of representation; at Bordeaux, Marseilles, Lyons, &c., every Ballet that has succeeded is performed; at Paris, on the contrary, those only are performed that have been introduced by private interest and favour. I remember at Bordeaux, upon one of my benefit nights, it occurred to me, in order to raise public curiosity, that my Ballet companions should represent a comedy. The attempt appeared very extraordinary, and was deemed impossible of execution. The performers, however, being all endowed with some talent, and very expert in Pantomime, boldly undertook the performance, and succeeded in giving a perfect representation of that delightful comedy, called *Folies Amoureuses*. A severe but just journalist, giving an account of this performance, thus expresses himself:—" The piece was played not only with *spirit,* which might be easily expected of dancers, but with *truth* also, a quality that becomes every day more rare. Regnard was both felt and expressed. The *novices in speech* did not stand in need of that indulgence which had been prepared for any failure in this hazardous attempt."

This occurrence ought to prove satisfactorily, that in France there are dancers capable of performing Pantomime perfectly ; and if they do not introduce more of it into their parts, the cause of it should be attributed to the composers who neglect too much this department, or who have not sufficient talent to put Pantomime upon an equality with dancing.

It is not consistent with the character of Ballets to treat of abstract things, nor to entertain the public with long details. This sort of representation ought only to exhibit such actions and images as create interest and pleasure, without giving the spectator the least occasion to guess at the intentions of the performer. A Pantomime must be simple, clear, and correct, if it be meant for a faithful interpretation of our sensations. All that cannot be understood at the moment of the action is mere imperfection, which it is the Ballet-master's duty to reject as useless.

Pantomime, like dancing, has its different kinds. Gesture, look, carriage, in short all the physical expressions, are not exactly the same in every person; they vary with the age, character, and condition of the actor, who ought, therefore, to pay the strictest attention to those kinds only of which he finds himself more peculiarly capable.

Unless the actor possesses certain physicial qualities, and a natural disposition to Pantomime, he cannot expect to see his endeavours crowned with success. It is an incontrovertible fact that, without the gifts of nature, it is impossible for us to become perfect in any one art or science whatsoever; but, at the same time, though endued with every requisite, were we to neglect the sage precepts of art, we should equally fail of our end. Those lessons of advice, formed into established laws by ages of experience, are essential, nay almost indispensable, to the attainment of perfection. The great Longinus says, " that nature is mainly instrumental in conducting us to the grand and the sublime; but unless art takes her by the hand, guiding her steps, she is as one blind-folded, knowing not whither her steps are leading her."

It was by such a direction of art that the chisels which creáted the *Apollo* and the *Venus* surpassed the hand of nature in the formation of beauty. *Ars naturam perficit.*

What is said of sculpture, painting, and all the fine arts, can be said with the same truth of Pantomime. A mime requires considerable assistance from art to be much valued; his imitations should be faithful, but at the same time finer than their original. This is the end he must try to attain. Experience, good taste, diligence, and study, will conduct him towards it. Art embellishes, while she corrects nature; the former assists the latter, and receives an ample reward for her aid[7].

The first study of the pantomimic actor ought to be dancing; to acquire which, he must devote a few years of steady application, that he may know it well, and be thus enabled to profit by its advantages. Some notion of drawing would be also very useful to him. Here let us observe, with the celebrated Hogarth, "that all those actions which are continually employed in our ordinary and daily occupation, are performed nearly in right lines, or as nearly so as possible; but all graceful movements, which display cultivated manners, are performed in undulated lines."— *Analysis of Beauty.*

This judicious remark is worthy of the attention of

every class of actors, as by it they may learn to give gracefulness to their actions and gestures. The study of oblique
lines is also of much utility in varying their gestures, and
in making their attitudes and motions appear more picturesque. By a knowledge of drawing, their performance
will present many attractions of the most pleasing kind,
and when united to that of dancing, afford them powerful
means to attain perfection. These two arts enable the
actor to be light, nimble, and flexible; all his motions will
be easy, graceful, and executed with taste; his attitudes
and gestures will be elegant and natural. Music, also, is
of equal service, and will contribute in no small degree to
the attainment of excellence. By the study of music, he
makes himself capable of following more exactly the
rhythm of the tune, and occasions his performance to accord more happily with the measure and cadence of
the notes. To these requisite accomplishments, let him
finally add an expressive countenance, always in strict unison with the subject he represents, and thus complete the
theatrical illusion.

It is very advisable for an actor to study history and
poetry; from them he will reap much profit. They enlighten his mind, enlarge his views, and give him true
notions of taste. They afford him the first lessons towards a knowledge of nature, the human heart in its full
extent, and the real character of those personages he
will be frequently called upon to represent.

We may see, from what has been said, that the modern
pantomimic actor does not require all those qualifications
which constituted the art of the ancient, who was obliged to
be at once perfect in pantomime, dancing, and composition.
These arts have, in our days, been carried to a degree of
excellence which neither the Greeks nor Romans ever
arrived at. This pre-eminence may be ascribed to the

better judgment of the moderns, who have made an appropriate division of each department.

Les sept chefs devant Thébes, Hercule furieux, Ajax, l'Adultère de Mars et de Vénus, Páris, and a few other Ballets of the ancients, are but weak and imperfect sketches when compared with *Télémaque, Psyché, Prométhée, Niobé, Les Amours de Vénus, Ulysse, Almaviva et Rosine, Cléopátre, Zéphyre et Flore, &c.* all modern productions, in which taste, genius, and reason are happily combined to charm the eyes and interest the heart.

With us, it is only young men that devote themselves to dancing and Pantomime, whilst those of more advanced years, who possess both talents and experience, apply themselves to composition.

Lucian says, that the stature of a pantomimic actor must be neither very tall nor extremely short; his limbs neither too strong nor too slight. He wishes his person to be as nearly as possible of the proportions of the statue of Polycletes[8]. But as this masterpiece of sculpture has not been transmitted to us, we must take as a substitute that of *Antinous.* A performer of this height and muscular construction may undertake a number of different characters, since his physical powers are adapted to all branches of the art.

An easy remedy for trifling defects is found in the manner of dressing and acting.

Our ballets have the advantage of being performed by a greater number of persons. Each mime or dancer takes that part which best suits his peculiar figure and talent. It is the duty of a Ballet-master to look into these particulars, and judiciously to distribute and appropriate the parts. The various characters of youth, manhood, and old age should be filled by different actors, whose stature and features resemble, in some degree, the idea we have of such personages. The theatrical system of the present time is not the same as it was formerly. Now, each actor and actress always takes one particular kind of character, by which means our dramatic representations are more naturally, and therefore much more perfectly, performed.

In France, the parts and lines of actors have been divided and sub-divided in the minutest manner, that all may be in a sort of exact accordance. The following is a classification of some of the principal parts : *Jeunes premières; jeunes premières ingènuités; amoureux; amoureux marqués; coquettes de Marivaux ; grandes coquettes; petits maîtres ; marquis ; premiers rôles; pères nobles; mères nobles; rôles à manteau; duègnes* (Spanish personage); *financiers; soubrettes; valets; Figaros ; soubrettes de bon ton; grandes livrées ; servantes et valets de Molière; travestis; Crispin; Scapin; caricatures; Cassandre; grimes; rois; reines; princesses; chevaliers; grands prêtres; confidents; utilités, &c. &c.*

This example deserves to be followed in every branch of theatrical art. But it frequently happens that, through motives of interest or ambition, an actor is induced to aim at acquiring a talent as universal as possible. This is well enough, if he finds himself really endowed with the requisite qualifications. Indeed I would then advise him to imitate every thing, to render himself a perfect master of mimicry in every kind. It may be here remembered that the Greeks called their players *hypocrites*. Among the ancients, one and the same actor used generally to represent a great number of personages (see Lucian, Cassiodorus, and others). Sometimes, also, two performers undertook to play every part in a piece ; but afterwards, their number having increased, there were as many actors as parts; still this was not always the case. A player ought to study the genius, character, manners, and customs of the various nations, the natives of which he may have to represent.

Let nature be his constant model. In this respect he then shares the labours and honours of the composer. The varied features of his countenance must exhibit the different sensations of his soul, and his eyes, particularly, must add to the expression of all those feelings which his gesture is intended to convey. The gesture of the mime, being ever in accord with his eye, should, as it were, speak.

Signat cuncta manu, loquitur Polyhymnia gestu.—
VIRGIL[9].

> " La passion toujours, selon l'âge et les rangs,
> Dans des signes pareils eut des traits différens.
> Pour nous peindre l'acteur, mesure son théâtre.
> La douleur d'un héros n'est point celle d'un pâtre ;
> Distingue par le sexe autant que par l'état,
> Les larmes d'une femme et les pleurs d'un soldat.
> Le même sentiment, selon les caractères,
> Se manifeste encor par des signes contraires ;
> Ce père en sa douleur, d'un courage assuré,
> Peint les livides traits de son fils expiré.
> Toi, malheureux Dédale, auteur de ta blessure,
> Deux fois tu veux graver ta fatale aventure,
> Deux fois ton cœur se serre, et tu sens sur l'airain,
> De ta main paternelle échapper le burin."

LEMIERRE.

Every thing must be well understood, every thing deeply felt, if we wish to represent it correctly. We hear that Polus, to enable himself to act with greater truth the scene in which *Electra*, in the most poignant anguish, brings the urn that encloses her brother's ashes, took that which did really contain the last remains of one of his own sons; the sight of this, by renewing his grief, could not fail of making him express, with an energy and perfection that art can never teach, that keen anguish under which his mind must have laboured [10].

Let nature, therefore, be most attentively studied, even down to her minutest operations.

It is the composer's duty to inform the actor of the subject, argument, and meaning of his Ballet, and especially to instruct him as to the nature of the part which he has to fulfil. He ought to show him the proper gestures that will express his own ideas in the Pantomime, and also guide him in all his motions, that the time and cadence of the music may be observed with precision.

Every action in Pantomime must be regulated according to the music, which ought also to participate in the expression of the passions. The effect resulting from this harmonious union creates the most pleasing emotions in the spectator. The Ballet-master should set the gestures, attitudes and steps exactly to the rythm of the tunes, and so manage that each sentiment expressed may be responsive to the measure. Let the mime or dancer, however, beware not to force his action, in order to prove that they really are in accord with the musical phrase. All must be blended together, and art be concealed as much as possible.

> "Sallé dont Terpsichore avait conduit les pas,
>
> Fit sentir la mesure, et ne la marquait pas." VOLTAIRE.

The accompaniment must possess the true tone and colouring of the pantomimic action.

The Ballet-master must avoid in his demonstrations all that is exaggerated, dull, vulgar, or trivial, particularly in subjects of a serious nature.

The expressions of violent passion, or of those which arise from any extraordinary situation, are not the most difficult task of a mime. " The great difficulty in the art," Marmontel observes, " is in a simultaneous expression of two sentiments agitating the soul, when the mind wavers from one to the other, or in the gradations and shades

either of one passion or of two contrary ones, in their de-
lusive momentary calm, in their rapid fury, their impetuous transports, in short, in all the varied accidents that
form together a picture of the storms which convulse the
human breast."

What skill is here required to offer a faithful representation of such emotions on the stage. It is, indeed, the
nec plus ultrà of the comedian's art! To this desirable
point of perfection it is, that such celebrated actors have
arrived as Garrick, Le Kain, Talma, Kemble, Kean, Young,
Demarin; Ekhoff, Iffland, Mayquez, Siddons, Oldfield,
O'Neil, Clairon, Duménil, Pellandi, Marchionni, Duches-
noy and some few others [11].

It is by that dumb action, and those energetic expressions, that we discover a truly good actor. One of a
middling talent may declaim a speech tolerably well ; but
it is the sublime artist alone that can paint, in one rapid
look, all the natural violence of a strong passion. In this
respect it is that a mime always surpasses a comedian or
tragedian.

The gestures and countenance of the performer must
express to the spectator all that passes in the soul, and
minutely point out every variation in its emotions. The
heart should feel all that is exhibited by the features and
gestures, which cannot act perfectly without its consent.

" ———— ogni membro all' animo risponde."—PETRARCH.

That accord which exists between our moral and physical faculties must be strictly observed. The most
studied dissimulation can never entirely hide the feelings
that agitate us. Nor are they ever so expressed as to be
glaringly conspicuous. It is very easy for the performer
to make the personage he represents perfectly dissimulate,
as his action is, of course, much calmer. He must always try
to throw a veil over all his expressions and gestures suffi-

ciently transparent for the spectator to perceive the shades of that secret passion which he endeavours as much as possible to conceal.

The performance of the mime sometimes depends on those who act with him; if they are not animated, he necessarily becomes cold. But the principal performer should rather take possession, as it were, of the stage, and give a tone to the rest, whose acting should be responsive to his, and form a part of it. It is this harmony between the characters of Pantomime which contributes most essentially to general theatrical effect.

It may be here observed, that an actor performing in a small theatre may restrain his gestures and moderate his exertions; but if, on the contrary, the theatre is of extensive dimensions, his pantomimic action must be increased in vigour also, and more strongly marked.

ON THE ORIGIN OF THOSE MASKED CHARACTERS WHO PERFORM IN ITALIAN COMEDIES.

The following short discourse upon *masked characters* is taken from *Pietro Verri.* Supposing it to be a subject not void of interest to theatrical amateurs, treating as it does on the origin of *Mimes,* whom we have already so often mentioned, we thought ourselves sufficiently authorised for introducing it here.

The custom of performing in masks, may be traced to the most remote antiquity. During the polished ages of Greece, no actor appeared on the stage without this peculiar appendage. In ancient comedy, masks were in such universal use that they were adapted to every species of character: there were the miser's mask, the parasite's mask, the mask for the good servant, and the mask for the

knavish one; an actor, therefore, had only to make his
appearance thus masked, when the nature of his character
was immediately recognized, even before a word was
spoken; this is precisely the case with respect to the mask
of the modern harlequin, which is always the same; while
those of Brighella, *(the Clown)*, Dottore, *(the Doctor)*, and
Pantaloon, present so truly their peculiar dispositions,
that it is impossible to be mistaken in the foolishness and
stupidity of Brighella, or in the tricks and roguishness of
Harlequin.

We must, therefore, establish it as fact and foundation,
that the custom of wearing masks, which never varied
when once adapted to its peculiar character, is derived
from the ancient Greek and Roman theatres.

Amongst the ancient Romans the profession of an actor
was divided into two branches, the *Mime* and the *Comedian*. The Mime had his face blackened, and appeared
upon the stage *fuligine faciem obducti;* for at that time,
the custom of performing in the high dramatic buskin
had not yet been introduced among the *Mimes*, the bottom
of their feet being bare, and on that account, indeed, they
obtained the name of *Mimes*, according to Diomedes:
"*Planipes Græci dicitur Mimus, adeo autem latine planipes
quod actores planis pedibus proscenium introirent.*" We
may hence gather how strong a resemblance exists between the modern Harlequin and Brighella *(or Clown)*,
and the *Mimes* of antiquity, particularly in those unvary-
ing characteristics, the blackened visage and the buskins.
Their general attire also bore a great similarity to that of
modern times; their Mimes were dressed precisely like
our Harlequins: see that passage of Apuleius, in which he
says, " *Num ex eo argumentare uti me consuevisse tragedi
sysmate, Histrionis cocosta, Mimi centunclo.*" Where observe, that to Mimes was assigned the *Centunclus*, which

means, *a dress of patches of a hundred colours, Anglicè* a Harlequin's suit. And further it may be remarked, that Vossius, in his *Institutes,* informs us that, *Sanniones Mimum agebant rasis capitibus ;* in which words two things are worthy of note; first, that *Sanniones* and *Mimes* were both in the same line of profession; and secondly, that Harlequin and Brighella are now called *Zanni* *, which word is doubtless no other than a corruption of the original term *Sannio.* Thus then a Mime with his head shaved, his face blackened, and a suit of party-coloured patches, bare-footed or nearly so, and bearing the name of *Sannio,* according to ancient historians, must have been the worthy ancestor of our magical Harlequin.

Perhaps it may be doubted whether the severe Cato, or the grave Cicero, had witnessed the performance of a Roman harlequinade, but the doubt will soon be removed upon reading the following passage, extracted from his book *De Oratore,* in which it may be seen he describes a harlequin exactly. *Quid enim potest tam ridiculum, quam Sannio esse, qui ore, vultu, imitandis motibus, voce, denique corpore ridetur ipso !* From this it must be concluded that the *Sanni* or *Zanni* of modern comedy are derived from the most ancient theatricals even of republican Rome, and thus transmitted down to us. It is not at all improbable that good and legitimate tragedy and comedy, might have been buried amid the barbarism that succeeded the fall of Rome, and with which all Italy was overrun, but the pleasure that unpolished ignorance would take in such gross representation of mimicry as that of the *Sanniones,* preserved them from oblivion, while nobler amusement was despised and forgotten. It appears, in short, that when the Italian drama was destroyed, those

---

* Zaney.

mimic farces continued to be performed, though it were only in open squares, or any corners where such shews could be conveniently represented. Proofs of this may be found as far back as the twelfth century [12], beyond which period the traces of the existence of the *Dottore* are not observable. Then it was that Irenerius opened, at Bologna, a school of jurisprudence, from which such institutions take their rise throughout the greater part of Europe, and so continue to the present time. And it appears that the origin of the mask called *Dottore* may be fixed at that epoch, when the two celebrated doctors, Bulgaro and Martino, disputed upon the question, whether the whole world belonged to the reigning emperor, as sole proprietor, or whether he was only a kind of tenant? Certainly it required some such an appearance as this grotesque mask, with black nose and scarlet cheek, which is supposed to represent exactly the man who could gravely inquire whether the world belonged to one man, or whether he was only a mere tenant? Some learned persons, indeed, contend that the original model of this mask was the only good ever bestowed upon posterity by the school of Irenerius.

With respect to Pantaloon, it seems that it was at the end of the fourteenth, or at the beginning of the fifteenth century, that this mask was introduced at the theatres; at a period when the extensive commerce of the Venetians caused the sum of 695,000 sequins to circulate annually through the state of Milan, the product of woollen manufactures, which were sent to Venice, and again sold in the Levant; this may be proved by reading a controversy of the time, of the Doge, Thommaso Mocenigo, as related by the historian *Sannudo, in Rer. Ital. Script. Tom. 22, page 954.*

NOTES

TO PART THE THIRD.

1.

Roscius and Esopus were the two greatest actors that Rome ever possessed, the first in the comic line, the second in the tragic. They gave lessons on declamation to Cicero, who always honoured them with his esteem and friendship. Horace also mentions these two performers : —

" *Quæ gravis Esopus, quæ doctus Roscius egit.*"

2.

About this time Rome had fallen into so much licentiousness that the players publicly performed the *Adultery of Mars and Venus*, with the most obscene gestures and particularities. Suetonius tells us, that under the reign of Nero the infamous loves of *Pasiphœ* were frequently represented on the stage, and in so natural a manner that many believed the real scene was passing before them : —

" Functam Pasiphaën dictæo credite tauro
Vidimus, accepit fabula prisca fidem."

MARTIAL.

3.

It may be here remarked that both Mimes and Pantomimes were anciently employed in the dance, with this difference, however, that the Mimes, by indecent motions and obscene gesticulations, described vile and ignoble characters only ; while, on the contrary, Pantomime described every species of personification ; the actions of the base, and the deeds of the illustrious ; great captains, heroes, and even Gods. See *Ger-jo Vossius*, Jstit. Poet. lib. 2. cap. XXX, § 3 et 5.

4.

See the learned dissertation of Doctor Zulatti.

5.

" Sentiments, mutually communicated, have a reference either to present or distant objects ; or, they relate to internal sensations. When the object is present the eyes are turned to it, while the staff or finger points it out ; the body either approaches or shrinks from it ; thus forming a kind of dictionary of this mute language. Signs made in this manner may be termed *indicative*.

" When the attention is directed to a distant object, as for instance when a savage would discover some animal to kill it, or would describe another by which he was attacked, he expresses its howling, roaring, or peculiar cry, by the effect of his own voice; its form and motions he describes by the gesticulations of his hands, arms, or head; and this species of signs may be called *imitative*.

" When the same person would express his own peculiar wants, fears, or any feeling which the eye cannot perceive, he first exhibits those peculiar attitudes which are produced by such feelings. B. seeing the place where he had been affrighted, will repeat the cries of fear, and the movements of terror, in order that his companion, A., may not expose himself to the same danger which he had experienced. A person deaf and dumb, wishing to show how he was trampled on by a horse, first describes the swift motion of the horse's feet with his hands, and then with his fingers he traces out on his body those parts that have been injured, showing at the same time how he fell.

" After exhibiting those external signs which accompany the affections, the savage, like a deaf and dumb person, seizes on the resemblance he finds between the internal sensations of the mind and the external qualities of bodies, employing the latter to express the former. Thus, violent anger is compared to the flame or the tempest; tranquillity of mind to a serene sky; doubt is expressed by the two hands that would weigh two bodies;—and such signs as these are called *figurative* or *symbolic*.

" These *indicative, imitative,* and *figurative* gestures then, provide a threefold means of communication between ideas and feelings, enlisting into their service all the aids afforded by the laws of association.

" To give a class of those elementary materials, of which this language is composed, we must reduce them into three kinds, namely gestures, sounds, and symbolic writing.

" The first class comprehends those actions and attitudes of the body employed to express the form or motion of a visible object; the second contains those sounds of the voice with which is described the cry of animals, or the noise accompanying the motion of inanimate bodies; the third comprehends those hieroglyphics which are frequently traced upon the sand, the bark of trees, or any other surface to indicate visible objects, or the motions appertaining to them."   M. GIOIA.

6.

Were it possible to put such a project into execution, would it not be more adapted to the formation of a universal language than the chimerical plans of George's '*Kalmar*' ? (See his Essay on a Philosophical and Universal Language: a work which, like all others that have been written by great authors upon the subject, is replete with useless speculative ideas, about as easy in execution as the ingenious method of Dean Swift, in his *Voyage to Laputa*.)

7.

Menzini says :—

" Sappi, che la natura ella Sovrasta
Qual nobile Regina ; e l'arte aggiunge
Un tal contegno, che beltà non guasta.

Anzi l'accresce e'l suo valor congiunge
All 'alma generosa, e rappresenta
A lei vicin ciò, che saria da lunge."

Art. Poet.

8.

The *Règle*, a celebrated statue of the famous sculptor Polycletes, of Syciones, which represented a guard of one of the kings of Persia. It was so called by reason of the just proportion and exact symmetry of all its forms, and was considered a perfect model of the human figure. Amateurs and artists came from all parts to see and consult it.

Polycletes was universal in his art ; and equally as successful in large works as in small. He much excelled in the carving of *basso relievo*, and possessed the same facility of execution on bronze, as on marble. He was also an eminent architect.

9.

This muse, Polyhymnia, also invented *chironomy*, a word signifying the art of making gestures in a graceful manner. The word is derived from χειρ hand and νομος law. This art also consisted in calculating and making expressive signs with the fingers.

10.

Polus was performing the part of Electra, sister of Orestes ; among the ancients, women were never permitted to act either in tragedy or comedy. The men took every part, and some there were who rendered themselves in a manner famous for their talent of performing in female characters. Nero, that monster of iniquity, who was so passionately fond of theatrical diversions, always gave them the preference. He performed in the character of *Niobe*, of *Canace in Child-bed*, and of several other women. In panto-mimes women played their respective parts, and produced a much better effect. Those who remain on record as having been distinguished in their art, are Arbuscula, Lucilia, Tymele, Denise Cytheris, (whose beauty, talent, and wit, inspired the poet Gallus with the most violent love for her,) and Valeria Cloppia, who also gained some repute by the composition of several Pantomimes.

Not long ago, in modern Rome, all the female parts, both in operas and ballets, were played by men.

This custom was also in fashion in France and England about the middle of the seventeenth century. Nearly every caricature part of women was played by the other sex. Jeurrain acquired much celebrity in them. The actor Hubert was so perfect in this line of acting, that it is generally supposed that Molière wrote expressly for him the characters of *Madame Pernelle,* *Madame Jourdain, Madame de Sotenville,* and of the *Comtesse d'Escarbagnas.*

11.

Baccio Ugolino, who had the honour of playing the principal part in Politien's celebrated piece *l'Orfeo,* may be regarded as the first actor who appeared upon the Italian theatre after the revival of the arts. Verato, surnamed the Roscius of his time, lived in the sixteenth century, and was celebrated as the original performer of Tasso's *Aminta.* Baron, Mondori, La Noue, Poisson, P. Susini, were Italian actors of the seventeenth century. Molé, Préville, Thomassini, Doggett, Watton, Gibbon, Zannoni, Petronio, Monvel, Vestri, Champmeslé, Le Couvreur, Gaussin, Contat, Ellena Riccoboni, Sainval, Silvia, Balletti, Lawrence, &c.

The following are the modern Mimes :—A. Vestris, Ferdinand, Molinari, Costa, Melle, Chevigny; Dutacq, Robillon, Théodore, Dauberval, Bigottini, Pallerini, Léon, Chéza, Pezzoli, Bocci, Conti, Olivieri.

The actors of antiquity are :—Esopus, Roscius, Nestor, Paris, Laberius, Pylades, Hylas, pupil of the latter, Bathylus, Mnesterius, Coramalus, Phabeton, Plancus, Sophronius, Polus, Aristodemus, Demetrius, Callistrates, Philonides, Neoptolemus, Apelles, and Stratocles, which latter was the Préville of his time.

12.

Those who would have a more detailed account of this subject may read *Nieuport :—Rituum qui apud Romanos obtinuerunt. Dubos:—Réflexions sur la Poésie. tom.* 3, and Riccoboni's Treatise.

PART THE FOURTH.

PART THE FOURTH.

THE COMPOSITION OF BALLETS.

" —————————————— éloquente et muette,
Elle (*la danse*) est des passions la mobile interprète :
Elle parle à mon âme, elle parle à mes sens,
Et je vois dans ses jeux des tableaux agissans.
Le voile ingénieux de ses allégories
Cache des vérités par ce voile embellies.
Rivale de l'histoire, elle raconte aux yeux :
Je revois les amours, les faits de nos ayeux :
Elle sait m'inspirer leur belliqueuse ivresse.
J'admire leurs exploits, et je plains leur faiblesse."

DORAT.

INTRODUCTION*.

IT appears to me that the plan and conduct of a Ballet should be nearly similar to those of a comedy or tragedy; since Pantomime is now capable of explaining our feelings almost as perfectly as the voice; and, as we have already observed, it expresses the transports of passion

---

* This Fourth Part has been already translated and published in Italian, by the Chevalier Bossi.

even more energetically.   Hence it may be concluded that
this art of expressing ourselves by looks and gestures is
sufficient to represent every species of action or historic
exploit; if the pantomimic performer, therefore, be well
understood he will awaken interest, and be finally triumphant.   Gresset, speaking of Terpsichore, the patroness
of dancing, expresses himself thus :—

" Her allegorical positions form a mute poetry, her attitudes are living and moving pictures, and become a faithful representation of sentiments and passions.   Rivalling
history, while she displays to the eyes (the Ballet) deeds
of renown, she exhibits to the spectator the peculiar genius of every nation ; by her steps she represents every
characteristic.   In her vehement movements, and uncertain wandering, I can perceive anger, indignation, and
despair ; her irregular and negligent gestures exhibit a
soft voluptuousness ; in the nicety of her *balancemens*,
and the exactness of her *equilibres*, we trace an easy languor; in the sudden agility of her steps, we perceive the
gaiety of the Graces, and the sprightliness of delight; amid
the labyrinth of her aerial bounds we are reminded of the
village *fête* and the joys of the vintage.   In short, dancing,
which at first view appears to be only a pleasure, conceals
a useful lesson.   Thus, anciently, the wise citizens of Sparta,
to inspire their children with the horror of intemperance,
caused their drunken slaves to *dance* before them.   This
dancing, however, cannot certainly be taken for a model,
but only as an example of the moral power contained in
the Ballet.   *Describo mores hominum,* is the motto of
comedy ; and might be applied to every kind of theatrical
representation.

Those laws and maxims which ought to guide the composer of Ballets, are no other than those which have been
laid down by the greatest critics on the drama.   I have,

therefore, laboured to make extracts from whatever work has treated on the subject; and afterwards to deliver them to my readers in a clear and condensed shape, in order that they may be enabled more easily to perceive my object.

Divesting the arguments and observations contained in certain authors of their obscurity and tedious verbosity, which so often confuse and repulse the inquiries of those who would otherwise have studied them, I have endeavoured to render them useful and advantageous to the professor of dancing; being well convinced that truth, clearness, and precision are the qualities required in delivering precepts.

The following subject has never yet been treated on, namely:—the application of dramatic principles in the composition of Ballets. The enterprise is not an easy one; in order to succeed in it, however, I have spared neither time nor labour; making an infinity of notes, and searching through a multitude of authors. This part, therefore, will treat on the object of the Ballet, its peculiarities, and the method in which it should be composed. An attempt will be made also to point out what kind of dramatic subjects are suitable to it; with the means necessary to be employed in order to insure success in the pantomimic department, and by what method the Ballet may be raised to anequality with tragedy and comedy. Thus, in the end, it may attain the same object as the speaking drama, though by a different rout. I have also shown that a more liberal application of theatrical scenery and decoration should be accorded to the Ballet; calling in the aid of those arts to which it bears a striking analogy. Each art, indeed, is united to the other, and all concur in mutual embellishment.

CHAPTER I.

<hr>

ON THE EXPOSITION, OR INTRODUCTION.

<hr>

Qualunque oggetto si vegga nelle belle Arti, si ha da conoscer subito che cosa fa, chi è, che significa, che vuole, che ci dice di bello e d'importante.—MILIZIA.

EVERY dramatic action represented upon the stage, ought to consist of three divisions, namely, the exposition, the plot *(nœud)*, and the catastrophe *(dénoûment)*. If any one of these parts be defective or ill-contrived, the action loses its interest, in proportion to its imperfect state; if, on the contrary, there exists a harmony in the parts, arising from a certain uniformity of arrangement, the dramatic action is perfect and complete; the effect that will be thus produced, aided by the illusion of theatrical embellishment must secure success to the author.

The unities also, as we shall shortly see, must contribute in some measure to the perfection of the work; and the composer should be exact to a certain degree in observing them, not attempting to introduce anything without a sanction from them. We must, however, remark, that a *Ballet* does not always oblige the writer to a strict observance of unities.

The *exposition* unfolds to us the subject upon which the author writes, and the nature of the action about to take place, and may be termed also the introduction. A good author should know how to awaken interest in this first part, and to keep it up by inspiring a desire of seeing the final consequence. This *exposition*, however, must be clear and concise; for here it is that many authors fail. In this division we expect a description of characters and manners, with the peculiar qualities of the persons about to appear upon the scene. Those who are to take an active part in the piece should be advantageously introduced to our notice, without, however, concealing from us their failings, when the latter are essentially necessary to the conduct of the subject. "Let your heroes be great but not faultless," says Aristotle; from which precept we may learn that nothing should be exaggerated, but rather probable and natural.

During the action every character should be sustained in a tone consistent with their beginning. The action itself, even from its commencement, should advance in such a manner as gradually to increase interest; an effect which requires some ability to produce; every effort, therefore, must be employed to raise emotion and pleasure; this, indeed, is the object at which true talent ever aims.

The exposition may be made either suddenly or gradually, according as the peculiarity of the subject may require. Sometimes, the veil which conceals from the spectator the actual state of things may be instantaneously lifted; at others, it must be slowly raised during the course of succeeding scenes. "When a subject is celebrated, and, consequently, well known, its exposition is both brief and easy; thus, on hearing the names of *Iphigenia, Œdipus, Dido, Cæsar,* or *Brutus,* not only are their characters immediately recalled to mind, but the peculiar events in which they have borne a part. To explain in such a case requires not many lines. But when a subject is not generally known, it should be both clear and striking of itself, and the characters marked by such strong traits of distinction, as to make an impression on the mind at their first appearance."—MARMONTEL. An exposition extended to too great a length, fatigues the audience and causes inattention. Do not promise too much at the opening, as it always raises a proportionate expectation.

CHAPTER II.

ON THE PLOT. (NŒUD.)

Que tout soit lié dans l'action principale, et que tout marche vers le même but.—ANONYMOUS.

THE poet or composer having informed the audience of the nature of the subject, he must raise interest, and, as it were, take the audience with him, by the emotion created by the incidents. A well-contrived episode, though proceeding from the action, crosses and embarrasses it, and interrupts its progress, yet at the same time its unexpected events excite curiosity, and agitate the mind: all these, aided by characters vigorously drawn, inspire an ardent desire to know what will be the end of so singular a history, without, however, being able to divine the catastrophe. Such is the state of things when the plot is well conducted and well sustained.

Episode[1] produces good effect and adds to the pleasure of the piece, by giving the imagination a kind of repose, or by diverting the attention from the principal personages. It must not, however, be too much prolonged, or it will injure the first action, and diminish the dramatic illusion which had been raised at the beginning.

By reading ancient dramatic writers, it will be seen that two or three actions are passing at once in their pieces ; but it will also be observed that their theatres were divided into several parts, so that, frequently, that which on the modern stage is recited by them, was exhibited in action. The Olympic theatre at Vicenza will fully prove what is here advanced. This masterpiece of Palladio is an imitation of ancient theatres ; and the most remarkable circumstance in its construction is, this identical threefold division[2].

CHAPTER III.

ON THE CATASTROPHE OR DÉNOUMENT.

> " Que le trouble toujours croissant de scéne en scéne,
> A son comble arrivé se débrouille sans peine.
> L'esprit ne se sent point plus vivement frappé
> Que lorsqu 'en un sujet d'intrigue enveloppé
> D'un secret tout à coup la vérité connue
> Change tout donne à tout une face imprévue."
>
> BOILEAU.

THESE verses of the celebrated imitator of Horace, who was the preserver of true taste [3], have already shown the signification of the word *dénoûment* (catastrophe).   If it is difficult to succeed in the *exposition*, and in the plot when incidents increase and obstacles embarrass, it is still more so, to contrive a happy or unexpected catastrophe; in this, even the greatest geniuses have sometimes failed; it is indeed a rock on which many have split, of which Molière and Goldoni are a proof. Diderot, therefore, has sufficient reason for the accusation he brings against most dramatic authors.   Shakspeare is often very defective in his catastrophes; the conclusion of *Othello* is void of all good sense, and produces nothing but horror [4].   The author should conduct the spectators gradually towards the catastrophe, by unknown ways, which continually excite interest as they develop themselves. At the end he surprises by the force of the sensations, whether they be of the terrible or gentler kind, according as the subject may demand; a fertile fancy, enlightened by the study of good authors, and, above all, by that of nature, will easily discover means for producing the necessary effect.

Thus the approach and completion of the catastrophe cannot be too much attended to; studying deeply the conduct of some sublime dramatic production, such as the *Orestes* of Alfieri. The plan and progress of this piece, with its final catastrophe, are constructed with admirable art; the interest goes on, gradually increasing, till at last the poet astonishes the audience by a catastrophe as terrible as it is unexpected. On such works as these we should continually meditate. Than the tragedies of this Sophocles of Italy, I know nothing in modern times more classic—more correct. The catastrophe, says Marmontel, to be unexpected, must proceed from uncertain means which lead to an unalterable conclusion. The fate of persons concerned in the plot is, during the course of the action, like a vessel tossed in a storm, which is at last terribly wrecked or happily conducted to a port, and this is the catastrophe.

CHAPTER IV.

___

OF THE UNITIES.

___

" Tous les beaux Arts ont quelque unité d' objet, source du plaisir qu' ils donnent à l'esprit: car l'attention partagée, ne se repose nulle part, et quand deux objets nous occupent c'est une preuve qu' aucun des deux ne nous satisfait."—J. J. ROUSSEAU.

IN order that the plan and progress of dramatic pieces may appear natural and probable, and that nothing may be introduced foreign to the plot; that the sentiments may be exactly what they ought to be, and the passions such as arise from the whole, the *unities* of action, place, and time have been established as essential qualities of dramatic writing; a law, indeed, enacted by taste and judgment.

Noverre does not wish to subject the Ballet to these three *unities;* but, considering the progress in the art of dancing, we shall adhere to whatever maxims may appear more admissible than the opinion of this celebrated artist. We shall, however, agree with him in a certain class of compositions, which we shall notice during the course of this work.

The plots of the Grecian dramas are too simple, and they are consequently often barren of interest. The moderns have escaped this error, by introducing into their works an amusing variety, but it should be done with moderation.

Unity of *place* requires that the action should always pass on the same spot on which it began, and that the scene should not be removed from it. Unity of *time*, that it should be completed in the space of twenty-four hours. These rules are, perhaps, too rigorously observed by French authors. The English and Germans disregard them totally [5], and widely wander from whatever regulation depends upon them.

Nothing, however, is more pedantic, ridiculous, or awkward than to oblige the poet or composer of Ballets to continue his characters in the same place in which they first appeared, and where the action commenced : an author would be thus constrained and enchained, by one of the most palpable blunders. If sometimes a talented performer do not answer general expectation, it ought to be attributed to some such shackles as these; and he may answer his censurers in the following words :

" Non mi lascia più ir lo fren dell' arte."—DANTE.

The celebrated Abbé Conti was one of those who piqued himself on paying a religious respect to the law of the *unities;* and fancying that any subject might be subjected to these rules, he was ridiculed by every sensible man. He wished every act of his tragedy of *Cæsar* to pass in the same place. The unalterable scene was a vestibule, and here every circumstance of the death of the illustrious Roman was to be transacted. But was it possible that the orations and every particular of that great event could pass on the same spot ? What improbability and absurd falsification ! A production of this sort might have been admired by Père Brumoy. Conti did what many have done ; he distorted history, and outraged common sense. La Motte, on the other hand, is not less to be blamed for having attempted to destroy the *unities* entirely.

This doctrine, Voltaire successfully attacked, and prevented any proselytes from being made, who, however, could not have obtained much encouragement. In England, it may be observed the *unities* are almost totally disregarded ; the audience are carried to and fro, almost from one side of the world to the other, and consequently during any indefinite space of time. The English have, indeed, some few tragedies in which the unities are preserved. One of these (*Cato*), though written by a celebrated genius, and containing great beauties, being considered dull from want of motion, is seldom performed. It is evident that Shakspeare is the father of that unbounded license, to be observed in the English dramas.

What fine opportunities for display have not been lost while paying too strict an attention to *unity* of *place !* I do not pretend that the composer should keep his characters journeying from town to town, or that he should transport us into another country at the beginning of every act ; but I am of the same opinion as those who, proceeding to neither of these extremities, do exactly what the plot and design of the piece require, and, if it is necessary, convey their characters from one city to another, or from one quarter to another in the same town. By this means dramatic pieces become more varied and natural, and, consequently, more interesting. The ideas of the composer, also, will have a greater latitude to range in, his resources multiplied, and he may rove indeed nearly in unlimited liberty : while the imagination, feeling itself thus unconstrained, invents with a greater facility. In short, taste and judgment have a right to destroy the works of pedantry[6].

With respect to unity of *time*, even the philosopher who first promulgated these laws, which many consider indispensable, remarks, that, when the nature of the action renders it necessary, the time of twenty-four hours may be either lengthened or abridged. This is a most reasonable exception, of which also I would make a free use, were I endued with talent which requires its assistance. It seems to me, that the great effects to be produced during an action that lasts two days instead of one, may well inspire us with a contempt for such ridiculous regulations ; when it is remarked also, that there is nothing in such a license either contrary to nature or probability. We have excellent pieces constructed on this plan.

In Ballets we may proceed still farther; we may allow ourselves still greater licenses, without, however, abusing them. The plot of a long historical piece may be contracted, and an abridged representation of it may be produced, but it must appear so probable that the audience may believe in what they behold.

> " ————— quel, ch'é d' incredibile, jo lontano
> E dentro a breve spazio non si chiude,
> Nol cercherai, perchè 'l cercalo è insano."
>
> Menzini.

The action must never appear to stand still; each part of it must succeed the other without interruption. For if, at the end of the first or second act, circumstances required a delay of some days, a week, a month, &c., before the thread of the story could be continued, good taste would never allow it, and the whole would be rejected. Almost every liberty is admissible in fabulous, mythologic, and fairy classes of pieces; the mind of the composer appears to be then in a certain *dythyrambic* state, if we may be allowed such an epithet, and he may be permitted every irregularity. However, the man of talent may be perceived in such productions, from the method in which he makes use of his freedom.

Care must be taken, therefore, not to compose after the Greek model, with respect to the dramatic *unities* of which we have been speaking. Metastasio, in his observations upon the Poetics of Aristotle, clearly demonstrates to us the defects of the most celebrated of ancient poets. Here then we must admire the genius of Shakspeare; but let us avoid following his system in every particular, or in adopting that of his imitators, in the same manner as we should avoid the renowned Schlegel, and his romantic sect.

CHAPTER V.

ON THE DIVISIONS OF DRAMATIC PIECES.

" Neve minor quinto : neu sit productior Actu
Fabula, quæ posci vult, et spectata reponi."—Hor.

This is the precept of the Roman satirist. Vossius makes the same division of dramatic productions

" Fabula, sive tragica, sive comica quinque actus habere debet."

Asconius Pedianus.

It is indeed an established law, that all the greater pieces should be divided into five acts. But there is a certain class of dramas, in which may be ranked the Ballet, that requires an exception to this rule. The *Grand* Ballet is capable of the same division as a tragedy;

this is done in Italy, and ought to be done in France; it augments the means of the composer, and on the other hand increases the stock of public amusement. Comic Ballets, and those of the melo-dramatic class, may be written in any number of acts beneath five, for generally that class of sentiments represented in these Ballets, from their sameness, want of force, and contrast, will not allow of an action so prolonged as that of the serious sort.

At the conclusion of each act a pause of the action should appear to take place naturally; the construction of the piece should be of a nature to demand such a rest. The imagination of the spectators should fill up this space by supposing what *might* happen with respect to the principal action during this cessation.   M. E. Gosse justly observes, that the moment the performers withdraw, is not that in which attention should be withdrawn too.   When retiring from our view, they should excite a desire for their re-appearance; though they are absent from our sight they should be present to our imagination; for if interest and curiosity languish but a very short time, the whole flags and dies away.   The exposition of a piece being effected in the first act, the plot begins properly in the second, and is continued during the third and fourth; and in the fifth we naturally expect the final catastrophe.

CHAPTER VI.

ON THE SUBJECTS PROPER TO BE SELECTED AND ADAPTED TO BALLETS, AND THE METHOD OF THEIR COMPOSITION.

" La virtù del *ballo* sta nel rimettere in atto le principali e le più vive impressioni che ricevono i nostri sensi."—Q. Viviani.

" Esso costuma più di affascinare il cuore, che concettizzare alla pensierosa ragione.—De Velo.

It is not every subject that can be rendered suitable to dancing; the composer, therefore, should know how to make a selection. A subject of the least importance may be worked up to interest greatly either as a tragedy or a comedy; but in a Ballet, the case is otherwise. Thus, for instance, the *Tartuffe ;* the *Légataire Universel ;* the *Grondeur ;* the *Philosophe Marié* ; *L'Ecole des Femmes ; Le Joueur ; La Métromanie ;* the *Déhors Trompeurs ;* the *Méchant,* and the *Coquette Corrigée,* are all excellent performances, but which, transferred to Ballets, would produce no effect. What could be substituted for the finished and witty dialogue of these pieces? Where is the pantomimic performer who could exhibit a true imitation of the minute details, delicate jests, or give an exact transcript of the characters, with all that striking originality so remarkable in these comedies? Could the Ballet-master attempt to introduce the heroes of the French Plautus and Terence dancing? Could he, in short, put a dancing *divertissement* into the *Orgonte* or the *Tartuffe?* In certain situations, speech possesses more power than gesture, and can give a far more effectual representation.

The soliloquies of Shakspeare possess an extraordinary sublimity; the thoughts contained in them are profound and beautiful; but what would become of these qualities if transferred to the Pantomime of a Ballet? No actor by gesture alone could give a faithful transcript of the fine scene to be found in the fifth act of *Richard III*, that great tragic production of the English Æschylus? The same difficulties attend the celebrated soliloquy of *Hamlet*[7]. Gesture is beautiful and effectual only when grief, tenderness, pride, or sprightliness is to be described; in logical reasoning, it becomes totally useless, and even ridiculous. —BATTEUX.

It appears then the province of the Ballet generally to exhibit a picture and imagery of things; action, striking situations, a peculiar life in all its motions; but vigorous representation of passions of the more powerful kind, and of exalted sentiments, are qualities essential to the *Grand Ballet*. The character and colouring of melodramatic and comic productions, require less vigour, but more of the agreeable; in these, a sprightly and interesting style must be preserved throughout. Hence it appears that the qualities of a good Ballet have a near relation to those of a good poem. According to Plutarch, the poet Simonides required that dancing should be mute poetry, and that poetry should be a speaking dance[8]. Consequently, the best poetry, is that in which we perceive the most action; the same may be observed of the Ballet[9].

The *Menteur* of Corneille, the *Plaideurs* of Racine, the

Turcaret of Le Sage, *L'Homme à bonne fortune* of Baron, all sparkling with wit and gaiety, would become vapourish and insignificant if changed into Ballets. The clever pieces of Marivaux, the amusing pieces by Collin d'Harleville (an author not sufficiently known and esteemed), together with the amusing comedies by Picard, would be flat and dull if represented by Pantomime. It is, therefore, a task of some difficulty, and requiring discernment, to select such subjects as will admit of Pantomime and dancing; they should be provided with a fund of interesting incidents, and the progress of the action should be sprightly and vigorous. No composer can succeed well in his work, if he has not, in the first instance, made choice of an appropriate subject, which, while furnishing the means of employing and displaying his talent, delights and inspires him. Every thing depends upon the selection of subjects. It sometimes happens, that a subject of very unimportant appearance, and that seems destitute of the requisites for a Ballet, unpromising, in short, in every respect, may still be essentially useful; but it must contain the germ of production, the spark that gives the hint, and illumines and warms the composer so as to awaken his powers of invention. He then by some appropriate additions, some well contrived episodes and embellishments of his art, augments and adorns the principal action; and thus, upon a small foundation, raises a sumptuous edifice. As it is a peculiar mark of genius, says L. da Vinci, to produce a great work with small means, so is it a sign of mediocrity to produce but a small matter from a plentiful fund. Frequently a word, a sketch, a fragment of sculpture striking the mind of a talented artist, forms the foundation of a masterpiece.

Subjects of universal interest and well known are very

proper for Ballets; when such is not the case, events should be as naturally represented as possible.

" Lo natural è sempre senza errore."—DANTE.

An intrigue may be invented, embarrassments cleverly contrived, and as cleverly cleared up; but all this must have the face of probability on it, if it is intended the illusion should be complete[10]. Truth may be mingled with fiction, provided it be done with art and prudence, and that such a composition proves moral and amusing. No complicated or compound action can be admitted, and but a very small portion of episode; in these particulars Alfieri and the French tragedy are good models. Nothing could be more ill-judged than to attempt to change into Ballets certain pieces of Calderon, or more foolish than to expect that Pantomime could express his twofold action, or gesture explain his entangled intrigues, still further confounded by his episodes.

All the dramas of the Spanish theatre, as well as a great many of the ancient English pieces, are scarcely any thing else but an assemblage of unconnected scenery, any imitation of which should be carefully avoided ; and the same may be observed with regard to the greater part of romantic productions[11]. Whatever is attempted in a Ballet, must be executed with clearness, precision, and a certain exactitude of manner. Digressions and long narrations are inadmissible; instead of which, action and incident must be employed; these alone are capable of conveying the meaning of the subject, and of making any deep impression. A recitation which the performer has closely studied in order to explain it by gestures, cannot be perfectly understood, unless some preceding action, upon which it must be founded, has been exhibited. The beautiful narration of *Théramène* in Pantomime would become downright nonsense, if the catastrophe which it describes had not already been represented.

We may be allowed to work up a subject that has already been treated on by others. History and fiction are open to all; the difficulty is, to know how to make a proper use of them; when the attention of genius is drawn to any part of them, it is then alone we may expect to see them successfully employed. Æschylus, Sophocles, Euripedes, Corneille, Racine, Voltaire, Metastasio, Zeno, and Alfieri, have often written on the same subject; but each has made it different by giving it after his own peculiar style and genius. The same observation may be made with respect to the great masters in painting. The tale of *Psyché* has been handled by Raphael, Gerard, Errante, and Appiani; that of *Galatea* by Raphael, An. Carracci, and L. Albano; *Aurora* was painted by Guido, Guercino, and Le Brun. D. de Volterra, Carracci, Guido, Tintoretto, and Rubens have all employed themselves upon the subject of *Goliath;* the *Slaughter of the Innocents* has occupied the talents of Raphael, Poussin, Rossi, Rubens, Gioseppino, and Le Brun. G. Campi, fearless of the rivalry of Titian, painted the *Assumption,* and in this masterpiece perfectly imitated the Venetian artist. Numerous other subjects were considered by the great masters as common property. Each embellished the same history or fable differently to the other, by introducing some new circumstance, or by adorning it with some beautiful episode; which traits of distinction would have been lost to us without this sort of emulation. Hence it appears that as often as the same subject falls into the hands of genius, it may be adorned by novelty and variety.

This is a sort of exercise of emulation very advantageous to young artists, since it gives rise to comparisons between their respective productions; faults are thus almost instantaneously perceived and as soon corrected. They would thus acquire experience also, without which we cannot attain to truth and perfection. While engaged in selecting a subject, be careful to make choice of one proportioned to your own peculiar ability : undertake nothing above your power.

CHAPTER VII.

ON DRAMATIC ACTION AND PASSION.

" Les passions sont les dieux du théâtre."—MARMONTEL.

GENIUS must be restrained by rules, and nature should be regulated by art.   How well contrived, and finely constructed is the *Saulle* of Alfieri! It is a masterpiece of the modern drama. But what absurdity may be observed in the arrangement and execution of the subject of the *Heraclius, or Famous Comedy*, by Calderon! Unbridled imagination quickly falls into senseless extravagance; but when guided by taste and philosophy, she produces an *Iphigènie* or an *Athalie.* " In order that the design of a work may be comprehended, it should be

simple, and independent of that general harmony which insensibly delights the eye or ear; any discordance between the lesser parts proves, not the genius, but, the stupidity of an artist. What obliges us to admire a noble work is a fancy at once fruitful and well regulated, which could conceive and reduce to uniformity any vast design."
MARMONTEL.

In Ballets, as in the *Grands Opéras* and lyric tragedies, the imagination may be allowed some irregularities; the scenery and embellishments that pieces of this kind require, give permission to such liberties, but they should be indulged in with care. In certain situations some license may and ought to be permitted, particularly to produce effect or increase the interest of the piece. Even the ancients themselves sometimes passed the limits of these severe regulations, but it was always done with good taste and great art. Their example in this instance may be imitated, as well as that of several celebrated moderns; and whenever the subject on which we are occupied can, by this means, be improved, it should be remembered that the unity of time and place is not a law that may never be broken.

Although a dramatic and pantomimic action may be perfectly conceived in all its parts, yet if not furnished with interest and incident, it will produce but little effect. To avoid falling into such defects, therefore, it is necessary to select a good subject, as has already been observed; one that continually exhibits a varied and striking picture of the passions [12]. When these are faithfully portrayed our attention is fixed, and our interest never flags. The *Varron* by De Grave, though a production full of art and contrivance, and very witty, could not retain its place on the stage from want of action and interest. Pathos is the most essential qualification of dramatic

pieces, and it ought to be the same in *Ballets d'Action.*
It is admirable in *Inès, Mérope, Iphigènie, Zayre,* and
Romeo and Juliet. Imitate in this particular the celebrated
Voltaire. Where is the writer who has treated on the passions in a more masterly manner, and with more philosophic knowledge, than this extraordinary man? He is the
most pathetic of tragic poets. He moves, inflames, and
transports us! What an endless variety of pictures does
he display! He is as much a painter as a poet; all is great
and true in his productions. He has beheld nature with
the eye of a Titian, and he has described her with all the
depth and energy peculiar to that divine artist. The
dramatic art was advanced by Voltaire to its highest perfection. In the plots of his pieces there is more life, and
in his characters there is more variety, than in those of any
writer who preceded him. He is also more diversified in
the choice of his subjects, and has exhibited more novelty
in his representation.

This philosophic poet understood better than any of
his rivals how to instruct, at the same time that he
delighted and interested the spectators. From whatever age or nation he took his subject, he had always a
moral end in view which tended to our improvement : at
once to delight and instruct, is the first axiom of dramatic
writers.

We may remark with men of learning that—the beautiful in sculpture, in poetry, in painting, and in dancing, is
not the geometrical beauty of proportion, but it is *expression,* and that vividly portrayed. The general action
and progress of theatrical exhibitions arrest our attention,
when accompanied by interest ; then it is they stir and
agitate the passions, and oblige us to take a part with the
characters of the piece. The art of taking possession of
the minds and affection of an audience constitutes the

highest praise of a dramatic author. It is then that the exhibition of a beautiful theatrical production, " vi sentite commuovere tutta la macchina : v' adirate, o temete a vicenda ; vi sentite raccapricciare i capelli, nascere il piacere, germogliar la speranza, &c. Un pezzo di pittura, o di scultura, il meglio fatto secondo le regole dell' arte, se non traspira azione, è un pezzo di maraviglia, come l'opera della Sfera, e del Cilindro di Archimede, le Galleggianti di Galileo, i principj di Newton ; ma non già bello. La prima sorgente di quest' azione, è che il poeta, o il pittore n' abbia molta nel suo temperamento, e sia capace di riceverne molta dagli oggetti o reali, o fantastici. Un temperamento lento o freddo potrá per avventura essere un gran geometra ma non un poeta, un pittore, uno scultore, che piaccia*."
—GENOVESI.

The passion of love, which is the soul of the stage and the source of so many other passions, whose variety and contrast produce numberless dramatic situations, is essentially necessary also to the Ballet. On it depends a multitude of striking and pathetic effects, which appear to be naturally allied to Pantomime and dancing. Love is the principal spring of action in a Ballet, the object of which

---

* It agitates the whole body, inspires us by turns with delight and gentle melancholy, then with lively sensations of pleasure, and sometimes with transports of admiration. In short the *beautiful* beheld in expressive action is capable of raising us to a state of rapture. That profound and discriminating philosopher, Genovesi observes, " that a painting or piece of sculpture, executed according to the nicest rules of the art, but wanting *expression*, may be admired, as we do the sphere and cylinder of Archimedes, and other works of geometric proportions ; beauty, however, excites within us feelings of a far different description. The source of the *beautiful* must be placed in the breast of the poet or painter ; he must be of a temperament susceptible of beautiful impressions, real or imaginary. A constitution cold and slow may, perhaps become a good geometrician, but never a poet, a painter, or a sculptor."

is to produce gentle, agreeable, and sometimes even terrible sensations. Love has been employed in a masterly manner by the authors of *Phèdre* and *Zayre*. These great poets will teach in what method love, of all passions the finest and most powerful, contributes to delight us on the stage; they were the organs of nature, which, together with their works, should be studied as models and guides.

The exalted stateliness of Corneille's genius appears above describing the scenes and events of this passion, which he has frequently treated in an episodical and even insipid style in his tragedies. In Alfieri, love is generally no more than secondary and accessary, excepting in the fine tragedy of *Myrrha*. The harmonious Metastasio, however, is a worthy rival of the great Racine, who may be termed the poet of the heart. The former treated the tender passion in a most elevated style; but what merits remark in him is, that a moral may frequently be traced in his most seductive scenes; he is superior to Alfieri in pathos. However, instances of tragic terror are to be found in his productions. His characters are drawn very much in the manner of Corneille. The delightful Quinault is also another dramatic model; he is tender, impassioned, and sometimes even sublime; his descriptions are frequently equal to the pictures of Correggio and Guido. Apostolo Zeno is full of dramatic fire and feeling, and treats on the passions with great energy. Shakspeare is another great painter of the passions; the truth and vigour of his conceptions are equally astonishing. Nature is his model, and his creations are not, in any particular, inferior to her. His pathos is often overpowering and sublime; his works are a mine, the gold of which must be extracted with care. In my opinion, however, the Avonian bard should not be consulted until after all the other great authors have been studied, since his numerous errors might spoil the taste of a young and inexperienced composer *.

The ancients neglected love as a subject for tragedies; we find in them but very weak representations of a passion which, however, I will venture to say, as handled in modern dramas, principally constitutes their superiority over the ancients. The classic poets contain nothing that can be compared to the character of *Phèdre*, or the last acts of *Zayre*, to Metastasio, or to the *Myrrha* of Alfieri. These seductive and powerful poets, to whom the modern drama owes all its interest and excellence, assisted essentially by the wise regulations of our theatres, must not be ranked second to any name mentioned in this work. In the mean time, it must be confessed, we are greatly indebted to antiquity, whose poets contain beauties that have never yet been equalled.

A Ballet, however, can still be made to excite interest without making love the sole subject, to the exclusion of all other passions, of which there is a numerous train, capable of fixing and amusing the mind of an audience; love, then, treated as an episode, produces a most agreeable contrast, and increases the effect of the other passions. Almost every species of passion may be produced in a Ballet, each in its place; but one should not be admitted to the exclusion of another, and particularly that of *love*, which even when introduced only as an accessary, often becomes a primary object. There are a number of historical and fabulous subjects that may be agreeably treated on, and in which it is not necessary that love should usurp despotic dominion.

---

* It must be observed that the author speaks of our great poet only from reading translations of some of his pieces, and then principally with respect to their plan and conduct.

CHAPTER VIII.

TERROR, RATHER THAN HORROR, IS SUFFICIENT FOR ANY
DRAMATIC PRODUCTION.   ON IMITATION.

" Nec pueros coram populo Medea trucidet :
Aut humana palam coquat exta nefarius Atreus."   HOR.

WHEN selecting passages from history for the purpose
of adapting them to the Ballet, it is not necessary to make
choice of those horrible deeds that have disgraced mankind, nor to extract from fiction those atrocities of which
human nature appears almost incapable.   The composer
should reject those shocking and sanguinary events which
generally form the subjects of the Spanish and English
dramas.   He should avoid also the slightest imitation of
that gloomy and improbable stuff with which certain
authors are filled; those poets who take a pleasure in describing all that is most desperate and dreadful in nature
are not to be followed.   Perhaps this species of subject
may be adapted to the deepest tragedy; but even then,
good taste would reprove and reject productions carried,
by an overheated imagination, beyond the bounds prescribed to imitative arts.   We must, in short, banish from
the Ballet the *Fausts*, the *Manfreds*, and the *Frank-
ensteins* [13]

It is not possible to atone for the horror and disgust inspired by these monstrous dramas, by any object they may finally tend to, whether useful or pleasing. I can compare such compositions to nothing but those hideous masks among the ancients, known by the name of *Mormolicia*, whose very name, according to Esichius and some others, pronounced by nurses and governesses, was sufficient to inspire children with dread. The greater part of these productions, indeed, contain neither solidity nor truth, and are only calculated, like the *Mormolicia*, to frighten children and women. In searching for subjects, therefore, among historians and poets, we should reject the atrocious deeds recorded in the former, and avoid imitating the reprehensible subjects exhibited by the latter. Exclude every subject, the nature of which will not allow of the introduction of dancing, and in which dancing would seem misplaced and ridiculous.

Æschylus, who was the father of tragedy, never stained the scene with blood; a conduct, the wise moderation of which can be never enough admired. This mighty genius, while occupied in creating the drama, knew how to restrain the flights of his imagination. He discovered and tried every means of arriving at theatrical perfection.

Horace also, as may be seen by our motto—the great lawgiver of Parnassus—condemns sanguinary deeds; he firmly forbids such an exhibition as Medea murdering her children; or the detestable butcher Atreus, preparing human flesh. One of the commentators on this poet says, that his precept is founded in nature and in reason; for that it is sufficient to excite terror and not horror; the heart is not amended by exhibitions of blood and murder, but by pathetic distress. This is in some measure only a repetition of the principles laid down by Aristotle. Let us now hear what that great philosopher delivers, who is almost always perfect in his conceptions: "Since tragedy" says he, " is an imitation of the noblest qualities to be found amongst men, we should follow the example of those good painters who give a true likeness, but at the same time beautified; thus a poet, who would describe an angry and outrageous man, or any similar kind of character, should exhibit what it is possible passion might do, rather than what it has in reality done."—*Poet.* Chap. XV.

These excellent precepts ought to be engraved on the memory of every writer who composes for the theatre. " If the arts are indeed imitators of nature, the imitation should be excuted in a wise and enlightened style, not performed like a servile copy: every trait should be preserved, but it should be described with all the improvement of which it is susceptible. In short, it should be an imitation that exhibits nature, not as she really is, but, such as the mind conceives she might be. How did Zeuxis proceed when he wished to paint a perfect beauty? Did he produce the portrait of some beautiful individual? No; he assembled the peculiar beauties of certain persons; he then formed in his own imagination a portrait in which all these separate perfections were united; and this imaginary portrait was the prototype or model of a picture, which was not true to nature except in its separated parts. This is a precedent for artists of every description; a path in which they should walk; a path, indeed, which all the great masters, without exception, have continued to follow."

This may be termed imitating *beautiful nature;* to do which is the business of poetry, music, dancing, painting, and sculpture; and which, says Le Batteux, does not prevent truth and reality from being the ground work of the Arts.

The muses themselves will explain this in the following
lines, imitated from Hesiod :—

> " When we the magic of our art apply,
> With truth's appearance, we can paint a lie;
> But by that art we can delight inspire,
> By showing simple truth in plain attire."

If a historical event happens to be so related as to be
susceptible of becoming a subject for a poem or a picture,
the poet or the painter would employ himself upon the
work, each making use of his peculiar powers, inventing
certain additional circumstances, contrasts, situations, &c.
When Le Brun painted the battles of Alexander, he found
in history the action, the actors, and the scene of action; but,
at the same time, with what invention, what poetry did he
adorn his work ; what design, what attitudes, and what
expression ! All these are the creation of his genius; they
are indeed models[14]."

The *Grand Ballet d'Action*, or serious Ballet, must be
principally modelled on tragedy ; but must be less gloomy,
substituting more cheerful traits for the latter quality.
The picture should be

> " Vrai, mais flatté, tel qu'il est, mais en beau."

BERNARD.

Corneille and other French tragedians, with Metastasio, were always of a contrary opinion to that which
allowed of sanguinary exhibitions.　Neither is there any
authority for effecting the catastrophe of a tragedy by
blood and murder, which can only then be admitted
when the subject absolutely requires it.　There are excellent tragedies that are quite free from scenes of horror;
this exalted department of the drama may, in short, be
composed without such assistance.　If the critics, who
are the guardians of Parnassus, have obliged even men of

taste to banish from the stage revolting spectacles, can we mention without blame those composers who would mix up dancing with the subjects of an ill-judged selection of pieces from Shakspeare, Otway, Crebillon, Schiller, and Nathaniel Lee?

Every style should be allowed its own peculiar characteristics; and it must be remembered, that nothing extraneous and foreign should be admitted. It is the province of history to relate every thing—she is the slave of truth. Tragedy portrays exalted nature: while deeply affecting us, she imparts the sublimest lessons. Let the Ballet-master seek and seize these and other beauties; and let him employ all his powers to turn them to the best advantage.

If a composer of Ballets, in his admiration of certain passages in some poets, who have otherwise exceeded the rules of Aristotle and Horace, by giving horrible descriptions, falls into the same error, his transgression will be greater than the others; for the peculiar object of his art is to excite gentle and sometimes pathetic sensations, but never terrifying and dreadful feelings.

CHAPTER IX.

ON THE METHOD OF RAISING AND IMPROVING A SUBJECT.

> " Il n'est point de serpent, ni de monstre odieux,
> Qui, part l'art imitè, ne puisse plaire aux yeux :
> D'un pinceau délicat l'artifice agréable
> Du plus affreux objet fait un objet aimable."—BOILEAU.

THE composer of Ballets should imitate those sculptors of antiquity who, in order to conceal the disproportionate length of Pericles' head, always represented that great man in a helmet[15]. If the author possesses sufficient talent to ennoble an indifferent subject, it will be sure of producing a good effect. How much genius does it require to perfect and embellish certain productions of nature, and, at the same time, to cover the art by which such improvement is effected! That peculiar and genuine ease to be observed in the works of the great masters was not produced without unwearied application. Whatever is added or withdrawn from a model should be done with a cultivated taste and a profound knowledge of nature. The best designs are drawn from nature, who also suggests to us every means of improvement and embellishment. Raphael is a model both for authors and artists; he imitated nature with profound judgment, and ennobled whatever he imitated. His exalted taste rejected whatever was mean, trivial, or indecent; whatever, in short, might offend the sight or wound the feelings. He imparted an air of novelty to the most ordinary subjects; and the simplest circumstance is rendered interesting by his pencil. To him, in his art, nothing was impossible. Often, when treating on subjects universally known, the fertility of his genius, aided by the profound knowledge of his art, surprises and delights by the manner in which objects are presented to us, and by the new forms in which they are clothed. We always find nature in him, but it is nature made beautiful and perfect. Whatever is disgusting and unworthy of representation, or that requires a veil, is but dimly discovered in his works.

Raphael has improved upon the beauties of the antique; he is as true, perfect, and sublime as the statuaries of Greece, and more universal and lovely: he, above all others, exhibits the *beau idéal.* Never did any man create and compose as he. An harmonious union is the characteristic of all his works, and produces the most wonderful effect. Every constituent part is arranged with taste ; his manner of grouping is charming ; every object being placed with unerring propriety. He has sometimes assembled things the most heterogeneous, but he has charmed them into union by the magic of his touch. The *Vision of Ezekiel,* together with some other allegorical pictures, exhibit a power of grouping at once gigantic and extraordinary. Here it is that the talent of ennobling every thing is carried to the highest point of perfection.

The great painters present to persons who are composing for the stage, advantages not possessed by writers ; for at the same moment that the former present the fable of a piece, they exhibit, also, the physical effect of the passions upon each actor in the scene. The imagination of young persons, while reading a dramatic piece, may indeed supply a representation of things described; but if they are not formed by study and nature, such imagery may be defective, and, accordingly, appear so at the theatre, by a flat and faulty style of performing. If, therefore, the best painters faithfully imitate the most beautiful parts of nature, let both the composer and performer of Ballets make them their study and model. The effect produced on the person who beholds a fine picture is more universal and striking, than that on him who reads a piece of poetry; for, our mind is more quickly and powerfully affected by impressions received through the sight, than by those conveyed through the ear and the memory.

CHAPTER X.

ON ORDER.

" ———————— des proportions la savante beauté
A joint la symétrie à la variété."   DELILLE.

IT is requisite that a perfect harmony should pervade the parts of every production. Every circumstance should be appropriately arranged, confusion avoided, and an exact order established throughout. That analogy which should subsist between each object must not, however, confound the traits of distinction, for if this analogy should cause a universal resemblance, the composition would then become void of that variety ever observable in nature, and the want of which causes monotony. Order excludes improprieties, transpositions of subjects, and a wild disproportion of parts. Every circumstance of a composition should have a mutual and natural relation to each other; and all should unite in forwarding the principal action,

Every thing should be rendered so clear, as to be felt and understood. Events ought to be artfully linked together, forming a clue of explanation at once useful and agreeable. It is such a skilful arrangement as this, where every circumstance is disposed exactly where it is required, which is called *order*. Unfortunately, however, this *order*, which is so delightful and essential also, to works of taste, is not always to be found in the productions of genius. Imagination often transports us, and the bounds prescribed by reason are then quickly passed. La Bruyère remarks, with his usual discrimination, that it is more easy for a great genius to excel in sublime compositions, than to avoid falling into any error whatever. Art, indeed, is not always the companion of genius.

The Pleasure arising from Order.

It is not sufficient, says Montesquieu, to present a multitude of objects to the mind; they must be presented with order. Then it is, that we can remember what is already past, and even imagine what is to come; and our mind congratulates itself on such an extent of its perception : but in a work where there is no order, the mind is continually labouring to introduce some sort of arrangement itself. The end the author has in view, and that which we have formed for ourselves, are thus confounded : the mind remembers nothing and foresees nothing, and becomes stupified by the confusion of her own ideas, and the senselessness of what she beholds; at length, being quite wearied, she is rendered totally incapable of tasting any pleasure; it is on this account that, though there is not an intentional display of confusion, order introduces itself voluntarily. Thus it is that painters group their figures; if the subject be a battle, they place in the foreground of their pictures whatever objects must be distinctly seen, while the confused part of the picture is shown in the distance.

CHAPTER XI.

ON VARIETY AND CONTRAST.

" Jucundum nihil est, nisi quod reficit varietas."

P. Syrus.

" Le contraste nous frappe en de contraires sens ;
Des termes opposés qu à nos yeux elle étale
L'imagination mesure l'intervalle." Delille.

Whoever desires to excite interest or pleasure, must introduce variety into his works. Nature is our model, and nature is never long the same. The composer must strive to display variety in the plot in each succeeding scene, and in every act ; the passions and the characters must also partake of this amusing quality. It must be observed also, even in the dances and decorations; and every where lend its aid to produce a pleasing effect. Avoid uniformity, for with it comes monotony, and monotony begets weariness.

Opposite qualities and striking contrasts are ever expected both in tragedy and comedy ; but in the Ballet, they are indispensable. It is the peculiar province of Pantomime to express the widely-differing classes of passions and sentiments ; without such an opportunity the art of gesture could not long excite interest. Contrasts are palpably remarkable in nature, and they must therefore be found on the stage; they are essential to the drama, and never fail in producing great effect. They impart life and vigour to the Ballet. It is by the remarkable contrast observable in their works that men of great talent may be recognized. Shakspeare, that giant of the British stage, is ever producing the most extraordinary contrasts. Voltaire, Racine, Corneille, and Metastasio, together with the best epic poets, must be our models in this respect.

" The contrasts between the gay and the noble, the great and the agreeable, the agreeable and the gloomy, do not excite deep emotion, but they are pleasing from variety, and free use should be made of them. The contrast which produces the greatest effect is the terrible and sublime, as opposed to cheerful and beautiful objects; but the assistance of this is seldom required : first, because this contrast is uncommon in nature, and, secondly, because the effect of the sublime is to excite astonishment; if, therefore, this contrast is frequently repeated, astonishment ceases.

" Contrasts may be sometimes raised from the peculiar situations of characters ; and from change of scenes, pleasure may be introduced amidst horrors, and melancholy into the garden of delight. Thus scenes may be produced capable of inspiring opposite emotions, of moving the affections, and of transporting the soul."—St. Lambert.

The contrast of *situations* must be particularly attended to, in order that they may be varied accordingly ; thus several scenes of love succeeding each other are wearisome; the same may be observed with respect to enraged passion.

Variety may be also observed in the arrangement of the scenery ; thus a gloomy representation should be succeeded by a bright and cheerful prospect. Let the sumptuous embellishments of a palace, be followed by the plain simplicity of private life. In the colours employed upon costume, also, sameness must be avoided. In short, the smallest circumstance in regard to contrast and variety should not be neglected, since it is the judicious union of these that produces the grandest effect.

CHAPTER XII.

STAGE EFFECT.

" C'est là ce qui surprend, frappe, saisit, attache."

BOILEAU.

MANY Ballet-masters, as well as dramatic authors, place great confidence in stage effect. Every opportunity of such a species of display is seized with avidity, and such persons think they have completely succeeded by representing an improbable and extravagant event, or by emblazoning forth some horrible scene of assassination. They imagine, also, that sudden changes of scenery, a multitude of supernumeraries, apparitions, showers of fire, and, above all, military evolutions by horse and foot, are all indispensably necessary, as producing stage effect. It is with such unmeaning noise and bustle as this that bad composers generally stuff the trash they produce, and, unfortunately, if through chance and ignorance they succeed, true taste and talent are despised. Such a triumph, however, cannot continue unchanged; clatter and tinsel cannot always drown the opposing voice of good sense.

" ———— il volgo ignaro, che non e bastante
A discernere il ver con vista acuta,
Tutto ciò, che ha del nuovo, e del brillante
Più che il solido, e l'utile valuta." CASTI.

These are the sort of connoisseurs who dictate laws, but it is the ignorant only who submit to them.

The meaning of stage effect is not generally understood; the real explanation of this cannot be gathered from what is so termed. I cannot do better, therefore, than supply an elucidation of this subject as contained in part of a letter from La Harpe to Voltaire :—" I continually hear people talk of the power of stage effect ;" says this writer, " but what is really stage effect ? Does it consist of sanguinary executions ? No. Orestes, in the tragedy of *Andromache*, loves Hermione ; he has just obtained permission to marry her, should Pyrrhus be united to Andromache ; in effecting which he appears determined, having refused to give up Astyanax, and making every sacrifice in order to get possession of the Trojan lady. Orestes is revelling in happy expectation ; Pyrrhus enters ; every thing assumes a new appearance ; he has been braved, and now again solicits the hand of Hermione ; and, yielding up Astyanax, he even invites Orestes to witness his espousal with the latter lady. Orestes becomes motionless with astonishment, and the audience partake of his distress." This is truly stage, or dramatic, effect : it is the production of a master.

How different is such dramatic effect as this, from that which we have mentioned above ; but which, however, is frequently applauded by the most considerable part of the public. In the drama it is not necessary to dazzle the sight, the heart must be affected. Stage effect, properly, consists of unforeseen events, sudden changes in the sentiments of the characters, and noble and extraordinary acts. Astonishment and admiration must be excited, but they should be accompanied by probability.

In the last act of the same tragedy, by Racine, Orestes, after having slain Pyrrhus to satisfy the desire of Hermione, returns to receive her hand, the reward promised to his crime ; but what is his situation on being attacked by the reproaches of her for whom he had committed such excesses ? She accuses him of the King's death, whom she still loves ; here is another terrible situation both for Orestes and the spectators. At the moment Orestes believes himself the happiest of mortals, he becomes an object of horror to her whom he loves. This is one of the most tragic situations of which the stage is capable ; and Racine has bestowed on it all the great talent for which he is so celebrated. This instance, in our opinion, is still more powerful than that which is cited above. They are both scenes that take forcible possession of our heart and imagination ; and such an effect as this the composer should endeavour to imitate. The poets who have adorned the French theatre; Metastasio, Alfieri, Ap. Zeno, and Shakspeare, must be deeply studied by those artists who would prosper in their dramatic career. The drama of Spain also frequently furnishes striking dramatic effects, instances of which may be found in Calderon. Excellent passages may be gathered from the pieces of Kotzebue and Schiller. While studying modern authors, do not neglect the ancients, their masters ; for they possess dramatic situations and the deepest pathos. Since their time, indeed, theatrical performances have made an astonishing progress, for which we are indebted to Poliziano, Trissino, Corneille, Racine, Molière, Crébillon, Voltaire, Maffei, Metastasio and Alfieri.

It is not necessary to be continually seeking after dramatic situations and stage effect ; nor to be ever introducing scenes in which contrasts are exhibited ; the most delicious dish may be too often served up ; and the same beauties, presented too frequently, become affected and monotonous. When incidents of the sublime are too much multiplied, the attention of the spectator immediately becomes fatigued. During every dramatic action, the poet and composer should occupy our minds entirely, by a natural description of the passions ; each by turns should delight us, the one by his poetic ideas, the other by the gaiety of the dance, and the pomp of decoration appropriately introduced.

CHAPTER XIII.

ON CHARACTERS, SOLILOQUIES AND MONOLOGUES.

> " Conservez à chacun son propre caractère.
> Des siécles, des pays, étudiez les mœurs :
> Les climats font souvent les diverses humeurs."
>
> BOILEAU.

AVOID introducing a crowd of characters; they cause confusion, and injure the effect of the piece. A useless part must not be admitted; when there are sufficient to explain the subject, no more need be added. In this respect Alfieri is the most perfect of models; all his characters are essential and indispensable to the subject; there is not one too many, and all are disposed of in the most interesting manner. To this poet we are greatly indebted for having banished from the scene those useless and troublesome personages called *confidents,* who generally answer no other end than that of exposing the barrenness of the author's invention. In French tragedy these idle characters impede the development of the subject; as do also certain amorous couples to be met with in Metastasio. The kindness of the latter poet to singers, who would all have principal parts, frequently caused his operas to be very monotonous. Horace wished not to see more than four persons performing a piece, considering that number sufficient to explain the subject to the audience.—" Nec quarta loqui persona laboret."

We may certainly be allowed to admit more characters than prescribed by the great poetical lawgiver; but whatever characters are admitted must be necessary to the piece, and should share in the general interest. We should take care, however, not to imitate Schiller, who, in one of his plays *(William Tell)*, has introduced fifty persons who speak, without mentioning an infinite number of mute parts, and characters who merely make their appearance. There are also twenty persons in the *Julius Cæsar* of Shakspeare. But this is one of the characteristics of writers in the *romantic* style [16].

A Ballet-master should make human nature his profound study; and should extend his observations over every class of society. He ought also to remark the customs and manners peculiar to different countries, even to their particular features, and whatever other mark of distinction is remarkable between them. Some resemblance may sometimes be traced between the manners of certain nations, still there is always a sufficiency of characteristic to mark the distinction. Nothing, in short, should escape the observation of a composer, for there is scarcely any thing in nature that may not be turned to his advantage. He must note particularly the peculiarities of the times or historical epochs in which his personages flourished. In classical representations, the audience should be enabled to recognize each character from his peculiar style of performing, and method of developing the passions. What a dissimilarity, for example, exists between the characters of Cæsar and that of Achilles; between Achilles and that of Paris ! The character and conduct of Mahomet are totally opposed to those of Trajan. What an immense difference is there between the characters of *Philip* and that of the father of *Virginia*[17] ; between *Rodrigue* and *Zayre;* between *Iphigénie* and *Agrippine!* The mind and manners of the inhabitants of *Africa* are of another nature to those of *Europe*. The education, manner, behaviour and deportment of a country person, or of a mere *bourgeois*, are entirely unlike those of a king or a hero. These marks of distinction are termed by Aristotle *costume*, and he recommends the study of them to every dramatic author :—

" Observez, connaissez, imitez la nature."

DELILLE.

Characters must be shown in contrast. If there appears in your production a *Clarissa*, her goodness and virtue must be opposed to the villanies of a *Lovelace*. The conduct of *Britannicus* heaps hatred upon the part of *Nero*. The abstinence of *Hyppolitus* is properly opposed to the unbridled passion of *Phœdra;* and, in Fielding's novel, the hatred we entertain for *Blifil* serves to increase our love for *Jones*. All dramatic characters must be prominent, every feature must strike us immediately, so as to be easily comprehended. The greater the contrasts, the more plainly does the eye find the peculiar traits. A character, when tranquil and inactive, says little, and exhibits but few peculiarities ; but the same being excited by reproach, immediately, as it were, starts into existence, evincing its own inherent qualities. Ovid, in one of his animated descriptions, presents us with a striking image in proof of this : " Envy is slumbering in her den, immersed in solitude ; her snakes find no object on whom to wreak their ire, and remain in motionless stupor. Minerva suddenly appears, Envy immediately exhibits signs of reviving action and agitation ; the deadly poison in her breast ferments, and livid fire flashes from her eyes. The serpents around her head dart forth their stings, and hiss for an opportunity to inflict their venom." The allegorical sense of this passage may be applied to the theatre. " Would we introduce an envious character, it is only necessary to bring it in contact with virtue, and its hideous deformity is immediately perceived. An assemblage of various descriptions of characters forms a relief to each other ; thus the *Misantrope* becomes enamoured of a *Coquette ;* while the *Glorieux* has an indigent unpresuming and secluded father. The integrity of *Severus*, in the *Polieucte*, defeats the suspicious policy of *Felix*."—DE CHABANON.

In the characters of Racine, we should frequently be glad to find more variety ; the same remark may be made with respect to Alfieri and Metastasio ; these great poets, adhering too strictly each to his peculiar style, did not perceive that they employed the same materials in describing characters totally opposite. Voltaire was aware of this, and we rarely find him in such an error ; he is varied and natural both in character and incident. Corneille may be termed the Michael Angelo of the drama, he is sublime and true to nature. Shakspeare frequently excels in the varied and striking style of drawing his characters, but his imitations of nature are not always finished, nor historically true ; he, however, appears as inexhaustible as nature herself ; he creates with ease, but his imaginings want finish, and appear never to have been corrected. When, however, the English poet does succeed, he surpasses all ; his characters are life itself, and their power over us is prodigious. Those inequalities we perceive in some of his personifications proceed, most commonly, from the nature of the events that happen during the piece, rather than from their own peculiar nature. The genius of Shakspeare was endued with a power capable of undertaking any thing, and of completing what it undertook ;

but taste and art seldom accompany his daring flights.
One of the peculiar qualities of Schiller, and which deserves notice, is, the almost endless variety he has spread
over his characters; and in this peculiarity, rather than in
any other, this poet ought to be imitated. Allow your characters some moments of repose, which will form, as it
were, a shadowing to their action. What is continually
before the eyes of the audience, and ever speaking on the
same subject, must necessarily weary them. A character,
for instance, that is mad from the beginning to the end
of the piece, becomes a disgusting and ridiculous object ;
a love-sick lady may be considered in the same light, who
continues throughout the play lamenting her fate. Let
sentiment be varied, therefore, and passion crossed.

The principal person of a piece should be more frequently before the audience than the less important
characters. The latter are, indeed, entirely subordinate
to the former ; they appear to be generally employed
either in causing the passions or in crossing them, and in
producing incident, and heightening the interest. Interest
must pervade every part of the production, but the greater
share of this must be attached to the principal subject,
rather than to the underplot. Two leading characters
may be opposed to each other, but in the end the hero
must triumph, though even by death. Your hero must be
kept sometimes out of sight, which causes that repose and
variety that are essential to his very being. Never withdraw him, however, so long that he may be forgotten, for
the interest with respect to his fate must not be suffered
to languish. The performance of secondary characters
lends a variety to the scene, securing, at the same time, a
sort of welcome for the return of the hero; whether fabulous
or historical, therefore, they are indispensably necessary.
The fate of the hero must be the universal object of hope

or fear, and his presence must be always impatiently expected; whenever, also, he re-appears, he should bring with him some subject for renewing the interest, and encreasing the animation of the piece.

Homer, Virgil, Ariosto and Tasso present a treasury of characters; in delineating which, these pictorial bards have excelled; they exhibit the finest and faithfulest description of mankind. Perhaps the great Torquato, in this respect, outrivals the rest. His characters are drawn with a philosophic hand, they are ever true and consistent. *Gofredo, Rinaldo, Argante, Tancredi, Saladino, Armida, Clorinda, Erminia,* &c., are perfect and finished portraits, and cannot be too much studied. The secondary personages of this poem are also drawn in an admirable style, and they are worthy of imitation.

Soliloquy; this word designates that reflection and reasoning a man holds with himself. *Monologue* is a sort of dialogue, in which a character performs at once his own part and that of some confidential person. If soliloquy may be frequently found in nature, it is not wrong to introduce it into the drama. There are certain interesting situations in ordinary life where a person finds, that it is in himself alone he can confide, and he accordingly enters into a monologue. It is, however, difficult to admit these sort of addresses into the Ballet; if they are attempted, the subject of them must be easily imagined, and they must contain only such ideas as can be expressed by pantomimic gesture. The action employed must be of a simple nature, calculated to convey the thought with clearness, ease and precision.

Soliloquies which suppose but one person are, therefore, not so difficult of execution as *monologues.* They require an exalted and imposing style. They produce a good effect when properly introduced, and when they appear a natural consequence of that part of the piece that preceded them. The pantomimic action of which they are composed, requires the greatest attention and study, otherwise they become totally unintelligible.

There should always appear a good reason for the introduction of soliloquies and monologues; and the composer should make an appropriate use of them. Some authors are too lavish in the employment of them in their productions; but this is extremely blameable[18]. Soliloquy is a refuge and resource for writers, but it ought not to be abused. They must arise naturally out of the subject, and be essential to its explanation. A person finding himself alone, gives himself up freely to his reflections; the feelings, under the influence of which he labours, break forth into exclamation from time to time, accompanied by a peculiar species of gesture; but all this is done in a sort of under tone, and generally lasts not long; he does not, however, ask himself questions and reply like any one deranged.

This appears to be the simple and original state of the soliloquy; and keeping this always in mind, we may heighten and adorn its expression by the power of gesture. Nature is generally content with very little gesticulation to explain her intentions; but those signs she does employ clearly express what passes within us, by their energy and propriety. The language of nature is simple, and if an actor will strive to imitate it, his Pantomime will triumph by such an effort. Scenes of a *monologous* nature frequently produce a powerful effect, particularly in the hands of a performer of talent, who will sometimes adorn them with all the beauties of his art.

Many of the ancient Pantomimes were nothing more than *monologues*, and were represented by a single performer, who undertook to describe every character mentioned in the programme. We shall conclude this chapter by recommending young composers always to show a reason for the entry of a character, and motive for its exit, since nothing can be imagined more improbable or preposterous, than that a character should appear and withdraw, because the author may have his own particular reasons for so doing.

CHAPTER XIV.

ON DRAMATIC MORAL.

"Se nessun componimento dee essere rettamente accostumato, e sano; ció si conviene a quelli, che debbono essere recitati in pubblico."

G. GOZZI.

THE drama may be said to have two principal objects in view—to please and to instruct; to compass such ends, therefore, works of a decorous character should be produced, tending rather to correct than to demoralize manners.

To authors and artists, therefore, should not be adjudged the palm of merit, except, after having realized this important intention as expressed by Horace, that is, by uniting the useful and amusing. Every artist of celebrity, and almost all great poets have conformed themselves to this wise regulation. Voltaire, Matastasio, Racine,

and Zeno ever aimed at some useful end in their productions[19].

" Qu'un sublime talent soit un talent utile "

LA HARPE.

Let this maxim be continually present to the mind of
the young composer: a piece is not perfect without a
moral. The learned and judicious Pompignan required
that every theatrical production should carry a moral with
it, considering that as indispensably necessary to render
the whole complete.

The greater part of Grecian tragedies are immoral; little
instruction, therefore, can be reaped from them. On the
other hand, the comedies of Greece are rather biting satires, than works of art produced with the intention of correcting the manners. It is with no pleasant feeling we
observe the same spirit of immorality prevailing through
many scenes of Molière and Goldoni, that defile the
dramas of Plautus and Aristophanes. The ancient
comedy of England is nothing but an abuse of morality
and good manners. Shakspeare is any thing but moral
in his comedies; and his tragedy is far different from
that required by Aristotle.

Metastasio, Voltaire, and Euripides may be termed
theatrical philosophers; the pictures they draw at once
delight and impart instruction. The first two, more particularly, are the most moral of all dramatic writers.
While presenting to us a living history of past ages,
mixed up with the passions of men, they provide us with
most excellent instruction, and inspire the most exalted
philosophy. And here the Italian poet surpasses every
rival, and Voltaire remains unequalled.

CHAPTER XV.

ON THE RELATION SUBSISTING BETWEEN MUSIC AND DANCING.

" Music and dancing are a married pair."—LUCIAN.

THE ancients required that a perfect agreement should exist between the expression of music and the movements of dancing.   Every gesture, and every change of countenance in the performer, was supposed to be produced by the peculiar measure and rythmus of the air, and the air was made to respond and reflect, as it were, every pantomimic movement in its melody and modulations [20].   In the cultivation of such an art, both taste and reason should be consulted.   This agreement was made by the Italians an important study, particularly with respect to their Pantomimes.   But, as has been already observed, it is not necessary to proceed to the extent of affecting to present a step and a gesture for every note. Dramatic illusion may be destroyed by being overacted.

Music is an essential part of the Ballet; by its powerful means, the truth, force, and charm of pantomimic acting is brought to perfection; and by their delightful union the most surprising effects are produced [21].

The music of the ancients, as well as their poetry, contained a variety of rythmuses, measures, and styles, the nature of which served to express the sentiments of the soul, in a most impressive manner.   The most particular attention was paid in suiting the action to the music exactly; and those who failed to observe this rule, were severely attacked and censured.

Scrupulous care should be taken to adapt the music with precision to pantomimic gesture. Particular attention also should be paid to avoid those mistakes to which we are but too often witnesses, namely, the ridiculous endeavour to suit an air taken from a serious opera to the action of those who are performing a comic scene ; and, on the contrary, pretending to represent the discourse of two grave characters by playing gay dancing music. This would be doing, as the satiric artist has it, — "Cantar su la ciaccona il miserere."—SALV. ROSA*. The music should describe the characters and passions belonging to it; striving to strengthen and complete the picture. The accent and melody of the airs, should always vary with the subject of the Ballet. The music of an Asiatic Ballet ought certainly to be of a different character to that of which the scene and action lie in a village; again, the rythmus and melody of the airs in a mythologic Ballet must not be of the same species as those of a ballet of chivalry and romance. A perfect analogous concord should subsist between what we see and what we hear. The ideas of the composer should accord with those of the author; and the labours of both should be ever most closely and agreeably united.

Let us profit by the examples of the ancients, and attend to the lessons of the great masters of Italy. By these means the multitude may be reclaimed to a just taste for music of a description truly pathetic, capable of delighting the soul as well as the sense; of a style, also, so pure that it ceases to delight as soon as the artist neglects the rules of science and the laws of reason[22].

---

* Or, dancing a hornpipe to the Dead March.

CHAPTER XVI.

ON DECORATIONS.

" Loin les ornemens froids, les détails superflus,
Tout ce qu 'on peint de trop pèse sur le tissus."

LEMIERRE.

ARISTOTLE recommends embellishment, and, indeed, productions of importance stand in need of such an addition. A theatrical representation, to be complete, requires decorations, properties, and costume ; for though acting and declamation may be fine, and singing charming, they still stand in need of these powerful and palpable illusions. D'Alembert justly remarks, how small and faint is the dramatic charm that is exhibited at the performance of French tragedies. Those productions, though of a noble nature, can never produce the effect intended, unassisted as they are by theatrical embellishment. It is an easy matter to dazzle the multitude by too great a display of machinery and ornament ; and when these are not required by the subject, I feel justified in treating them with contempt; with respect to the Ballet, it is rather on pantomimic expression, and on dancing, that I would rest my claim to approbation ; and from the proper application of these two arts I dare augur entire success. I should not seek merely to satisfy the eye, I would attempt also to touch the heart, and good Pantomime, explained by good music, is capable of moving the heart deeply.

Costume, properties, machinery, and decorations are particularly requisite in embellishing the *Grand Ballet*[23]. This theatrical display is indispensable also in pieces of the fabulous or heroic kind. If the study of painting be considered necessary to a full knowledge of the art of dancing, the assistance of that art is required in adorning the entire action. When, however, these embellishments do not arise out of the subject, and so become necessary to it, they lose their charm, and become useless and heavy. " It appears to me," says Dauberval, " that the most essential parts of the Ballet are dancing, Pantomime, music, painting; and all other embellishments, should be—

> " Per bellezza di parti aggiunte insieme,
> E con giusta misura in un composte."

Tasso.

It is a systematic and harmonious union of these by which the senses are delighted, nay, even ravished. Though embellishment should be properly introduced, still it is not upon that alone success depends. The heart must be first interested, and the study of ornaments may follow as secondary; and it belongs to taste and judgment appropriately to arrange them, placing them only where they seem to be required. Pantomimic action must claim our principal care throughout the piece, to which scenery and embellishment are certainly necessary, but subservient.

When an indifferent composer is determined to obtain success, he finds himself obliged to display to the public tinsel finery, dazzling colours, properties of every description, dresses bedecked with gold and silver, a multitude of mechanic tricks, and a crowd of characters. He expects by all this theatrical noise and parade to excite interest, but he is deceived. His production pleases for a

while, until critics and connoisseurs inform him to what
rank he belongs.   These self-constituted artists, who
would wish to adorn themselves with the laurels of talent,
act like the pupil of the celebrated ancient, who, unable
simply to represent the beauty and grace of *Helen*, dressed
her in jewels and embroidery. "You must paint her handsome, not rich," said his master.   That which pleases the
eye without satisfying the mind, is not received long.

Scenery and embellishment naturally belong to Ballets.
They should be appropriately varied, and whatever is introduced should be founded on the nature of the piece;
every ornament must have a meaning and a reason [24].
If it is a fault in plays to be continually changing
the scene of action, even in the same act, so as to
confuse the attention and spoil the interest, it is still
more blameable, not to avoid such an error in Ballets,
where pantomimic action, in certain situations, cannot, like
words, either connect one scene with another, or show a
reason for sudden changes.

Hence, it appears, that whatever changes we make, whatever novelty and variety we introduce into a Ballet, our
first and principal care must be, not to break the thread
of its history, which thread is represented and sustained
by *pantomimic gesture*.   This gesture is the only means
in which the mind confides for an explanation of what is
going forward; and which is now interrupted and destroyed, by dancing continued to a most unreasonable
length of time.   To this practice, perhaps, principally
may be attributed, the just complaints so frequently vented
against the prevailing system of Ballet representation.

CHAPTER XVII.

ON COSTUME.

"La leggiadria del vestirsi, che tanta vaghezza a natural beltade accresce."—ALGAROTTI.

EACH performer should be obliged to wear that species of costume which is exactly appropriate and peculiar to the character he represents.   Every remarkable characteristic of dress should be carefully studied; after which they may be modified and embellished as theatrical taste shall dictate.

This is an art that should not be neglected in theatres, since it greatly increases stage effect, and is advantageous both to the dancers and to those who perform Pantomime. Persons of our profession cannot be too studious to dress in such a style as not to prevent the display of attitudes used in dancing, and yet at the same time to preserve the true character of the costume.   Dancers are frequently obliged to make great alterations in their dresses, when the peculiarity of shape or make might prevent or conceal the grace of their motions.   They require, in short, to be lightly and elegantly habited ; and their costume should be so arranged, as to add a new charm to the art.

If, for instance, it is necessary to introduce a Turk or eastern caliph dancing, could such a thing be effected with their usual enormous costume ? To attempt it would be ridiculous to the utmost; the dancer would be imprisoned in his apparel, and deprived of the means of displaying the simplest movements. Or, could it be expected that any performer in the part of an ancient knight, should attempt to expose himself in a dance, habited in boots and spurs, military gloves, mantle and scarf?

It may be admitted that the court dress of those times was chivalric and picturesque, but were it preserved by dancers in all its severe formalities, it would be found impracticably heavy. Would any one require of us to execute well struck positions, clothed in the furred robes of Russia, or the thick stuff gowns of Poland, accompanied by caps and boots of a fashion almost barbarous? Truth and nature cannot appear simply as such at the theatre. A certain resemblance to these can be always preserved, but still remember to display so much only, as is pleasing and decorous. Adorn the original model, and reject what is faulty in it.

In Italy, and particularly at the great theatre of Milan, the most scrupulous attention is paid to the peculiarities of costume in their Ballets. With them nothing is of greater moment than the dressing a piece. Every habit is constructed after authentic monuments of art; and nothing is left unessayed by the management to complete the theatrical illusion. It were indeed sometimes to be wished that Italian artists would not copy with so severe an exactness those costumes, the form of which restrains the easy movements of the body, and prevents a freedom of pantomimic action; for in such a case the Ballet-master should certainly sacrifice something to the graces.

In France, excepting at the *Opera* of Paris, every one has to find his own dresses; and he arranges them, consequently, according to the imperfect ideas he may have formed of peculiar styles in costume. Hence it happens that the characters of a piece are very rarely seen to be habited either with truth or dignity. Many of those performers, indeed, want the means to perfect their imitations. In provincial theatres, neither actor nor audience pay any attention to costume; if they are but gay, and fit the shape well, nothing further is required. The principal performers indeed are more appropriately dressed; but those of the secondary and lowest class are habited in the most paltry manner. These glaring faults belong to the peculiar system of management in France, and consequently the *artistes* must not be exclusively blamed. Some means, indeed ought to be suggested to remedy the defects attending the French theatrical government; that, however, cannot now form a part of our inquiries. In the mean time, it is impossible to forbear condemning certain performers, who, through ignorance and inattention, commit the most palpable blunders, not caring to preserve a shade of resemblance between their habits and what is really original; yet these are well provided by the management with all that is requisite for costume, and have, besides, at Paris, every opportunity of consulting productions of art and of inquiring of men of learning. Their faults therefore are inexcusable; let those young persons who follow the theatrical profession avoid their example *.

Talma performed the part of *Coriolanus* in a rich *tunic* and a *Grecian* helmet, which he had worn in the part of *Achilles*. Thus exchanging the appropriate and unadorned simplicity of the Roman casque, for the magnificence of Grecian armour. The same performer, also, played *Niomède* in the costume he had displayed as

---

* From such remarks as these it must appear that M. B. is universal in his intentions; he endeavours to establish dramatic truth; and to expose theatrical absurdities wherever he finds them.

Orestes. This might appear incredible when related of such an actor, who is esteemed the founder of tragic costume in France. Lavigne, the celebrated singer, who held one of the first places at the *Academy of Music*, played the part of *Orpheus* with the helmet and sword of *Achilles.* Thus the Thracian bard appeared in the borrowed arms of the Grecian hero. This performer also appeared before the audience as a Roman consul, adorned with the costume of *Greece*, the magnificence of which was worthy of Alcibiades himself; and certainly the severe and plain republicans of ancient Rome never dreamt of beholding their chief in such sumptuous garments. The same Lavigne performed the shepherd in the *Devin du Village*, or *Village Conjuror*, dressed in a shirt, the bosom of which was plaited with the greatest nicety, worked and trimmed with lace. His coat was silk, decorated with satin ribands, and cut after the fashion of Géliot, the singer. His waistcoat was dimity; while his cap or hat was carried to a point like a conjuror's, and thus this piece of extravagance was completed. Vestris danced the part of the lover, in the Ballet entitled *La Fille mal-gardée*, in one of those fashionable dresses in which an *exquisite* would go to some ball. He played also the part of *Mars* beardless as a boy, and barefooted too; not being buskined, he might at least have appeared in simple sandals.

In his Ballet of *The Barber of Seville*, where he sustains the character of *Count Almaviva*, instead of disguising himself as a farrier, according to the piece, he performed that amusing scene of the second act in an elegant officer's uniform, wearing silk stockings. The same *artiste* danced in the opera of *Aristippe* in a *tunic* and *turban!*

Melle. Georges appeared in the part of *Clytemnestre* wearing the same scarf and tunic she had worn in the part of *Idamèe.* A certain critic observed upon this, that she was more excusable for having dressed a Grecian lady in Chinese costume than Voltaire was for having endued a Chinese with virtues of so sublime a description. This actress frequently confounds the garments of Greece with those of Rome. She has also the weakness and affectation of displaying her diamonds on every occasion, and in every species of character. She decks herself with them even when personating *Antigone,* who accompanies her father in circumstances of misfortune and wretchedness. There are those who can remember Lafond performing *Pygmalion* in the same magnificient attire he had worn as *Nero. Niomedes,* who should be plainly habited, as he appears *incognito,* at his father's court, was played by this actor in the splendid dress of *Ninias.*

When the Ballet-master issues out his orders for costume, let him pay attention that there be some sort of unison between the character of the dresses and that of the scenery; the colours of which may be different to the scene, but not more splendid. In dressing the costume peculiar to a country, the period in which the scene is laid should be carefully examined and imitated. The selection and disposition of colours and shades must be intrusted to taste.

Costume, in short, may be defined to be a kind of epitome of history, geography, and chronology; for it not only determines the country, but, if exactly adhered to, declares even the epoch of time to which the piece relates; a man of sense and general information will require nothing but costume, strictly true, to direct him to the country and period of a drama, though he had never read or seen it before. Perhaps it is impossible to give more cogent reasons than these, to show the importance of paying rigorous attention to costume.

CHAPTER XVIII.

ON FRENCH COMPOSERS AND MIMES, OR BALLET PERFORMERS.

L'âme veut être *émue*, et sentir est son sort.
L'inaction, pour elle, est une lente mort,
Et cette activité, partage de son être,
Au feu des passions, elle le doit peut être.

DULARD.

GENERALLY speaking, French Composers, or Ballet-masters, neglect in their productions to preserve the interest of the action. They are defective both in variety and incident; thus, weak and void of theatrical effect, it is impossible they can please long. As it has been already observed, action, passion, and intrigue are always looked for on the stage, and without these the attention can be neither fixed nor pleased.

The French composers should model their scenes upon the most celebrated works of the great masters, and particularly upon those important compositions that adorn the drama. These writers deal too much in the mythologic style; they seem determined to repeat, without intermission, the same tales and descriptions contained in ancient fiction, and in the *Metamorphoses*. This renders their productions flat, monotonous and wearisome. The characters of their pieces are ever *Venus, Cupid, Flora, Zephyr,* the *Graces,* sports, and pleasures; and with these the audience are doomed to be treated *ad nauseam.* Though only a *Divertissement,* Olympus and its inhabitants are still crowded in. Were this style but altered, agreeable novelties might succeed, and public attention would be drawn and amused.

The ancient and modern history of every country and people, the accounts of celebrated men of every age, the relations of travellers, and the writings of great authors, present an infinite number of fine subjects, perfectly fitted to be represented as Ballets; to such, artists should direct their abilities and attention; while, by clothing these in a dramatic garb, their own names would become distinguished. A selection of these events, exploits, and deeds of renown

> " ——————————— argomento grande
> Porge a i più dotti ingegni ————————." PINDAR.

It has often been wished that persons of talent would apply themselves to composing on those subjects, hitherto totally neglected at French theatres; and that enlightened composers would prefer history to mythology, selecting, with taste, such parts as may be appropriated to dancing, and which are susceptible of beautiful scenery. I am of opinion that subjects of this class, worked up with talent and art, would be certain of success. By thus varying the amusement of the public, the Ballet would gain in the end, and become more popular. Sometimes a fable, an anecdote, a romance, or a poem, may suggest the plot of a Ballet. A hint of this sort is often sufficient for the man of genius; he seizes, illustrates, augments, and embellishes it; and theatrical mechanism brings the whole to perfection.

A great number of operas, by Quinault, by A. Zeno, and Metastasio, have been altered and adapted to Ballets in Italy: why then should not the same thing be done in France? The pomp, parade, and magnificence peculiar to the *Grand Ballet d' Action* would even heighten the interest of a fine play. Let, therefore, productions of a noble and pathetic nature be sought after; a national theatre requires great and powerful representations. Several Ballets indeed have been represented at the opera of Paris composed in a style somewhat different from those usually produced: *L' Enfant prodigue, Le Retour d' Ulysse, Nina, Cléopâtre,* and some others of the same class, were very well received by the public; why, therefore, do not the authors of these strive to obtain new honours, by continuing in such a career? They were not even followed by imitators bold enough to continue in what had been so happily begun. The enterprise was noble and worthy of praise; and had they proceeded steadily in the path they had discovered, success must have crowned their perseverance. The most plausible reason, I suppose, that can be advanced for such indolence or irresolution, is the defective state of their Pantomime, which is incapable of explaining sentiment, and which fails even in those necessary gestures that are employed to indicate surrounding objects; consequently, it cannot enter into detail, and its language is often obscure[25]. Pantomime failing in that class of gestures which describe sentiment, and those other natural and imitative motions not being clearly made out, the whole must become languishing and uninteresting.

With such means as these, it is impossible to exhibit the intrigue of a piece; frequent interruptions by intervening scenes, which suspend the action, require the most exact explanation. Thus, not being able to obtain a clear elucidation of their ideas, French composers are obliged to

confine themselves to subjects of a plain and simple construction, to well known events, and to such as have already been treated on.   Added to these, a faulty system,
and certain foolish customs, prevent the progress of this
art amongst them.   Every one fears to attempt an innovation, and would imagine himself ruined the moment he
dared to quit the track marked out for him by preceding
authors.   Ignorance is satisfied, and envy triumphs at such
imbecility.

A profound study of Pantomime will discover the means
of explaining every description of subject.   It will augment the resources of the Ballet-master, and will contribute to vary his compositions.   Were this study pursued
in France, they would consequently soon enlarge the limits
of their subjects.

In selecting originals, seek variety ; choose of every style,
of every class.   Always copy from productions of talent,
not from those of mediocrity ; and in this we should not
be swayed either by caprice or private interest.   Nature,
ever varied and fruitful, will continually supply entire subjects, or hints at least.   Neither are the works of poets
and historians yet exhausted, they still present great resources to the Ballet-master.   The same subjects, too, may
be again and differently treated.   It is no difficult matter
for a man of genius to give a fresh form and a different turn
to what has already been before the public.   Art can add
a new interest to a known subject.   A lively and active
imagination surmounts every obstacle.   Thus there appears
to be a crowd of characters to describe ;   and the French
artist will dispose of them in a manner the most advantageous to his production.

CHAPTER XIX.

ON ITALIAN COMPOSERS AND MIMES, OR BALLET PERFORMERS.

" Les arts imitatifs òtent à la réalité ce qu' elle a d'odieux, et n'en retiennent ce que qu' elle a d'intéressant. Il suit de là, qu'il faut épargner aux spectateurs les émotions trop pénibles et trop douloureuses."—BARTHELEMY.

IF French composers give up too much to the fabulous style, the Italians appear to abandon themselves too much to the tragic, and in their productions scenes are rarely exhibited that are calculated to relieve the depression of mind caused by the gloominess of the subject. These mournful pieces are characterized by scenes of a horrible description; and the stage appears like the theatres of old, where gladiators came to combat and die. The imagination of such writers delights to revel amid slaughter and tombs; the furies of destruction seem to attend all their conceptions; and their dark and dreadful exhibitions generally terminate with crimes or revolting executions. Cold enthusiasts may applaud such a style, while they remain unmoved at representations of true pathos; sublime composition has no attraction for them. The multitude also delight in such exhibitions ; but it is in the power of true taste to destroy the charm [26]. The dance withdraws itself from such terrible scenes ; Terpsichore flies from the sight of murder, death and corpses. There are certain things that should be kept entirely away from the scene, and there are others of which a glimpse is sufficient.

Too much attention cannot be paid in selecting subjects intended for Ballets. Those in which dancing may be introduced, must not be appropriated to the tragic style ; and on the contrary, the gay movements of the comic ought to have nothing to do with tragic gravity and pathos. When working up serious subjects, the original, as has been already observed, must be modified and embellished. Those representations that are rather horrid than tragic should never stain the scene ; they are rejected by good sense, and our feelings are wounded by them. Many artists are aware of the defects of such pieces ; but still do not avoid them while composing for certain audiences, whose taste appears to rival that of the more serious and calculating inhabitants on the banks of the Thames*.

The Italians like to be deeply affected and agitated by the power of theatrical representation. Melpomene holds strong dominion over them, while the empire of her sister Thalia is weak. Such a predilection may be attributed to the force and fire of their imagination, and to a deep and characteristic sensibility. They require to be as much moved and transported by a Ballet as by a spoken piece. They require of pantomimic performers the utmost exertion ; and criticise a Ballet-master as unsparingly as they would a dramatic poet. This severity, however, is advantageous to the art, since it excites talent,

---

* M. B. does not yet know us *à fond*.

and is a proof of the great interest taken in it by the public.
It may be remarked of those artists to whom this chapter
is dedicated, that the Pantomime of their pieces absorbs
all the action, to the exclusion of dancing. That, however,
cannot be called Ballet that consists of Pantomime only.
Those plots, therefore, should be chosen in which dancing
can be appropriately introduced, for it would be impossible and ridiculous to exhibit a *Divertissement* on a subject
of a character too tragic for such joyous amusement. Let
the colouring of your picture be varied, but let that variety
be disposed with art. Thus, let gloomy scenes be insensibly
shaded off into the light and gay. Painful and pleasant
emotions depend upon such an arrangement, which, if
managed with taste and judgment, enable us to witness,
without surprise, tragic scenes succeeded by the graceful
movements of the dance.. Such well-disposed contrasts
as these constitute the Ballet, instead of the simple Pantomime. And in this method certain tragic subjects also
might be treated, which, at first, might not seem adapted
to the object of a Ballet.

In Italy, excellent historic and mythologic Ballets have
been produced, and represented with such magnificence and
perfection as have remained unrivalled ; and the severest
critics found themselves obliged to applaud. These,
however, exhibited no disgusting horrors, nor any circumstance tending to corrupt the manners. Those who
wish to attain celebrity as composers should constantly
refer to such models, keeping them ever in view, even
amidst their own inventions; thus would they secure the
applause of men of taste. By this method, young composers would avoid committing these two palpable errors :
first, that of seeking to inspire horror instead of pathos ;
and that of making Pantomimes instead of Ballets. In a
Ballet the dance should partake of the plot and interest of

the piece, at the same time that it becomes an ornament to it. Some Italian artists, either from an ignorance of the art, or from a determination to give up all to Pantomime, neglect dancing. French composers, on the other hand, pay not requisite attention to the art of gesture, treating as secondary the principal and most important part of a piece. But each department claims its due share of attention ; when one encroaches upon the rights of the other, the performance must become extravagant.

To the greater part of Italian composers, it might be suggested, that to enlarge the limits of their productions, and in order to become less tragic, and more varied, they should examine the best ancient and modern romances, the renowned deeds of chivalry as described in certain poems, eastern fictions, and fairy prodigies. These works present a treasury of excellent materials, capable of enriching the *répertoire* of Ballet-masters with every kind of novelty.

There are certain composers, not content with the system of performing already established by taste and reason, who would introduce a new method, of which the following are the principal. They declare that Pantomime should be regulated, not only by the *rythmus* and *cadence* of the air, but that an actor should mark with his arms or his legs every bar, and even every turn in a phrase of music. They require also that a step should be executed, in certain passages, to every note. Thus steps and gestures would be multiplied to infinity, while the spectator, dazzled and confused by rapid motion, finds himself unable to attend to the plot of the piece. The performer, too, exhausted by incessant exertion, finishes the scene, but without producing the least effect. The consequence of this false system is, that the dancer, being obliged to take for each single gesture, two or three steps, to keep up with the measure of the air, and being obliged also to fly over the stage in diverse directions, his steps must absolutely become *pas dansans*, that is to say, *pas de bourée, des chassés, des contre-tems, des glissades, &c.* It is easy to imagine what would be the laughable effect of Pantomime thus executed. What would be more ridiculous than to see the most important characters, such as heroes and divinities, dancing with rapidity at a time when interest should be raised by gentler and pathetic action ? Composers who would exhibit Pantomime in this style, are defective even in those gestures and positions they pretend to exccute by extravagance of method. How widely different is this affectation from a true imitation of nature !

It is impossible that an actor, constrained to observe the rules of such a system, can express himself with grace or ease ; nor can he find any opportunity to give vent to the feelings that agitate him. His spirits receive a damp, and his gesture partakes of the same quality, and he performs his part ineffectually. This new method, indeed, considered in its most advantageous light, and even when sustained by talent, must ever appear paltry and insignificant, producing only the effect of a puppet set in motion by wires. To such a pass must a performer come, who falls into the hands of a composer of this class, that would bind him to observe the rules of this school, in order that he might, as it were, sacrifice him to this extravagant idol of innovation.—Follow rather the rules of truth and beauty :

> "——i' vo' credere a' sembianti,
> Che soglion effere testimon del core."
>
> DANTE [27].

CHAPTER XX.

ON THE DIFFERENT KINDS OF BALLETS.

" Sua cuique proposita lex, suus decor est; nec comœdia in Cothurnos assurgit, nec contra Tragœdia socco ingreditur."—QUINTILIAN.

OF the Ballet there are three kinds:—the *serious,* the *melo-dramatic* or *demi-caractère,* and the *comic.* The serious Ballet embraces the following subjects:—the tragic, the historic, the romantic, the mythologic, the fabulous, and the sacred [28]. The melo-dramatic Ballet is of a mixed description; certain passages in history, some romantic subjects, marvellous, oriental, allegoric, pastoral, and anacreontic tales are admissible to this class, provided they be of a cast neither too serious nor too comic. Subjects of a triumphant, national, *bourgeois,* satirical, trifling, burlesque, heroic, comic, or tragi-comic nature, are peculiar to the comic Ballet. The *Divertissement,* or *Fête,* is that theatrical spectacle in which dancing alone is the constituent part. The action of the piece, indeed, excludes this exhibition, as not belonging to it; notwithstanding which, however, it not only represents the celebration of some public or private event, but serves to render homage to some illustrious characters, or to revive, in a solemn and ceremonious manner, the remembrance of some renowned deed.

It may be thus perceived that the Ballet consists of as many varieties as other theatrical performances. It follows, also, that in pursuing this object, great authors should be deeply studied, together with the whole range of the drama, and those good Ballets, also, that may fall under observation. Nor can the talents of young composers be better employed and developed, than in uniting the principles of art to the remarks of experience.

Pity and terror appertain to tragedy; those authors, therefore, who, in order to produce striking effects, dispose of events so as to produce unmixed horror, rather than simply to inspire terror, cannot serve as models in the art of moving the affections, or of raising interest. Feeble minds are greatly alarmed by auch productions; and this, in fact, in the judgment of men of taste, who can properly appreciate what is good, is the only object they attain. These representations merely serve to augment such horrible and disgusting productions as the *Parthenius de Nicée*, and the romances of the Radcliffe school. The great Arouet requires that the scene should not be stained by blood, except upon extraordinary occasions, when it becomes indispensable, and even then it should be executed with such care, that the public may be spared, as much as possible, the sight of such horrors. We may remark, also, with Dubos, that "it is not the *quantity* of blood that is shed, but the *manner* of shedding it, which constitutes the character of tragedy. Besides, tragedy, when extravagant, becomes cold; and we are rather inclined to laugh than to weep at the productions of a poet, who fancies that he is pathetic in proportion to the quantity of blood he spills: some wicked wag might even send to him for a list of killed and wounded." It is rarely necessary at the theatre to deepen terror into horror; the pathetic alone should be deemed sufficient to produce tragic illusion.

It was a custom with the ancients that government should furnish poets with subjects for tragedy, and upon these the writers were obliged to treat. The most celebrated deeds of history or of fable were chosen, in order that, as they were generally known, they might be the more certain of exciting general interest; and in the end the custom proved very advantageous to the poet. Comic poets, on the contrary, were allowed to make choice of their own subjects, each selecting whatever was most agreeable to his own peculiar taste and genius; they might invent their own subject, and the piece became entirely their own. Blair does not give sufficient latitude to comic authors in the choice of their subject. Some limit is necessary in the selection of a plot; but it is my opinion, the more universal a comedy is, the better it is, and the more likely to meet with success.

Comedy, in its beginning, was nothing more than a representation of the simple truth, which exposed upon the stage some transaction of private life. Writers having at length ceased to adopt actual occurrences, betook themselves to imaginative subjects, to the great peace and satisfaction of the public.

The same remark cannot be made with respect to tragedy, because, in treating on great and exalted subjects, it was always necessary that they should be founded on truth, or on fables which, by becoming well and universally known, assumed the appearance of truth. The truth, however, was not always scrupulously adhered to by some writers, who paid little attention to public opinion with respect to place and time. They even differ from each other in these particulars, when bringing the same subject before the public. Upon this, Gravina, as well as Aristotle,

observes, that *Medea* did not kill her children; that was
a crime invented by Euripides. In the *Œdipus* of Sophocles, *Jocasta* strangles herself; according to Seneca, she
died by the sword. Both Sophocles and Euripides have
written upon the subject of *Electra;* but one represents
her a virgin, always dwelling in her own country, while the
other describes her married and living out of her native
land. The latter poet, in his *Trojans*, sacrifices *Polixenes*
at the tent of *Achilles;* and in his *Hecuba*, the same *Polixenes* is slain in Thrace.

When a poet is engaged in describing imaginary beings,
he sometimes allows his fancy to transport him beyond the
bounds of probability, but some resemblance to nature
must always be preserved; some meaning or allegorical
sense should always be perceptible. The poet, in short,
must imitate those sculptors who, though producing colos-
sal statues, of dimensions immensely super-human, yet
still preserved the proportions of man in his ordinary size.
Taste and judgment thus ever avoid folly and extravagance; and thus treated, subjects of the fabulous, allegorical, or fairy nature, may insure success.

Numerous examples of this kind might be cited. We
may, therefore, conclude, that there is no necessity for making any alteration either in history or fable as it is generally received; the authors, however, may be allowed to
make some slight changes in the action, provided they are
of a nature uniform with the subject, and calculated to increase dramatic effect. Additions as well as retrench-
ments should be made judiciously, and in those places only
where they are required, particular care being taken that
the general resemblance between parts be not destroyed.
In such compositions the author has permission to exercise
his invention; but let him remember that his fictions
should wear the garb of truth.

The Greeks did not confine themselves to comedy, whose province it is to describe the ridiculous; nor to tragedy, which inspires only terror and pity. They understood how to introduce serious scenes into their comedy, as may be seen in Aristophanes; while tragic pieces frequently admitted the gaiety of comedy, as the works of Euripides will prove:

"Interdum tamen et vocem comœdia tollit;
Et tragicus plerumque dolet sermone pedestri."

HOR.

The Greeks had also other kinds of dramas, namely, the *Satirical*, the *Ilarodia*, and the *Magodia*, which being ranked between tragedy and comedy, partook more or less of each, and formed a very agreeable and convenient connexion between the two extremes of the dramatic art.

With such a license poets would present every species of character, with every shade and gradation of passion. Nature in her course advances not by leaps; nor does she fly in an instant from the obscurity of night to the brightness of day; or from the frosts of winter to the heat of summer; on the contrary, she proceeds gradually and imperceptibly.

Of all the varieties of drama to be found in the two principal divisions, the *tragi-comic* is most remarkable. The characters of this class are those of princes and great men, who, though preserving a certain noble and imposing style, perform with a kind of condescending cheerfulness. The aid of deep and powerful passion is not required; and the catastrophe is never of a terrible description.

Very few French authors have availed themselves of this literary license; they have left it to the Spaniards, English, Italians and Germans, who have cultivated this kind of composition eagerly and successfully. By such a neglect variety is excluded, and a multitude of subjects to be found in nature remains entirely untouched. The tragi-comic class of pieces present a vast field in which a fertile fancy may range at pleasure. It requires, however, deep discrimination to succeed in this style, nothing being more difficult than to pass

      " From grave to gay; from lively to severe." POPE.

      " Passer du grave au doux, du plaisant au sévère."

                                      BOILEAU.

Were we to admit nothing into tragedy but horror and dread, and nothing but the jocular and ridiculous into comedy, what would then become of that immense space that lays between these two extremes? Should not this blank be adorned by representations of those sentiments and incidents which are neither terrible nor trite, neither grave nor gay?

Thus it appears there are several kinds of tragic and comic productions. Can the style of Corneille be termed tragic in his *Nicomède*, as it is in *Rodogune?* How widely different is the style of *Tancredi* from that of *Otello!* Yet both are of the tragic cast. The style of Alfieri is entirely different from that of Racine. The comic humour of the *Misantrope* is not the same with that of the *Femmes Savantes,* and the style of the *Etourdi* differs from that of the *Glorieux.* Goldoni presents still another sort of comedy in his *Padre di Famiglia,* not at all resembling that of *Gl' Innamorati. Le Dissipateur, Nanine, La Gouvernante,* &c., are all dissimilar.

The same characteristics are perceptible in the style of Ballets as in that of poetry, and it belongs to the man of talent to appropriate to each its peculiar colouring.

There are many French comedies, however, which, had they been written in verse, with a classic change in the names, might pass for legitimate tragedies. On the other hand, there are tragedies in which it would be necessary only to change the names, with a little alteration in style and action, to render them complete comedies. But care should be taken to avoid this latter error, as well as that of choosing subjects too elevated and serious for comedy; neither should Melpomene be divested of that interest which moves and melts the passions, and gives rise to situations of pathos and terror. In tragedy the characters should be sustained as heroes; in comedy they should move and act like ordinary men.

The dramatic style may be adapted to the Ballet, but it is not necessary to make use of it as those authors do who would raise it upon a level with tragedy, when making choice of subjects.

The greater part of those who manufacture *Drames Bourgeois, Drames Sombres* and *Drames Honnétes* attain no other object but that of making the spectator tremble with horror, while presenting him with pictures which dishonour humanity, and shock the feeling, by the exhibition of that wretchedness to which nature and fate have subjected us; and nothing is left untried to arrive at this very amusing object.

Dramas include at once the pathos of tragedy, and the gaiety of comedy; and they should convey the same moral as tragedy or comedy separately considered. When this mixture is made with talent, its effects are novel, agreeable and interesting. Without bestowing on this class of theatrical performance all that panegyric with which a sort of fanaticism inspired Diderot, Beaumarchais, and some others, to load it, I shall only remark that it is more suited to the intention of a Ballet than might be supposed, for it affords a great variety of scenery, together with very striking and contrasted situations, in which dancing and Pantomime triumph by turns. A piece of this description furnishes also a great variety of characters and passions, developed in scenes alternately serious and gay. The Avonian bard is often successful in this medley of tragedy and comedy ; he handles with ease the pencil of Æschylus and the pen of Molière, painting with equal talent the comic and the sublime. If Denina* and some others had taken the trouble to observe this, they might have spared themselves their unjust criticisms upon this celebrated man.

It must be repeated, that discernment is necessary in the choice of ornament and effect. The theory of bad composers, who, without taste or genius, would impose upon the multitude by noise and show, is similar to that of many play-wrights, who suppose that every thing to be found in nature will produce an effect upon the stage ; and, provided that some emotions are awakened, and a certain quantity of tears shed, they trouble not themselves about the means by which that object is attained. This new system of poetics appears to have been created by some German writers. I prefer the *Proverbes Dramatiques* of Carmontelle to all such extravagant and unmeaning commotion as attain no useful end. The pleasant morality spread over this work amuses the mind, and becomes extremely serviceable.

While discoursing on the different styles, it will not be unseasonable to say something on the *romantic*, and such productions as may prove useful to the composer, by introducing variety into his works. A fragment of M. Chaussard, relating to this subject, may furnish a kind of preface to our observations.

" The followers of the romantic," says he, " declare that imagination alone is the essential soul of poetry. The classics, on the other hand, lay it down as a principle, that reason and imagination united is the essence of poetry.

* A celebrated literary character of Italy.

Each of these, according to his own position, draws the following inferences :—the first say, all the wanderings and extravagances of fancy constitute the beauty of the romantic style; the others admit of these, but always on condition that they be not contrary to reason. Hence, it is evident that the romantic system is the direct road to absurdity, and that the classic system leads to liberal and enlightened reason. still leaving to the imagination sufficient opportunity for the most lofty flights ; then is fancy a fiery steed guided by reason, who does not impede his course, but prevents him from stumbling."

" And further, let fact decide the question. When those of the romantic school shall produce a man equal to Homer or Ariosto, we will yield to their opinion; but Homer has united deep reasoning to exalted imagination, while the very simplicity of Ariosto is concealed wisdom. When we come to reflect upon the circumstances attending the appearance of the *phantom* of romance, for I cannot bring myself to call it *style,* we shall be something surprised at the result: it has no less a tendency than that of leading back to barbarism. In a word, all the horrors of feudal times, all the superstitions of the thirteenth century, together with the legends of the *Autos Sacramentales* of Calderon[29], form the *material* and the essential elements of these depraved compositions, which are a part of that dark conspiracy, whose end is again to impose fetters on the human mind, even after reason has burst them asunder."

" In short, to develop the imagination according to the system of some, is to place implicit faith in the most ridiculous absurdities, of which error and degradation are the consequences. Rather[30] let reason be followed; it is the basis of a good education, and hence will arise a race of powerful, enlightened, and virtuous writers. The poets of antiquity were no trifling and unmeaning seducers into amusement; they were rather masters in morality, and the first instructors of mankind. This consideration will, doubtless, separate from the *romantic* school every person of credit, that otherwise, perhaps, would not have perceived its fatal and lamentable consequences. The above cited author says elsewhere, " It (the romantic) certainly affords specimens of charming compositions, and I could wish to applaud them ; but they are always inferior to the great classic productions. The strain of the Syrens is not equal to the song of the Muses."

The romantic class is of a mixed nature, it embraces almost every style, for every object in nature becomes the property of the poet of romance. Taste or art is rarely employed in the choice or embellishment of subjects of this description. If, however, this medley were generally treated as it is by certain authors, it would have an effect infinitely more agreeable and interesting, considering its great variety and striking contrasts. A fruitful imagination should ever place before it the image of the *beau idéal*, without which, as it has been shown, the descent into the absurd and ridiculous is easy and immediate.

As models, I would rather propose certain works of its followers, than the system itself. They should be followed with taste and discretion. It is impossible that a production truly romantic can be a model in all its parts ; it ever presents a great disparity of objects ; notwithstanding, parts may be found of great utility to the artist.

There are many critics and innovators who give the preference to this style above all other kind of dramatic composition; accusing classic authors, who keep within the bounds of reason, of being sterile, flat and cold. May it not be said that these critics resemble Demonatus, who, being opposed to the laws of a certain state, first declared them useless, and then, by consequence, superfluous ?

The craving that authors, and the public also, have for novelty, is frequently injurious to the arts; hence it is that men of talent have united themselves to extravagant systems and styles, and it must be confessed that their inventions are of the miraculous order.

" Humana natura est novitatis avida."

Let us seek for novelty, but let not our compositions be void of good sense.

" —— des chemins nouveaux, il est un heureux choix."

LEMIERRE.

Racine, Voltaire, Metastasio, and Alfieri, opened each for himself an untried way, through which they have passed like great and creating geniuses. Reason readily bestows on them admiration and applause; and the style of unaffected beauty to be found in their works is universally admired.

Concerning English dramatic poets who are of the romantic class, Montesquieu observes that, " their genius is of a singular description; they do not even imitate the ancients whom they admire; their productions bear less resemblance to the regular course of nature than to those happy freaks in which she sometimes indulges; and this may be proved by Shakspeare and all his numerous imitators; and on this system it is that their style has been formed. The same may be observed with respect to Calderon and his rivals,[31] Vondel, and the tragic poets of Germany."

These authors, however, have not always represented the *happy freaks of nature;* for, what puerilities, absurdities, and extravagances may not be found mixed up with their natural and sublime passages ! They must be examined with peculiar care, for we can obtain no profit from the good things to be found in such authors, except we bring to their perusal a taste already firmly established.

The crowd of imitators whom the splendid genius of these great men has attracted is very pernicious to young artists, who flatter themselves that they have faithfully reproduced their originals by copying all that is faulty in them.   Void of both taste and fancy, these theatrical apes believe they work miracles, by straying from the road marked out by good sense.   The vulgar, surprised and even astonished, second such efforts by vehement applause, and the frenzy endures a short period in opposition to the better understanding of connoisseurs; and, it even gives birth to other and similar productions.

> " Credite, Pisones, isti fabulæ fore librum
> Persimile, cujus, veluta egri somnia vanæ
> Fingentur species : ut nec pes, nec caput uni.
> Reddatur formæ ————————."
>
>   HORACE.

CHAPTER XXI.

ON MODELS, AND THE METHOD OF STUDYING THEM.

" The subject selected should be both known and appropriate."
                                             ARISTOTLE.

THE origin of tragedy may be traced to the immortal poems of Homer; and it is to his *Margites* and his other satirical poems, that we are indebted for the discovery of comedy. According to Suidas, Alceus Epigenes and Thespis made the first attempts at tragedy, which was soon after to be fully developed by the genius of Æschylus. Phrynicus, a disciple of Thespis, introduced female characters upon the stage. Thespis himself was the first actor of whom we have any account.

Thelestes made great progress in his art by performing in the pieces of Æschylus: he was both actor and Pantomime. Aristocles loads him with panegyric as having brought to perfection the art of gesture. The masterpieces of Æschylus, Sophocles, and Euripides followed almost immediately the *Alcestis* of Thespis, with an astonishing and gigantic stride towards perfection. Under Solon, lived Susarion and Dolon, who were the first that produced farces on the stage. Æschylus, Acheus, and Hegemon also distinguished themselves in this class. But it is to Epicharmes we owe the model of legitimate comedy. Cratinus, Mænander, Philemon, and Aristophanes brought it to perfection. Livius Andronicus, Ennius, Nævius, Varius, the second Pomponius, Pacuvius, the Sophocles of the Romans, Plautus, Trabea, Terence, &c., adorned the drama of ancient Rome by imitating the Greeks.

The plots or intrigues of the dramas of Æschylus are extremely simple, and I may compare his manner to that of Michael Angelo. It must, however, be objected to him, as well as to Alfieri, that he has not given sufficient attention to the pathetic. The Italian poet seems to have modelled himself upon the Greek; they are nearly similar in style; and the lofty genius of both has frequently directed them to objects of a moral or political character.

Sophocles, on the contrary, manages the plots of his tragedies with more skill and address. He is ever pathetic, and often sublime. In the works of this great poet, and in those of Alfieri, nothing is said uselessly, or without a meaning. Their characters neither act nor speak but when the subject requires them. Their productions are not at all overcharged with false or superfluous ornament; and indeed they well understood where to stop, by observing that limit beyond which it is absurd to pass; this is a point of perfection, at which it is not in the power of every genius to arrive. Mediocrity ever misses this mark, and even men of talent cannot always impose needful restraint upon their flights. And here, unfortunately, it must be confessed how very much out of place are those fine *tirades* in French pieces, together with the poetic and philosophic airs even of Metastasio, bearing no relation to the principal subject, and serving only to interrupt the progress of the action. Euripides is regarded, and with reason, as the most tragic of ancient poets. He is true to nature in the pictures he draws, and he possesses more variety than is to be found in his rivals. He is both pathetic and moral, and well deserves the name of the theatrical philosopher.

Modern Italy, to whom Europe owes the revival of letters, has greatly contributed also to the rise and progress of the drama. Albertino Mussato was the first who wrote a regular tragedy; and Sicco Polentone signalized himself by giving to the modern the first comedy. *L'Ezzelino* and *La Catinia*, the first of our essays in the dramatic art, were written in Latin, which at that epoch was the language of authors. *Orpheus*, a tragedy of the celebrated Poliziano, and the comedy of the *Calandra* by Bibiena, succeeded the above productions, and being written in Italian, they became models to all who wrote for the theatre. Poliziano did for Italy what Jodelle, with far less talent, did for France; and every French writer of that period both imitated and translated Italian authors.

The tragedies of Trissino, Speroni, Torelli, Tasso, Ruscellai, Giraldi, Dolce, Anguillara; the pastorales of Tasso, Guarini, Bonarelli, Beccari, Buonaroti, Cortese; the lyrical dramas of Rinuccini, the comedies of Ariosto, of Aretino, Firenzuola, Groto, and Lasca; and above all the *Mandragora*[32], of Macchiavelli have each contributed to polish and perfect the drama from the time that it arose out of barbarism. The Italians imitated the ancients, but their comedy possessed more sentiment, and had a greater regard for decency[33]. Nearer approaches to those almost faultless models of antiquity were reserved for more civilized times.

The great Corneille, Molière and Racine effected prodigies, and arrived very nearly at perfection. The Italians, in their turn, profiting by the example of their neighbours on the other side of the mountains, produced *Crœsus*, *Cleopatra*, and *Octavia*, which were regarded as their best tragedies during the seventeenth century. S. Maffei, and P. J. Martello, in the following age, distinguished themselves in the same career. Shakspeare, Calderon, Lope de Vega, and Guillin de Castro, have rendered themselves illustrious, by the untried ways they have trod, but they have made very small advances to the classic idea of perfection.

Gottsched obtained the glorious title of reformer of the German theatre. Holberg created the Danish drama. P. J. Martello, Voltaire, S. Maffei, Zeno, Metastasio, Goldoni, Alfieri, Monti, Kotzebue, Schiller, and Moratin, the Molière of Spain, carried their art to the highest pitch, each according to the peculiar genius of his nation.

Racine felt deeply what is due to the worth of the ancients; he studied them learnedly and philosophically, or, in other words, as a man of talent. It was from these models of perfection that he formed for himself a style which, in grace, beauty, and pathos, rivals the originals. Nothing finer can be imagined than his tragedies of *Phèdre, Iphigénie, Athalie, Britannicus,* and *Andromaque* [34]. Whenever this illustrious man handles a subject that has already been treated on by the ancients, he has, as it were, brought it to greater perfection, or imitated them to rivalry. But Racine studied nature as well as the classical productions. The moderns too often neglect the study of nature for that of authors; and Le Batteux justly observes, "that the ancients are to us, what nature was to them." The works of nature will bear a deeper study than those of men.

It may be said of the French Euripides, that he has avoided the faults of the illustrious ancients by exchanging their defects for his own natural beauties; and fortunate are those who can pursue a similar system [35].

Since even models possess defects, care must be taken to avoid them when studying. Feebleness and mediocrity would frequently appeal to their authority as precedents for the faults they commit. The vanity of young artists is easily flattered in perceiving that some slight resemblance may be seen between certain parts of their own productions and those of the great masters; but it is in their beauties and perfections only that this resemblance must be sought. Men of genius may be accused of errors, but their excellence never wants admirers; and he is justly despised who presents in his works nothing but an imitation of their failings. Favour and excuse may be easily procured from the generality of observers; but *connoisseurs* bestow praise only in proportion to real merit.

Voltaire also possessed the rare talent of perfecting his originals. Endued with the double advantage of vast experience, united to a brilliant genius, which was adorned with almost universal erudition, he was well fitted to enrich the stage with productions at once varied and natural.

Things apparently of very small importance are often turned to great account in the hands of genius. Thus it has been seen that talented artists have greatly profited by the simple frescoes of Herculaneum, and from the time-worn bass reliefs of the Parthenon.

The *Torse* of Belvidere has served as a model to crowds of painters and sculptors; indeed this precious relic of antiquity has formed a school. There are, however, men of great talent, who having first conformed themselves to certain styles, have afterwards left them, and entered upon others. Amongst these may be instanced Annibal Carracci, who, subsequent to studying Raphael, M. Angelo, Titian, Correggio, and the antiques, created a style for himself, which has rendered him immortal. The same may be observed in literature. Theophrastus, the pupil of Aristotle, followed another style than that of his master. Menander, after studying the characters of the former, produced the most perfect comedies of antiquity, and which served as models to Terence, who was imitated by Molière, till the latter, following the example of other great geniuses, traced out a way for himself, and became an original of the first order [36].

The tragedies of Corneille, who was the father of the French drama, are filled with poetic and tragic beauties, but the conduct of his plots is sometimes defective. He must, therefore, be examined with care ; nor should we suffer ourselves to be overcome by the enthusiasm of the poet. He is sometimes sublime, and often original; but his pieces have never any moral object in view, paying, at the same time, but little regard to certain theatrical regulations.

The author of *Cinna, Rodogune, Polieucte,* and the

Cid, filled with the fire of poesy, and endowed with an exalted genius, created for himself a new style. He appears to have disdained to subject himself to many of the laws prescribed by theatrical legislators. Some of his models he took from a nation whose taste and character were more conformable to his own peculiar manner. The Spanish drama has the honour of having furnished materials to some of the principal productions of the French Sophocles. Spanish pieces, during a certain period, found a good reception in France, and theatrical writers readily imitated them. Exhibitions of heroic Moors, together with extraordinary events, attended by stage effect and bustle, were capable of some attraction, and amused the generality.

Racine brought tragedy to perfection; he was well versed in the theatrical art; the conduct of several of his pieces is admirable. He is a master who cannot be too much studied. He is always true, interesting and pathetic; while nothing interrupts the advance of the action. Unfortunately, however, those idle characters, called confidents, sometimes prevent him from being perfect in the formation of some of his productions. Thanks are due to Alfieri for having delivered us from this trifling set of creatures, who have only owed their existence to mediocrity of talent. And it is custom alone that has continued them in modern masterpieces; but genius does not require their ineffectual assistance. These confidentials ought not to make their appearance, except when it is absolutely necessary to the plan of action.

In the plots of Racine and of Metastasio, too much uniformity may be observed. In the first, this defect is owing perhaps to that pathetic style to which his genius inclined him; and in the second, it has been caused by his complaisance in conforming himself too much to the desires of musicians, who require that the action of a piece should be subservient to their inspirations. Metastasio is one of the greatest philosophic poets that ever existed. In him the most useful and important truths are adorned by poetry. Being deeply versed in the movements of the human heart, he has painted passions and characters in the most striking colours. Ever under the direction of nature, he is, like her, true, elegant, noble, and sublime; no dramatic writer has shown greater resources. He had also the advantage of writing in a language which, of all modern tongues, is the most suitable to poetry. M. Schlegel, in one of his unaccountable criticisms, affirms that in Metastasio nothing can be found that *strikes the imagination*, and that Alfieri is only read in Italy because it has been *fashionable* to study him. This writer can have but merely turned over the pages of these two great writers, or otherwise he has but a slight acquaintance with the language of the authors upon whom he has made these observations. This in a critic is unpardonable; for a sound opinion cannot be thus formed of the productions of genius. In every country, where taste and nature prevail, the tragedies of Alfieri must always be *fashionable*, and admissible to the *bon ton;* and the works of Metastasio will ever be admired in nations where learning flourishes.

How has it happened that M. Schlegel, with all his information and great talent, should have forgotten to notice the genius of Molière and Goldoni, and the excellence of the *Aminta?* A malady, caused by the study of the romantic, must have deceived him into these omissions. He requires that Greece, France, and Italy, should yield to England and Spain in dramatic works. This Coryphæus, in the above style, pretends to quote a scene from the opera of *Raoul de Créqui,* as a *chef-d'œuvre* of theatrical effect, and as a model for writers both of tragedy and comedy in France. The extraordinary penetration of his mind has induced him to panegyrize the operas of *Nina* and *Richard Cœur de Lion*, passing over in silence productions of acknowledged excellence. This German critic has not spared even the writer of *Vaudevilles*, for he cites the miserable piece called *Le Désespoir de Jocrisse*, as the only performance of that kind worthy of notice. Such criticisms as these are extremely injurious to rising talent, and very little attention should be bestowed on them.

Zeno was one of the restorers of the modern Italian drama, and he served as a model to Metastasio. His manner is learned, free, and full of fire. He treats on the passions like a master; working on the affections, and keeping interest awake. It were to be wished that in some of his pieces there had been fewer incidents, for they are in some cases so abundant as to draw the attention of the spectator too much from the principal action. A pomp of style is every where observable in his works; he is ever varied, and always dramatic; his language is always equal to his subject; in short, he may be considered as the *Julio Romano* of the Italian theatre. It ought to be observed, also, that all his scenes are accompanied by a moral.

Alfieri modelled himself at once upon the Greek, English, and French theatres. Of the first, he imitated their beautiful simplicity; he followed the peculiar manner of the second in the vigorous pictures they have drawn of strong passion; and conformed himself to the classic regularity of the third. Such a learned acquaintance with national style, joined to his own creative genius, rendered him equal to the greatest dramatists. According to my humble opinion, Alfieri is the most irreproachable and correct of all dramatic writers.

Molière, the father of modern comedy, is the most perfect of comic poets. To the composer of Ballets, he presents an extensive field for study, and his pieces may be turned to great account in the pursuit of this object. The design, conduct, and characters of these excellent comedies should be most carefully examined : they are pictures of nature.

The numberless traits of genuine comedy with which the writings of this great man abound cannot be too deeply studied. The author of the *Tartuffe* and the *Misantrope* is more delicate, elegant, correct, and even more decorous (at least in his higher comedies) than Goldoni. He is also more universal, learned, and finished than the Italian writer; but the latter seems to surpass him in invention; in Goldoni, there is indeed to be found an astonishing variety of subject and intrigue. He is always true and natural, and appears to paint by inspiration. On whatever subject he is occupied, he treats it with a certain delightful facility ; nothing can embarrass or obstruct his course ; and the fountain of his ideas appears inexhaustible. Several of his pieces, which have deservedly attained a brilliant celebrity, are founded upon very unimportant subjects. It was, perhaps, this great facility of imitation which gave him a disinclination for correcting and perfecting his comedies, which may, therefore, be regarded rather as sketches than finished pictures ; but, it may be added, they are the sketches of a great master.

Molière surpasses his rival of Italy in the composition of his pieces, in what may be termed elevated comedy, particularly in his method of writing, and in the energy of his versification. In this department of his art he is infinitely superior to the Italian poet. Goldoni paints with fire and truth, and his humorous scenes are replete with a sly gaiety. His comedies present perfect pictures of vice turned into ridicule, and they are, therefore, always moral. He may, however, be justly reproached with having always represented characters and manners of a vicious description; a peculiarity in which he excels; but he should either have made his comedies universal, or have confined himself to exhibiting the characters, mind, and manners of Italians. He was equal to the task, and Italy might then have been indebted to him for a national comedy. He is an author whose genius is equal to that of the first dramatists, and his works offer to the composer a numerous train of characters, dramatic situations, bright pictures of manners and passions, which may be easily transferred to Ballets of the comic or melo-dramatic class. From some of Goldoni's pieces, also, may be learned the art of arranging a plot, and of raising interest by an adroit progress of the action, without introducing useless episodes or unlooked-for incidents. This is a writer who, possibly, is not always guided by art, but he always follows nature.

The greatest poet of England was created and formed by nature, and for her alone. " In works of art, it is the labour and ingenuity that attract attention; but in those of nature we are astonished by the sublime and prodigious." This passage of Longinus may be applied to Shakspeare; he can only be considered as a prodigy of nature : study contributed little to the formation of his mind. He is great, unequal, sublime, fantastic, like his model — nature; and he who can at once imitate his beauties and avoid his defects, may be regarded as one possessed of a happy discrimination. We might sometimes even suppose that this poet had formed himself upon the Grecian school; for it is well known that, in some ancient tragedies, certain characters were introduced, who, by the jocularity of their manners, witticisms, ribaldry, and satire, pleasantly broke in upon the monotony that characterizes tragedy, particularly when written by mediocre authors. These interlocutors relieved the audience from that oppressive melancholy attendant upon tragic representation. But when tragedy was brought to perfection, an equal tone was preserved throughout, as it should be. Shakspeare, however, and his followers admitted this medley of tragedy and comedy; and, for the sake of a ridiculous variety, they allowed scenes of the most trivial, irrelevant, and extravagant nature; and it must have arisen from a desire to please the depraved taste of the vulgar of that period, that these authors fell into such errors. The plan and disposition of parts in the dramas of him who produced *Hamlet* and *Romeo and Juliet* form, as it were, an irregular order of architecture; grandeur of design, however, frequently prevails. There is a want of harmony and classic uniformity of tone; still there is more life and energy in the tragedies of the great English poet than in those of the principal part of French dramatists. There must be a movement of action caused by incident, if it is intended to raise interest or to move the passions. Sterne justly observes on the tragedies of certain French writers, that they resembled *sermons*. Voltaire, also, and D'Alembert tax the French tragedy with a want of action; and Blair is of the same opinion. Tragedy divested of scenic embellishment, and lifeless for want of incident, can engage the attention but slightly, and can awaken no interest. Voltaire availed himself of the good qualities to be found in English dramas, and, with great taste, transferred from the British Æschylus the beauties expanded over the tragedies of *Hamlet, Othello, Julius Cæsar,* and some others, into his own productions. It is owing to this acquaintance with the theatres of foreign nations, that he has been enabled to give the drama of

France a new, more varied, and more interesting structure. The English have a predilection for the dark and terrible style of writing. The muse they invoke frequently frightens away the graces, and unhappy consequences attend their flight, for the former immediately bedecks herself with the gingling bells of *Momus*[37]. Such writers may be regarded as the Riberas, the Calabreses, the Rosas, and the Caravages of the stage; Crebillon is weak, and Alfieri is but demi-tragic in comparison with them.

To such authors as these, inequalities and transgressions may justly be objected as well as to their imitators, the Germans and Spaniards. But we must also remark with Le Tourneur, that, "If the English frequently transgressed through too much license and daring, the French may be accused but too often of want of courage on the the dramatic field; they permit their genius to be stifled under the influence of a slavish subserviency to taste." Moderns, however, are generally more free from such a reproach; the progress of art has incited them to throw off the yoke of cold and formal regularity.

The words of the above-cited celebrated translator should be engraved on the memory of young composers, who, engaged in bringing each class to perfection, are also honourably availing themselves of the mine of riches to be found in the works of foreign writers. Care must be taken not to listen to those who are enslaved to a certain fixed idea, that there can be but one particular style of beauty. They will deceive you, for the more universal an artist is, the more universally will he be admired.

CHAPTER XXII.

THE COMPOSER, OR BALLET-MASTER.

" Rapproche les climats, les peuples et les tems,
Réalise la fable, et reproduit l'histoire ;

. . . .

. . . .

Et des feux de son âme embrase tous les cœurs."

DELILLE.

THE Ballet-master should unite to a perfect knowledge of of the arts of dancing and Pantomime an acquaintance with music and painting. The study of polite literature, and particularly of celebrated authors, will prove essentially serviceable to him. He should also have a just idea of the various mechanical arts, joined to some instruction in geometry ; which will enable him to execute the design and movements of his dances with truth and precision; besides, a certain degree of mathematical learning imparts clearness and exactness to all our conceptions. But the study most requisite to a theatrical artist, and which claims his deepest attention, and on which depends the entire effect of his compositions, is that of nature and the human heart ;—without this no dramatic work should be attempted [38]. In short, a complete Ballet-master is at once author and mechanist ; in him should be joined an experience, almost universal, to a fertile and varied imagination. Let it not be thought extraordinary that so much should be expected from a composer. He never loses his time who knows how to employ it. There is nothing prodigious in such an extensive acquisition; besides, nature herself assists the progress of those whom she destines for celebrity.

Maffei remarks that, in the list of qualifications deemed indispensable for a composer of dances, according to Lucian, "the study of morals is not required." Why, it may be asked should not a Ballet-master complete the course of his studies? Is not his art essentially considered equal to that of Corneille, Alfieri, or Molière? Should not he, whose business it is to display men and their passions on the stage, be acquainted with a science which introduces us to a knowledge of the virtues and vices of our species? This criticism, therefore, of the Italian author is inconsiderately pronounced. Without a knowledge of mankind, he could never have produced so fine a piece as *Mérope*, which subject also, as treated by Voltaire, is a masterpiece. The former could not have been ignorant of this truth, but perhaps he thought it would not be expected in a composer of Ballets. Manufacturers of Ballets are plentiful, but talented composers are rare. The office of composer is often filled by ignorant impostors, and the imperfections in this department may, in some measure, be attributed to audiences which have become too easy and indulgent towards avaricious managers, and to performers who are too indolent to acquire perfection in an art which, however, they are proud of professing.

The intrinsic value and excellence of a picture, fresh from the hands of an artist, consists in its perfect imitation of nature; the same observation may be made with respect to Ballets. A Ballet should represent a picture

put into motion; its colouring should be varied; its shadowing clear; and its drawing correct : grace must be its
predominant characteristic ; the groupings, positions, and
scenery should be elegant and clearly delineated :—

> " Ne nous présente point dans tes folles peintures,
> Ce désordre jeté par l' amas des figures,
> Ces corps s'entrechoquant, ces groupes mal conçus,
> Montrant une melêe au milieu des tissus ;
> Mais que dans le tableau la figure première
> Frappe d'abord les yeux par sa vive lumière [39]."
>
> LEMIERRE.

A taste for painting and an acquaintance with its masterpieces are of the utmost utility to a composer.   What
assistance may he not derive, with respect to action, expression, and pictorial effect, from a contemplation of the magnificent compositions of Raphael, the Carracci, Andrea
del Sarto, J. Romano, Tintoretto, Dominichino, M. Angelo,
P. di Cortona, Poussin, Le Brun, Rubens, Ricciarelli,
Joseppino, Albano, Guido, &c.   The powerful designs of
Flaxman, and some other moderns, will also add greatly to
his resources.   Painting, Sculpture, and dancing have,
indeed, a most intimate relation to each other ; and as they
are expected to produce similar effects, each of them
should possess the same inherent qualities.

It frequently happens that a fine picture, or a good
piece of sculpture, suggests the design of a dramatic representation.   Of this, the *bass-reliefs* of the sumptuous
urn of Alexander Severus, which was discovered in the
capitol, may be adduced as a proof.   The following is
the description of the urn, given by the keeper of the
Musée Capitolin:—" The *bass relief* in front epresents
the dispute between *Achilles* and *Agamemnon* for the possession of *Chryseis* : *Achilles* appears in the centre, with
his sword drawn, and in the attitude of aiming a blow ;
Agamemnon is seated before him ; *Minerva,* supposed to

be invisible, is restraining the wrath of *Peleus'* son, and *Chryseis* is standing, apparently in great fear, near *Achilles.* The other figure is most probably intended for *Menelaus.* The group behind represents the Greeks assembled round their kings in council.

"Side view.—*The seizure of Chryseis :*—She is embracing and taking leave of her father *Chryses ;* her head is turned towards *Achilles,* who appears looking at her with impatience; the latter is also holding his horse by the bridle, while he makes a sign of departure to his attendant *Automedon,* who is near him. Two damsels, bearing small parcels, follow the prisoner.

" Opposite side view.—*Achilles resuming his arms to avenge the death of Patroclus :*—He appears in the midst of his armour, holding with his right hand the bridle of his horse, while his left hand grasps a sword; the other figures surrounding him are the princes come to implore him to return to the combat.

" The hinder side.—Here *the ransoming of Hector's body* is described:—*Priam,* the aged king of Troy, is on his knees before *Achilles,* whose hands he embraces, while entreating for the remains of his son; the chariot, placed behind the monarch, is filled with costly articles destined for the ransom."

This subject has been dramatized, and frequently and variously treated by theatrical writers. Numerous are the examples of such adoptions, which, on the part of the artist, only require arrangement and adaptation to the taste of the modern audience. Moral as well as allegorical subjects may be clearly explained in a picture, and, indeed, on such the talented painter may employ all the riches of his art. Jordan has handled a great moral truth both as a painter and as a philosopher; and his picture exhibits a fine dramatic representation. The following is the manner in which Dupaty expresses his admiration of the painted ceiling in the palace of Ricciardi, at Florence. The subject is *The Destiny of Man.*

The attention is first drawn to the representation of the birth of man. *Fate, Time,* the *Parcæ,* and *Nature* appear waiting in expectation; *Fate* is beckoning to *Time,* and *Time* makes a sign to the *Parcæ;* the spindle of the latter seems to have been just put in motion, and a child is discovered in the arms of *Nature.* *Prometheus* approaches, waving his torch; a spark falls, and inspires life. The child now appears creeping at the feet of *Nature;* he rises, walks, and wishes to leave his foster-mother; in vain does she endeavour to detain him, in vain she weeps, already is he far from her, and he soon loses his way. After having wandered for some time, two roads present themselves to the youth; one of which appears steep and rugged, paved with flints, and hedged with thorns; but the other is represented smooth, level, and enamelled with flowers. At the entrance of these roads two troops of men and women are seen. Those in the first evince a sweet but sedate air; their apparel is decent, and without any ornament, except a simple wreath of laurel in their hair : they are standing near the thorny road. Without attempting to mislead the traveller, they merely address him in these words :—" Young man, this is the way to happiness." They are the *Virtues.* The troop upon the smoother road are far more numerous than the first, and exhibit a more interesting appearance; their countenances appear joyous and animated ; they laugh, sing, and exhibit a wantonness in their movements ; their attire is of the most luxurious description. Their hair is decorated with flowers; they are crowned with flowers ; and flowers are in their hands. So lovely and smiling do they appear, that it is easy to mistake them for the *Graces ;* however, on observing where the fillet binds their hair behind, it may be seen that their charming faces are but masks; from this aperture, visages of the most hideous description can be discovered. This deceptive troop hasten to meet the traveller; they smile on him, carress him, and take his hand, " Lovely pilgrim," say they, " behold the way to pleasure ; so come with us." He follows. Wretched youth! they are the *Vices*.

Very little alteration would be required to transfer the action of this piece to the theatre, in the Ballet form ; the allegory has already been well dramatized in a lyrical tragedy, by Metastasio.—*(See Alcide al Bivio*[40].*)*

The Ballet-master should know how to adapt such subjects to the theatre, and to bend them, as it were, to his purpose. A poetical description, also, can furnish a composer with ideas, and aid him in the selection of characteristic scenery. The objects of representation should be chosen with taste, and constructed with art. The author should study the peculiar taste of that public for which he labours, and which it is his duty to please. The natives of certain countries think slightly of their own national productions, and laboriously search for whatever is foreign ; others, on the contrary, despise every thing that is not of " home manufacture." Certain characters and events have, however, invariably been received with universal respect. Such as those illustrious men, and celebrated deeds, which are enshrined in the works of the best and most accredited historians ; they are of all times and all countries. From these the composers may select with great advantage ; for in them spectators of all nations may be interested.

CHAPTER XXIII.

GENERAL ADMONITIONS.

" Sia vergogna il giacer vile, e sepolto,
E'l risorger sia gloria."   A. GUIDI.

" ———— se tu segui tua stella,
Non puoi fallire a glorioso porto."

DANTE.

OCCUPY yourself according to your own peculiar inclination and talent: if your mind is formed for the grand and serious, those laws must be observed which such a style requires; if you attempt to counteract a natural bent or disposition, your productions will not succeed.

" Ne forçons point nôtre talent,
Nous ne ferions rien avec grâce."

LA FONTAINE.

If, on the contrary, your genius and taste tend to the gay and comic style, should you assume the robe of tragedy you will most probably become flat and ridiculous, instead of great and sublime. " Non omnia possumus omnes;" a Raphael and a Voltaire occur but rarely in the family of man. Be convinced of this, and undertake nothing without consulting your own peculiar powers. If, upon examination, extraordinary qualities are discovered attempt, without hesitation, to realize whatever ideas may fire the fancy; boldly enter upon your designs, at the same time be guided by prudence and judgment, and success will, in all probability, attend you.

To attain celebrity, it is necessary to possess a certain sensibility of soul, which is instantly struck, moved, and interested by surrounding objects, and which is ever alive to the least emotion; without that kind of sensibility which raises in the mind a sort of enthusiastic energy, we cannot attain renown. It too frequently happens that an ardent desire to equal our superiors, or to produce things which may honour or perpetuate our memory, springs within us, in proportion as we find ourselves capable of accomplishing the desired object, and we are rarely deceived. The mere desire of doing something praiseworthy inspires us with a certain extent of power. Vanity and envy also may suggest a wish to equal, or even surpass, the works of genius; but there is not then the same foundation for such pretensions. If ordinary and uninstructed artists continue in their ridiculous attempts, they will become rivals only to Le Moiné, who pretended to equal the heroic poetry of the ancients with his ridiculous verses; or Borghese, who undertook to write a poem which should suspass that of Tasso.

Let your application be continual; meditate on and analyze your productions; reflection and examination lead to perfection. Compare your own works with those of others which are generally acknowledged to be truly beautiful; nothing can be more beneficial than comparison. A spirit of remark and review (so necessary to dramatic authors) should accompany all your studies, if you wish to render your imitations of nature perfect. Let the rules of art curb the impetuosity of your imagination, whose flights frequently transport us beyond the bounds of reason and taste, which should never be offended. In order to secure universal approbation, let the beauties of nature shine throughout your productions. Never forget that the sound critic is generally sitting and ready to pass judgment on your production. D' Alembert says, reason is a severe judge and ought to be respected! A man of the lowest class and the least enlightened would cry down a piece in which neither consistency nor true imitation appears ; and the author of the *Metromania* has justly observed—

" Le bon sens du maraud, quelquefois m' épouvante."

But although it is indispensable that we should respect the acknowledged rules of art, we need not be enslaved by the dogmas of mere pedants; pay no attention to the maxims of those who, without talent and void of invention, seek only to fetter genius and encumber its progress. The writer of *Sulmone* observes, that envy is never so severely punished as when it witnesses the glory and success of another.

Although nothing should be thrown hastily out of hand, and improvements may be made on reviewing our productions, yet it is a fault to be incessantly retouching ; for too elaborate a finish often destroys expression. Apelles reproaches Protogenes with this error. The latter was ever by the side of his pictures, endeavouring to give them a finish that frequently degenerated into affectation. This failing must be avoided, and the example of the Grecian painter may become useful to artists of every class. We are sometimes content to see in the productions of art a certain carelessness and easy negligence, which serve to conceal the labour and study which the artist has undergone.

A suitable and appropriate subject should be fixed on ; on this the success of a piece in a great measure depends. An interesting plot, cleverly treated by the author, and sustained by performers of talent, must necessarily meet with applause. Every circumstance in the piece should be connected and dependent, and the whole should tend to produce the final catastrophe ; avoid the example of certain authors of the *romantic* style, who, by continually multiplying incidents and episodes, cause the principal subject of action to be totally forgotten. Boileau, deriding a writer who had produced a piece of this description, sings thus :—

> " Son sujet est conduit d'une belle manière,
> Et chaque acte en sa pièce est une pièce entière."

When the thread of the tale is too often broken and interrupted, the interest is weakened ; the attention of the audience being diverted to too many objects, fixes on none.

> " Pluribus intentus, minor est ad singula sensus."

While your characters are natural, the action must create interest ; theatrical embellishment will then indeed adorn your work; and the powerful assistance of music render the illusion charming and complete. Seek not the society of such pretended critics as flatter without ceasing ; but rather court the company and opinion of men of sense, who will speak with sincerity : their criticisms are of the utmost utility, and beneath their observations talent strengthens, and advances nearer towards perfection. Happy is that artist who finds in his friend an able and impartial critic ! the very difficulty we experience in satisfying such a friend, is the sure way to avoid error [41]. It is no easy matter to judge of our own productions impartially : self love, together with a certain propensity to prefer one part to another, prevents us from forming a just opinion. Attend, therefore, to the observations of others, and profit by them. If you adopt a subject let your imagination embellish it, but remember that it is better to produce an indifferent original than to finish a faultless copy. Aspire to place your name amongst those whose originality and genius have rendered them illustrious. *Non parvas animo, dat gloria vires.*—OVID. Essay to deserve the praise of able judges ; but despise and avoid stupidity, envy, and cabal [42].

CHAPTER XXIV.

ON PROGRAMMES, OR WRITTEN PLOTS.

" Que ————— l'action préparée,
Sans peine du sujet applanisse l'entrée."—BOILEAU.

SEVERAL professors have averred that a good Ballet needs no programme, provided the plot is well and clearly displayed ; and the Pantomime so executed as to give a perfect idea of the passions and sentiments meant to be expressed. This opinion is just, and I am persuaded that the composer should be understood by means of the art itself, rather than by the reading of a written plot or programme. According to this plan, it is sufficient to print the title of the Ballet on the theatrical bill, together with the names of the characters. I must, however, observe, that programmes are necessary to explain certain mythological and allegorical subjects; and also where some circumstance or event has preceded the principal action, and on which the progress and catastrophe of the piece depend. Without programmes, which acquaint us with what is about to be represented, and inform us of each principal event, upon which the whole action is hinged, a number of interesting and agreeable circumstances would pass unnoticed and not understood. Without such an expedient, the Ballet-master must necessarily employ himself during the whole performance, in explanation and directions to actors how to execute their parts. Every composer, not being equally endued for such a task, programmes become extremely useful. Those who are thus situated would be infallibly undone, should the custom of distributing programmes at the entrance of the theatre be forbidden, or should the practice of exhibiting certain devices and explanatory bills during the piece be abolished.

Programmes are found to be extremely serviceable to those artists who wish to produce the Ballets of another composer, as they mark particular passages, which must otherwise escape the observation of him who did not originally compose the piece. They serve also to direct the attention of spectators to certain scenes and situations, which would have passed off unregarded.

The ancients were in the habit of distributing a sort of programme before the performance of their Pantomimes; in these the piece was announced, and whatsoever preceding event had produced the subject of the drama about to be represented was particularly noticed [43]. Sophrones and Xenarques always wrote programmes to their compositions.

It requires great talent in an artist clearly to exhibit to the spectators that progress of events which completes the subject of a Ballet; upon this depends the entire interest of the composition. If the representation is confused or obscure, dramatic effect is lost, and the programme then becomes a feeble aid to the public, and almost useless to the artist. The mode of representation should be clear, simple and exact. It is not necessary to employ an infinity of gestures though even there are many ideas to be expressed, for this practice is only calculated to mislead the spectators; be rather brief and precise, and avoid long pantomimical narrations. Render your plot interesting at its commencement, and the final dénoument will then be expected with a pleasing impatience.

Programmes should be written with clearness and simplicity. Every circumstance in the Ballet should be there detailed with the utmost perspicuity; the succession of scenes should be described in exact order. The intention of the composer being thus perfectly explained, each performer is enabled to form for himself a just idea of the successive order of scenes, peculiarities of characters, the depending class of passions, and the nature of his own part. A plot may often, however, be more easily composed than developed on the stage. In writing programmes, it is usual to omit a quantity of details useles and uninteresting to all except the Ballet-master, whose business is to superintend rehearsals, and to conduct the representation. A quantity of pantomimical business, therefore, instructions for dancers, and mutual explanations, are only expressed in stage directions, in giving which, particular care should be taken that every circumstance tends to produce clearness and general effect.

NOTES

TO PART THE FOURTH.

1.

Episode is a poetical term, signifying an action of a different nature from the principal action, but connected with it. An episode should be skilfully treated, and its connexion should be made with every appearance of probability. It must not divert the attention of either the spectator or reader; it should, therefore, not continue too long a time, but should be proportioned to the nature of the subject. After having made a well-contrived progress, and produced its effect, it should disappear.

Poets have employed episodes with great propriety, to acquaint their readers with those events that have preceded the action of the poem; showing how the hero arrived in that position in which he appears at the beginning of the piece. This artifice is used by the greatest poets, in order that unity of action may be preserved, and that whatever is requisite to be known may not be left in uncertainty and obscurity.

2.

The centre division was called the *Imperial Gate*, through which persons of distinction passed; the other two divisions on each side were termed the *Strangers' Gates*, being constructed for foreigners; the lower class of people, also, went in by these latter named entrances. The scenery generally represented merely a street, a public square, or the country.

3.

Some regard Despréaux as the lawgiver of Parnassus, as the restorer of good taste, and as the first who wrote good verses. This, however, is wrong; for Corneille, Molière, Racine, and La Fontaine had already produced their masterpieces, when, as a certain author remarks, Boileau *had not yet written but a few indifferent satires.* He afterwards instructed young persons by describing to them the beauties of those great originals. While waging war against bad writers, he certainly merited the title of preserver of true taste, rather than *restorer.* This great and celebrated versifier might be followed on every subject, had he not been guilty of some false criticisms, which may be found in what he has said against Quinault, as good a poet as himself, and possessing all the sweetness we admire in Metastasio. But when Boileau was jealous, he traduced the greatest geniuses of Italy, England, and even of France.

4.

In other respects we are not insensible to the beauties of this great production; above all, to the deep and terrible pathos of *Othello* himself. Many actors, and authors too, are indebted to this tragedy for a great part of the fame they have acquired. Ducis, taking Shakspeare for his model, on this subject has given an excellent tragedy to the stage. Voltaire has introduced into two of his pieces several passages taken from the English poet. In the character of *Othello* Talma greatly added to his reputation ; the same may be observed with respect to Kean. Garrick, according to the relations of that period, always excited astonishment when depicting the ardent passion of the Moor, and concluded by inspiring at once both horror and pity. At length music took possession of this tragic tale ; and, perhaps, the *Otello* of Rossini is the noblest opera he ever produced. With respect to the latter, it may be observed, that to find an actor who could at once sing and act the character of *Otello* was no easy task. Signor Curioni, however, of the present day, has particularly distinguished himself in this part, both by his singing and acting ; he possesses, perhaps, the finest tenor voice at present in existence, to which he joins every physical power necessary to such a performance. In short, no singer would attempt to take the part out of his hands, as there is no performer now on the Italian stage who could give it equal effect. Connoisseurs are aware of the difficulty of representing all the powerful energy of this character, and at the same time to do justice to the fine but difficult music with which it abounds. From his first appearance to his final exit, *Otello* sings and acts without intermission ; a gigantic effort totally unknown to singers of the last century.

5.

It is not long since that E. Gosse said, unity of time and place is too great a restraint on the dramatic art, and particularly when applied to tragedy.

6.

The witty and judicious Marmontel observes, with respect to unity of place, that those poets who would restrain themselves to a rigorous observance of unity of place, have been frequently obliged to force the action in a manner quite opposite to that probability which might have accompanied a liberty of changing the place ; for if the act of changing the place destroys the illusion but for an instant, when the action passes where it is impossible it could have passed, the idea of the place being continually at variance with what is passing in it, the illusion is thus far more materially injured, and every probability of dramatic illusion is entirely destroyed.

7.

Let but any person give himself the trouble to peruse those pieces mentioned, or to read extracts from Shakspeare, and he will be convinced of the truth of what we have advanced.

8.

Questio. Conviv. trad. de M. A. Gandini. Questio. 15, lib. 9, tom. 2, page 303.

9.

Amateurs should read, upon this subject, Gravina's learned work, entitled *La Ragione Poetica*, liv. 1.

We must esteem poetry as the mother of the fine arts ; in her bosom, they have had their birth, and were not distinguishable from her until, arrived at a state to sustain themselves, they adopted different functions, and each followed appropriate principles. The fine arts follow poetry as an original, and advance in the same path towards the same object, that is, to move and delight us by powerful and beautiful imitations of nature.

10.

> " ——————— a dilettar bisogna
> Eccitar meraviglia, ed ogni evento
> Atto, a questo non è. L' arte conviene
> Che inaspettato il renda,
> Pellegrino, sublime, e che l'adorni
> De' pregj ch' ei non ha. Così diviene
> Arbitra d'ogni cor ; così gli affetti
> Con dolce forza ad ubbidirla impegna,
> E col finto allettando il vero insegna.
> Che nuoce altrui, se l'ingeguosa scena
> Finge un guerriero, un cittadino, un padre ?
> Purchè ritrovi in essi
> Lo spettator se stesso, e ch' indi impari
> Qual' è il dover primiero
> D' un cittadin, d' un padre e d' un guerriero."

Metastasio.

11.

Our observations here relate solely to the theatrical business of a piece ; for no person can be blind to the poetic beauties contained in the dramas both of England and Germany.

12.

The *Varron* of De Grave is a production both witty and well-contrived ; but, being defective in interest as well as incident, was soon rejected at the theatres. Numerous are the pieces of this kind, and similar is the fate of them all.

> " Non satis est pulchra esse poemata : dulcia sunto,
> Et quocumque volent, animum auditoris agunto."

Hor.

Perhaps no dramatic writer abounds more in dramatic action than Shakspeare. Schiller also, following his great model, is fruitful in incident. Calderon, too, notwithstanding his defects, is another instance of dramatic motion.

13.

Faust, a drama by the celebrated Goëthe; *Manfred,* by Lord Byron; *Frankenstein; or, the Modern Prometheus,* by Mr. Shelly, are works of the terrific class.

" Simile mostro visto ancor non fue."

DANTE.

14.

The celebrated *Pagano* has also written a treatise on the beautiful; it contains observations that may prove very useful to performers.

15.

Apelles being desired to paint the portrait of King Antigonus, who had but one eye, in order to conceal this defect, painted that king in profile.

16.

" The multitude of actors employed by some tragic poets, frequently, for want of invention, become very embarrassing as the catastrophe approaches, when it is necessary to get rid of them by some means or other. The author, therefore, finds himself obliged to seize the first opportunity of despatching them by sword or poison."

What this writer has said with respect to the number of characters is perfectly true; but it may be added, that it is not necessary the poet should kill a troop of characters at the *dénoûment* of his piece. Tragedy, as we have aleady remarked, may still be *tragedy,* and produce effect, without sanguinary scenes; this may be proved by examples: the dagger and the poisoned bowl are not the only objects necessary to excite terror and pity.

17.

Philip and *Virginius* are two characters from Alfieri's tragedies. The following characters from Corneille, Racine, and Voltaire are models for the deep study of performers;—*Curiace, Auguste, Don Carlos, Le Cid, Sertorius, Nicomède, Chimène; Acomat, Néron, Mithridate, Achille, Agamemnon, Narcisse, Phèdre, Hermione, Bérénice, Athalie, Roxane, Clitemnestre, Andromaque; Œdipe, Brutus, L'Orphelin, Tancrède, Mahomet, Orosmane, Gengis Khan, Mérope, Alzire, Sémiramis, Adelaïde.*

For characters of comedy, Molière alone will supply a sufficient quantity.

18.

" If a *soliloquy* has neither object, interest, nor consequence, it must necessarily become puerile; for children, idiots, and drunkards are accustomed to soliloquize in this manner.

" The *monologue* appears absurd if employed to give a historical recital which is neither expected to arise from the situation of the person who delivers it, nor from the general progress of the action; this is, in effect, not a monologue but rather the author, who is thus prating, while the character through whom he speaks ought to be acting instead of trifling away his time, and exposing the poverty of the poet's genius."—Roubaud.

19.

See D'Alembert, Batteux, *Beaux Arts*, Part III., chap. iii. ; Marmontel, Gravina, Du Bos, Maffei, Montesquieu, &c. The last writer had a particular predilection for the comedy of *Esope à la Cour*, on account of the moral it conveyed. This production of Boursault's gives, indeed, the most useful instruction, and is capable, without any other assistance, satisfactorily to answer J. J. Rousseau's theatrical paradoxes. Beaumarchais, also, in his sprightly and satirical prefaces, inculcates the dramatic moral of his pieces.

20.

The measures, movement, and character of Grecian music.

The Pyrrhic (∪ ∪) and the tribrach (∪ ∪ ∪) are employed to express the light and joyous movements of the satiric dance ; slow and sedate movements are accompanied by the spondee (— —) and the molossus (— — —); passions of a quiet and pleasing character may be represented by the trochee (— ∪), and sometimes by the amphibrach (∪ — ∪), which latter is a sweet and gentle measure. The iambic (∪ —) is full of force and fire ; the anapaest (∪ ∪ —) is nearly of the same nature, expressing violent and warlike movement. To express gaiety and joy, we should employ the dactyl (— ∪ ∪), whose character corresponds very well with such feelings. The antipast (∪ — — ∪) gives a striking idea of whatever is rude and clownish. If we would express rage and madness, not only should the anapaest be employed, but the fourth Paeon also (∪ ∪ ∪ —), which is still more effective.—Vossius.

21.

See, *Traité Elémentaire Théorique et Pratique de l'Art de la Danse.* See that part which treats on music.

22.

The science of music appears unhappily to be somewhat on the decline. The styles of music peculiar to each class of the drama are now confounded; modern musicians seem to have forgotten that such men as Pergolese, Jomelli, Sacchini, and Cimarosa, ever existed ; at least such a conclusion may be deduced from the fact of their paying so little attention to the models for every style that those talented men have left behind them ; were the works of these composers deeply studied, dramatic music would, perhaps, become more appropriate and natural. But I have spoken more at length upon this subject in *Observations upon Singing, and the Expression of Dramatic Music*, and also in an *Essay upon the Introduction of Italian Music into France.*

23.

The properties (*accessoires*) of a theatre consist of whatever, in scenery and decorations, is of a detached and portable nature, such as furniture, fire-arms and instruments of every description, whether for use or pleasure. In Italy, a most particular attention is paid to this department.

24.

I am aware that Addison has observed, speaking of tragedy, in words nearly to this effect, " Ordinary minds are as much delighted with the decorations as with the words ; but a man of sense is inspired with admiration from what a hero says, not from what accoutrements he wears. All the pomp and parade of royalty bestows not on Brutus one half of the majesty with which a single verse of Shakspeare adorns him."

The theatre displays its pompous scenery and gorgeous decorations equally to the learned and to the illiterate ; and, if necessary, to the subject and conformable to truth, such exhibition will not be blamed by men of taste. But when an author, confiding in these aids, neglects the interest of the plot, and leaves the characters imperfectly delineated, to give the painter and mechanist an opportunity of displaying their talent, he becomes a proper subject for the severity of criticism. In order that the charm of dramatic illusion may be perfect, decorations should accompany and help to explain a piece in its progress, but should never be made principal objects.

25.

Who among an audience could possibly conclude that in the second act of the Ballet of *Psyché*, the person whom *Psyché* supposes to be her mother is *Venus* herself, concealed beneath that disguise in order to deceive and destroy her hated rival ? Without the assistance of a programme, or a knowledge of *Apuleius*, or of *La Fontaine*, this piece could never be understood. This inconvenience must be attributed, in the first instance, to a meagre supply of panto - mimic action, or, in other words, *explanatory gestures*. It is the composer's business to exert his utmost, that he may avoid falling into such incertitude : even the Italians, when the subject is complicated, are not always sufficiently clear.

26.

" If it is against the principles of morality to endeavour to debauch the mind by licentious exhibitions, in which every sense appears lost in pleasures. Should it be permitted to display to the eyes of an audience execrable and unnatural passions ? Which is more scandalous, the fury of a tyrant, or the ecstacies of licentious pleasure ?" LEMIERRE.

27.

We shall here quote some verses by Riccoboni, which occur very opportunely to sustain our argument and to assist young performers in counter-acting the force of bad example. The poet is addressing an actor :—

> " Non stupir se ti esamino e ti squadro ;
> Quel moverti per arte e col compasso
> Ti rendon, se nol sai, scipito e ladro.

Per numero tu calcoli ogni passo,
E per linea le braccia stendi in giro
Con molta attenzion per l'alto e il basso.

Talor bilanci un guardo ed un sospiro
Volgi il capo, e la mano movi, o il piede
A battuta, quat canta un semi-viro.

. . . .
. . . . in te ogni membro si contiene
Così che un parte, un resta, e uno altro riede.

Parmi veder, come sovente aviene
Quei fanciulletti che un pedante in scuola
Ammaestra per porli in su le scene.

Imparata che s' han la cantafola,
Che devon recitar, quegli innocenti
Ti fan cinque o sei moti ogni parola.

Non crederesti, e pur non altrimenti
Far ti vedo talor comico sciocco,
Tanto prodigo sei di movimenti."

Art. Rappres. C. II.

28.

In Spain, composers are permitted to select subjects from the Bible. The same thing has been frequently done in France ; they may be termed a sort of *Oratorios dansans.*

29.

For the hero of the romantic, see Schlegel. This writer may be very properly contrasted with an excellent work upon the romantic by Count Ségur, a production remarkable for purity of taste and elegance of style.

30.

If any person reflects deeply on this, he will find that the imagination is a passive faculty, but reason an active one. Upon this subject many are greatly mistaken in their ideas.

31.

A Dutch poet, whose genius, according to his countrymen, is equal to that of Corneille or of Shakspeare.

32.

Voltaire said of this piece, that the *Mandragora* alone, by Macchiavelli, was, perhaps, worth all the comedies of Aristophanes.

33.

About this period, Hardy, Ronsard, Duché, Follard, Boisrobert, Boyer, Desfontaines, Mayret, Roy, Scudéry, Du Ryer, Desmarest, Coypel, La Calprenède, le P. la Colonie, &c., inundated the French stage with their productions.

34.

This piece, with that of *Britannicus*, are noble productions ; and those critics who pretend that this great poet wants tragic vigour, both in style and in the arrangement of the subject, betray their own want of judgment. The same observation may be made with respect to those detractors from the merit of Metastasio, who deny him energy when describing the passions, and elevation of style, when treating on heroic subjects. Let such persons read his *Temistocle, la Clemenza di Tito, Regolo, &c.*

35.

There is as much difference between the *Phèdre* of Racine, and the *Hippolytus* of the Greek poet, as there is between the latter piece and that of Seneca upon the same subject.

36.

There are certain authors who would have the public believe that they are not indebted to the ancients either for style or invention. Even Metastasio, Alfieri, Goldoni, and some others may be accused of this species of ingratitude. Such authors insist that their best works were produced before having become acquainted with those of the celebrated men who preceded them ; the excellence of their talents, however, stood in no need of the support of falsehood. Virgil was not the less a great genius for having modelled himself upon Homer ; and would these moderns conceal their imitations of the Greeks and Romans ? This, indeed, is a contempt and negligence almost unpardonable in men of genius. Would not that curiosity and emulation, so natural to talent, inspire Goldoni with the desire of becoming intimate with Plautus, Terence, Aristophanes, and Molière ? Could the learned Gravina keep his scholar, Metastasio, from a knowledge of the Grecian drama? Again, it is certain Alfieri could never have carried the Italian tragedy to such a pitch of perfection, if he had not previously studied the Greek and French drama, and even Shakspeare too. Voltaire, Boileau, and Molière also, have not been always sincere in acknowledging literary obligations. Justice should be done to those who have had so great an influence on modern fame ; without the aid of the ancestral antique, should we have had a *Gierusalemme*, a Raphael, and a Racine.

37.

" A nation of a character confessedly gloomy and melancholic, where the enjoyment of society is so difficult of attaining, where men are divided into a species of *castes* who seldom communicate with each other; such a people require theatrical representations of a peculiar description, perhaps such as are intended for the eye rather than the heart, something shrewd and witty, rather than tender and pathetic. The more solitary men are, the deeper and stranger are their passions; it is only, therefore, by a representation of these passions in all their power and energy that such can be moved or interested. At Paris, a tragedy, whose subject is love, is required only to draw tears of tenderness; in London, tragedy is expected to be infuriated with passion and filled with horror. A Frenchman is delighted with the pathos of *Zayre*; an Englishman, with the terrible frenzy of *Orosmane*. The haughty *Achille*, raging and menacing to preserve the object of his affection, opposed by the anger of *Agamemnon* and of all Greece, would draw more attention at the theatres of London than the dark and deep dissimulation of the jealous *Eriphile*. Thus it appears, that a study of the theatrical taste of different nations is an excellent means of attaining a knowledge of both individual and national character; indeed it is almost impossible to be perfectly informed upon such a subject without the aid of the drama."—*L' Observateur Français à Londres.*

With respect to English comedy, the same species of remark still holds good. The connoisseurs of England generally require representations and characters to be finished in such a style of extravagance as almost to approach carricature; such productions as those of Molière, Regnard, Destouches, and Goldoni are not conceived with sufficient vigour for the generality of an English public; they prefer a species of nondescript pieces, in which appear characters of the strangest and drollest description, incidents of a most extraordinary nature, and situations conceived with all the grotesque of Scarron.

The Harliquinades, or *Pantomimes*, as they are improperly termed, may be cited as a good example of national comic taste in England; they are truly national, whatever may be said to the contrary, for old and young, rich and poor, the nobility of the boxes, the learned of the pit, and the whole of the middling and lowest classes to be found in the galleries, all universally join in broad laughter at a *Christmas Pantomime.*

Of these farcical extravaganzas the principal characters are, *Harlequin, Columbine, Pantaloon,* and *Clown;* with respect to the latter personage, so great is his influence, it seems doubtful whether he or *Harlequin* ought to be considered the hero of the piece. Nothing is left untried to excite both laughter and astonishment; metamorphoses, called *tricks,* are, by the assistance of the most powerful and excellent machinery, carried to a point of perfection unknown both in France and Italy.

38.

Among the moderns, Shakspeare, Racine, Metastasio, Molière, and Boccacio must be considered as the great organs of nature. These writers should be ever present with you; nature speaks in their persons.

The *Decameron* is more useful to the composers of Ballets than is generally supposed. It furnishes an infinity of interesting subjects, in which are to be found faithful portraits of mankind ; every character and passion is described in the liveliest colours. From these learned and witty *novels* of this great writer, we may learn to delineate perfectly the magnanimity of a king, the prudence of the counsellor or courtier, the valour of the general, the virtue of the matron, the modesty of the virgin, the looseness of the courtezan, the knavery of a servant, the fidelity of a friend, the ecstacy of love and the jealousy that often attends it, the fury of despair and idiot simplicity, the misery of a miser and the munificence of a great mind, village rusticity and polite libertinism, &c.

39.

" Though every person present at a scene becomes an actor in it, yet every one must not be equally affected at what is passing : thus, the soldier who witnesses the sacrifice of *Iphigénie* ought to be moved by such an event, but certainly not so deeply as the brother of the victim. A woman present at the trial of *Susanna*, and who does not appear from any outward mark to be related to her, must not evince the same degree of affliction as the mother or sister of *Susanna*. Again, a young man appears with more spirit than an old one. A young man will appear totally absorbed at a pathetic scene ; while the man of more years and experience exhibits less feeling, though more consideration. When the features of a spectator are marked by sense and study, he does not become so wrapt in imagination as one whose phisiognomy exhibits a kind of idiot simplicity. Astonishment, as seen in the part of a king, is different from the same passion as displayed in an ordinary man."

A person placed in the distance does not appear so visibly affected as he who is nearer to the spectator. Attention, as portrayed in him who sees, is different from that of him who hears. A person of lively temperament sees and hears with gestures differing from those of a melancholy character.

These observations may, perhaps, appear too nice and over-laboured ; yet it is by this appropriate and universal expression, that a scene is rendered complete in all its parts ; the principal actors in a scene always exhibit the necessary feeling ; but it is over the secondary parts that this feeling should be spread and continued, thus rendering the picture an entire imitation of nature. And it is the Ballet-master's business to give the instructions necessary for producing such an effect.

40.

We have thought it requisite to introduce here the following description of the *Loves* of *Venus* and *Adonis*—a picture by Albano :—*Venus*, impatient to try the effect of her charms upon the heart of *Adonis*, is beholding herself in a glass, and seems confident of the conquest. As she reclines upon the bank of a river, she is surrounded by *Cupids* and the *Graces*, who are still occupied in adorning her The God of Love is already singing the delights of the expected union ; while winged children are employed in feeding the swans about to be harnessed to the Goddess's chariot.

Vulcan is observed sleeping at the feet of his wife ; while little *Cupids* are manufacturing and sharpening their arrows, and stringing their bows ; and to prove their unerring aim, others are showing to *Venus* a shield pierced in every part. *Diana* and her nymphs, borne on the clouds, are anxiously observing the labours of the *Loves*. After their work is finished, the winged children sink into a pretended sleep ; in this state, *Diana's* nymphs surprise them, break their bows, and destroy their arrows ; the wounds of which they so much dreaded. *Calisto* is going to awaken the deities, but is deterred by her more prudent companion. *Diana,* viewing the scene from above, enjoys her victory.

The little *Loves*, however, soon repair their loss, when every thing in sea, earth, and air yields to their power. One of them conducts *Adonis* to the feet of *Venus*, who seems slumbering. The faithful dog of the young hunter vainly essays to draw him back to the forests, the charms of the Goddess have rivetted him. The winged boys near the bed of *Venus* appear, by their signs, to command silence and secrecy.

41.

Many authors owe their celebrity to the counsels of those wise and enlightened friends whom nothing could deter from speaking the truth. From their remarks, men of talent have sometimes even destroyed their productions, and have improved by repetition. Perfection is obtained by docility and perseverance. An inordinate love of vain flattery conceals the truth from us.

Euripides, Virgil, Ariosto, Boileau, Pope, and Gray, all of whom were men of the greatest celebrity, found a great difficulty in satisfying their own judgment, and were ever ready to listen to the voice of sound criticism. They frequently effaced what they had written, and were never hasty in publishing their productions. Such examples as these, together with the *Epître aux Pisons*, which every lover of the fine arts ought to know by heart, are surely sufficient to restrain vanity, and to point out the way in which we ought to proceed.

42.

When our cowardly Zoiluses are opposed by talent, they quickly return to the mire from whence they sprang. " Untoward circumstances, disputation, envy, jealousy, and ignorance, very often contribute to the development of talent equally with good criticism, and thus become the prime cause of their celebrity. Sergent rightly observes, that if a Cardinal Minister had not excited, through jealousy, some wretched scribblers against the author of the *Cid*, the great Corneille would not, probably, have bestowed on us so many masterpieces. The protection afforded to bad taste, by a powerful party at court, doubtless induced Molière to imagine the designs of his two comedies, the *Femmes Savantes* and the *Précieuses Ridicules*. Who can say whether we do not owe the excellences of Racine to Boileau, who did not pass him over, while satirizing the Pradons, the Brébœufs, and the Cottins of that day.

Thus Fréron was very serviceable in establishing the fame of Voltaire : and, had not La Harpe quarrelled with Clémeot, probably he would never have become so finished a judge of literature.

How many pigmies, elevating themselves on stilts to climb Pindus, and having violated *Melpomene* and *Thalia*, have at length been precipitated amongst college drudges by such fearful critics as Royou, Aubert, Suard, Geoffroy, &c. !"—See *Lettre à l'Auteur du Mercure Encyclopédique*.

PART THE FIFTH.

PART THE FIFTH.

PROGRAMMES,

CONTAINING

EXAMPLES OF EVERY SPECIES OF BALLETS.

COMPOSED BY C. BLASIS.

" Miroir universel ———— ———— ———
Les siécles reculés, les grands évenemens,
Tous les faits consacrés dans la Fable et l'Histoire."

DULARD.

PRELIMINARY REMARKS.

THE reader is here presented with the different kinds of Ballets, each being treated in a style peculiar to its class. In doing this, the author has endeavoured to enlarge the sphere of this sort of composition, by introducing a great variety of subjects, by producing more striking contrasts of sentiments and passions, and by giving to certain scenes, hitherto not adapted to the Ballet, their appropriate tone of expression. I have frequently considered the Ballet as a kind of poem or romance, reduced to those dramatic rules and principles which must be observed on their production at the theatre.

Compositions that can speak to the eye, and interest the heart, should be honoured with the same attention as any production of the fine arts ; for what else is a good classic Ballet but a picture in motion, with the additional charm of well adapted music ?

It has here been thought necessary to recal some observations made in the Fourth Part of this work. In composing programmes for Ballets, we must remark, First, that the programme may please the reader, while it is useless in explaining the performance ; for it frequently happens that a bright and well written description becomes flat and void of effect, when put into a state of theatrical action. Secondly, what is easily comprehended by means of words, is not explained with the same facility by gesture. Thirdly, the subject may be interesting and well contrived and yet not be dramatic. Fourthly, what really is dramatic, is not always exactly conformable to reason and probability. In order, therefore, to avoid falling into these errors, to make the programme answer the performance, and to show the real object prescribed by our art, it is essentially requisite, First, that the subject should be of a sustained sprightliness throughout, representing nature beautified by art. Secondly, that the passions be picturesque and strikingly contrasted ; characters deeply shaded and strongly made out (if we may make use of these terms), and, that incident and action be employed rather than long dialogues, which latter must be particularly avoided. Thirdly, the imagination must be continually amused by a variety of scenery, capable of exciting surprise and admiration ; to which must be added costume, machinery, and every species of appropriate decorations, for they are indispensably requisite to dramatic effect. Fourthly, let nothing of the marvellous and supernatural be admitted, unless it is well founded on the nature of the piece, and executed with a good taste. What is called theatrical show and stage effect become puerile, insignificant, and absurd display, unless closely connected with the incidents of the play in which they are exhibited. It is presumed from the author's own experience, which has guided him in this selection, that whatever effect the following examples may produce in the reading, they will not fail to tell well in representation, some of them having been already performed on the continent.

THE WRATH OF ACHILLES,

OR THE

DEATH OF PATROCLUS.

A HEROI-TRAGICAL BALLET, IN FIVE ACTS.

ARGUMENT.

The subject of this Ballet is borrowed from the Iliad. The action opens at the time when *Achilles*, swayed by his resentment for the insult offered him by *Agamemnon*, who had conveyed away his dear *Briseis*, withdraws into his camp and refuses to assist the Greeks. In the mean time *Patroclus*, having been permitted to appear in the armour of his friend to encounter *Hector*, revives among the Greeks hopes of seeing again the son of *Peleus* in the field of battle. He goes forth, fights with *Hector* and perishes by his hand. The fate of the unfortunate *Patroclus* induces *Achilles* to alter his resolution; he advances against the *Phrygians* to avenge the fall of his friend. *Hector* being slain, *Agamemnon* acknowledges himself to have been in the wrong, and makes ample amends to *Achilles* for the injury he had done him. The affectionate *Briseis* flies to the arms of her lover, and the banishment of discord is succeeded by a lasting reconciliation between all the Greeks.

CHARACTERS.

Achilles, *King of Thessaly, son of Thetis.*
Patroclus, *a Grecian Prince; a friend of Achilles.*
Calchas, *Chief Priest.*
Ulysses, *King of Ithaca.*
Agamemnon, *King of Argos and Mycenæ, Commander-in-Chief of the Grecian army.*

THETIS, *a Deity of the sea.*

BRISEIS, *daughter of Brises, Chief priest of Jupiter, in love with Achilles.*

AUTOMEDON, *armour-bearer of Achilles.*

MENELAUS.

NESTOR.

AJAX, *son of Telamon.*

AJAX, *son of Oileus.*

DIOMEDES.

PHŒNIX.

MERION.

ANTILOCHUS.

Grecian Soldiers; Thessalians, under the command of Achilles; Trojan Soldiers; Princesses, attendants of Briseis; Grecian Princes; Priests, attendants of Calchas; Nereides, attendants of Thetis; Sea Deities; Cyclops; nine slaves alloted to Achilles; Phrygian slaves; Smiles, Sports, Pleasures, and Graces.

ACT I.

SCENE*.—*At the right, the camp of* Achilles *; at the left, afar off, a large plain bounded by hills, above which rises the city of* Troy. *The tent of* Peleus' Son *stands partly on the stage, his armour hangs on a pillar. The prospect is limited by the sea, and the Thessalian ships are seen along a part of the shore.*

ACHILLES is seated near a table, striking a lyre. After he has stripped himself of his armour, and withdrawn into his camp, the workings of his countenance express deep resentment of the injury inflicted on him by *Agamemnon,* and concern at the loss of *Briseis,* with whom he is enamoured. He endeavours to smooth his cares with the charms of music, which seems to afford him some relief. Its sweet modulation is expressive of the delights of peace and the charms of friendship. *Patroclus* is near him, bewailing the misfortunes of the Greeks and his friend's obstinacy.

Of a sudden the sky is rent by the sounds of war. The song of *Achilles* is interrupted by the clang of clarions and trumpets, which is a signal for the Trojans to attack the Greeks. The Trojan army is discovered filing off in the distance. Grief of *Patroclus!* *Achilles* is thrilled with the din of war; his lyre falls from his hands; he snatches up his armour, as on the day when, disguised among the daughters of *Lycomedes,* he betrayed himself at the sight of a sword. His emotion is perceived by *Patroclus,* who draws a favourable omen from it, points out to *Achilles* where the Phrygian warriors are advancing, and solicits

---

* It will be observed, that the word Scene, in the following Ballets, does not always denote a change of *scenery,* but frequently only a change or addition of *characters.*

him to assist his allies. But the hero is presently checked
by the remembrance of the wrong done him by the
Greeks; he retraces his steps, inflamed to the highest
pitch of anger, peremptorily refuses his assistance, and
makes vows for the success of *Hector*. He lays down his
armour and resumes his lyre. He turns a deaf ear to the
entreaties of his friend, who represents in strong colours
the misfortunes consequent upon his inflexibility. But
Achilles is sensible only of his affront. Grief of *Patroclus!* He implores the hero's clemency, and comforts
him with the hope of Agamemnon's making him ample
reparation. *Achilles*, however, remains unmoved, and
entreats him not to intercede for his dastardly enemies.
A celestial symphony is heard. The sea divides, and
Thetis is seen wafted in a concha by sea Gods, and surrounded by *Nereides*, attending upon her. The mother
of *Achilles*, delighted with her son's inactivity, conceives
hopes of the non-fulfilment of the predictions respecting
him. She endeavours to strengthen his resolution and
induce him to return to Thessalia. *Achilles* and *Patroclus* express their joy at the arrival of the august Goddess. *Thetis* and her train emerge from the waves.
Achilles gives his mother an affectionate welcome, and
shows himself sensibly affected by the tokens of her love
and the vows she offers up for his happiness. *Thetis*
commands her train to entertain her son and beguile his
grief.

The scene changes, and clouds are seen descending
from all parts, wafting down *Smiles, Sports, Pleasures,*
and *Graces*, who, joining the sea nymphs and the women
of the suit of *Achilles*, form grottoes of coral and other
phenomena. *Thetis* and her son seat themselves upon
a throne just erected, and *Achilles* is presented with
crowns of laurel and roses, in token of homage. He views

with pleasure the dances and sports which the sea deities indulge themselves in, for his entertainment. Every thing is calculated to give him a relish for pleasure and a distaste of the dangers of war. When the dancing is over, *Thetis*, her son, and *Patroclus*, come down from their thrones. Before departing *Thetis* wishes to see her son in a disposition to return to his own states; but all her entreaties are of little avail to change his frame of mind. He prefers the pursuit of glory; the effects upon his mind of the delightful entertainments he has just beheld, are of short duration, and he avows his resolution of resuming arms when his injury is avenged.

Thetis is anxious about the fate of *Achilles*, and grieved that he maintains his resolution. During this scene *Patroclus*, fearing lest he should be persuaded by *Thetis*, departs hastily, as though to execute a project that seems to engross all his thoughts.

Thetis endeavours to appease her son, and entreats him to preserve his life. *Achilles*, sensible of her tenderness, expresses his gratitude. *Thetis* bids him farewell, and ascends to heaven with a view to his happiness. She is wafted up in a cloud and soon disappears. The *Smiles, Sports, Graces*, &c. fly up with her. Her numerous retinue plunge into the sea. *Achilles* bids his mother farewell, and withdraws to his tent, musing on his fate.

ACT II.

SCENE.—*Interior of the camp of the Thessalians. At one side is the tent of* Achilles.

ACHILLES appears absorbed in reverie. Full of the remembrance of his *Briseis*, he expresses his love and grief at her loss. He threatens with dreadful vengeance *Aga-*

memnon, the author of all his misfortunes. He cannot for one moment forget his affront, and feels a transport of rage. The Thessalian trumpets and the clamours of his soldiers are heard. *Achilles* stands amazed, unable to account for the noise. *Patroclus* comes in, acquaints him with the disasters of the Greeks, the triumph of *Hector*, and the rebellion of the Thessalians, who, tired of repose, wish either to march against the enemy or return to their country. *Achilles*, surprised, gives vent to his indignation, while *Patroclus* tries to excite his compassion in favour of the Greeks. *Achilles* puts him in mind of the outrage committed against him. As he is going forth to chastise the insolence of his soldiers, *Patroclus* stops him, and excuses them on the plea that they are animated by honour. He prays to the Gods that his friend may lead them to combat; but *Achilles* remains inflexible.

The soldiers enter in disorder, headed by *Automedon*. They complain of their inactivity, and show their ardent wish to be led to battle. The son of *Thetis* scarcely contains himself, and burns with desire to punish their rebellion. *Patroclus* endeavour to calm him; entreating him to yield to their wishes. *Achilles* restrains his impetuous temper, and commands his warriors to await with him the command of the Gods to encounter the Trojans ; but their minds continue in the same agitation, and grief preys upon their hearts. At last *Patroclus*, seeing his friend's resistance, snatches up a weapon, with an intent to stab himself, unless *Achilles* will comply with his request. *Achilles* withholds him, is moved, and promises compliance. *Patroclus* demands his armour, which is proof against all weapons, and the command of the army, to take vengeance on the enemy. *Achilles* yields reluctantly, and seems apprehensive from his friend's zeal. A general expression of joy. *Achilles* delivers his armour to *Patroclus,* and helps him to buckle it on. All give thanks to the immortal Gods for hearkening to their prayers. *Achilles* bids them return quickly after the victory they are about to gain over *Hector* and not increase his own sorrow. He bids *Automedon* drive up his car, which he causes *Patroclus* to ascend: the charioteer mounts beside him; and *Achilles* bids adieu to *Patroclus,* recommending to him moderation in victory. The army, preceded by the chariot, commence their march to the walls of Troy. The Thessalians, rejoicing in expectation of the combat, point to the hostile towers. Being departed, *Achilles* follows them with his eyes ; puts up prayers for the success of his friend ; then enters his tent.

ACT III.

THE stage represents the magnificent tent of *Agamemnon,* who appears in council, surrounded by the Grecian chiefs, profoundly affected by the misfortune consequent to their enterprise. Doubt and embarrassment prevail ; some propose another attempt against the Trojans, while a few advise to inquire the will of the Gods, and each to return to his country. At length, *Nestor,* rising, proposes to effect the return of *Achilles,* showing how necessary the valour of that hero is to insure success, and that the Oracle must be obeyed in order to become victorious over the Trojans. He adds, that the past should be forgotten ; and that, by atoning for the injury done to *Achilles,* that hero might be turned from his desire of revenge. Deep silence follows the oration of *Nestor,* every one being wrapt in reflection upon this proposition. *Calchas, Ulysses, Menelaus,* the two *Ajaxes, Diomedes, Phœnix, Merion,* and *Antilochus,* unanimously fix their eyes upon *Agamem-*

non, and await his decision with impatience ; he approves of the counsel of *Nestor*, and appears prepared to do any thing for the public good. As a proof of the change of his sentiments with respect to *Achilles*, he restores *Briseis*, whom he had detained from the hero. He sends away the damsel, accompanied by magnificent presents. Universal expressions of joy ; every one evincing his gratitude to the King upon the happy occasion. *Phœnix*, *Ulysses*, *Calchas*, and *Ajax Telamon* are deputed Ambassadors to *Achilles*. *Agamemnon* gives them instructions on the nature of their mission, and receives their protestations of fidelity. A warrior now enters, and announces that *Achilles* having listened to the entreaties of *Patroclus*, the latter was on his march against *Hector* and Troy. Expressions of joy, every one drawing a happy presage from the event ; hope animates every heart. *Calchas* beseeches them to invoke the propitious aid of the Gods. All obey ; and each, pouring out the contents of his cup, makes libations in honour of Jupiter. The embassy departs, and the remaining chiefs retire to await the happy result.

ACT IV.

Scene.—*An extensive prospect adorned by trees. The camp of* Achilles *appears at a distance on the left ; on the right a Statue of Jupiter is discovered.*

Calchas, *Ulysses*, *Ajax*, *Phœnix*, and their suit arrive. *Briseis* appears preceded by slaves, destined for *Achilles* : she is followed by warriors bearing presents of tripods, vases, armour, &c., intended for the hero ; *Briséis* evinces the pleasure she feels at being restored to the dwelling of her lover. *Calchas* prays Jupiter to prosper their undertaking, and to punish the Trojans. Approaching the statue of Jupiter, they all implore his assistance ; while *Briseis* appears to anticipate her tender reception.

Achilles, followed by warriors, enters from his tent ; he seems agitated by deep thought. He is discovered by the Greeks, who prepare to address him ; *Achilles,* recovered from his meditation, appears astonished at their presence. *Ulysses* advances to speak, but remembering the ancient hatred between them, his indignation returns ; he is on the point of drawing his sword, but is restrained by *Calchas* and *Briseis;* the former of whom prevails with him, from the reverence due to his character, and the latter calms him by the power of her love. *Ulysses* now endeavours to appologize, and joins with *Calchas* in persuading the hero, by the will of the Gods, and the welfare of Greece, to change his resolution, displaying at the same time their rich presents. *Briseis* is now brought forward and led towards him, accompanied by more gifts. *Achilles,* notwithstanding, remains inexorable ; he turns a deaf ear to the prayers of the Greeks, and even resists the tears of *Briseis,* who embraces his knees ; he lifts up the latter, but with eyes averted from her. She continues to give expression to her love and grief, representing to the hero what glory awaits his return. The Grecian chiefs remind him of the atonement made by *Agamemnon;* but vengeance alone seems to inspire the son of *Thetis.* *Calchas,* advancing, denounces celestial wrath against him, and, in the style of prophecy, menaces him with every misfortune, should he continue insensible to the woes of Greece.

This solemn warning seems to move *Achilles;* he becomes agitated, and sinister presentiments appear already to have taken possession of his breast. This is remarked by every one present, who now expect a happy change : a movement is made to induce him to decide favourably, and prayers are repeated. But *Achilles,* resuming the haughtiness of his ungovernable character, exhibits all his former rancour, and refuses his aid, while the Ambassadors, hopeless of success, abandon him to the wrath of the Gods. At this conjuncture, as they are on the point of departing, *Automedon* arrives in despair, bringing news of the defeat of the *Thessalians*, and the death of *Patroclus*. Universal consternation! *Achilles* is plunged into an agony of grief. His friend being dead, life becomes insupportable to him; he rushes upon his sword with the intention of slaying himself; he is, however, instantly prevented and disarmed; but he conjures his friends to put him out of his misery. Despair now takes full possession of him; he raves deliriously, and refuses every attempt that is made to console him. The regions of eternal darkness appear opening to his disturbed fancy; the shade of *Patroclus* seems advancing towards him, weeping and pointing to the mortal wound; he groans, and commands *Achilles* to fly to the combat and revenge his death. The latter swears to sacrifice *Hector* to appease his ghost. The hero now gradually regains his spirits. The Grecian chiefs applaud his resolution, and implore the Gods to crown him with victory. *Achilles* now no longer hesitates, no longer refuses; he furiously seizes a sword, gives the signal to his companions in arms, and rushes forth at the head of them, breathing revenge and death to the slayer of his friend. Prayers follow him for his success *.

---

* In the Iliad, *Achilles*, before going to battle, waits until *Vulcan* has forged his arms; and Homer cannot be too much praised for the method in which he has profited of this circumstance by offering a sublime piece of poetry to the reader, and raising his curiosity by a description of interesting events. But it appears to me, that the manner in which *Achilles* proceeds in the opera of M. Barincou, is far more suitable to the rapidity of dramatic action; besides, it presents a true picture of

ACT V.

THE scene represents the adjacent part of mount Ida, which appears in the distance. The Trojan army is routed. The growling of a tempest is heard, and lightning illumines the gloom. Companies of soldiers, supposing they are still pursued by the sword of *Achilles* aided by celestial wrath, are seen traversing the mountain in disorder. The storm now relaxes ; the clouds roll off, and light appears. The Grecian trumpets rally their victorious army and proclaim their victory. They enter and arrange themselves at the foot of the mountain. *Agamemnon* and *Achilles* arrive, accompanied by the Grecian princes. The King acknowledges his injustice, for which, however, he has just atoned by contributing to the late victory. *Achilles* appears fully satisfied and reconciled. The services of *Agamemnon* have calmed every feeling of resentment. Notwithstanding the joy at having revenged his friend, *Achilles* cannot recover from the sorrow he feels at his own loss ; *Hector's* death cannot remove the rankling dart of grief in his bosom ; *Patroclus* is ever before his eyes. All partake in his sufferings ; and the hero expresses a wish that his friend should receive the last honours due to his valour ; upon which *Agamemnon* orders preparations to be made for celebrating the funeral ceremonies. A tomb is quickly erected, constructed of the spoils of the vanquished. Every one crowds around this monument to do homage to the memory of the warrior, placing upon it coronets of laurel and garlands of cypress ; *Achilles* himself deposits a laurel crown ; and the rites are thus completed.

---

the impetuosity of that hero, and the spectator does not grow inattentive by delay.

During the funeral hymn, *Achilles*, his face bathed in tears, bends over the tomb of his beloved friend, strewing cypress and evincing symptoms of the deepest anguish ; then swears again to satiate his revenge upon the Trojans. After this melancholy scene, he sinks into a trance of grief upon the trophied monument, embracing the urn that contains the ashes of the valiant warrior.

Agamemnon and *Calchas* arouse *Achilles*, and recall him to himself. *Calchas* assures him of the immortal happiness of his friend, and announces the arrival of *Thetis*. Celestial music is heard spreading a charm over the whole scene, and reviving every heart. The Goddess appears accompanied by *Briseis*. The immortal mother, deeply affected at her son's misfortune, comes to administer consolation, and to restore his beloved *Briseis*. The lovers evince marks of mutual affection. The heart of *Achilles* becomes cheerful, and he thanks his mother for her care. The Greeks invoke the Gods to crown their efforts with success, while *Agamemnon* commands that the presence of *Thetis* and the glory of *Achilles* should be appropriately celebrated. The princes seat themselves in state, and preside over the games and dances. By order of *Thetis*, the *Cyclops* are now introduced, bearing the magnificent armour forged by *Vulcan ;* they advance towards *Achilles* and present the heavenly gift ; the hero is wrapt in admiration, and expresses his deep sense of gratitude to his august mother, promising to make the best use of them. A *Divertissement* follows, after which the Ballet terminates with a general and pictorial grouping.

HERMANN AND LISBETH.

VILLAGE BALLET.   *(BALLET VILLAGEOIS.)*

IN TWO ACTS.

ARGUMENT.

CAPTAIN HERMANN, son of the *Baron de Botzen,* is deeply enamoured of the beautiful *Lisbeth,* a young villager, whose father, *Scharff,* an old veteran, is now become a rich farmer.   The young officer determines to disguise himself as a peasant, in order more easily to procure interviews with her he loves, and to secure unbiassed affection, by laying aside the signs of his rank.   The design succeeding, he gains the affections of *Lisbeth ;* and the only obstacle to their union is, the nephew of the Burgomaster, a person enjoying a title.   In the heat of his affection, the Captain forgets the importance of his rival ; besides which the father and mother of *Lisbeth* are determined to marry their daughter to the above-mentioned personage, whose name is *Tunder,* a simple and ridiculous character.   Preparations are making for the wedding, which is on the point of being celebrated. The two lovers are in despair, and know not how to proceed ; at length, blinded by affection, they decide on flight.   The nephew of the Burgomaster becomes acquainted with their intentions, of which he informs his uncle and the parents of *Lisbeth ;* and they are followed and taken.   The *Baron de Botzen,* coming by chance to the dwelling of *Scharff,* learns the whole affair ; he severely reproaches his son with his wild and extravagant conduct, while the parents of *Lisbeth,* refusing to pardon her, remain irreconcilable.   The villagers, hearing of the adventure, assemble at the scene, and soon join in demanding forgiveness for the young delinquents.   At length, the anger of the two fathers being somewhat allayed, they satisfy the general desire, by granting their pardon to the lovers.   The *Baron,* forgetting pride and prejudice, consents to bestow his son upon *Lisbeth,* thus uniting himself to the family of the worthy *Scharff.*   Joy and congratulation become universal. The Burgomaster and his nephew, upon the representation of the *Baron,* finding that *Lisbeth* would never have married *Tunder,* excepting by force, submit to a compromise.

CHARACTERS.

THE BARON DE BOTZEN.

CAPTAIN HERMANN, *his son; in love with Lisbeth.*

SCHARFF, *a veteran soldier; now a rich farmer.*

DAME WOLF, *his wife.*

LISBETH, *daughter of Scharff, and in love with Hermann.*

ROFF, *a Burgomaster.*

TUNDER, *his nephew; rival of Hermann.*

FRANCK, *Hermann's servant.*

Village lads and lasses; Tyrolese; Guards, and attendants on the Baron.

The scene passes in Germany, on the estate of Baron de Botzen, *near the Tyrol.*

ACT I.

The Scene represents a village. In the distance a hill is seen, at the foot of which stands the Burgomaster's house. On the right is the dwelling of Scharff. Trees are promiscuously scattered over the prospect.

SCENE I.—At the rising of the curtain a storm is heard, during which two men appear enveloped in long cloaks;

having passed over the scene, they are at length driven by the inclemency of the weather to seek shelter, and retire.

SCENE II.—The storm ceases, and the sky becomes clear ; the sun shining forth, the whole landscape rejoices in his rays. Shepherds leaving their huts on the hill, call, by the sound of their pipes, their companions to labour; the summons is answered by other pipes, and villagers enter, bearing their rustic tools ; and, displaying health and cheerfulness in their countenances, they prepare to go into the fields, indulging before they depart in a rural dance.

SCENE III.—*Franck* appears cautiously advancing, as unwilling to discover himself; observing no one near, he calls his master, assuring him that there is no danger. *Hermann* expresses his joy at the sight of *Lisbeth's* dwelling. *Franck* declares his wish to be made acquainted with his master's designs; the latter confides the secret to his servant, telling him, the motive of his present disguise is to secure more easily the affections of the beautiful young villager, *Lisbeth*. *Franck* evinces great surprise ; but his master engages him to acquaint no person with his intentions, and to obey in whatever is commanded him. The servant assures the Captain of unshaken fidelity. The hour of appointment arriving, *Hermann* and *Franck* lay aside their cloaks, and appear in the habits of peasants ; the Captain signs *Franck* to retire, and wait for his orders.

SCENE IV.—*Captain Hermann* now advances and fixes his eyes upon a balcony, in which he has before beheld his pretty *Lisbeth,* who not appearing, he seems anxious and impatient. A noise is heard, and the door of the Burgomaster's house is opened; while *Hermann,* disappointed at the unlucky circumstance, immediately conceals himself in a tree, to observe what is passing.

Scene V.—*Tunder* enters from his uncle's house. He wishes, no doubt, agreeably to surprise *Lisbeth*, by presenting her with a bouquet of flowers, which he carries carefully in his hand ; she, however, does not appear; he calls her several times, and grows angry at her absence. At length, supposing it is her beloved *Hermann*, she appears, but soon evinces her disappointment on seeing *Tunder*. *Hermann*, having witnessed this scene, contrives to discover himself to *Lisbeth ;* and looks of love and delight are quickly exchanged between them. *Tunder*, supposing they are meant for him, rejoices in the happy omens, and, taking advantage of such a favourable opportunity, encourages himself to declare his passion, and becomes a laughing-stock to his rival *Hermann*. He entreats *Lisbeth* to accept of his flowers, but she refuses ; he threatens to throw them at her, but she prevents him. Her lover having motioned her to descend, she tells *Tunder* she will come down to accept his present ; upon which pleasure is visible on the countenances of both the rivals, and *Tunder* exults in his triumph. *Lisbeth* enters from the house, and *Tunder* immediately throws himself at her feet and presents the flowers ; she accepts them, but at the same time, unperceived, presents her hand to *Hermann*, who covers it with kisses; while the simple *Tunder* becomes the ridicule of both the lovers. He proceeds even to greater lengths, expressing a sort of grotesque triumph ; while the bouquet gives rise to various and beautiful groupings and mutual attitudes between the enamoured pair.

Dame Wolf comes into the balcony, and discovers the whole intrigue ; she at first laughs, but, resuming a serious air, she prepares to surprise the harmonious trio.

Scene VI.—The noise made by *Dame Wolf* opening the door disturbs the lovers ; she enters, and scolds *Lisbeth* for her intriguing behaviour with *Hermann,* who entreats for pardon, while *Tunder* joins with the old lady in threatening and accusing them both. The Dame orders her daughter to enter the house, she obeys; but on going casts a significant glance at *Hermann.* Her mother then forbids both the rivals ever again to come near her house ; and they attempting to intercede for themselves, she shuts the door in their faces.

SCENE VII.—*Hermann* evinces gloom and disappointment ; he seems meditating on the consequences of the adventure, and appears unable to leave the dwelling of his love. *Tunder,* on the other hand, at once indignant at such treatment and jealous of his rival, seems forming projects of revenge. The presence of the Captain preventing him from executing his intentions, he wishes to get rid of him. At length, finding him not disposed to go, and weary of waiting, he calls to him and makes a sign, as if desiring his absence ; *Hermann,* deeply engaged in his own reflections, pays no attention to his signal. *Tunder,* supposing this silence to be intended as a mark of contempt, approaches *Hermann,* and taking his hand, shakes it most violently, in order to arouse his attention, while endeavouring to affright him by the tragi-comicality of his anger. *Hermann* is surprised at such liberties, but excuses them, and begs that he may not be interrupted. *Tunder,* mistaking this moderation for fear, boldly demands why he still continues to stay in a place which he has been desired to quit. *Hermann,* darting a threatening look at him, pushes him away ; *Tunder* returns to the attack in great anger ; the Captain, unable longer to restrain his wrath, takes him by the arm, and twirls him off to some distance. *Tunder* again returns to the attack, when the Captain seizes and throws him to the ground. *Tunder,* not expecting

such usage, becomes affrighted ; *Hermann* making a certain sign, the other rises and runs away, seemingly to seek
means of revenge, and to relate the whole affair to his uncle.

Scene VIII.—*Hermann* now calls his man, and informs
him of the óbstacles that have arisen to cross his intentions. Both appear determined to bring the adventure
to a more happy conclusion, and retire.

Scene IX.—The Burgomaster enters, accompanied by
his nephew, and followed by a troop of guards. *Tunder*
has related the whole affair to his uncle, and now returns
prepared to take revenge upon the supposed peasant; for
whom, after searching in vain, they are compelled to post-
pone the intended arrest ; not, however, without leaving
a watch to prevent his escape. *Tunder*, in the mean time,
takes the opportunity of reminding his uncle of the promise he had made to demand for him the hand of *Lisbeth*,
and expresses an impatient desire to have it realised.
Roff promises to keep his word and secure happiness to
his nephew. He desires him to go and change his dress,
which has suffered in the scuffle ; and that afterwards he
will present him to the parents of *Lisbeth*. *Tunder*, overjoyed at this information, leaps upon his uncle's neck, and
they both enter the house, the guards accompanying them
with a laughable air of severity.

ACT II.

*The stage represents the interior of Scharff's farm. In
the distance is discovered a shaded walk, enclosed by a
wall with a gate. On one side a part of the house of
the Burgomaster is perceived.*

Scene I.—A troop of peasantry enter dancing, as

they return from labour. *Roff* and his nephew appear habited for the ceremony. *Scharff* makes a sign to his people, and they retire.

Scene II.—After compliments being exchanged, the farmer inquires the reason of the Burgomaster's visit. The latter replies, that his nephew being deeply enamoured of *Scharff's* daughter, he is come to ask her in marriage. The former and his Dame appear to consent to the proposition ; while the Burgomaster boasts of his nephew's birth and fortune. The father and uncle appear to consult further upon the affair; when the former, representing that his daughter is disengaged, there can be no obstacle to the match, requiring, however, to retire for the purpose of considering on the affair, and of acquainting *Lisbeth* with their intentions ; *Roff* immediately consents to this, while *Tunder* exhibits an expectation of success.

Scene III.—*Roff* partakes in the triumph of his nephew, expressing his satisfaction at seeing the prosperous progress of *Tunder's* designs. During this scene *Hermann* is perceived endeavouring to gain admission to *Lisbeth's* house, in order to acquaint her with his projects ; he employs every precaution to prevent discovery. Finding the gate of the walk open, he immediately enters. He already understands the motive of the Burgomaster's visit, and that *Scharff* has consented to the propositions in favour of *Tunder ;* he is accordingly greatly disappointed, appears very gloomy, and conceals himself behind a projection to overhear what is passing.

Scene IV.—The farmer enters, conducting his daughter, who is followed by her mother. But how great is the surprise evinced by *Lisbeth* on beholding her intended husband ! Her parents informing her of their design, express their entire approval of the expected union.

Lisbeth appears in great trouble and agitation. Her emotion is remarked, and every one is desirous to know the cause of it, but she is unable to give an answer ; she is urged to satisfy their inquiries, but eludes them by giving an uncertain reply. At this moment she perceives that _Hermann_ witnesses her distressing situation. He consoles and encourages her by his gestures. She is on the point of giving a decided refusal to the proposed match, but is deterred by the motions of her lover, who would inspire her with hopes of defeating the projects of _Roff_ by other means. _Tunder_ and the Burgomaster are greatly disconcerted at the conduct of _Lisbeth._ _Scharff_ and his wife endeavour to assure them that the emotion of _Lisbeth_ must be attributed to the approaching separation from her parents ; upon this assertion the nephew and uncle appear satisfied. _Lisbeth,_ wishing to prepare for her approaching change, demands permission and retires ; as she is going, she casts a significant glance of love and hope at _Hermann,_ who, by gestures, bids her be confident of success.

Scene V.—_Scharff, Dame Wolf,_ the Burgomaster and _Tunder,_ consult upon the preparations for the wedding, which they fix for the next day; satisfied with their projects, each takes his leave and retires ; during this, _Hermann_ evinces marks of deep concern.

Scene VI.—_Hermann_ now quits his concealment and comes forward ; he appears undecided as to what means he should employ to counteract the designs of his rival. At length, after some consideration, he is resolved to carry off _Lisbeth,_ and to be united to her.

Scene VII.—_Lisbeth_ enters and flies into the arms of _Hermann,_ who, though crossed in his career, swears that nothing shall now separate them. They express mutual

sentiments of unalterable affection; but the recollection
of the intended marriage destroys their moments of
delight, and they appear dejected.

SCENE VIII.—*Tunder* enters; he brings certain orders
from his uncle to *Scharff*. Scarcely has he passed the gate,
when he perceives the two lovers supported in each other's
arms; he becomes motionless with astonishment. Having
recovered himself, rage and jealousy take entire possession
of his heart. He is ready to rush upon them, but recollecting himself, he dares not, and seems determined to
await the sequel of this interview ; fearing to be observed,
he creeps into the hollow of a tree, and so hides himself.
From time to time he puts his head out to spy what is
going forward ; but whenever the Captain displays a
gesture of menace, supposing it relates to himself, he
immediately draws back. *Hermann* proposes flight to
Lisbeth, and a secret marriage ; but the latter fearing
such an attempt, she refuses with tears in her eyes, while
Hermann laments his unhappy fate. *Tunder* exhibits the
most grotesque gesticulations ; he will hear no more ; and
leaving the tree, runs to his uncle to inform him of the intended flight; vowing vengeance as he retires.

SCENE IX.—*Hermann* employs every means of per-
suasion to induce his mistress to follow him ; but still she
dares not consent to his proposal ; upon which *Hermann*
reproaches her with indifference, and as being the cause
of his misfortune. *Lisbeth* weeps, wavers, and at last
yields to the desire of her lover. *Hermann*, transported
with joy, now discovers his real rank in life, and on his
knees he swears eternal fidelity to her. *Lisbeth*, struck with
astonishment, scarcely believes what she hears ; and supposing the Captain would deceive her, she reproaches him
with inconstancy ; *Hermann* protests the truth of what he

advances, and the purity of his intentions; but she still evinces great anxiety and agitation, while *Hermann* is deeply affected by her unbelief.

Scene X.—*Franck,* who has never neglected the interest of his master, enters hastily to announce the arrival of the Baron, who, returning from the chase, has fixed upon this farm as a place of repose; the consternation is general; in the mean time *Franck* assures *Lisbeth* of the honourable intentions of his master. *Lisbeth* falls into the arms of *Hermann,* who tells her they must now depart instantly; that it must be done quietly and secretly, to avoid the anger of their parents; *Lisbeth* gives herself up to the guidance of her lover; and all three hasten away.

Scene XI.—But scarcely have they began their flight, when they are stopped by *Tunder,* accompanied with a troop of peasantry armed with cudgels. The Captain is immediately attacked, but he, snatching a stick from the hands of the affrighted *Tunder,* and aided by *Franck,* makes so vigorous a resistance, that his opponents betake themselves to flight. *Hermann* then attends to the distressing situation of *Lisbeth,* endeavouring to encourage and console her. As they are about to continue their journey the Burgomaster is discovered, followed by a troop of his guards.

Scene XII.—He causes the Captain to be arrested; the latter demands an explanation, and surprises every one present by his spirited conduct. The Burgomaster, however, is inexorable, and *Tunder* increasing his anger against his rival, desires instant revenge. The sound of a horn is heard, announcing the arrival of the Baron, while *Hermann* and *Lisbeth,* without making further resistance, wait the result in silence.

Scene XIII.—The Baron enters, accompanied by

Scharff and his wife; but what is their surprise on beholding the lovers fall on their knees before the Baron.
Hermann's rank is now discovered; and the astonishment
is universal.   The report spreading, a number of villagers
assemble to witness the event, and every one waits respectfully for the decision of the Baron.   The latter severely
reprimands the conduct of his son, and finally disowns
him; while *Lisbeth* vainly strives to regain the affections
of her parents; and the two lovers are accordingly deeply
dejected. In the mean time, *Tunder* and his uncle tremble
for the consequence of their treatment of the Baron's son.
At length, the father of *Hermann*, moved by the repentant
grief of his son, and the distress of *Lisbeth*, joined to the
prayers of all present in their favour, is resolved to pardon
and forget the offence, wishing also to avoid general
scandal by settling the whole amicably.   *Lisbeth's* parents
readily consent to so advantageous a match.   All express
their joy and gratitude, and the Baron receives the
homage of his vassals; he embraces his children, and
evinces his satisfaction at being allied to the family of the
brave and respectable *Scharff;* while the delight of the
lovers is extreme.   The Burgomaster and his nephew
excuse themselves to *Hermann*, who is not long in granting
pardon.   The Baron orders the celebration of the happy
union to begin, and all withdraw to make the necessary
preparations.

SCENE XIV.—The stage represents the village green,
where sports and frolics usually take place.   The Baron's
mansion appears in the distance. Peasants enter, and raise
a seat of state adorned with flowers, and ornament every
place with garlands.   They construct also a swing and a
balance, and arrange tables for the feast.   The Baron
now appears, accompanied by the bride and bridegroom,

Scharff, his wife, the Burgomaster, and *Tunder ;* he is conducted to his seat, and presides at the ceremonies. Universal joy and gaiety reign around ; sports and dances now begin ; *Hermann* and *Lisbeth*, at the general request, mingle with the dancers. Every one seems by his cheerfulness to evince his attachment to the Baron. The *Divertissement* being concluded, the Baron rises and expresses to his tenantry the happiness he feels at the joyful event. A general group is formed, conveying an idea of the sentiments with which all are inspired, and terminating the Ballet.

HIPPOLYTUS.

A GRAND PANTOMIMICAL BALLET,

IN FIVE ACTS.

ARGUMENT.

THIS Ballet was founded upon what has reached us of Euripides, upon Seneca, and more particularly upon the *Phèdre* of Racine. The plot has given me great trouble in forming, from the necessity of explaining that part of the fable which precedes the action, and which cannot be related or expressed by gesture.—BOURDEAUX, 1814.

In the first Act, therefore, I have supposed the incident of a dream, which, by representing all that is necessary for unfolding the subject, enables the spectator easily to comprehend the whole of the following intrigue. Before my performance, no one had attempted a Ballet upon this subject; no Ballet-master, I believe, has yet adapted it to his purposes in any shape.

CHARACTERS.

THESEUS, *Son of Egeus, King of Athens. He is returning into his Kingdom, after having vanquished the tyrant, who detained him long a prisoner for having assisted his friend Pyrithous, the companion of his labours.*

PHÆDRA, *wife of Theseus, and daughter of Minos and Pasiphæ; in love with Hippolytus.*

HIPPOLYTUS, *Son of Theseus and Antiope, Queen of the Amazons; in love with Aricia.*

Aricia, *a princess of the blood-royal of Athens; the last survivor of her family; now a prisoner at Theseus' Court, and beloved by Hippolytus.*

Theramenes, *Governor of Hippolytus.*

Oenone, *Nurse and Confidant of Phædra.*

Ismena, *confidential attendant on Aricia.*

Neptune; *Esculapius; the Winds; Hunters attending Hippolytus; Huntresses attending Aricia; Women attending Phædra; Guards and Soldiers of Theseus; Princes and Princesses of the Court; Priests of Diana; Priests and Priestesses; the People.*

CHARACTERS OF THE DREAM.

Venus.

Love.

Phædra.

Hippolytus.

Theseus.

Princes and Princesses of the Court.

The Scene lies at Threzene, a town of Peloponnessus.

ACT I.

A forest; mountains are seen in the distance, and several clusters of trees are dispersed over the scene. On the right appears the statue of Diana, and further on a green bank.

Hunters in the train of *Hippolytus* are discovered on the mountains. Having spread themselves over the scene they take various paths, and prepare for the pursuit. Hope and joy animate them to the chase, they brandish their javelins, while the air re-echoes with the sound of their instruments, until they disappear.

Hippolytus enters, he seeks his beloved, he has not yet beheld his *Aricia*. Exhausted by the fatigues of the chase, and a fruitless search for his love, he sinks down upon a bank. In a short time sleep takes possession of his senses; his imagination is, however, disturbed by a terrible dream.

THE DREAM.

The back scene changes, and discovers a charming rural prospect. The remaining parts of the stage with the front scenes are darkened, consequently the representation of the dream becomes more brilliant. *Venus* and *Cupid*, borne through the air, in a chariot drawn by swans, descend. Rage inspires the breast of the Goddess, she breathes nothing but revenge, and menaces by her gestures. Her son inquires what are her designs: she reminds him of the hatred she bears the house of *Phœdra*, and declares her intention of destroying even *Phœdra* herself; she requires of him to assist in her projects, by wounding her victim. *Phœdra* arrives accompanied by her consort; they are attended by a part of the court. *Venus* directs the attention of her son to them; he promises obedience to her commands, and each withdraws to some distance.

Theseus and *Phœdra* repose themselves beneath the umbrageous shade; they exchange mutual marks of affection. *Venus* causes *Cupid* to approach, and incites him to strike *Phœdra* with love for *Hippolytus*. The malicious God replies with a smile. He draws from his quiver one of his deadliest darts, and menaces *Hippolytus*, who is seen ranging through the forest and hurling his javelin at the timid inhabitants.

Theseus, obliged to depart, reluctantly takes leave of his Queen, who shares deeply in his sorrows, and conjures him to hasten his return.

The implacable *Venus,* seizing this opportunity of revenge, makes a sign to her son, who levels a dart, and *Phædra* is wounded. Whence the pain with which she is seized? In vain does she endeavour to discover the cause; she laments her fate, and implores for aid ; her attendants endeavour to administer relief; *Venus* causes *Hippolytus* to approach, and desires him to console *Phædra,* and to alleviate the sorrow she feels at the absence of his father ; the young Prince obeys and presents himself before her. *Phædra* evinces great emotion! The society of *Hippolytus* suspends her grief: joy succeeds to woe; and she seems revived and happy. It is *Hippolytus* who causes this change ; he is the author of the charm; and she cannot exist without him. He redoubles his attention, and assures her of his father's love; but *Phædra* requires something more than such an assurance. Being now recovered, she thinks both on the duty she owes to the father, and on what may be the sentiments of the son ; obstacles insurmountable! Pleasure is already fled, and woe has taken her place. *Hippolytus* knows not what to conclude from her deportment. He tries to tranquillize her; but *Phædra,* unable longer to resist the torments of her passion, and the power of *Venus,* confesses her love to *Hippolytus;* he recoils with horror and remains motionless with astonishment. The daughter of *Minos* tries to allure him by prayers, caresses, and tears ; but nothing can shake the virtue of the young *Hippolytus.* He essays to break from her, while she employs every art to detain him ; but her strength failing, she beholds him hastening from her for ever.

Venus, triumphing in success, then offers herself to the eyes of the wretched Queen. *Phædra,* recognising the divinity, flies to her and throws herself at her feet, imploring mercy. She next addresses herself to *Love,* but in vain. The two powers, deaf to her prayers, and rejoicing in her pain, abandon her to her fate, and ascend towards the skies. This last trial convinces *Phædra* that her enemy is implacable. Every hope forsakes her, she becomes distracted, and unable to support the weight of her sufferings, till oppressed by wrath divine, she falls and expires. The scene disappears, and the stage resumes its former aspect.

Hippolytus, awakened by the terrible conclusion of the dream, shudders with the impression it has produced; he is wrapt in the recollection of it, and dreads the future consequences: he revives a little, but again falls into a deep reverie. The echoing of distant horns is heard; *Hippolytus* is aroused, and recognizes the signal of the arrival of *Aricia;* his gloomy thoughts are dissipated, and pleasure takes possession of his heart. His love appears upon the mountain side, and he flies to meet her. *Aricia* is attended by huntresses, she presents her lover with the game taken in the chase. They express to each other their mutual flame, while their companions partake in their delight. *Hippolytus,* at the height of his wishes, receives an oath of fidelity from his affectionate *Aricia.* Preparations are now made for a fête in honour of their patroness. Offerings are made to Diana, and each takes a part in the dances and sports. After the celebration, *Hippolytus* commands to depart to the city.

ACT II.

The interior of a magnificent Temple dedicated to the worship of Venus. In the centre appears a statue of the Goddess, before which an altar is raised.

THE adorers of *Venus* enter dancing, some bearing baskets of flowers, others garlands, coronets, &c. Sacrifices are made to the divinity; and dancing accompanies religious ceremonies.

Phædra now enters, attended by *Oenone*. She slowly approaches, and prostrates herself before the statue. Every one follows her example; a basket of offerings is then given to *Oenone*, who receives it and presents it to her mistress, who places it upon the altar. The sufferings caused by a violent and unfortunate passion appear deeply marked upon the features of *Phædra;* her deportment evinces the dreadful state to which she is reduced. She invokes the Goddess, and implores aid in her distress. After the gifts are offered, the dances are renewed. *Oenone* has closely observed her mistress; greatly surprised, and sensibly affected at the pain she appears to suffer, she desires to know the cause. The amusements are now suspended, and *Phædra* motions all to retire but *Oenone*. (During the preceding ceremonies, *Phædra* commands *Oenone* with a mysterious air to seek for *Hippolytus*, to whom she would speak; her confidant obeys, and after some minutes returns.)

The looks and gestures of *Phædra* express the disturbed state of her heart; *Oenone* observes it with astonishment, and wishing to interest herself in the fate of her mistress, demands the cause. The distress of *Phædra* increases, she shudders at the idea of disclosing her griefs. *Oenone* presses her with prayers and tears to reply. *Phædra* is unable longer to resist these importunities, and the declaration of her abominable passion escapes her bosom. The name of *Hippolytus* and the vengeance of *Venus* make so terrible an impression upon *Oenone*, that scarcely can she believe what *Phædra* has avowed. The Queen, overwhelmed by woe, implores the Gods to annihilate her.

Her deplorable situation greatly affects the sympathetic *Oenone*, who endeavours to raise her drooping spirits and to inspire consolation by directing her to confide in the goodness of the Gods. *Phædra* throws herself at the feet of *Venus* and implores her pity; *Oenone* joins in the prayer. The woe of *Phædra* appears to augment, and *Oenone* is in despair. At length both are resolved to confess every thing to *Hippolytus,* and to plead the death of his father (a report of which is already in circulation) as an excuse for the Queen. *Oenone* flatters *Phædra* with a happy result.

They are interrupted by the arrival of *Hippolytus,* who comes in obedience to the Queen's command. *Phædra* is agitated at his approach, while *Oenone* tries to support her. The place which *Phædra* has chosen for the interview awakens in *Hippolytus* a melancholy remembrance of his dream, which seems to have presaged some misfortune. Banishing, however, these gloomy ideas, he respectfully approaches *Phædra* to know her pleasure. She receives him graciously, but at the same time betrays unusual emotions of pleasure, caused by his presence. Grief seems to have given place to hope and joy. She at length informs *Hippolytus* that she has dedicated this temple to the most amiable of the deities, whose favours are so dear to mankind, who causes happiness, and to whose empire all should submit. The son of Antiope shows some surprise. *Phædra* continues, that as he was made to love, he should prefer this worship to every

other, desiring him to devote himself entirely to the
service of the Goddess of Cythera. She feels her heart
palpitate while waiting the reply of *Hippolytus.* *Oenone*
incites and applauds her. *Hippolytus* blushes at the
words addressed to him, and appears agitated. Is the
dreadful dream about to be realised? He evinces surprise and embarrassment. *Phædra* would induce him
to sacrifice to the Goddess; but the severity of his education, and the sobriety of his manners will not permit him;
and beholding the resemblance that exists between the
dream and his present situation, he entreats permission
to withdraw. *Phædra* detains him, while her looks and
behaviour begin to unveil the secret of her heart. *Hippolytus* dreads the consequence of what he sees, and is
astonished at the deportment of *Phædra,* who, incapable
of containing her transports, and emboldened by *Oenone,*
declares to the son of *Theseus* her unlawful love for him.
This avowal strikes *Hippolytus* motionless; recovering from
his stupor, the first feeling he evinces is that of horror: his
dream was but too true an image of the dreadful reality.
The offence against nature and his father fills him with
indignation. *Phædra,* a prey to her destructive passion,
endeavours to calm *Hippolytus,* and to extort his pity for
her fate. But he, unwilling to offer violence to the wife
of his father, and fearing to be overcome by her entreaties,
is about to leave her presence, but is prevented by *Phædra*
and *Oenone.* Terrible is now the situation of *Hippolytus!*
The Queen and her confidant essay by prayers to soften
him, but he is immoveable, and threatens them with the
wrath of heaven. *Phædra,* forgetting her rank, throws
herself at his feet, entreats his regard, paints the grief
that destroys her, the hatred of *Venus,* and the death
that awaits his cruel refusal. *Hippolytus* obliges her to
rise from her abject position, then repulses her, and is

flying from her, but is again detained by *Phædra*, who demands the punishment due to her crimes, since he will not listen to her love. In vain does *Oenone* try to bend the young Prince; his virtue remains unshaken. At length the consort of *Theseus*, lost to every hope, and transported at once by love and rage, rushes upon *Hippolytus*, seizes his sword, and is on the point of stabbing herself, when *Oenone* employs every effort to disarm her, and then drags her out, lamenting her own error and the insensibility of *Hippolytus*. The latter, filled with fear and consternation, implores the assistance of the Gods, and, confiding in their protection, hastens from a place so fatal, and goes to prevent greater misfortunes.

ACT III.

Scene.—*The Palace of Theseus; on the right appears a statue of Neptune, raised by that hero in gratitude.*

Aricia enters, attended by *Ismena;* she awaits with impatience the approach of her lover. Her faithful attendant endeavours to remove every doubt. *Hippolytus* enters haggard and pale, nor can the pleasure of beholding his mistress restore peace to his mind. She perceives his situation and demands the cause. He tries to dissimulate by answering dubiously. Suspicion seizes *Aricia*, and she entreats *Hippolytus* to conceal nothing from her; but he begs her not to require of him a confession painful to both. The inquietude of *Aricia* increases, and she implores to be allowed to share in the pains of her lover. The latter endeavours to avoid an answer; but the tender solicitations of *Aricia*, and the proofs of her affection, at length obtain an explanation, and he informs her of the unhappy passion that possesses the breast of *Phædra*.

Aricia is astonished; and the consternation is equal on both sides. They are alarmed at what may ensue: their enemy is powerful; and the fury of her passion may set no bounds to revenge.

The son of *Theseus* is resolved to quit Threzene, and communicates his determination to *Aricia*, entreating her to accompany him; this being the only method to avoid both the love and hatred of *Phœdra*. *Aricia* hesitates, modesty will not permit her to accept of *Hippolytus* such an invitation; but he assuring her of safety and protection, dissipates her fears and expresses to her the transport and delight he shall experience in being united to her by sacred ties. *Aricia* consents, and both swear eternal fidelity, and implore the protection of the Gods.

During this scene, *Oenone* appears in a distant part of the palace; she perceives the two lovers, and is witness of their tenderness. Her surprise increases on discovering her mistress's favoured rival, and she flies to inform *Phœdra*.

Theramenes enters to announce the unexpected arrival of *Theseus*. The two lovers express their joy at this happy news; hoping now, for a fortunate result. *Hippolytus* causes *Aricia* to withdraw, promising to endeavour to prevail upon his father to consent to their union.

Theseus appears; he is followed by warriors and a part of his court; on beholding again his family and his people, the King rejoices. His son approaches to embrace his knees, he raises him, and presses him to his heart; while the young Prince exhibits traits of reverence and love.

Theseus now expresses his surprise at the absence of the Queen. He demands her of his son, who replies, he knows not where she stays. The distress and agitation with which *Hippolytus* answers, is remarked by his father, who desires to know the cause. The Prince's silence raises his suspicion; and he commands *Theramenes* to go and announce to the Queen his arrival. *Hippolytus* evinces embarrassment and dread. The Queen enters, accompanied by *Oenone;* sadness is spread over all her features. *Theseus* is surprised at the languor and melancholy of *Phædra*. He hastens to her, declaring the joy he feels at beholding her, demanding at the same time to be informed of the cause of her grief; she replies with sighs, her agitation increases, and *Theseus* presses her to reply. *Oenone* too encourages her to declare it, but still she refuses; *Theseus*, impatient of suspense, at length obliges her to answer. *Phædra*, transported with hatred to her rival and to *Hippolytus*, and determined to rescue her character from suspicion in presence of the King, accuses *Hippolytus* of her own crime. *Oenone* produces the sword left in her possession, adding, that it was thus he had threatened her refusal to comply. *Theseus* is struck with amazement, and *Hippolytus* becomes motionless. *Phædra*, stung by remorse and unable to endure the presence of those she had injured, retires, supported by *Oenone*.

Hippolytus trembles with indignation, and implores the assistance of the Gods. *Theseus*, recovered from his stupor, gives way to his wrath; and menaces his son with the most cruel punishment. The air of innocence displayed by *Hippolytus*, his oaths, and his prayers, avail nothing. The too credulous King, incapable of curbing the fury of his temper, curses his son, who is kneeling at his feet, and inhumanly shakes him off. Blinded by his rage, he hastens to the statue of *Neptune*, invokes his aid, and resigns the punishment of *Hippolytus* to the will of that God. The Prince appears overwhelmed with distress; the King then commands him to quit the kingdom, and, giving him over to divine vengeance, retires.

The wretched *Hippolytus,* not having ventured to render *Phædra* an object of disgust to his father, yet finds himself labouring under paternal hatred; and dreads the fatal consequences.

Aricia appears. She comes to learn the result of the interview, and is astonished to see the grief into which her lover is plunged. He revives at her presence, but it is only to inform her of the horrors of his fate. *Aricia* shudders with surprise. The abominable crime of *Phædra* and the wrath of *Theseus* is about to force them into exile. *Aricia,* her heart oppressed and torn with what she has heard, gives new proofs of her affection to *Hippolytus,* by swearing to be his for ever. After having implored the protection of the Gods, they give orders for departure.

ACT IV.

The scene discovers the sea-port of Threzene in the distance. Farther still appear the tombs of the ancestors of Hippolytus. In the centre stands a temple of simple but majestic architecture, dedicated to Diana. A vessel lies near the shore.

PRIESTS open the temple; they appear occupied in the service of the divinity they adore; and are preparing for a religious ceremony.

Hippolytus, Aricia, Theramenes, and their equipage arrive. The young Prince directs attention to the temple, and to the scene, as objects of his dearest wishes, it being here that he hopes for the joy of being united to the beautiful *Aricia,* who then expresses her entire affection for him. Every one appears to take a lively interest in their fate; and the sacred Priests receive them with kindness. *Hippolytus*, taking the hand of his intended bride, advances with religious reverence towards the altar. He expresses the delight he feels in uniting himself to the object of his heart, and calls heaven to witness the purity of his love. *Aricia*, overjoyed at the happy event, evinces all the tenderness of affection. The High Priest then unites them, and implores the divine favour for the welfare of so virtuous a couple. The happy pair express their joy. *Theramenes*, forgetting awhile his grief, partakes of their pleasure. The whole company are delighted. The offerings being placed on the altar, every one supplicates the immortal power favourably to regard the august alliance. The Priests await in solemn silence some manifestation of approval from their divine patroness.

The figure of *Diana* suddenly appears in the skies, and the victim is consumed by sacred fire. The joy is universal! The happy prognostications reanimate every breast. *Hippolytus* and *Aricia*, beholding their prayers regarded, take leave, and prepare for departure. *Hippolytus* embraces his faithful and respected tutor with marks of the fondest attachment. *Theramenes* desires to accompany him, but the Prince engages him to remain with his father; at which request, tears flow from the eyes of *Theramenes*. The newly espoused pair, accompanied by their attendants, embark, and the vessel departs from Threzene.

Scene changes, presenting that of the Third Act.

Theseus appears musing on the unhappy event which destroys the peace of his family; his looks and gestures are disturbed and agitated. He is assailed by gloomy presentiments, and fears the approaching confusion. He fancies he hears sighs and groans; and his troubled imagination presents him with sights of woe. He complains bitterly to the Gods, prays for death, and then falls into a state of deep dejection.

Phœdra, accompanied by her accomplice *Oenone,* enters. She has learned the fate of *Hippolytus,* and, torn by remorse, she comes to implore his pardon and return, whose banishment has redoubled her grief. Her presence serves but to increase the fury of *Theseus,* and to render him inexorable to his guilty son. He evinces, however, surprise at the intercession she would make for one who had attempted her honour and her life. He would rather persuade her to unite her prayers with his in obtaining of the Gods, speedy and terrible vengeance, as a punishment due to the abominable crime of their son. He then leads *Phœdra* to the feet of the statue, and commands her to obey; she turns pale with terror, and trembles. At this instant *Theramenes* arrives, bringing intelligence of the departure of *Hippolytus* and *Aricia.* This last act of his son's seems to *Theseus* a new proof of disobedience. His rage returns and increases; he demands of *Neptune* the accomplishment of his ancient promise. So great are the jealous torments of *Phœdra,* that her emotions attract the attention of *Theseus* and astonish him; he seems to have discovered in them some new misfortune; he requires of her a full explanation. She tries to conceal her feelings and endeavours to dissimulate still. *Theramenes* darts a look at her, which seems to reproach her with the destruction of *Hippolytus.* She appears disconcerted, and guilt is depicted on her features. Nothing has escaped the observation of *Theseus;* suspicion distracts his soul. The growling of thunder is heard; and it bursts with a terrible crash. Lightnings blaze forth awfully bright: the statue of the God of the Ocean moves and emits fire, attesting the accomplishment of *Theseus'* vow. Dread seizes on every heart. Overwhelmed with woe, *Theseus* laments, but too late, the rashness of his rage ; he darts at *Phædra* a look of indignation ; suspecting the cause of all his un-happiness, he fears to behold the effects of his prayers. *Theramenes* attends the King with the most respectful solicitude. *Phædra* can no longer resist the divine power by which she is stimulated ; while love and despair appear in every feature. Her mind becomes disturbed, reason seems to have abandoned her ; she declares to the King the passion that consumes her, and exculpates the in-nocent and virtuous *Hippolytus.* Having made this con-fession, she draws a poniard concealed beneath her robe, stabs herself and falls into the arms of *Oenone,* near the statue of *Neptune.* The storm increases ; *Theseus,* sinking beneath the weight of his sufferings, is supported by *Theramenes ;* he expresses horror at having been united to the daughter of *Pasiphæ.* He weeps for the fate of his son ; and asks of the Gods the punishment due to his rash anger. He hates the light, and seeks to terminate his existence.

His faithful servant *Theramenes* employs every art to persuade him from so terrible a resolution ; endeavouring to recall his scattered senses, and to restore tranquillity to his soul, he represents the time may come when his son will return ; and this hope revives the drooping powers of the wretched father. Every one now hastens to pre-vent the fate of *Theseus.*

ACT V.

THE scene presents the shores of Threzene. A storm. *Neptune* appears drawn in a chariot ; he is armed with a trident ; and every circumstance announces the rage of the God. At his command the winds are raised around him, which shake his dominions. Thunderbolts and lightnings add to the horrors of the dreadful scene. Every thing announces the approaching fate of *Hippolytus;* and *Neptune* departs satisfied. The vessel conveying *Hippolytus* and *Aricia* appears struggling against the fury of the waves; while the seamen strive in vain to resist their turbulence. The ship is shattered, and becomes the sport of the tempestuous billows. The distress is universal. Every one prepares for death. *Hippolytus* and *Aricia,* locked in each other's arms, endeavour to effect an escape, or to find an equal fate. The sea opens and engulfs the vessel.

All now appear entombed in the waves. *Aricia* alone is thrown upon a huge rock ; she moves with pain ; and, gradually recovering, she seeks her lover, but finds him not ; his companions have perished, and he must have shared the same fate ; she shudders, her powers fail, and she prepares to die. Suddenly the body of *Hippolytus* floating on the sea meets her eyes; it is washed by the waves on the rock where she reclines; she throws herself upon the remains of her lover, embraces him, covers him with kisses and tears, and then supplicates the Gods to be permitted to join her lover in death ; thus ending her woes.

Theseus and *Theramenes,* followed by the people, enter in haste, and become witnesses of this terrible spectacle. They surround the body of the unhappy *Hippolytus;* and the affliction is universal. Despair has taken possession of *Theseus.* Each prostrates himself, and implores the mercy of the Gods. The virtues, misfortunes, and prayers of *Aricia* at length prevail; and the immortals are moved. Melodious music is heard, as the first sign of the favour about to be bestowed. Every circumstance announces the immediate descent of some deity.

The scene brightens, and becomes filled with clouds of azure and gold, and *Esculapius*, seated on a throne, is beheld descending. Sent by the Gods, he comes the bearer of health and happiness to man. Hope and joy appear in every face. By the peculiar power of the God of *Epidaurus*, the body of *Hippolytus* gradually revives, and becomes completely reanimated ; during which the scene changes into a princely palace, embellished by art and nature ; on one side appears a throne. *Hippolytus*, restored to the desires of all, and beholding the scene of calm delight, falls at the feet of *Esculapius*, who unites him to *Aricia*. The happy *Theseus*, shedding tears of joy, presses to his breast his son, and shares in the pleasure of his children.

Esculapius having executed his beneficent commission, reascends the skies ; while on the spot which he leaves, rises a golden image of the God ; and *Theseus* commands a feast to celebrate the power who has restored life and joy to his dear *Hyppolitu Virbius*.

A Divertissement and General Picture.

Note.—The death of *Hippolytus* has been altered, for it is impossible to represent it on every stage in the manner in which it has been related in the fable. The resources of managers, and the talents of mechanists are not alike in every theatre. The chariot, therefore, drawn by sea horses and marine monsters, have been changed into a vessel, which is wrecked in the tempest, an incident easier and less expensive to perform. At greater theatres, where expense is not so much regarded, and where good mechanists may be procured, it is preferable to perform the death of *Hippolytus* as described by antiquity, besides, it is a novel incident, and the scene of it is more striking.

THE FESTIVAL OF BACCHUS,

OR THE

LOVES OF CYLLENIUS *.

AN ANACREONTIC BALLET, IN THREE ACTS.

CHARACTERS.

CYLLENIUS, OR MERCURY.
ZEPHYR.
EGLE.
FLORA.
TERPSICHORE.
NYMPHS.
SHEPHERDS.

The Scene lies at Nysa, a city of Greece.

------

* A surname of Mercury.

ACT I.

The stage represents the prospect of a pleasant country; on one of the sides, and beneath a bower, are seen the statues of Love and the Spring; higher up is a cluster of trees, and in front, opposite, a fountain. The sea appears behind.

At the rising of the curtain, groups of nymphs, beneath some trees, make the air re-echo with the melodious sounds of their instruments ; other nymphs join their dancing to the melody of their companions. Others at a distance, the friends of *Egle,* arrange their dresses by the crystal reflection of a fountain, whilst part of them amuse themselves in gathering flowers, and in forming garlands and wreaths.

The frolicsome *Egle* comes on dancing. Her companions go to meet her; they are profuse in their expressions of friendship. *Egle* informs them of the arrival of *Zephyr* and *Flora,* who are come to celebrate with them Love and the Spring. They all evince the utmost joy at it.

Flora reclining in a light bark, and *Zephyr* fluttering over her, arrive at the bank. The *Nymphs* receive them with joy, and sports and dances follow their delightful meeting to celebrate their divinities.

During these floral sports, *Zephyr,* busied in wantoning with some of the *Nymphs,* seems to have forgotten *Flora,* who, hurt at his neglect, consults with *Egle* for some moments, and determines to abandon her inconstant lover, in order to punish him for his inconstancy.

They depart without being noticed by him. The

Nymphs, surprised at the disappearance of their companions, at length guess the cause, finish their sports, and fly off, laughing at *Zephyr.* He, astonished, knows not what can be the reason of his being abandoned. He can no longer see *Flora,* she has also fled. He endeavours to discover which way these *Nymphs* have directed their flight. He finds himself sported with, is piqued at it, and promises to be revenged on them. He is just going off. At this instant *Mercury,* cleaving the air, flies after him, and stops him.

The son of Maia appears agitated, a soft languor is visible in his countenance. *Zephyr* expresses to him a wish to know the purpose that brings him, and what can be the cause of his agitation. *Mercury* confesses to him the passion *Egle* has inspired him with, and the desire he has to make an impression on her, and to be by her beloved under the disguise of a mere mortal. *Zephyr* interests himself in his fate, and assures him of success in his project. Hope brightens in the eyes of *Mercury. Zephyr* advises him to personate *Faunus,* and to be present at the Dyonysian Festivals, which are celebrated in honour of Bacchus, as there he might enjoy the pleasure of beholding her he loves, and accomplish his designs.

The son of Jupiter, arrived at the summit of his wishes, testifies his gratitude to him. They both direct their flight towards heaven, and proceed to the commencement of their project; then insensibly disappear.

ACT II.

*The Stage represents the magnificent temple of Bacchus.
The statue of the God is placed in the midst of the
Scene.*

TERPSICHORE comes in dancing, and is to preside at
the festival. *Egle* and her companions, in the habits of
Bacchanalians, follow her steps, and form groups around
the statue of Bacchus.

Zephyr and *Flora*, being reunited, appear, and strew the
portico with flowers. *Terpsichore* encourages them, every
one imitates them, and they accompany the action with
dancing.

The sound of the instruments of shepherds, disguised as
Fauni, makes the sacred walls re-echo, and announces the
votaries of the God of Nysa. *Cyllenius,* in the dress of a
Bacchanalian, is at their head. Love and gaiety prompt
their steps and movements. *Zephyr* and *Mercury* make
signs to each other of a mutual understanding. *Egle*
notices this strange *Shepherd;* there are visible in him an
air and manner different from the rest of the train. The
divinity seems to betray itself involuntarily.

However, the rites begin by order of *Terpsichore,* and
from her example, *Flora, Zephyr, Mercury, Egle,* and
the Bacchanalians, taking urns and goblets filled with
wine, pour out libations, and drink in honour of the
God who inspires them. During this scene, *Cyllenius* has
not ceased to attract the attention of the fair *Egle.* The
nymph seems already to feel a tender attachment to this
amiable stranger. *Mercury* expresses to *Zephyr* the
joy he feels at the happy auspices of his love.

The ceremony commences, and they all devote them-

selves to dancing. The son of Maia is noticed for the
grace and excellency of his steps, and his total object is
to delight his nymph. *Egle* is agitated, and her heart
begins to beat. At the conclusion of a dance, and in a
group, *Cyllenius* whispers to *Egle ;* she blushes at his discourse, and hangs down her head. *Zephyr* perceives
them, interrupts them, and thereby prevents their being
discovered by the assemblage. The dance recommences ;
the sound of the horn puts an end to it, announcing their
departure for the chase. A Bacchanalian, holding a bow,
gives a signal, and each of them separates to prepare their
arms, expressing pleasure in devoting themselves to the
pursuit of the tenants of the forest.

The amorous *Cyllenius* prepares to avail himself of the
opportunity, and to see himself crowned with success.
Zephyr encourages him, and they both follow the lovely
Egle. They all depart.

ACT III.

The stage exhibits the interior of a thick Forest.

Mercury appears ; he seeks the object of his passion ;
he does not perceive her ; he evinces the deepest impatience at it ; he calls in vain ; he falls into a mournful
languor. A noise of hunting is heard ; several *Nymphs*
cross the stage. *Egle* follows them ; she is herself in
quest of her successful lover. She at last espies him, she
pretends to wish to fly. *Mercury*, at the summit of his
wishes, rushes upon her, and stops her.

Egle becomes agitated, *Mercury* endeavours to calm
her, and assures her that his passion for her is as pure as it
is sincere.

The nymph, abashed, gently withdraws herself. Her lover attempts to seize her hand ; she withholds it ; agitation is betrayed in all her demeanour ; she will listen to him no longer. *Mercury* tenderly presses her, complains of her cruelty. *Egle* languishingly turns her eyes upon him, and begins to tremble. The God exhibits the most lively joy at it ; he redoubles his entreaties, throws himself at her feet, conjuring her to return his affection. He assures her of the constancy of his passion by oaths. *Egle* can no longer resist the passion which impels her, and the ascendancy of the God who has triumphed over her. She abandons herself entirely to the pleasure of receiving from her lover assurances of his constancy, and she avows her own tender sentiments towards him.

Mercury enjoys the pleasure of being beloved on his own account ; he vows to his fair one the most tender passion, and they sink into each other's arms. At this instant the *scene changes, and represents the temple of Mercury.*

Zephyr, holding the *caduceus* in one hand, and with the other pointing to the amorous Faun, discovers *Mercury*. *Flora*, the muse of dancing, as well as the *Nymphs* and *Shepherds*, express the surprise they feel at the disguise of the God.

Mercury throws himself at the feet of the trembling nymph, and swears to her to continue ever the tender and faithful shepherd who found means to please her.

Egle can scarcely believe her felicity ; all applaud so excellent a choice, and joy summoning each of them back to the dance, thus are celebrated the amours of *Egle*.

MARCUS LICINIUS *,

AN HISTORICAL BALLET, IN FIVE ACTS.

CHARACTERS.

LICINIUS, *Emperor of the East.*
CONSTANTIA, *his wife, a Christian.*
STATIRA, *maid of honour to the Empress, a Christian.*
BENIN, *captain of the Emperor's Guards.*
NARSIS, *the lover of Statira, a Christian.*
AGENOR, *father of Statira, a Christian.*
Guards; Princes and Princesses ; Pagan Priests, Popu-
lace ; Retinue of the Emperor and Empress.

The action of the Ballet takes place at the commencement
of the Fourth Century.   The scene lies at Nicomedia, a
City of Bithynia.

---

* The subject of this Ballet has never been theatrically represented.

ACT I.

The scene represents the neighbourhood of Nicomedia. A temple dedicated to the Christian faith is seen in the middle of the stage.

Narsis outstrips the dawn; he is waiting with impatience for the arrival of his beloved. He expresses the love he feels for that fair one, and invokes the protection of the God he adores. *Statira,* accompanied by her father, and a group of Christians, presents herself to the notice of *Narsis.* Tender transports of the two lovers; they fly into each other's arms, and fall down at the feet of *Agenor,* who raises them, and presses them to his heart. That venerable old man unites them in the sight of Heaven, and bestows upon them his benediction. *Narsis* and *Statira* vow an eternal attachment before the altar, and every one present participates in their happiness. Harps make the air resound with a hymn, and they all with one consent invoke the Eternal. Sacred dances celebrate the religious festival. *Agenor* commands them all to retire, and he goes off attended by his children.

ACT II.

Magnificent apartment in the Imperial Palace.

Licinius appears; he seems to be agitated by some violent passion. He seats himself by a table, and meditates on his condition. Love is the cause of his sufferings. He shows himself indignant at being a slave to this tender passion. The fierceness of his disposition in vain prompts him to despise it; the charms of *Statira* have attained too much influence over him : he adores her ! The attractions of that young Princess have enchanted his heart. He knows not what stratagems to use to put him in possession of the object of his love, and to make himself beloved by her. He is in the greatest agitation, and appears to have lost all hope.

He is surprised by *Benin*, who has been a witness to his transports of love. His confidant evinces a wish to be made acquainted with the cause of his sorrows, and makes him an offer of his services. *Licinius*, unable to resist the transports of his soul, and his situation needing some consolation, confesses to *Benin* the passion *Statira* has inspired him with. *Benin*, delighted at this proof of confidence and attachment which he has received from his master, avails himself of this opportunity of making himself serviceable. This artful courtier flatters the passion of *Licinius*, devotes himself entirely to him, and promises him success over the heart of *Statira*. The Emperor is restored to the most delightful hopes, and retires depending upon the promise of his confidant.

Benin reflects upon the means he is to use to win over *Statira*, and render his master happy. Should his projects succeed, his ambition points out to him, in anticipation, the most brilliant prospects.

Statira appears ; she desires to speak to the Empress. The secret joy of *Benin*. He begs that Princess to condescend to listen to him for a moment, having a secret to impart to her which may render her the happiest of woman kind. The astonishment of *Statira*. *Benin*, after having flattered the vanity of the young beauty by the most fulsome compliments, which greatly surprise *Statira*, informs her of the impression her charms have made upon the heart of *Licinius*, and of the desire he feels of finding his love returned. *Statira* stands petrified at these words. *Benin* attentively watches her. He does not abate his efforts, he portrays to her the advantages and the honours which would accrue to her from the Emperor's affection, and, in short, that she would become mistress of the Emperor's will by submitting to his desires.

Statira, deprived of utterance, knows not what reply to make. The glory and honours which are offered her are, in her mind, but so many insults, and so many degrading affronts. She blushes on seeing herself thus despised, she is aware of the inflexibility of *Licinius*, and she trembles at her situation.

Benin endeavours to allay her agitation, and to weaken her notions of virtue; he tries to dazzle her mind by the splendour of *Licinius'* rank. However, prudence demands of *Statira* that she should manage the perfidious confidant, and that she should not affect the character of her worthy master. She answers evasively, dissembles, and begs for time to reflect upon her destiny.

Benin, fearful of losing the golden opportunity, warmly urges her to give him a favourable answer; but *Statira*, no longer able to brook such humiliation, and resuming her resolution, manifests to him by her gestures the most profound contempt for her vile seducers. The energy which virtue inspires her with renders her superior to all fear, and she forbids *Benin* ever more to approach her. He stands dismayed at the firmness of *Statira*, which his base soul did not expect from her. Recovering himself, he shows his resentment towards *Statira*; vengeance alone can console him for the ill success of his base attempt, and he hastens to inform *Licinius*.

ACT III.

CONSTANTIA, surrounded by the ladies of her court, presides at a festival. Each of them is endeavouring to testify her love and respect for her.

The dances and sports are interrupted by the arrival of *Statira* and her father. *Statira* implores the Empress to grant her a moment's private audience; *Constantia* makes a sign, and her court retire.

Statira describes in the most lively colours the sentiments and desires of *Licinius*, and her own unfortunate situation. The astonishment of *Constantia*. *Agenor* and his daughter prostrate themselves at her feet, and implore her to protect them. *Constantia* promises to save them ; she pities their condition, and expresses the indignation which the conduct of *Licinius* inspires them with.

Agenor introduces *Narsis*, and presents him to the Empress as her daughter's husband.

Constantia seems to be meditating upon the plan they ought to adopt. At length she sees no other means of rescuing them from the fury of her husband but by flight. She proposes to *Statira* to disguise herself in man's attire. She promises them her assistance. *Agenor* and his children depend on her kindness for every thing. *Narsis* goes to make preparations for their departure. *Constantia*, *Agenor*, and *Statira* implore the protection of heaven.

During this scene *Benin* appears, he discovers the understanding that prevails amongst these personages, and he hastens to acquaint his master with the movements of *Statira*.

Constantia invites *Agenor* to follow her, to communicate to him her ultimate intentions relative to the flight.

Statira remains, and waits for the arrival of *Narsis*. She reflects upon her situation; the fate of her husband distresses her more than her own. A slight noise is heard, she expects to see her lover appear, but it is *Licinius* who presents himself. The dismay of *Statira*. Rage at first transports the tyrant; the virtues of this young female act as stings to him, but soon the charms of *Statira* soften the asperity of his impetuous nature. Love has taken possession of his soul. *Licinius* strives to appease the fears of the object of his passion. He endeavours to give to his countenance a less terrible aspect, and tenderly declares his sentiments.

Statira with difficulty recovers her spirits; she finds herself undone. *Licinius* tries to render himself more agreeable, he assumes a less haughty mien, and his countenance seems, for the first time, to wear a smile, that he may better carry his aims. *Statira*, trembling, meets him with respect and modesty. *Licinius* declares to her how fondly he loves her, and all the sacrifices he is prepared to make for her sake. The agitation of *Statira* is increased, she sheds tears. *Licinius* implores her to compassionate his fate; she points out his obligations, alluding to what he owes his wife. Nothing can move him; he uses the most tender entreaties. *Statira* conjures him to relinquish his designs, and to spare her. He throws himself at her feet; she attempts to escape from him; he ardently presses her; she repels him, he redoubles his entreaties, but *Statira*, arming herself with noble resolution, tells him that she will never be his. Fury and threats of *Licinius*. But nothing can allure *Statira*. She endeavours to fly. *Licinius* stops her, and threatens her with death, if she persists in her resolution. *Statira* points out to him the vengeance of heaven. Transport of rage of *Licinius;* he completely relapses into his terrible character. He calls his guards. They enter; *Benin* is at their head. *Constantia*, attracted by the noise of this transaction, comes in attended by a part of her retinue. Aware of her husband's disposition, and of the impetuosity of his raging passions, she endeavours to appease him by her prudence, and pretends to be unacquainted with a part of the adventure. But all in vain. *Licinius* orders *Statira* to be dragged off and imprisoned. He goes off animated by a desire of vengeance. *Constantia* deplores her own fate, and that of the her husband's victim.

ACT IV.

Interior of the temple of Jupiter ; it is adorned with the statues of the principal divinities of Paganism. An altar stands in the middle.

SACRIFICE to Jupiter. The Priests burn incense on the altars of their Gods, and religious dances, accompanied by the sound of various musical instruments, celebrate the festival.

Licinius, attended by his court and guards, makes his appearance. He comes to worship his Gods. He orders all his subjects to revere none but them, and to banish every other kind of worship from his territories, under pain of death. They all submit to his will.

The ceremony is interrupted by *Benin*, who comes to announce the escape of the prisoner, favoured by the arms of the Christians. *Licinius* is in the height of fury. He

places himself at the head of his warriors, and after dreadful threats, he rushes out to effect the destruction of his
enemies.

ACT V.

*The City of Nicomedia is seen in perspective at the back
of the stage. The ruins of ancient edifices are scattered
about the scene.*

NARSIS, at the head of his faithful companions, pursues a
party of *Licinius'* soldiers. The latter brings assistance
to his warriors, whom he sees on the point of being overpowered. He has the advantage on his side, and the
Christians are obliged to yield to the numbers which
overwhelm them. *Licinius,* wounded by *Narsis,* rushes
upon him, and aims a terrible blow at him, which a warrior, who has placed himself before him, purposely to
shield him, receives.

The young hero totters ; his helmet falls, and his hair
and features discover the person of *Statira,* disguised
in the garb of a man, in order to escape from the tyrant.
Universal surprise ! Mournful feelings of *Licinius.* Despair of *Agenor* and *Narsis,* the latter of whom rushes
upon his sword, and falls by the side of his beloved.

Constantia arrives at the moment of this terrible scene.
She sheds tears over the unfortunate objects of her protection. *Statira* recommends the fate of her father to
Licinius, and conjures him to pardon his Christian subjects. She embraces *Agenor* and *Constantia,* and dies in
the arms of her husband.

At this moment a celestial brightness illumines the
clouds, and on a sudden the heavens are darkened, and

the thunder rolls in grandeur. The spotless soul of *Statira* appears translated to the abode of the blessed.

Constantia invokes the eternal in favour of her husband, whom this distracting scene has rendered motionless with terror.

General and pictorial grouping, in which is portrayed the contrast of the different sentiments of the characters.

SIDONIUS AND DORISBE.

CHIVALRESQUE BALLET, IN FIVE ACTS.

CHARACTERS.

ARGENIA.

SIDONIUS, *son of a Phœnician King.*

DORISBE, *daughter of Argenia and Morastus, who was killed in battle by Sidonius.*

ARSENIA, *confidential attendant on Dorisbe.*

NARBAS, *an aged servant in the Palace.*

GRIFFE, *his wife.*

A Page of Dorisbe's ; a Squire attending Sidonius ; Priests, People, Court, and Guards.

The Scene passes at Memphis.

ACT I.

SCENE.—*The country about Memphis. A temple is discovered dedicated to Nemesis, the Goddess of Revenge, whose statue appears covered with votive funereal ornaments. Upon an altar is placed an urn, containing the ashes of Morastus.*

ARGENIA enters, she is followed by her daughter, guards,

and people. A sacrifice is made to Nemesis, at which all assist, taking a remarkable interest in the solemnity. *Argenia* promises the hand of her daughter to him who shall revenge the death of her husband by slaying *Sidonius*.

The latter is conducted by chance to this scene, and enters disguised, and unknown to any; he learns with astonishment the motive of the sacrifice; he passionately loves the beautiful *Dorisbe*, but dreads the consequences. *Argenia* again proclaims the promise with its conditions; and the more deeply to impress her subjects with a desire of revenge, she directs their attention to the ensanguined armour of her husband. A general expression of indignation follows; while *Argenia*, in tears, calls down the wrath of heaven upon the victor's head, whose life all swear to sacrifice. The distress of *Sidonius* becomes extreme; and he complains to the Gods of his cruel fate.

ACT II.

The Palace and Royal Gardens.

DORISBE is discovered sporting amidst a troop of young companions; music and dancing contributing to their pleasure. *Sidonius*, disguised as an Arabian shepherd, appears, and endeavours to gain admission to the Princess whom he loves. He accordingly promises the old governor of the gardens to discover a treasure for him, if he will grant him admission into his dominions. *Narbas* seems to raise great difficulties, but *Sidonius* informing him that the enchantment that will put him in possession of this wealth must take place in the palace, both the old man and his wife immediately grant him an asylum, and *Sidonius* passes for their son.

He is then presented to *Dorisbe*, who receives him graciously, and *Sidonius* endeavours to attract her attention by the amiability of his conduct, and by offering a bouquet of flowers recently gathered. Already does the young Princess feel a certain pleasure in beholding the youth, who soon perceives this, and becomes inspired with a modest confidence. He plays upon certain instruments, dances, and evinces qualities far above his apparent rank in life. *Dorisbe* is surprised at such abilities, and examines the pretended shepherd with a pleasing curiosity, while her heart becomes unusually perturbed, and the affection of *Sidonius* increases. *Narbas* and *Griffe*, his wife, inspired by avarice, now advance and remind the supposed peasant of the promised discovery. *Sidonius*, to appease their avarice, and to gain time for his designs, presents them with a cup of gold, procured, as they imagine, by his knowledge of magic. They seem peculiarly delighted with the gift. Here a banquet takes place, at which *Sidonius* fills the office of cup-bearer, and offers wine to the young Princess. Their eyes encounter each other as by accident, when a certain tender and lively expression informs each of what is passing within. *Dorisbe*, taking the cup given by *Sidonius*, admires the beauty of its workmanship, and asks him how he got possession of it? The shepherd replies that he won it at rustic games. All that *Dorisbe* sees fills her with suspicion and a curiosity to know more; tranquillity, in short, no longer reigns within her bosom.

ACT III.

Scene.—*A grove in the garden; break of day.* Enter *Narbas* and his wife; they display the cup of gold lately given by *Sidonius.* Unable to take rest, from an insatiable desire to increase their possessions, they now consult on the means necessary to be employed to oblige *Sidonius* to discover the promised treasure. They indulge the flattering hope of changing their present servile condition : inspired by such sentiments, they hasten away to find *Sidonius*, and force him to keep his promise. *Dorisbe* enters alone, she exhibits signs of those feelings with which the shepherd stranger has inspired her breast; but remembering the meanness of his birth, she becomes greatly agitated, and laments her fate. *Sidonius* appears; love and fear by turns affect his breast. Upon perceiving *Dorisbe* he is greatly surprised; his agitation increases, but inspired by his passion, he approaches and presents himself before the astonished *Dorisbe.* After some gestures of fear and restraint on both sides, nature at length triumphs, and the lovers reciprocally express the sentiments of affection they entertain for each other. *Sidonius* discovers his rank; he informs her of the stratagem he has practised to gain admission, but conceals in the deepest silence his real name. *Dorisbe* seems unprepared for so much happiness.

The sound of horns is heard—*Dorisbe* takes a hasty leave of her lover, and retires; but *Sidonius* remains and joins the train of the Queen.—Squires announce the approach of *Argenia;* she appears and gives orders to prepare for the chase, and departs in procession. *Scene, a forest—the chase.* Excursions are discovered in various directions; at length a furious boar rushes toward the Queen *Argenia*, upon which *Sidonius* instantly flies to her relief, and slays the sanguinary animal; while the whole company are overjoyed at the victory ; and *Sidonius* becomes an object of royal and universal congratulation, and is distinguished by peculiar marks of honour.

ACT IV.

An *apartment in the Palace.*—*Dorisbe* and *Sidonius* are discovered exchanging marks of mutual affection; they express their determination to be united for ever.   In the midst of this, however, a deep melancholy appears on the countenance of *Sidonius*, and mixes itself with their hopes of future happiness.   *Dorisbe* perceives this with anxiety, and fears that she has been deceived by her lover ; but *Sidonius* assures her of his constancy, and entreats her to forgive the feelings caused by a secret woe.   *Dorisbe* instantly seeks to know what is the concealed grief that so affects him; unable to resist her affectionate inquiries, *Sidonius* discovers his name; when both are immediately plunged into the deepest woe.   *Sidonius* protests his innocence, but *Dorisbe* dares not pardon him; he implores forgiveness on his knees, and bathes with tears the hand of *Dorisbe*.   At this moment *Argenia* appears, and immediately exhibits marks of indignation.   The lovers throw themselves at her feet, and beseech her pardon, but in vain; both are seized as equally guilty.   Death is the sentence adjudged by the law, unless their innocence be proved by two knights who must enter into combat, as their representatives.   *Sidonius*, unwilling to augment their mutual sufferings, still keeps his real name and rank concealed from the Queen.   *Scene, a prison.*— *Sidonius* appears in the deepest distress.   He, however, prevails by a present of gold, and the gaoler allows him to escape; he flies upon the wings of love to seek and save *Dorisbe*.

ACT V.

Scene.—*An open place, in the centre of which stands a funeral pile.*

Argenia and her court assist at the solemn ceremony. Combat between two warriors, one being habited in white armour, the other in black; the first appears as the champion of *Sidonius*, while the second sustains the cause of *Dorisbe*.   The black knight is victorious, and discovers that his antagonist is no other than *Dorisbe* herself; while he proves himself to be the Arabian shepherd; the astonishment and joy become universal, all admiring such an unequalled example of love and valour. *Argenia* is deeply affected, and loses all power of inflicting further punishment.   All hasten to the assistance of the fainting *Dorisbe;* she gradually recovers; the real name of the unknown conqueror is now demanded; *Sidonius* declares himself, and the consternation becomes universal! The indignation of *Argenia* is immediately kindled; while *Dorisbe* remains unnoticed and oppressed by the weight of her woes.   *Sidonius* declares that, though innocent, he is ready to sacrifice his life to satisfy *Argenia*, and appease the manes of *Morastus*.   The court is moved at the unfortunate situation of the young hero.   The Queen, though not forgetful of what she owes to the Prince, suffers the desire to revenge her husband's death to overcome every

other consideration.   At this moment *Dorisbe* rushes on
a sword to stab herself, but is prevented from doing the
horrid deed ; the nobility implore the Queen's mercy for
the lovers; at length *Argenia*, yielding to sentiments of
justice and gratitude, grants a pardon, to the joy of all her
subjects, and the delight of the happy pair.   Universal
fêtes and rejoicing in honour of the Queen's magnanimity
terminate the Ballet.

APHRODITA*,

A MYTHOLOGICAL BALLET, IN FIVE *TABLEAUX.*

ARGUMENT.

THE following is nearly a literal translation of the description of the birth of *Venus* from Hesiod :—

" ——— He threw the bleeding mutilation into the stormy sea of Epirus ; it floated long amid the waves, till at length a white and foamy scum gathered around ; a charming child appeared, and soon a lovely nymph arose.

" To Cythera first she passed, isle divine ; then she fled to sea-surrounded Cyprus.   She went forth an adored deity, divinely fair ; beneath her tender foot the grass more gladly grew.   Gods and men have named her Aphrogenia and Aphrodita ; she is entitled, also, the garland-crowned Cytherea, because begot on froth, and first received

---

* The subject of this Ballet, whose intention is to represent the most remarkable actions in the life of *Venus,* as well as her birth, has never been treated on by any Ballet-master before me.   The idea of it was first suggested by reading the entertaining Letters of Demoustier ; and in early youth the design of the piece was formed.   Since that period, I have made such alterations as study and experience have dictated, and I flatter myself that those alterations are improvements.

The first scene represents the birth of *Venus;* the second, her education ; the third, the reception of the young Goddess into Olympus, and her marriage with *Vulcan;* the fourth, her amours with *Mars;* in the fifth, the daughter of Ocean, persuaded by the counsels of *Minerva,* returns to her duties, and reunites herself to the affections of her husband ; upon which a celebration takes place in honour of the Goddess of Beauty.   C. B.

upon the Cytherean shores.   She was surnamed Cypria too, because bred up on Cyprus isle.

" The wonder of her birth endows her with the name of Philomedia.   When first presented to the assembly of immortal Gods, Love and Cupid * bore her company.   These are the honours and the titles adjudged to her by Gods and men.   She holds dominion over sweet discourse, innocent deceits, smiles and gentle flatteries; loves and pleasures follow and surround her as their Queen."   THEOGONY.

Cicero mentions four Venuses ; the first is the daughter of the Sky and the Day ; she had a temple at Elis ; the second sprung from the froth of the Sea, and was united to *Mercury*, who begat *Cupid;* the third, was the daughter of *Jupiter* and *Dione*, was married to *Vulcan*, and had a son by *Mars*, named *Antirus;* the fourth was the child of *Sirus* and *Siria*, and was worshipped by the Phœnicians under the title of *Astarte*.   All these Venuses, however, are generally included in one, namely, the second mentioned above.   Boccaccio, in his work on *The Genealogy of the Gods;* Poliziano, in his *Stanze;* Sannazzaro, Marino, and a number of other moderns, have followed the opinion of Hesiod.

---

* Cupid, from the Greek word HIMEROS, a desire, for which word the Latins substituted CUPIDO, signifying indeed the same thing, but afterwards confounded with LOVE, whereas Hesiod distinguishes Love and Cupid into two persons.

CHARACTERS.

VENUS, or APHRODITA.	PAN.
JUPITER.	PALES.
JUNO.	FLORA.
NEPTUNE.	ZEPHYR.
CERES.	THE GRACES.
MINERVA.	HYMEN.
MERCURY.	HEBE.
VESTA.	NYMPHS.
APOLLO.	FAUNS.
DIANA.	SATYRS.
MARS.	SHEPHERDS.
VULCAN.	SHEPHERDESSES.
THE FATES.	HUNTERS.
SATURN.	LEMNIANS.
GENIUS.	NEREIDS.
PLUTO.	TRITONS.
BACCHUS.	CYCLOPS.
CUPID.	WARRIORS *attending Mars.*
CYBELE.	BELLONA.
PROSERPINE.	

TABLEAU I.

The stage represents the sea-coast of Epirus. A bright prospect of fields stretches down to the ocean. On the right is perceived the statue of Spring. The light of the scene shows the break of day.

FLORA, *Zephyr, Pan,* and *Pales,* followed by *Nymphs, Fauns, Satyrs, Shepherds, Shepherdesses* and *Hunters,* enter dancing ; they carry baskets of fruits and flowers ; garlands and coronets; the sound of their rustic instruments regulates and animates their steps.   After a measured march, they proceed to deposit their offerings at the feet of the statue of Spring, adorning it with flowers and the gifts of Pomona.   The feast is celebrated by sports and dances, until they are interrupted by a rumbling noise, which seems to proceed from the earth.   The sea is observed to be greatly agitated, tossing on high its foaming waves; every one, struck with astonishment and dread, hastens to the shore to discover the cause of this unusual commotion; when *Venus* is seen rising from the troubled ocean; she is borne in a marine shell* by *Nereids* and *Tritons* †.   The Goddess, enveloped in a great veil, and reclining in an attitude of repose, appears in all her splendour.   When the daughter of Ocean has arisen from her wavy bed, *Apollo* arrives in his chariot of fire; he comes to dissipate the twilight that hangs around her, and to illumine her charms; he then remounts on his course.   In the skies are seen the assembled deities who

---

* " Et faveas concha Cypria vecta tua."   Tibull. El. III.

† " Par le plaisir émus, mille flots caressans
   S' entrepoussaient autour de ses charmes naissans;
   L' un baise ses cheveux que le Zéphyr dénoue,
   L' autre près de sa conque et bondit et se joue;
   D' autres avec respect demeurent suspendus,
   Fiers d' ouvrir un passage à la belle Vénus.
   Le Triton recourbé, fendant l'onde écumante,
   Change en soupirs les sons de sa voix éffrayante,
   Et sème de corail les courans fortunés
   Qu' en glissant sur les eaux le char a sillonnés.
   Vous filles de Thétis, de vos grottes profondes,
   Vous élevez vos fronts sur la cime des ondes;
   Mais éveillé soudain par tant d'attraits nouveaux
   Le dépit vous oblige à rentrer sous les eaux."

                                                    Leonard.

presided at the birth of *Venus*.   Both gods and mortals
are wrapt in admiration at her extraordinary beauty.—

> The youthful Goddess, lifting now her eyes,
> Throws round a gaze of terror and surprise ;
> She wonders at the waves, the skies, the light,
> Whose brightness wounds her unaccustom'd sight ;
> Sighing she speaks, and her first accent tells
> The future mistress of enchanting spells.
> Where am I ? whence awaked ? what bliss I feel !
> What gentle gales perfum'd around me steal !
> How beautiful is nature, and how blest !
> What genial warmth pervades my heaving breast !
> What's this that beats so quick beneath my hands ?
> And as it beats the gentle heat expands.
> On breasts exposed, her downcast looks are stayed,
> Vainly she tries their nakedness to shade ;
> O'er the soft hills, her pressing fingers stray,
> She droops confus'd, and seems to die away.
>
>   *From the French of* DEMOUSTIER *.

> * La jeune déité levant enfin les yeux,
>   Promène ses regards, craintifs et curieux.
>   Elle admire le ciel et l' onde et la lumière
>   Dont l'éclat blesse encor sa timide paupière.
>   Sa bouche s' ouvre, et son premier soupir,
>   Son premier mot est l' accent du plaisir.
>   Où suis-je ? quel réveil ? quelle volupté pure !
>   O que cet air est doux ! que ce jour est serein !
>   Que tout est beau dans la nature !
>   Quelle douce chaleur circule dans mon sein ! . .
>   Que sens-je battre sous ma main ? . . . .
>   Vers son cœur palpitant alors baissant la vue
>   Elle admire, sourit, et rougit d'être nue !
>   Ses mains volent, mais ces mobiles remparts,
>   Ses trésors innocens, percent de toutes parts.
>   Quelle confusion ! . . . . . .
>
>   DEMOUSTIER.

At the sight of this seducing beauty all hearts are filled with admiration. *Zephyr* flies around *Venus*, he gathers together his azure clouds, and envelopes the Goddess in them ; and then transports her into the skies, conducting her to those scenes she is destined to adorn with her presence. The attendants of *Zephyr* and *Flora*, gazing still on *Venus*, follow her until she disappears. *General Picture*.

The marine powers regain their watery dwellings, and *Flora* departs, accompanied by her train.

TABLEAU II.

The stage exhibits the enchanting abodes of the island of Cyprus. The sea is discovered in the distance. To the right rises a lofty rock ; on the same side appears the statue of Jupiter. The scene is filled with Nymphs, *indulging in light dances and joyful sports.* Venus *and* Zephyr *now appear in the air, and descend into the isle. (They enter on the right.)*

THE *Nymphs*, in surprise, admire the charming visiter. *Zephyr* confides to their charge the care of the Goddess ; he describes to them her birth, and after having taken leave, he departs on a bed of roses, composed by some nymphs, who, grouping around him, follow him with their eyes till he disappears, presenting an agreeable picture. The *Nymphs* having joyfully received the orders of the God of gentle gales, signs of mutual kindness are exchanged, and each seems charmed with the happy event. A troop of nymphs hasten to enrobe the daughter of Ocean, and adorn her with flowers ; others invite her to prepare a sacrifice to the Gods. She obeys, and following their example, prostrates herself before the statue of *Jupiter*, whose nature and worship is taught her by one of the nymphs, her companions; *Venus* then burns incense upon the altar of the governor of Gods. After this religious ceremony, the feast is celebrated by dances, in which *Venus* is instructed by one of the amiable *Nymphs*. These amusements are interrupted by the unexpected arrival of *Mercury*, who, descending from the skies remains motionless before the resplendent charms of *Venus*. Every one is attentive in listening to the celestial messenger, who, by order of *Jupiter*, is to conduct *Venus* to Olympus. The command of the consort of *Juno* fills the nymphs with grief, which is displayed in their gestures. The sovereign decree must, however, be obeyed, and after an affectionate adieu, *Venus*, accompanied by *Mercury*, ascends a flying chariot, and leaves with reluctance her beloved companions, who show lively emotions of sorrow at the loss of their divine charge

TABLEAU III

Represents the interior of Olympus; the edifice is supported on masses of azure and golden clouds spread entirely over the stage. Jupiter reclines majestically amongst the other divinities.

The Gods appear to pay homage to their governor. A distant noise is heard, which announces the approach of *Vulcan:* the clouds dividing discover the Lemnian God ascending into the heavens. He is come from his island, and, advancing respectfully towards his father, he begs him to arm his powerful hand with the bolts he has just forged. The son of *Saturn* shows signs of satisfaction; while the performance is beheld by the other powers

with admiration.   In the mean time *Venus*, accompanied
by *Mercury*, attains the palace on the same side at which
Vulcan had entered, and presents herself to the observation
of the celestial assembly.   The admiration and astonishment become universal.   Jealousy takes possession of the
hearts of the Goddesses.   The thundering King admires
the divine stranger.   The flame of love is already kindled in
the breasts of *Vulcan, Mars,* and *Apollo.   Jupiter* descends from his throne, the deities follow him; he approaches *Venus*, embraces her, and, placing a crown upon
her head, proclaims her Goddess of Beauty.   The ruler
of the skies declares, that as *Juno* partakes with him the
empire of heaven, and that as *Pallas* is patroness of wisdom, so shall *Venus* be the mistress of beauty.   He commands also that the young Goddess should have as inseparable companions, *Love** and the *Graces. Venus* seems
confused and modestly displays her joy.   The rival Goddesses, endeavouring to dissimulate, conceal their real
envy.   Her reception is celebrated by dances, in which
Apollo, Mercury, Hebe, the *Graces,* and *Love* take a
part.   *Venus* is distinguished by her seducing manners
and voluptuous attitudes.   *Vulcan,* deeply enamoured
with the charms of this ravishing beauty, finds himself
excited to demand her hand of *Jupiter*, as a reward for
the service he had just performed.   *Mars* and *Apollo,* also,
as much overcome as their rival, entreat possession of the
charming deity, as a recompense of their heroic deeds;

---

* Several writers of the highest antiquity, and more recently certain
mythological authors, have placed the birth of *Love* prior to Chaos.
We have followed this tradition, although contrary to the general opinion that *Venus* was his mother.   We, therefore, thought ourselves sufficiently authorised, yet deemed it requisite to inform our readers of
that authority.

but *Vulcan* having made the first demand, and in consideration of his late services, and reiterated supplication, is preferred, and obtains the accomplishment of his desires. Anger and resentment take possession of *Mars* and *Apollo*. *Cupid* appears inclined to take part with the first, in whose fate he interests himself, and approaching him slily, by a sign, inspires him with sentiments of hope. The Thracian God, revived at the happy intimation, expects every thing from the assistance of *Love;* he essays to engage the attention of *Venus* by pleasing assiduities. In the mean time *Jupiter* unites *Vulcan* to *Venus;* the latter, submitting to his orders, becomes the ridicule of her jealous rivals, who observe with pleasure this preposterous union with the hideous offspring of *Jupiter; Hymen* presides at the ceremony. *Vulcan*, his wishes being now gratified, returns thanks to his father, and taking possession of his bride, he departs from Olympus, and returns to his island. The divinities attend *Jupiter* into his palace, while *Mars* and *Cupid*, slily slipping from the assembly, hasten away to forward their designs.

TABLEAU IV.

A view of the beautiful and fertile fields of the Island of Lemnos.

Venus and *Vulcan* descend in a golden chariot ; the inhabitants receive them with marks of reverence and love. *Vulcan* introduces to them their charming Queen ; they are surprised at her beauty. He expresses his own love and delight, and *Venus* returns in an agreeable manner the advances of her husband. Various occupations call *Vulcan* to his forge, he is obliged to leave his consort, but promises shortly to return. The men of Lemnos follow their king, leaving their wives to attend upon *Venus ;* each of whom endeavours to pay homage to the Goddess, placing her on a throne of flowers which they had constructed.

This pleasing scene is interrupted by the noise of warlike instruments ; fear taking possession of their breasts, the *Nymphs* disappear, while *Venus* seems overpowered with dread. It is the God *Mars,* who appears in a chariot driven by *Bellona ;* he is armed with terror, accompanied by *Love* and attended by warriors. *Venus* gradually recovers, but her timidity cannot support the sight of the warlike deity ; trembling she attempts to fly. *Mars* pursues, stops her flight, and throws himself at her feet. *Cupid,* seizing this propitious moment, draws his bow, and *Venus* is wounded by his dart. *A Picture.* The young Goddess, for the first time, feels the pains of love, inflicted by a deity, powerful though a child. She feels emotions at her heart ; she is confused and agitated, yet beholds *Mars* with pleasure, who adores her. She listens with pleasure to his enamoured language, and receives with joy his oaths of love and sincerity. Notwithstanding this, the habiliments of the God of battles and the warlike train attending him still alarm the timid Goddess, and she expresses her fear of them to *Mars.* The condescending hero obediently lays aside his arms, and causes his attendants to withdraw. *Love,* who has not remained idle in this scene, now presents his new convert to *Venus* more agreeably dressed, and suitable to his present situation ; and having woven a crown of flowers, he presents it to *Venus,* who places it upon the head of her lover. The Goddess contemplates with delight the change that has taken place, expressing to *Mars* how much more pleasing and amiable he appears in his present attire. The God accosts her with a peculiar ardour of passion ; *Venus* blushes, is confused and hesitates ; *Mars* perceiving her irresolution, redoubles his solicitations, and conjures her with increased fervor to satisfy his wishes; but it is *Cupid* who completes the conquest, and the two lovers fall into each other's arms, while he triumphs in their reciprocal transports. *Mars* and *Venus*, in the excess of their delight, swear eternal fidelity, and then betake themselves to the pleasure of dancing.

Their enjoyment is now interrupted by the arrival of *Minerva* and *Mercury*, who descend in a chariot drawn by owls. They are commissioned to announce to *Mars* the necessity of his departure into Thrace to subdue the Titans ; such being the royal pleasure of *Jupiter*. The two lovers appear thunderstruck by this news ; they become motionless ; and all their vows of affection must be broken. The Ocean's daughter feels the most poignant grief. Rage and revenge inspire her breast. *Minerva* persuades them to be calm, and induces them to act promptly and resolutely. The son of *Juno*, unable to withstand the power of *Jupiter*, takes an affectionate farewell of his mistress, and departs fully armed, but a prey to despair. *Minerva* consoles *Venus*, and covering her with the Ægis, protects her from the fatal passion. *Love*, to try the effect of his arrows, engages in a contest with the Goddess of Wisdom, but he is vanquished, and finding himself deceived, and his designs frustrated, he wings his way into the skies, the daughter of Jove laughing at the rage of the malignant boy.

Vulcan now enters, accompanied by his attendants, he revisits his wife with delight, the influence of *Minerva* having entirely obliterated every trace of what has happened. The happy couple exchange marks of mutual attachment, while *Vulcan* invites *Minerva* and *Mercury* to attend him into his palace to partake of a banquet.

TABLEAU V.

A magnificent interior of the Palace of Vulcan.

THE Gods arrive; a superb throne is prepared to receive them, and they preside at the dances and games. The court of *Vulcan*, the *Lemnians* and the *Cyclops*, who are armed with hammers, and whose grotesque gestures and dancing form a marked contrast to the graceful attitudes of the *Nymphs*, complete the entertainment. *Mercury* partakes of the dancing, and *Venus*, to satisfy the wishes of the assembly, joins the troop of Terpsichore, unfolding new charms by the graces of her motion. After a general dance, the Ballet finishes by the formation of a group intended to convey an idea of the homage due to the Goddess of Beauty.

DIBUTADE*,

OR

THE ORIGIN OF DESIGN.

A HISTORI-FABULOUS BALLET, IN TWO ACTS.

ARGUMENT.

THE ancient traditional allegory, which relates Love to have been the inventor of the wonderful art professed by Apelles and Raphael, suggested the design of this dramatic performance. Love, who is every day producing prodigies, and who gave birth to all the fine arts, incited the young *Dibutade* to this discovery : warmed by his inspiration, and animated by his genius, she made the first essay in Design. This young damsel, in the excess of affection for her absent lover, which amounted to a delirium, fancied him present to her eyes. She instantly desires to preserve his image. Love, guiding the ardour

---

* The subject of this composition, and part of the scenes are nearly the same as those of the Opera bearing the same name, the author of which is M. Barincou, and the music by M. Blasis, senior ; both of whom produced the Grand Opera of *Omphale,* and *Achilles ; or, The Death of Patroclus.*

The novelty of this subject, which, excepting by painters, had never been treated on before the above named poet undertook it, having engaged my attention, I found it both agreeable and well adapted for the plot of a Ballet. In its peculiarly dramatic situations, and in every succeeding scene that unfolds the fable, I have endeavoured to substitute pantomime for speech, and to exchange the melody of song for the delights of dancing.   C. B.

of her fancy, teaches her to trace the likeness of *Polydore*, and the sight of these simple lines supplied to mankind the idea of the admirable art of painting.

According to the writings of Pliny, the inventor of this art was Gyges of Lydia, who taught it to the Egyptians. This author relates that Gyges being near the fire, and perceiving the reflection of his shadow, he took a coal and drew the outlines of his body upon the wall. Apollodorus afterwards invented the pencil.

Philocares of Egypt, and Cleanthes of Corinth, passed also as the inventors of painting. Enchires, brother-in-law to Dædalus, calls him the original discoverer, as his relative had been of sculpture.

Further, it may be gathered from the ancients, that Crato of Sycion was regarded as the inventor of painting, he having traced the outlines round the shadow of his horse, while the sun was shining upon the sand. The name of *Corinthia* has also been assigned to *Dibutade* when relating her essay; but the name and anecdote of *Dibutade* being more generally known, they have been preferred.

CHARACTERS.

PHILOCLES, *manufacturer of earthen vases.*

DIBUTADE, *in love with Polydore, and daughter of Philocles.*

POLYDORE, *a Greek Officer, enamoured of Dibutade.*

CUPID.

APOLLO.

THE MUSES.

DRYADS.

SYLVANS.

SHEPHERDS.

SHEPHERDESSES.

PEOPLE OF SYCION.

The scene is laid at Sycion, a town of Greece.

ACT I.

The scene represents a rural retreat consecrated to the God Pan, whose image, together with that of Cupid, adorns the prospect. In the distance the sea is discovered. Trees of majestic growth and verdant bowers, swelling banks and glittering fountains delight the eye. The silver rays of the moon illumine the landscape.

WITHIN the bowers, and beneath the spreading trees, *Dryads* and *Sylvans* are reposing. Shepherd swains, each accompanied by his partner, enter dancing to the sound of rustic music. The woodland divinities awaking, join in the dance and celebrate their patron, *Pan*, and the God of Love. [During this *Divertissement*, night disappears, and rising day chases the moon beneath the horizon.]

Towards the end of these amusements, the sky becomes darkened, and every circumstance indicates an approaching storm. The dances are suspended; the sea is agitated; lightnings blaze forth, and the thunder roars; the woodland train hastens away to seek shelter. A vessel appears struggling amidst the waves; it drives towards the shore; unable to resist their fury, it is at length run aground, and dashed upon the rocks. A few moments afterwards, *Polydore* is seen clinging to a wreck of the vessel, and, impelled by the billows, he is at length tossed upon the land. He appears exhausted by exertion, yet he strives to keep himself on his feet. He essays to discover on what country he is thrown, but finds no mark of information; he knows not which way to direct his steps, and is ignorant of what may be his fate. The wretched lot of his lost companions, who are become the victims of the storm, presents itself to his mind, renders him miserable, and plunges him into despair. He now recalls the image of *Dibutade*, it revives his drooping powers, and fortifies his breast against misfortune. His woe is alleviated by the remembrance of his love; she alone, even in idea, transports him amid distress; and could he but behold her, that distress would be forgotten; but, how shall he discover her dwelling? distressing situation! He now perceives the statue of Love; hoping for aid from that divinity, he implores for pity and protection, and to have his desires granted. Oppressed by his woe, he then sinks upon a bank.

Love at length appears, he comes to console *Polydore*, and to restore his mistress. · The God seems occupied with some important project; and he intends to render his suppliant instrumental in his designs. He approaches the young lover, and touches him with his bow; *Polydore* awakes, restored by the magic application; he is lost in astonishment at the sight of the deity; he prostrates himself; *Love* encourages him, and on the pedestal of his own statue traces these words:—

> While hast'ning to bring thee desired delight,
> I discover an art that shall ravish the sight *.

Polydore is scarcely able to contain himself, so greatly is he overjoyed. *Love* again encourages him, and striking the earth with his bow, the scene changes, and they are at once conveyed to the dwelling of *Dibutade*.

Scene, *the house of Philocles. To the right and near*

---

* ' Je vais ici produire en exauçant tes vœux,
  L' origine d'un art qui doit parler aux yeux.'

a projecting wall which forms a kind of portico, are observed various kinds of earthen vases. *Polydore* throws himself at the feet of *Love*, and appears anxious to behold his dear *Dibutade*. The young God commands him to announce his arrival in writing, directing him to perform it with the point of a dart upon a papyrus. *Polydore* obeys, and writes what *Love* dictates, who takes the epistle, and causes *Polydore* to conceal himself until the accomplishment of his wishes; the lover submits. The mischievous boy of Cythera then disguises himself as Anthenor, a pupil of *Philocles*, and betakes himself to the manufacture of vases. He seems meditating on his designs, and expresses himself confident of success.

Dibutade enters; love appears to engross all her thoughts; the absence of *Polydore* causes all her woe; *Cupid* watches her motion, and shortly after approaches and presents himself before her. His sprightly air and gay behaviour are offensive to *Dibutade;* and she desires him to show more respect to her situation; *Love* smiles and continues his roguishness; *Dibutade*, impatient of such effrontery, is going, but is prevented by the pretended Anthenor, who entreats her to pardon his jocular humour, which is caused by a piece of good news that he is going to inform her. *Dibutade* is surprised! does it concern her love? *Cupid* replies in the affirmative. *Dibutade* implores him not to keep her in uncertainty, but to explain himself without further delay. The mischievous boy gaily resumes his discourse, smiling at the torments of the affectionate girl. He at length satisfies her request, by telling her that a message has been sent to him announcing the arrival of *Polydore*, and that probably she may soon behold him at her feet. After this information he delivers the letter from her lover. *Dibutade* seizes it with transport, she cannot contain her joy;

she devours with her eyes the much-beloved and long-desired characters. *Philocles* is introduced by *Love* to partake of the happiness of his beloved daughter; they embrace; but the epistle of her lover again attracts her attention, and she becomes immoveable with admiration; it inflames and transports her, until she falls into a sort of delirium. She imagines she is addressing *Polydore*, and describes to him the feelings he has inspired and the ardour with which she burns. *Philocles*, greatly affected, endeavours to calm her. *Love*, seizing the propitious moment, leads forth *Polydore* in one hand, while in the other he bears his torch. The scene is brightened by its flame. *Cupid* and *Polydore* are standing behind *Philocles* and his daughter. Immediately upon their entrance, the shadow of *Polydore* is reflected upon the wall of the apartment. Both parties are equally surprised. Inspired by affection, and burning to preserve the traits of the beloved youth, *Dibutade* seizes a pencil, and, guided by *Love*, she traces the outlines around the shadow of *Polydore*.

Satisfied with the success of his intentions, the young God waves his torch over *Dibutade* and she is restored to her senses; he then resumes his own shape and resigns *Polydore* into the arms of *Dibutade*.

Love recalls the recollection of *Philocles* and his daughter, who are struck motionless with surprise: all now prostrate themselves. The performance of *Dibutade* is universally applauded; and all do honour to the art that ravishes the sight.

ACT II.

SCENE.—*A charming prospect, representing the sacred Valley.*

APOLLO appears seated on Parnassus, in the midst of the Muses; *Love* advances with those whom he has patronized. The rural divinities, &c., assemble themselves to witness the solemn celebration. *Cupid,* accompanied by the two lovers, offers his own and *Dibutade's* performance, which *Apollo* receives graciously and presents to the Muses, who, decorating it with flowers, do honour to the newly discovered art. The son of *Venus* receives from the hands of *Apollo* a resplendant crown, as the reward of his genius. His deeds are duly celebrated; while *Dibutade* is united to her lover by their divine protector. The Ballet is terminated by universal dancing, and allegorical representations analogous to the subject.

THE FALSE LORD*.

A COMIC BALLET, IN TWO ACTS.

___

CHARACTERS.

THE MARQUIS.
FRONTIN, *his servant*.
THE STEWARD.
LOUISE, *niece to the Steward*.
COLIN, *in love with Louise*.
MATHURIN, *in love with Louise also, a simpleton*.
 Village Lads and Maidens; Servants of the Marquis.

The Scene is laid in France.

___

ACT I.

SCENE.—*A green bower adjoining the chateau, the front of which appears on the right. On the left is discovered the village. Near the bower rises a green bank.*

COLIN and *Mathurin* are rivaling each other in endeavouring to procure the smiles of *Louise*, who is inclined to

___

* The subject is taken from an Opera.

favour the first, but rejects the latter. The two lovers amuse themselves with the simple *Mathurin*, who exhibits all the marks of disappointment.

The *Steward* enters, he holds a paper in his hand, and seems occupied in preparing a speech he is to deliver. *Mathurin*, perceiving him, leaves *Colin* and *Louise* and hastens to make complaint of his treatment. The *Steward*, busily engaged in his own affairs, pays no attention to him. *Mathurin* is offended, and all present themselves before the *Steward*, to acquaint him with their several pretensions ; but the latter, not attending to their request, wishes them to listen to the address he has prepared for the *Marquis ;* they turn away from him offended ; upon which the *Steward* forbids both the pretenders to speak to his niece, adding, that he shall not make known his intentions until the arrival of the *Marquis ;* he then withdraws, taking *Louise* with him; *Colin* steals after, unperceived.

Mathurin, left to himself, is in despair; he knows not on what to resolve, and falls into a reverie.

Frontin enters ; having left his master at the house of a favourite lady, he has preceded him to announce his arrival. He examines the place in which he is. *Mathurin* perceives him, and observing a dress and air he is unaccustomed to see, mistakes *Frontin* for the *Marquis*. He bows without knowing when to have done. *Frontin* appears surprised at such a reception. *Mathurin* gives him to understand that all are impatient to behold him in the village, and describes the honours that will be paid him, and the fêtes intended to celebrate his arrival. *Frontin*, charmed at this description, and dazzled with the honours of distinction, makes several awkward reflections. An idea strikes him, he appears delighted at it ; but hesitates before attempting to put it into execution ;

at length, however, he is determined to personate the *Marquis*. He buttons up his coat to conceal his livery. He imitates the manners of persons of rank, gives himself awkward airs, and promises his patronage to the peasant before him ; at which *Mathurin* is overjoyed, and begs the pretended gentleman to take some refreshment. *Frontin* instantly accepts the invitation with pleasure, and in a trice finishes a bottle of wine, so great is his thirst, while the villager stares in astonishment. The footman, finding his courage rise under the influence of the wine, is determined boldly to continue the cheat. *Mathurin*, observing his good humour, profits of it, and makes a confession of his love for *Louise*, begging *Frontin* to procure him her hand ; the latter engages to satisfy him. *Mathurin* returns a thousand thanks, and hastens to announce his arrival in the village.

Frontin now exercises himself in imitating the manners of his master, whom he apes in every action. Knowing his indulgence, he is not at all troubled with the idea of punishment, and prepares himself to enjoy the fruits of his successful deception. No time, however, must be lost ; he is going out to change his dress, but is detained by the entrance of *Louise*, who asks him, with modest fear, if it is to the *Marquis* she has the honour of addressing herself. *Frontin* replies it is. She then entreats him to pay no regard to *Mathurin*, but to unite her to *Colin*, whom she loves. *Frontin* has remarked her interesting appearance, and becomes enchanted with her amiable simplicity. He evinces a design upon her ; but does not yet venture to inform her; unwilling, however, to disappoint the pretty villager, he bids her entertain hopes that she shall be satisfied. He desires her to see that every thing is prepared for his reception in the village ; and then withdraws, casting significant glances at her. *Louise* is overjoyed at her success, and confides in the kindness of the supposed Marquis.

The *Steward* now arrives, accompanied by country people of both sexes, together with *Colin* and *Mathurin*, the latter of whom has informed them of every thing. Preparations are made to receive the *Marquis*, and the *Steward's* orders are promptly executed.

Frontin now appears dressed in his master's clothes; he receives, with an amusing air of assumed grandeur, the compliments of the villagers, acknowledging, in a burlesque style, their declarations of attachment. The *Steward*, in the name of the tenantry, assures him of their devoted affection; at the same time presenting his niece with her two rivals, and asking his consent to the marriage of *Louise*. The pretended Marquis, having his own views upon her, defers giving his decision from some certain secret motive, and gives orders for the fête to begin. Every one obeys. The enamoured party appear in great anxiety. After the *Divertissement, Frontin* rises, and declares his intention of giving a dinner at the chateau, to the surrounding nobility and gentry. Every one now prepares himself for the new fête.

The joyous peasantry and the *Steward* accompany *Frontin* to his residence. *Colin* and *Louise* steal away from the crowd and return to complain of their fate.

The *Marquis* himself now appears, he seems extremely disappointed at not having met his lady; at being obliged to hasten his journey, which he has performed on foot: he is exhausted by fatigue. Perceiving the two villagers, he inquires of them if they had observed any person arrive in the village? They reply yes, and that the *Marquis* is arrived at the chateau. The *Marquis* is astonished! On making further inquiries he learns clearly what has taken place, and suspects his roguish footman to be the author of the deception. He, however, conceals his indignation, and seems meditating on some new project. The two lovers appear desirous of knowing who he is. He replies that he is an agent of the *Marquis,* and also his banker. *Colin* and *Louise* apprise him of their mutual passion, and entreat him to conciliate the consent of his master to their union. The *Marquis* appears interested in their behalf, and informs them that he wishes to be secretly introduced into the chateau. They consent to assist him to the utmost of their abilities. The *Marquis* seems prepared to take revenge, and to punish his impudent servant. He withdraws, attended by *Louise* and *Colin.*

ACT II.

The scene represents the hall of the chateau; the garden is discovered through the entrance at the lower end.

THE *Marquis* enters, and waits the arrival of *Frontin*, in order that he may observe his conduct. The latter soon makes his appearance, accompanied by the *Steward;* they are discoursing on affairs. The *Marquis* conceals himself to make remarks. The *Steward* draws from his pocket a quantity of money, and deposits it on the table; then makes up his accounts. *Frontin* is electrified at the sight of the gold. The *Steward* gives him to understand that the money belongs to him as his right. *Frontin* knows not how to contain himself; his eyes devour the money, while his hands are employed in counting. He, however, recollects himself, and shrinks from dishonesty; but finding himself unable to resist the temptation, he orders the *Steward* to take it, and lock it up himself, and to prepare the fête immediately. The *Steward* obeys, though surprised at the indifference of his master. This action of *Frontin* at once appeases the resentment of his master. The fellow muses on his new condition, but the entrance of *Louise* puts an end to his meditations, and changes them into joy. She does not venture to approach him, but *Frontin* encourages her by his gestures. She informs him that she is again come to implore him to unite her to *Colin*, and to appoint the day of marriage ; but this proposal not answering the intentions of *Frontin,* he turns the subject of the conversation, flatters, and compliments her on her agreeable qualities. The young village maid blushes, and appears confused. *Frontin* growing impertinent, *Louise* attempts to escape from him, but he arrests her flight. He now makes confession of his love, on which *Louise* becomes greatly agitated. Fearing to offend the supposed Marquis, she knows not how to proceed. At length she sees no hope, but in artifice ; she pretends to faint, and is on the point of falling. *Frontin,* fearing discovery, is greatly perplexed. He places the maid in an arm chair, and searches on all sides for assistance ; he knows not what to do. The design of *Louise* has succeeded, and while *Frontin* is seeking for aid, she rises and runs away unperceived, thus avoiding his disagreeable advances. *Frontin* now returns to the spot where he had left the young villager ; but what is his surprise on finding her gone ! He perceives himself tricked. He storms and menaces *Louise* with the effects of his rage, and meditates on the means of revenge. The *Marquis* has observed all that passed, and has been much amused at the scene, particularly at the vexatious predicament of his man *Frontin.*

The *Steward,* the two lovers and the peasantry enter. The repast is prepared, and each takes his place. *Frontin* endeavours to overcome his agitation, and to effect an easy and genteel air.

The villagers enliven the fête by dances and pantomimic gestures. *Frontin* unmercifully devours whatever is set before him, from time to time casting a leer at *Louise*, at once reproaching her indifference, and striving to regain her favour.

The *Marquis*, who is continually straying about, arrests the attention of the *Steward*, and he inquires of his niece who it is that is standing near her. *Louise*, upon this, acquaints him with the secret, begging him not to divulge it. Her uncle, not hearing this, asks *Frontin*, who being surprised, demands who that man of business may be, and soon recognizes his master ! He finds himself greatly embarrassed, and is running towards the *Marquis*, when the latter stops him by a gesture, which is observed by none but *Frontin*. The company, remarking the change in the countenance of their supposed master, believe that he is taken ill, and inquire if he is unwell, but he is not prepared with an answer. At length, leaving the table, he entreats his master to take his place. He declares, that finding himself indisposed, he must withdraw into the air, and instantly makes off.

The *Marquis* now sits down to table, laughing at the affair. The *Steward* not discovering who it is, finds himself offended at this liberty, and rises from his seat. *Colin* and *Louise* alone are undisturbed, for they have not forgotten his promise of protection.

Frontin appears in his livery, with a napkin under his arm, and takes his usual place behind his master. Astonishment seizes on all ! All rise but the *Marquis*, who is infinitely amused at the scene. Each thinks proper to continue standing before his master, which redoubles his laughter. *Frontin* throws himself on his knees before his master, confesses his folly, and implores pardon for what he has done.

The kindness of the *Marquis* disposes him to overlook every thing, while amusing himself with the adventure, and enjoying the good humour of his people. All do obeisance before their lord, and express their dislike of *Frontin*. But the *Steward* is his irreconcilable enemy, having allied his family to a servant.

The *Marquis* tries to calm him, and unites *Louise* to her lover, consoling the disappointed *Mathurin* with a well-filled purse.

The village rejoice at the presence of the real lord, who graciously receives the marks of their attachment.

General Picture.

ACHILLES AT SCYROS*.

A HEROIC BALLET, IN THREE ACTS.

CHARACTERS.

ACHILLES, *married to Deidamia, under the name of Pyrrha, a supposed female attendant on Deidamia.*

DEIDAMIA, *daughter of Lycomedes, and wife of Achilles.*

ULYSSES, *Ambassador from the Greeks.*

LYCOMEDES, *King of Scyros.*

HIGH PRIEST.

ARCAS, *confidential attendant on Lycomedes.*

Princes of the Court of Lycomedes; Princesses attending Deidamia; Officers attached to Ulysses; Priests; Priests of Bacchus; Troops of Bacchantes; Satyrs, Fauns, Shepherds and Shepherdesses; Soldiers of Lycomedes; Soldiers of Ulysses; People of Scyros.

The Scene is laid in Scyros.

---

* Of all writers who have treated on this dramatic subject, none have succeeded better than Metastasio; and I have endeavoured to follow the footsteps of that great poet. M. Gardel's Ballet of *Achilles* at *Scyros* differs greatly in its plot from mine.

ACT I.

Scene I.—*A view of the country near the sea, which is discovered in the distance. Towards the centre of the scene appears the temple of Bacchus. On the right stands a wood consecrated to that God. The Scene is obscurely lighted, to represent the break of day.*

On the rising of the curtain, the temple of Bacchus is observed surrounded by groups of Bacchantes, who are assembled before the dawn to prepare a feast. The Bacchanalian priests enter from the temple, and command the Bacchantes to dispose every thing for the ceremony, and to arrange the processions: the latter retire to execute these orders. The priests withdraw into the wood, to invoke the assistance of the Gods. *The stage has become gradually and fully lighted.*

Scene II.—*Achilles* and *Deidamia* now appear; joy is depicted on their faces, and they express mutual delight at meeting each other. Unobserved by any intruder at this secret rendezvous, they exchange marks of affection; and then betake themselves to the pleasures of the dance *(pas de deux)*, during which they describe the sentiments of love. They are interrupted by the instruments of the Bacchantes, who are approaching; they suspend their amusement in surprise. *Deidamia* counsels *Achilles* to withdraw instantly, and to disguise himself to prevent discovery. *Deidamia* retiring entreats *Achilles* to be prudent, lest suspicion should arise; he obeys, and they depart on the left, to avoid encountering the Bacchantes.

Scene III.—The music plays some few minutes prior to the entrance of the Bacchantes, after which they appear brandishing their Thyrses, and attended by Fauns, striking on cymbals, and Satyrs playing the syrinx, shepherds and shepherdesses. They surround the fane of the God they are celebrating. At the same time the priests reappear and ascend into the temple; they invoke their deity and sacrifice to him. *Achilles* and *Deidamia* enter, each disguised as a Bacchante, and join the company in the games. [From time to time these bacchanalia are interrupted by *pas seuls* and *pas de deux* executed by the leaders of the groups of bacchanals, Fauns, Satyrs, shepherds and shepherdesses.] At the end of the *Divertissement*, the warlike sound of trumpets is heard echoing along the shores.

Struck with fear, every one seeks to discover from whence it proceeds; they hasten towards the sea. *Deidamia* trembles, and *Achilles* is surprised; they direct their attention to the shore; vessels suddenly appear filled with warriors, while the sounds of the instruments increase, and the bacchanalian troop, seized with dread, fly into the woods.

SCENE IV.—*Achilles* detains *Deidamia,* assuring her of safety by his own example; but the timid lady draws him away with her, entreating him not to expose himself to the hazard of a discovery. The brilliant appearance of the warriors awakens the military ardour in the breast of *Achilles.* He beholds with delight a sight till now unknown to him. In the mean time the vessels disappear on the right to disembark. His wife endeavours to detain him; but the attraction of arms, and the desire to become acquainted with the strangers, overcome every other consideration, and render him deaf to the prayers of the distressed *Deidamia.*

SCENE V.—*Ulysses*, followed by his officers, now advances in sight, while *Achilles* and his wife appear amazed. *Ulysses* salutes them. *Achilles* being recovered, demands who he is, and for what purpose he is come? urging a reply with threats. In vain does *Deidamia* strive to restrain his rashness. *Ulysses*, surprised to behold so much effrontery in a woman, already begins to suspect that it is *Achilles*, the object of his pretended embassy; but concealing his suspicion, he answers to the satisfaction of both, who now, but too late, perceive their imprudence. *Achilles* wishes to apologize, but *Ulysses* informs them he came not to interrupt their tranquil enjoyments, and presents them with an olive, as the symbol of peace; adding, that he would be introduced to the King. *Deidamia* answers, she will procure him an interview, and that *Lycomedes* will receive him graciously. She then takes leave, and is retiring, when *Achilles* again attempts to address *Ulysses*, but is prevented by his wife, who commands him to follow. In fear of being discovered, he submits to her wishes. The eye of *Ulysses* is in the mean time incessantly upon them.

Scene VI.—The crafty ambassador does not for an instant lose sight of *Achilles*, of whose renown he has already been informed, and whom, he flatters himself, he has here detected. This fortunate commencement inspires him with hope; and he thanks the Gods, supposing that he will have the honour of delivering up to the Greeks the man they so ardently desire. He acquaints his attendants with the discovery; they are astonished. *Ulysses (aside)* forms a stratagem which seems to fill him with confidence; he commands his suite to follow, and they take the way to the palace of *Lycomedes*. They withdraw on the right, the side at which *Deidamia* and *Achilles* had retired.

Scene VII.—*A magnificent interior view of the Palace of Lycomedes; on the right a throne with seats.*

Lycomedes enters, preceded by guards and accompanied by his suite; he conducts *Deidamia* by the hand, *Achilles* following at a respectful distance. The King orders preparation to be made for receiving the Greek Ambassador. *Lycomedes* is attended to his throne; he takes his seat, and places *Deidamia* at his side, the princes and princesses of his court surrounding them. *Achilles* contrives to place himself near to *Deidamia*.

A prince enters to announce the arrival of an ambassador who desires an audience. The King commands him to be presented; the prince makes obeisance and retires; while the intelligence excites general curiosity. *Ulysses* now appears, followed by military attendants, he salutes the monarch respectfully, who grants him a gracious reception. *Ulysses*, on the part of his allies, the Greeks, demands the assistance of *Lycomedes*' troops and vessels to furnish out an expedition against the Trojans. *Lycomedes* agrees to his demands, informing him that he may ever rely in his friendship. *Achilles* pays a most marked attention to the proposals of *Ulysses;* he feels himself highly excited; an ambition of glory is awakened within him; scarcely can he restrain his feelings; he blushes at his effeminate apparel, and is on the point of tearing them off, but the affection he bears his dear *Deidamia*, on whom his eyes are continually fixed, restrains and calms his internal heat. During the discourse, the vigilant *Ulysses* has attentively observed him; he smiles triumphantly; the disguise of the hero is no longer unknown to him. He now hastens to terminate the negociation.

The King, descending from his throne, convinces all who surround him of the union that should subsist between them and the Greeks; and particularly between himself and the hero who merits both their esteem and admiration.

Lycomedes invites *Ulysses* to remain with him; he consents with pleasure. The King commands to retire, and, giving one hand to *Ulysses* and the other to *Deidamia*, he withdraws. The latter princess expresses great agitation; she darts a look at *Achilles*, who appears lost in reflection upon his condition; he recovers, starts, and follows. The princes and princesses are near the King; and guards close the procession.

ACT II.

SCENE I.—*Sumptuous apartments in the Palace of Lycomedes. In the back ground are perceived the royal gardens. Statues representing Gods and Heroes adorn the sides of the apartments, and embellish the gardens also.*

PRINCES and princesses of the court, together with the suite of *Deidamia*, enter dancing *(on the left side)*. Pleasure animates their steps; they precede the King's entrance into this retreat of pleasure. *After a general Dance*, *Lycomedes* appears, and they environ him. In one hand he leads *Deidamia*, with the other he conducts *Ulysses*; a part of his train attends him. The guards retire to a distance. *Achilles* follows *Deidamia* with his eyes, which are now fixed on her, and now on *Ulysses*. *Lycomedes* commands all to celebrate the arrival of his illustrious friend, who appears sensibly alive to the noble conduct of the King, and acknowledges the homage paid to him by a respectful obeisance. Every one now hastens to fulfil the orders of the King. Both *Deidamia* and *Ulysses* watch respectively every motion of *Achilles*, who appears wrapt in meditation.

Lycomedes commands the dance to commence, wishing all to partake in its pleasures. Seated between *Ulysses* and *Deidamia,* he presides at the entertaiment. (*Divertissement* by the whole *Corps de Ballet.*) A prince and two princesses dance a *pas de trois.* The women attending *Deidamia* dance a measure to the sound of *lyres.* They then invite the spouse of *Achilles* to join them. *Ulysses,* seconding the request, entreats her to condescend to delight them. *Deidamia* consents and rises. *Achilles* presents her with a harp, she accepts it with a secret pleasure; she then executes a *pas seul,* with peculiar grace and science. Every one applauds, and she receives the praise with modesty. In dancing, she has essayed, however, more particularly to fix the attention of *Achilles.*

Ulysses now rises, returns thanks for the gracious reception *Lycomedes* has granted him, and prays him to receive the offerings of friendship which he is about to present; they are produced before the King, who is pleased to accept them. Vases, rich stuffs, &c. are exhibited before the court; on beholding them the admiration becomes universal, during which *Ulysses* narrowly watches *Achilles.* A complete suit of armour forms part of the presents, upon this the son of Thetis rivets his attention; he wishes to contemplate it nearer; he examines it, while his eyes sparkle with joy. *Deidamia* perceives it, hastens to him, and fearing for his imprudence, by looks and gestures allures him from the snare. The crafty *Ulysses,* satisfied at the success of his penetration, already sees the happy termination of his enterprise. While these offerings occupy the entire attention of the court, *Deidamia* being in fear, and *Achilles* in agitation, they are disturbed by the clash of arms. Surprise pervades the court, their attention is diverted. A prince, attached to *Lycomedes,* enters, and announces that the soldiers of *Ulysses* are engaged in an obstinate combat with those of the King; and that the presence of the latter is necessary to restore peace. *Ulysses* secretly enjoys the success of his stratagem. Every one appears to feel deeply the event. *Lycomedes* commands his soldiers to follow him; they arrange themselves in array of battle, and march off to meet the rebels, with the King at their head. The princes and officers withdraw on the left, following the King.

Deidamia, accompanied by her women, makes a sign to *Achilles* to follow, when hastening away; he heeds not, and allows the timid *Deidamia* to fly. *Ulysses* feigns to follow the King, but remains behind, to profit by an opportunity of a private interview with *Achilles*.

SCENE II.—A deep silence prevails. The son of Thetis remains immoveable; recovered from his stupor, he reflects upon his fate. He ruminates on what he has heard and seen; his spirits returning, the love of arms gradually inspires him, and takes possession of his breast. At length he seems determined to depart, but hesitates. He approaches the armour and contemplates it with a lively pleasure; he then casts a look on his own apparel and blushes to behold himself so disguised. Unable longer to restrain his feelings, he tears off his female attire with rage and indignation. The impetuous hero then seizes the shield with one hand, while with the other he grasps the sword, and prepares to depart. During this *Ulysses* observes *Achilles* at a distance; he expresses joy on beholding the success of his designs—his commission has prospered; he is in possession of *Achilles*, it is enough; he therefore advances to meet him, and prevents his departure; he embraces the hero with delight, and congratulates *Achilles* on the happy change. He now turns the attention of *Achilles* to the contemplation of the glory that awaits him, and which will exalt him to the rank of the most renowned heroes. While representing these results, *Ulysses* points to the statues of those heroes who have distinguished themselves by their deeds and their virtues, expressing at the same time contempt for those who have debased themselves. The heart of *Achilles* burns at the words of *Ulysses*, who having thus become acquainted with his character, persuades him now to hasten away. *Achilles* hesitates; tender recollections arise; love presents to him the image of his affectionate consort; her faithful attachment is about to be rewarded by his own ingratitude; these thoughts cause him to be undecided. *Ulysses*, unwilling to lose so favourable an opportunity, treats these emotions with contempt, and exhorts him to go forth, and eradicate those debasing recollections which must wound the heart of a soldier; he even commands a compliance. *Achilles*, feeling the ascendancy that *Ulysses* has over him, is decided on the pursuit of glory, and, forgetting the past, he triumphs over himself and departs. *Ulysses* accompanies him, satisfied with the conquest he has made.

ACT III.

SCENE.—*A tent is discovered on the right. The sea of Scyros appears covered with vessels. To the left stand the statues of Mars and Venus.*

AT the rising of the curtain, *Achilles*, completely armed, appears standing in a pensive attitude, meditating on his fate; *Ulysses* is at some distance from him, and observes him. Both are in the tent. The soldiers of *Ulysses* are at the end of the stage, reposing in various positions. *Achilles* seems affected at the loss of his *Deidamia*, the thought of whom greatly agitates him. *Ulysses*, remarking this emotion, approaches to tranquillize him and to cheer his gloom. He endeavours to sustain his fortitude by representing the honour and glory that await him. *Achilles*, recovering, resigns himself wholly to the pursuit of arms, and is entirely directed by *Ulysses*. The latter makes a sign to his warriors, and they commence an *Armed Dance*. *Achilles*, unprepared for such an exhibition, is agreeably surprised. *Ulysses* extols his soldiers, and *Achilles* is transported. At the close of the measure the warriors prostrate themselves before the statue of Mars. *Ulysses* draws the attention of the hero to these tutelar deities, and both do homage before the statues. *Ulysses*, to prevent loss of time, orders to depart immediately. The soldiers prepare to march, and he tells *Achilles* he must now quit this abode of effeminacy, and fly to the field of Mars; he obeys. As they are departing, a noise is heard and *Deidamia* enters; *Ulysses* hastens to draw away *Achilles*, who would stay, so great an effect has the unexpected arrival of *Deidamia* upon him.

Scene II.—*Deidamia*, her face bathed in tears, expresses unrestrained grief, and deplores her situation; she arrests the progress of her husband, who is leaving her for ever. She then breaks out into reproaches, and evinces the strength of her attachment. She upbraids him with his cruel ingratitude, violated oaths, and deceitful conduct, and then endeavours to recall the first sentiments of their affection. *Achilles* is silent; he is anxious to rejoin *Ulysses*, who appears something disconcerted at the scene. *Deidamia*, perceiving her husband deaf to her entreaties, renews her supplications, and again reminds him of the oaths of fidelity they had sworn to each other before the Gods, oaths that should unite them for ever; she taxes him with her injuries, and employs prayers to dissuade him from departing. *Ulysses*, by contrary counsels, sustains and fixes the resolution of the hero; yet he fears the susceptibility of his heart. *Achilles* is mute and turns from *Deidamia;* the beauteous princess clinging still to her husband, at length moves him; he hesitates between love and glory. *Deidamia*, perceiving him irresolute, and still entertaining hopes, throws herself at his feet; the sight of this abasement recalls his affection, he is on the point of yielding; when *Ulysses*, constant to his purpose, essays to draw him away. *Deidamia*, unable longer to struggle with her misfortunes, and weak with exertion, falls into a swoon before him. *Achilles*, breaking from *Ulysses*, hastens to assist her, and employs every means for restoration; his heart, subdued by love and pity, is wholly occupied with *Deidamia*. The latter gradually recovers, and finding herself in the arms of her husband, her joy is extreme. *Ulysses*, on witnessing this affecting scene, appears something moved, yet is he impatient to be gone, and even to abandon *Achilles;* but the latter detains him, entreating his indulgence for the object to whom he owes so much; he implores a short respite; *Ulysses* consents, finding it impossible to counteract the present emotions. *A noise is heard.* At this moment *Lycomedes* enters, followed by his guards and attendants; information of what is passing has caused his presence.

SCENE III. They are struck motionless at the unexpected appearance of the monarch, who seems astonished. Recovered from his surprise, he perceives the whole intrigue; he bursts out into the heat of passion, and loads them with reproaches, showing them their ungrateful conduct in abusing his credulity.

His daughter and *Achilles* fall at his feet; but he attends not to their entreaties; their tears and supplications are incapable of appeasing his just resentment; he feels deeply the injury offered him. *Deidamia* still employs tears and prayers to calm her incensed father, and perse-

veres in her endeavours to prove her innocence and her
hapless fate; *Lycomedes*, still remembering the wrongs
done to him, repulses, with grief and indignation, his affectionate child; *Achilles* joining himself to the princess,
they prostrate themselves before him, and assist in the
entreaty. At length *Ulysses* discovers to the King that
it is *Achilles*, the son of Thetis the Goddess, who is
united to his daughter by the ties of Hymen; and that
the Gods now demand the services of that hero against
the Trojans.

At this intelligence the monarch is both calmed and
surprised; he turns, and raises *Achilles* and *Deidamia*;
and, submitting to the will of the Gods, he pardons them;
he embraces them, and congratulates himself on such an
alliance. This discovery fills the couple with delight; and
all partake in their joy.

To celebrate the happy day, the King commands all
to return thanks to the Gods, and to enliven the rejoicing
by dances and games. The priests enter and prepare an
altar for sacrifice; they invoke the Gods, and implore
their protection. All surround the altar to partake in the
rites. The High Priest begins the sacrifice, beseeching
the favour of the Gods; he prays them to decide the lot of
Achilles by some supernatural sign. All, bending before
the altar, await the supernatural signs in solemn silence.

The growling of thunder is heard, attesting the will of
the Gods. Every one now prostrates himself; *Achilles*
submits with pleasure; but *Deidamia* cannot restrain her
sorrow. *Lycomedes* endeavours to console her; he commands the celebration to begin, seating himself by his
children and *Ulysses*. [*Divertissement, Corps de Ballet,
pas de deux, pas de quatre, and Finale*]. The *Divertissement* is performed by the princes, princesses, and
the whole assembled court.

At the end of the Ballet, *Ulysses* advances and informs the King of the approaching departure; for which preparations are now made; the soldiers stand ready to march. *Achilles* takes leave of *Lycomedes*, and of his wife, whose grief is still visible; he consoles her with hopes of a happy return when the foe shall be vanquished. *Ulysses*, attended by his soldiers, bids adieu to *Lycomedes*, acknowledging his kindness. *Ulysses* and *Achilles*, now ascending their vessels, glide from the shores of Scyros amidst the acclamations of the people. *A general grouping*, while *Ulysses*, placed by the side of *Achilles* on the deck, triumphs in success, and departs.

MOKANNA*.

AN ORIENTAL BALLET, IN FOUR ACTS.

CHARACTERS.

MOKANNA, *a false Prophet.*
ZELICA.
AZIM, *her lover.*
KALED, *father of Zelica, and principal officer of Mokanna.*
HAROUN and MESROU, *officers of Mokanna.*
Women of Mokanna's Harem; Soldiers of Mokanna's Army; Soldiers of the Caliph's Army.

The scene is laid in Persia, in the year 163 *of the Hegira* (785 *of our Æra), and during the reign of Caliph Mahai.*

---

* The subject of this chorographic performance is taken from an English poem (*The Veiled Prophet*), by Thomas Moore, a celebrated poet, who imitates, with equal talent, the style both of Correggio and Guercino.

The peculiar character of a Ballet has obliged me to make some alterations in the action of the author's production. I have, however, particularly endeavoured· to embody his ideas upon the stage, and to preserve his beautiful local incidents.

This tale, I believe, has never yet been adapted to the form of a Ballet, or represented in any dramatic shape whatever.

ACT I.

The stage represents a sumptuous vestibule. Pillars of porphyry support an arched roof of Moriscan architecture. A throne is placed at the upper end, near which soldiers of the Harem are discovered.

MOKANNA, in the midst of his followers, receives their homage, oaths of allegiance and blind obedience. He prides himself on the ascendancy he has acquired over the minds of the people, who are become fanatical from the success of the impostor, now become secure of complete triumph in his designs of ambition, cruelty and love.

Every one, allured by his flattering promises of happiness and another life free from pain, allows himself to be overcome by the prospect of this deception, and adores him as a God.

Mokanna imagines himself, more than he finds himself, master of the lives of his subjects, and endued with sufficient power to oblige them to advance his sanguinary designs. The most unbridled passion burns within him; amongst all the women in his possession, the unfortunate *Zelica*, whom he intends to seduce, is preferred. He shows his preference of her, and endeavours to conciliate her by hopes of future happiness. The young maiden allows herself to be deceived by his imposing falsehoods. All prostrate themselves at the feet of the barbarous impostor, who pretends to grant them eternal protection.

Haroun enters to announce the arrival of *Azim*, a young and valiant warrior, who is about to join the standard of the heaven-appointed Prophet. He is returning victorious from a military expedition. Attracted by the extraordinary actions of the great *Mokanna*, he devotes himself to his worship, and burns with impatience to assist in advancing a belief in the happiness promised by the man who vaunts himself inspired. The appearance of *Azim* produces emotions of general joy. He is attended by some followers. They prostrate themselves at the feet of the Prophet, and take an oath to sacrifice their lives in his service. *Mokanna* inflames their ardour, by promising to place them amongst the number of the elect in heaven.

Azim has now discovered his love, the beautiful *Zelica*, who can scarcely conceal her joy at the unexpected arrival of her dear *Azim*, whom she thought dead. The lovers evince great joy. *Mokanna* boasts his power, and encourages his followers to propagate the new faith, and threatens death as the punishment of rebels. He promises to conduct his army in person, and thus to secure victory to his adherents; and peace will be but the beginning of their happiness. The enthusiasts agree to every thing. The banners of the soldiers, floating in the air, display these words: " *Freedom to the World.*" They swear upon their swords to deliver nations. Warlike music sounds forth the battle hymn; and the glory of the Prophet is celebrated by martial dances.

ACT II.

The stage represents a vast subterranean vault, from which livid flames are continually seen darting, supposed to be caused by putrefaction. Mokanna, bearing a light, is seen to enter this receptacle of the dead, by a secret staircase.

HE ruminates upon his horrible designs, and the smile of a villain seems to announce success. He now waits with impatience the object of his desires, for he is soon to become the possessor of the charming *Zelica;* he displays a barbarous joy. He wishes beauty to contribute to the success of his arms, and to augment by its attractions the number of his followers; and he instigates them to cruelty by promises of laurels of victory. *Zelica* appears, accompanied by *Haroun.* They are come in obedience to the commands of the Prophet; they bow before him.

Mokanna motions to *Haroun,* who retires. *Zelica* is astonished to find herself in so gloomy an abode; she waits to know the Prophet's pleasure. *Mokanna* tells her that the time is arrived in which the decrees of heaven must be accomplished; that it is her whom heaven has chosen to be a partner in the disposal of the fates of mankind. Surprise of *Zelica! Mokanna* endeavours to convince her of the purity of his sentiments, his noble disinterestedness, and his wish to see her the object of divine favour; he therefore expects her to show feelings of gratitude for his kindness; but the young maid is in the greatest agitation. What she has just heard, and her affection for *Azim*, throw her into great distress. *Mokanna* represents to her a happy futurity,

and promises her a share in his throne, if she will consent
to become the dispenser of human happiness to mortals.
He now proceeds to declare his passion to her. Astonishment of *Zelica*. The seducer shows marks of his affection, and conjures her to hasten his happiness, by submitting to the divine will.

Zelica can scarcely believe what she hears. No longer
does she find him the man who could subjugate the mind
of the people. Her faith wavers, and she fears the dreadful consequences; the remembrance of the faithful *Azim*,
too, draws tears from her eyes. The impostor, *Mokanna*,
fearing his prey may escape him, and that his deceptions
should be discovered, endeavours to impose upon the
young *Zelica*. He threatens her with the wrath of
heaven and the most terrible punishments; *Zelica*
shudders, but fanaticism still enthrals her. *Mokanna*
perceives that his intentions succeed, and he entreats her
to become his for ever. *Zelica*, driven to despair, at
length confesses that her heart is pledged to *Azim*. The
furious rage of *Mokanna* upon this: and the maiden reads
her own fate, and that of *Azim* also, in the countenance
of *Mokanna*. She throws herself at his feet and implores
for mercy. *Mokanna* is inexorable, and even seems
ready to attempt her life, but interested thoughts restrain
him, and he promises to let *Azim* live; but informs *Zelica*
that she must become his, and commands her to forget all
upon the earth, and to take an oath that she will be united
to him. The distress of *Zelica*. *Mokanna* drags her to
a tomb, and forces her to swear by the infernal powers,
and by the shades of the dead, to dedicate her life to his
service. *Zelica*, scarcely supporting herself, makes a
sign of consent. Upon this, flames dart from the tombs,
and a tremendous report resounds through the vault.
Zelica, unable longer to endure the emotions produced

by the scene, falls into a swoon. *Mokanna*, triumphing in his wickedness, smiles with a malignant satisfaction, and even boasts his success.

ACT III.

The stage displays a magnificent saloon, which looks into a delightful garden, illumined by the moon.

AZIM appears; he seeks *Zelica;* he burns with impatience to find her, and to prove to her his affection. Deprived of the pleasure of her embraces, he has for some time experienced the most cruel torments.

Melodious music breaks on the silence of night, while *Houris* enter dancing to their instruments. *Zelica* follows, but melancholy and sorrow prevent her from partaking in the joy of her companions, who are celebrating the glory of the Prophet by their games and dances. They congratulate *Azim* on his attachment to the banners of *Mokanna*, and they conjure him to deserve the happiness promised to him. *Azim* has already discovered his love, but is prevented from approaching her to declare his tenderness. *Zelica*, now esteemed the favoured of the Prophet, makes a sign to her companions, who retire.

The two lovers now fly into each other's arms. Transports of affection ensue; but they are soon interrupted by the distressing recollections of *Zelica*. *Azim*, in surprise, demands the cause of this emotion. *Zelica* hesitates; he presses her, she replies by tears: *Azim*, greatly agitated, conjures her to tell him all. *Zelica* represents to him the dreadful character of *Mokanna*, and his impostures; and at length reveals the cruel oath he has drawn from her by promising to spare the life of her lover. Rage, instead of grief, now possesses the bosom of *Azim ;* he swears to release her from his hated bonds, and to deliver the earth from such a monster. Nothing can appease the anger of *Azim ;* he is ready to attempt any thing. *Zelica* succeeds in calming his rage, persuading him that great prudence is necessary, without which they are both lost.

Kaled enters in haste ; he seeks for *Mokanna* to inform him of the approach of the Caliph at the head of his army, coming to engage the followers of the new sect. *Azim* and *Zelica* hasten to embrace him. *Kaled* bestows a blessing on their union. He discovers their painful anxiety, and desires to be informed of the cause of it. *Azim* explains to him the infamous character and horrible designs of *Mokanna.* Amazement of *Kaled !* Recovering, he throws himself into the arms of his children, and communicates to them with what horror *Mokanna's* character inspires him. They now appear greatly embarrassed. The time presses, and *Azim* engages his love and her father to seek safety by flight, and immediately to secure means of complete and speedy revenge.

Mokanna has appeared, he observes them and discovers their design. At the moment they are going to escape, he arrests their progress, gets possession of *Zelica,* and, by a menacing gesture, recalls to her mind the oath she had taken. *Zelica* trembles, totters, and is on the point of swooning. *Kaled* and *Azim* draw their poniards and rush upon the infamous seducer. But he, anticipating them, calls his guards, and commands them to be secured. *Kaled* and *Azim* vainly endeavour to defend themselves, they are made prisoners ; while *Mokanna,* menacing them with the most cruel revenge, drags off *Zelica.*

The approach of the Caliph's army is announced. Sudden terror of *Mokanna*. Appearance of hope on the part of *Azim* and his followers. *Mokanna*, vaunting his own strength, gives orders to prepare for the combat.

ACT IV.

A vestibule in Mokanna's residence. The ramparts of the City are seen in the distance. Night.

AN engagement between *Mokanna's* soldiers and those of the Caliph. The latter are victorious, and pursue the conquered. *Kaled, Azim,* and *Zelica* appear, having escaped the vigilance of their guards. They are animated by revenge, and, the better to obtain it, they join the army of the Caliph. *Zelica* enjoys the protection of her lover, but she cannot yet forget the villain who seduced her; she is, however, animated by the hopes of success. *Kaled* discovers a way that leads to the Mussulman army, and all hasten to follow him.

Mokanna enters, attended by his warriors; his thoughts are employed on his situation; he foresees the end of his reign approaching with certain death. He still essays, by his looks and promises of futurity, to impose upon those men whom he has seduced. He shows them the end of their labours, and the immortal glory that must ultimately crown them. He causes them to take an oath to destroy the Caliph, and to venture their lives in the holy cause. All obey. News is brought of the escape of *Zelica*. The furious rage of *Mokanna!* He swears their destruction, brandishes his scymitar, puts himself at the head of his warriors, and advances to battle.

Azim enters, followed by his brave soldiers, seeking every where his enemy, to destroy him. He descries

Mokanna's standard floating in the air, and flies to it. *Mokanna* re-enters in despair. Hope has forsaken him; he prepares for death. A ferocious smile expresses the joy he feels in beholding himself the destroyer of his species. His reign is at an end, but he has been the assassin of mankind. This abominable thought seems to give him pleasure to the last. The happiness, however, of *Zelica* and *Azim* torments him, and he is furious at not having prevented it, and it even inspires him with a sort of remorse. The conquering army approaches; part of the ramparts are beaten down, and several edifices become a prey to the flames. *Mokanna* then procures a flambeau, and fires one side of the palace. He falls near the ruins, and breathes out his soul in horrible blasphemies. *Kaled* and *Zelica* enter in time to behold the last moments of the impostor; and the victorious armies, headed by *Azim* and the Caliph, now arrive at the scene.

Each returns thanks to heaven at the happy event which delivers the people from a barbarous tyrant. *Kaled* unites *Zelica* to her lover, and peace bestows untroubled joy. *A General Picture.*

THE DUTCH PAINTER,

A SEMI-SERIOUS *(DEMI-CARACTERE)* BALLET,

IN TWO ACTS.

ARGUMENT.

CIRCUMSTANCES of an unfortunate and disagreeable nature at court obliged *Teniers* to assume a disguise, and to retire into a village. Having continued for some time in this retreat, chance conducted the *Archduke Leopold* and his *Duchess* to his place of concealment; and having recognized the great artist, they wished to atone for the injustice that had been shown him, and accordingly recalled him to the court, and again honoured him with their protection and friendship. Upon this last mentioned event the plot of this Ballet is founded.

CHARACTERS.

TENIERS *(under the assumed name of Dominic), a painter.*
ARCHDUKE LEOPOLD, *Governor of the Low Countries.*
THE ARCHDUCHESS.
FRITZ, *an innkeeper.*
DAME FRITZ, *his wife.*

CARLO, *a young villager.*
ANNA, *daughter of Fritz, in love with Carlo.*
TUNDER, *a daubing sign-painter.*
THE DROSSART, *a kind of beadle.*
*Peasantry; Officers of Leopold; Huntsmen in the suit
of the Princess.*

*During the first act, the scene lays at a village near
Lackin; during the second in the gardens of Lackin,
a summer residence of Leopold.*

ACT I.

*The centre of a village; on the right is an inn; on the left
the cottage of Tunder, against which are affixed boards,
representing grotesque and caricature paintings, as signs
of his profession. A hill appears in the distance.*

TENIERS is discovered occupied in painting the figure
of a man completely armed; beneath which is inscribed:
" *To the Great Leopold.*" The artist seems to reflect
upon the peculiarity of his condition; living under
an assumed name, and obliged to paint sign-boards in a
village.

The hostess of the inn and her daughter enter, and
appear to be engaged in preparing for a wedding. During
what follows, *Fritz,* the landlord, is discovered spying
into the conduct of his wife, of whom he is jealous.
Teniers advances to meet her; she inquires whether the
work upon which he is engaged is finished? He replies,

nearly. The mother and her daughter then admire the painting, and compliment the artist. *Fritz* enters, apparently in ill humour ; and, casting a jealous look upon his wife, he informs his daughter that he intends *Tunder* shall be her husband. *Anna,* instantly embracing her father, implores him not to be the cause of her wretchedness by marrying her to him she hates, and while her heart is wholly devoted to *Carlo.* *Fritz* becomes angry, and refuses her request ; while his wife obstinately contradicts all her husband advances ; *Teniers* endeavours to appease this strife, and to console the unfortunate *Anna,* whose whole reliance is upon the opposition of her mother.

Tunder now enters, carrying a picture under his arm ; he salutes the company, and throws a tender look at *Anna.* Observing *Teniers,* he gives him the compliments of the day with a contemptuous grin. He is civilly received by *Fritz* alone, who desires to see his performance ; *Brush* obeys, and courts the admiration of all while exhibiting his daub ; but it is ridiculed, except by himself and *Fritz,* who treat the work of *Teniers* with contempt. *Tunder,* however, wishing for a more decisive proof of excellence, draws an immense magnifier from his pocket, and after having examined each performance, finally gives the preference to his own. The admiring landlord being of the same opinion, immediately presents his daughter to him as his future wife ; at the same time *Anna* and her mother discover by their looks a resolution to defeat this project. Upon this the merry *Carlo* enters, and interrupts the discourse ; he salutes all present, giving his rival a rude push as he passes ; the latter, however, does not notice it. *Carlo* announces further orders concerning the approaching nuptials, and *Fritz,* with his wife, re-enter the house to make preparations. *Tunder*, angry at this awkward circumstance, and disappointed at being unable to conclude the match, enters his cottage greatly chagrined.

Carlo and *Anna*, notwithstanding the vanity of *Tunder*, place the sign painted by *Teniers* over the door of the inn. *Anna* relates what has passed, and proposes means to effect their union. The two lovers then exchange proofs of affection, which inspire the delightful movements of the dance. They are suddenly interrupted by a noise of hunters; *Anna* enters the inn, and *Carlo* retires on the opposite side.

The *Archduke Leopold* enters, habited as a hunter; having separated from the train, he has discovered this agreeable retreat to repose and refresh himself. The hostess, entering from the inn, soon perceives him, and taking him for an officer of the Duke's, asks him if he wishes for any refreshment; *Leopold* answering in the affirmative, *Dame Fritz* calls her daughter, and desires her to attend to their guest. The latter pays a particular attention to the peculiar gentility of *Anna's* person; and demands the name of the inn; the girl replies by pointing to the sign; the Duke is instantly struck with the subject of the picture and the beauty of its execution; he expresses feelings of gratitude at the zeal of his tenantry in thus honouring his effigy. The music to be employed in the celebration of the approaching wedding is now heard, and *Leopold* is invited to form one of the party. *Carlo* enters at the head of a gay troop of villagers; *Fritz* enters from the house, and *Teniers* and *Tunder* appear. *Carlo* draws the attention of his companions to the newly painted sign, while *Leopold* secretly enjoys the effect produced by his own portrait. Loyalty to *Leopold*, and praise to the painter, become the general theme.   *Teniers* discovers *Leopold,* but conceals his knowledge. *Tunder* is tormented by jealousy. The feast is prepared ; the bride and bridegroom take their seats, and dancing begins ; *Leopold,* meanwhile, seems highly to enjoy the scene. *Tunder,* after having been with some difficulty prevailed upon, dances in an awkward and grotesque style ; he then requires others to exhibit their abilities in this way, and, taking a fiddle, mounts a tub ; wishing to mark the time with a scientific precision, he stamps with such force, that the top of the tub breaks, and he tumbles heels over head into it; while the whole assembly bursts out into a universal shout of laughter. *General Picture.*

The *Archduchess* arrives, attended by her suit, and the whole assembly prepare themselves to meet and welcome her ; she causes inquiries to be made concerning the Duke, her husband ; the answer is, that no person belonging to the court has been except the officer whom they point out to her highness ; upon this *Leopold* is immediately recognized by all present, and the whole company do homage before him, in great astonishment. The Duke embraces his wife, who is equally surprised, and both express their sentiments of condescension and gratitude at the respect paid to them by their subjects. The Duchess having remarked the painting on the sign signifies her wish to know the artist who executed so fine a likeness, and *Teniers* cannot longer keep concealed, being soon discovered by his royal patroness ; he immediately throws himself at her feet ; the Duchess raises and presents him to *Leopold* as the artist whose departure she had continually regretted. The Duke reproaches him with his retreat from court, and demands what he can do for him. *Teniers,* with an air of modesty, only desires that his highness would make some provision for the enamoured couple, *Anna* and *Carlo*, having found in the family of the former an agreeable asylum, and the most hospitable treatment. *Leopold* grants his request, and being charmed with the artist's generosity, he desires him to return to court. *Fritz* and his wife, perceiving this advantageous and unexpected change, express their gratitude both to *Teniers* and the Duke. Every one appears delighted excepting *Tunder*, who has lost his lass ; but how can he oppose a prince ? Certain of the company undertake to represent to him that there is nothing unreasonable in *Anna's* choice, and at length prevail upon him to join the general gaiety. The *Archduke*, in order the more completely to celebrate this extraordinary event, commands his tenantry to follow him to his residence, upon which a suitable procession is formed.

ACT. II.

SCENE.—*The gardens adjoining the chateau of* Leopold ; *the chateau appearing in the distance.*

PEASANTS enter and prepare a seat of state decorated with flowers. The *Drossart* enters with a solemn air, and is observed perusing the oration he is about to pronounce. The peasants show him their work, with which he appears entirely satisfied. The approach of the procession is heard, and the *Drossart* hastens to meet it. *Leopold* and the *Archduchess*, accompanied by *Teniers* and a long train of servants, officers and tenantry, enter and take their seats. The *Drossart* prepares with an important air to deliver his harangue ; but as he is on the point of commencing, the Duke signifies by a sign that he will dispense with this part of the ceremony, and orders the marriage to be forthwith performed ; after which the villagers celebrate the union of *Anna* and *Carlo* by joyous and varied measures, and the Ballet terminates with a Flemish dance.

THRASIMEDES AND THEOPHANIA,

OR

THE FEAST OF ELEUSIS,

A SERIOUS BALLET, IN THREE ACTS.

CHARACTERS.

THRASIMEDES, *a Grecian Prince, disguised as a shepherd.*

THEOPHANIA, *beloved by Thrasimedes.*

ALCANDER, *father of Theophania, Governor of Eleusis and master of the Temple of Ceres.*

NARSES, *confidential friend of Thrasimedes.*

Shepherds, Nymphs, Priests of the Temple, and Greek Soldiers.

The scene passes at Eleusis.

ACT I.

*An extensive prospect ; in the distance mountains are
seen, the sides of which are adorned by copses of trees
and winding rivulets.   On one of the declivities there is
a little enclosure of myrtles and laurels, decorated with
garlands, ears of corn, and instruments of husbandry ;
from the midst of these rises the statue of Ceres, she
holds in her hand two lighted torches, and is seated in
a chariot drawn by serpents.*

Scene I.—*Thrasimedes* and *Narses* are perceived upon
the mountains disguised as shepherds ; the former is
hastening to meet his love, and he expresses his delight
at again beholding the spot upon which they are accustomed to meet daily.   He intrusts *Narses* with his
love secret, on understanding which, the latter appears
surprised ; *Thrasimedes* continues, that, being deeply enamoured of the Governor's daughter, he wishes to pursue his intentions habited as a shepherd, and so to owe
his conquest rather to personal qualifications than to
those of rank ; *Narses* approves the project, and offers
his faithful services in assisting his prince ; while the
latter solemnly protests his fidelity to *Theophania*.   He
recommends to *Narses* a conduct of the utmost caution,
and desires him to be ever prepared to execute his commands ; the former promises to obey, and retires.   *Thrasimedes* evinces all the anxiety of an expecting lover.

Scene II.—A slight noise is heard, seeming to indicate the approach of *Theophania ; Thrasimedes* hastens to
discover whence it proceeds ; the maid appears, and flies
to the arms of her beloved.   By turns they express to
each other the feelings of their hearts ; and before the

image of the chaste Ceres they vow eternal constancy, and invoke her protection. They call the Goddess to witness the purity of their love, and entreat her to preside at their union. They now betake themselves to the delights of the dance, in which every attitude does but the more clearly develope their sentiments. The arrival of the companions of *Theophania* interrupts their pleasure, and they take a hasty leave of each other, promising soon to revisit that spot. *Thrasimedes* seeks his friend *Narses*, and *Theophania* hastens to meet her companions, who are coming to prepare a ceremony which is to take place in this part.

Scene III.——A troop of nymphs appear, bearing branches of myrtle in their hands, and crowned with chaplets of wheat-ears. They enter dancing, led on by *Theophania*.

The procession to Ceres advances in sight; priests and shepherds are uniformly crowned with corn, each carrying a myrtle branch. These are followed by *Alcander* accompanied by his officers of government. The procession being fully arrived it halts, and all do obeisance to the Governor, awaiting his commands. While this is passing, *Thrasimedes* and *Narses* intermingle with the shepherds unperceived, and take part in the solemnities. *Alcander* invokes the Goddess; and the whole assembly implore her to be propitious, and to preside at the feast about to be celebrated by *Theophania*, as mistress of the religious ceremonies. The Governor now causes his daughter to approach him; she advances, agitated at finding herself in a situation which excludes every sentiment of love. Being aware of her own feelings, she fears her father may perceive the cause; but the latter attributes them to a mixture of modesty and awe; he embraces and encourages her; she bends before him, and he places a coronet of flowers on her head.

Theophania expresses her gratitude, while the whole company applaud the choice of *Alcander*, and regard the nymph as worthy of presiding over the worshippers of Ceres, both from her rank and chastity.   Curling clouds of smoke now arise from the incense lighted up by the priests.

Thrasimedes is discovered in a torment of anxiety, he perceives insurmountable obstacles to their union; *Theophania*, by her gestures, evinces a mutual concern; they exchange significant looks, but dare proceed no further; all hope, however, has not forsaken them, and they are supported by love.   *Narses* encourages them, and by certain signs counsels them to dissimulate.   *Alcander*, his daughter, and the priests, take their seats near the myrtle bower and preside at the feast.   Universal homage is done to the Goddess of the golden grain, and prayers are put up for the welfare of *Theophania*; a *Divertissement*; after which *Alcander* commands to depart, and retires, accompanied by his daughter.   The nymphs and shepherds, carrying their garlands and wheat-ear coronets, their myrtle branches and torches, playing also on cymbals, flutes, and other instruments, follow their Queen and Governor in dancing measures.

Thrasimedes and his friend remain and appear plunged in gloomy meditation.   Having recovered themselves they seem engaged in forwarding their enterprise; *Narses* expresses to his prince certain hopes, with which he is inspired, and advises *Thrasimedes* to withdraw to avoid suspicion, while he himself will endeavour to advance his interests.

ACT II.

Scene I.—*Narses* and *Thrasimedes* enter in haste and agitation; the latter appears a prey to anguish; his friend essays to calm him, but cannot succeed. *Theophania* has signified to him that her new office will effectually prevent their union. *Thrasimedes*, however, returns to meet his love once more, perhaps, for the last time, a thought that deeply wounds his heart. *Narses* tries to console him by a ray of hope which seems to gleam through the apparent gloom; he then retires.

Scene II.—*Thrasimedes* seems assailed by various and conflicting thoughts; dreading what may happen, he prostrates himself before the statue of Ceres, supplicating the Goddess to pardon the passion of two who cannot cease to love.

Scene III.—*Theophania* enters, and witnesses the emotions of her lover; she rushes into his arms, expressing the excess of her affection, and tears soon bedew the faces of the hapless pair; *Theophania* informs *Thrasimedes* that the Gods are averse to their union, and that they must now separate for ever; at these words the youth appears overpowered; having in some measure recovered, he reproaches *Theophania* with insensibility while delivering such cruel conditions; he appears sunk into an abyss of woe. The affectionate girl, deeply wounded by such expressions, assures him of her unalterable love, till, unable to support herself under such a conflict of emotion, she falls into the arms of *Thrasimedes*, who presses her fervently to his breast; he tries to reanimate her, conjuring her to satisfy his desires by sharing with him his unhappy fate; *Theophania* becomes deeply agitated, while anticipating the dangers to which they are exposed; her lover, however, sees nothing but happiness in the possession of his adored. *Theophania* is affrighted at the idea of forsaking her country, her gods, and her father. The impetuous youth, however, entreats her to accompany him; she rejects such a proposal; he essays to force her away; she still refuses, and seeks protection at the feet of the statue of Ceres. Transported by his passion, *Thrasimedes* tries to drag her even from the altar. At this instant, *Alcander* and his attendants, drawn to the spot by the necessity of attending to sacred duties, enter, and behold the temerity of the youth. The astonishment is indescribable.

Scene IV.—*Alcander* remains motionless at this spectacle; *Theophania* is nearly sinking, and *Thrasimedes* appears oppressed with woe. All the attendants remain also in a stupor of surprise and dread; while the whole assembly expect to see the vengeance of the Goddess visibly displayed. The rage of *Alcander* now becomes ungovernable; he calls down the wrath of the Gods upon the guilty pair. The latter throw themselves at his feet, but he repulses them, cursing his daughter, and condemning *Thrasimedes* to death; to the horror of all present. Every one endeavours to conciliate the pardon of *Alcander*, but he remains inexorable. Despair takes entire possession of *Theophania*, she is horror-struck at the fate of her lover, and, rushing into his arms, demands to be made a partner in his punishment. *Alcander* continues to rage with inextinguishable wrath; he orders the lovers to be divided, and to be conducted to separate confinement. *Narses*, attracted by the unusual commotion, enters, and can scarcely credit his eyes. Perceiving the danger of his prince, he is on the point of discovering the real rank of the latter, when *Thrasimedes* by a sign intimates that such a proceeding would be useless, and would expose both to the Governor's anger. *Narses*, however, pledges himself to bring his royal friend aid, whatever may be the event of his fate; he further motions him to confide in his zeal, retires unnoticed, and flies to effect the deliverance of his prince. The latter and *Theophania* are conducted away in opposite directions, exchanging, as they are going, mutual expressions of the utmost grief. *Alcander*, deeply concerned at what has just passed, retires, accompanied by his officers.

ACT III.

A wild and desert country near Eleusis. The trees on each side the scene stretching their umbrageous branches, intermingle and form a leafy vault. In the centre appears an image of Ceres, before whom an altar of incense is burning. This gloomy abode is the place destined for the punishment of criminals.

Scene I.—A funeral march is heard; priests enter advancing slowly; they surround the statue of Ceres, whom they seem to supplicate, as they bend in worship before her. Shepherds appear conducting *Thrasimedes;* they are followed by a troop of nymphs, and *Alcander* walks in the rear. The procession being fully arrived, the shepherds place themselves on one side, the nymphs on the other. Nothing appears to move *Thrasimedes* but the idea of an eternal separation from her he loves; this alone breaks his heart, and suffuses his eyes with tears.

Alcander, standing near the altar of Ceres, addresses that deity, and indicates, as her victim, the man who has dared to profane her worship. A universal emotion of terror follows his imprecation. *Alcander* then makes a sign to *Thrasimedes* to approach, desiring him to address his last prayer; the young prince prostrates himself, and prepares to receive the cup of death. The poisoned chalice is borne to the Governor, who presents it to *Thrasimedes;* at the moment that the latter is about to take it a noise is heard.

SCENE II.—*Theophania* rushes in, presenting a figure in the utmost disorder; she flies to her lover, snatches from him the fatal cup, and falls down at the feet of her father, the whole company appearing astonished at the action! The Gods, however, seem deaf to her entreaties; *Alcander* remains fixed in his resolution, and *Thrasimedes* must perish. She then flies into the arms of her lover, protesting that no power shall drag her hence; while despair and tenderness are depicted in the countenance of the young prince. *Alcander,* trembling with rage, commands the guilty pair to be forced asunder, which, after some struggle, is effected ; *Theophania* swoons and falls into the arms of the attendant nymphs, while *Thrasimedes* prepares to submit to his fate. Scarcely has he again taken the cup into his hand, when universal attention is attracted by the approaching clash of arms ; a cohort of warriors enters, and the astonished assembly fly for refuge towards the statue of Ceres, while the progress of the execution is again interrupted.

SCENE III.—The brave and faithful *Narses,* in complete armour, rushes in to save his royal friend, who cannot conceal his joy at such an unexpected deliverance. The warriors beholding with indignation the wretched state to which their prince is reduced, instantly fall upon both the judges and executioners of such a law; whose fate would have been certain, but for the interposition of the noble *Thrasimedes*, who, by signs, commands them to await his orders, expressing at the same time his gratitude, and embracing *Narses* as his deliverer. *Theophania*, having recovered, witnesses the generosity of her lover; she hopes for future happiness, and grief gives place to pleasure. *Thrasimedes* wishes to bury all in oblivion, and to signalize the event by a general pardon; he then fully discovers his rank, at which the surprise is universal. He advances towards *Alcander*, who has not yet recovered from his astonishment, and informs him that love had united him to *Theophania* before the latter had been dedicated to the altar of Ceres, declaring also that the purity of his intentions ought to procure for him the concurrence of the Governor. *Theophania* joins her entreaties to those of the prince, and conjures *Alcander* to crown their wishes. *Alcander*, moved by the generous conduct of *Thrasimedes*, and having considered his exalted rank, bestows the hand of his daughter upon her beloved prince, and the happiness of both is expressed by their attitudes. *Alcander* then desires that prayers be addressed to the Gods, in order that their favour and protection may be secured. All immediately surround the altar of Ceres, and implore the consent of that Goddess to the marriage of *Theophania*. The company now depart from this gloomy place, and, by the order of *Alcander*, proceed to celebrate the union elsewhere.

The scene changes and represents a magnificent square of Eleusis, destined for the exhibition of public ceremonies.

Nymphs and shepherds in troops enter dancing; they raise thrones for the Prince and Governor. *Alcander, Theophania, Thrasimedes,* and *Narses* enter sumptuously attired. The soldiers of *Thrasimedes* close the procession. Joy reigns universally, and finally, dances celebrate the happy union of *Thrasimedes* and *Theophania.*

VIVALDI.

A GRAND BALLET, IN TWO PARTS.

ARGUMENT.

VIVALDI and *Orsano*, Venetian noblemen, having conceived an inordinate passion for *Rosamond*, daughter of the Doge, avow their affection for her. *Orsano* having been rejected, and perceiving the preference given to his rival, resolves to rid himself of *Vivaldi*, unmindful of every consequence that might ensue. He accuses him, as well as his father, of treacherous designs against the state ; and on the false evidence brought against them, the two innocent noblemen were condemned unheard. The mother of *Rosamond*, affected by the situation in which her daughter and her affianced husband are placed, consents to a private celebration of their nuptials. *Vivaldi* and his family quit Venice, and retire to Sicily till the decree of death issued against them shall be revoked. *Vivaldi's* father having through grief terminated his mortal career, his son, leaving the asylum which sheltered him from his persecutors, goes (under the name of *Fernando*) to offer his services to the King of Spain. *Vivaldi* having, by his martial achievements and noble sentiments, acquired the favour of Charles V., that monarch confers on him the most honourable distinctions in the army. Honoured by the confidence of his sovereign, he unbosoms himself to him and reveals to him his real name, and informs him of his ardent desire to avenge his father. The King approves of his designs and promises to serve him. The republic of Venice standing at this period in need of a captain, whose superior talents should stand forth as a bulwark against her enemies, the Emperor profits of the opportunity, and offers the Senate the services of *Vivaldi* to command the troops of the republic. The lover of *Rosamond*, still retaining his fictitious name, having signalized himself by his exploits returns to Venice after several years absence, and is loaded with honours by the Senate. He endeavours by his conduct to vindicate his innocence. Chance enables him to discover a conspiracy, which, by his courage, his sentiments, and ingenuity, he succeeds in suppressing. The ambitious *Orsano*, the author of the conspiracy, is betrayed by his accomplices. Venice is saved, her generous deliverer recognized, and the Senate, regretting its past injustice, bears witness to the nobleness of soul that *Vivaldi* has displayed, and finally the nuptials of the lovers are openly solemnized.

CHARACTERS.

Vivaldi, *a noble Venetian.*

A. Gritti, *the Doge.*

Rosamond, *the Doge's daughter and wife of Vivaldi.*

Alfieri, *a Senator, friend of Vivaldi.*

Orsano, *a Senator, chief of the conspirators.*

Anselmo, *another chief of the conspirators.*

A Spanish Officer.

Abelino, *a Bandit, carrying on his depredations in the vicinity of Florence.*

Senators; Conspirators; Venetian noblemen; Venetian ladies; Venetian soldiers; Spanish soldiers; Masks; Gondoliers; Moors; Abelino's comrades.

The scene takes place at Venice, about the middle of the Sixth century.

PART THE FIRST.

ACT I.

The theatre represents the entrance of the Ducal Palace.
Every thing is prepared for the reception of the Spa-
nish General, and to celebrate his triumph by a public
festival; the edifice is magnificently adorned.

THE Doge, seated on a throne, is surrounded by *Rosa-mond, Alfieri, Orsano,* and *Anselmo,* as well as by senators and concealed conspirators. The Venetian army is drawn up on both sides of the scene. The people give loose to gaiety. In the harbour, which is at the back of the stage, are discovered vessels of every kind covering the sea, and the standards of the republic are seen waving in the air; a number of gondolas add, by their diversified appearance, to the brilliancy of the spectacle. A discharge of artillery gives a signal that the vessel in which *Fernando* is sailing approaches; music accompanies its arrival; several Venetian noblemen receive the Spanish general, and present him to the senate. The hero is accompanied by his officers and a part of his soldiers.

Vivaldi, under the name of *Fernando,* sent by the King of Spain to the help of the republic, is presented with the most lively marks of acknowledgment.

He returns after the conquest of the enemies of Venice, and the joy that is diffused through all ranks of persons is to him the most flattering tokens of respect, and he anti-

cipates future felicity.   He has already perceived his
adored wife, but endeavours to suppress the agitation
which the sight of her occasions in his breast.   *Orsano*
alone beholds the new comer with regret, he fears lest
he should prove an obstacle to his designs.   His companions participate in his forebodings.

Vivaldi offers his services to the state, and devotes
himself unreservedly, by an oath, to its welfare.   The
Doge, in the name of the senate, thanks him, and *Vivaldi*
(as *Fernando*) is already regarded, on account of his talents, his virtues and his courage, as the support of Venice.   Happiness begins to dawn anew in his bosom.
The Doge seats him at his own side; *Vivaldi* darts from
time to time secret glances at his beloved *Rosamond*,
whose grief no object can allay.

The feast begins, national dances are performed by
the Venetians, the Spaniards, and the Moors.   The *Divertissement* terminates by a general finale, in which the
variety of the steps and attitudes peculiar to each nation
in the joyful moments of the dance is portrayed.

The Doge, his daughter, *Vivaldi*, all the senators, &c.
then retire in procession, and the people accompany them
in measured march.

ACT II.

Armoury in the Arsenal.

SPANISH warriors, dispersed over the stage, are awaiting
the orders of their general.   *Vivaldi* appears, he is apparently engaged in his plans and in the employment that
he holds.   He orders one of his officers to intimate to
Alfieri that he wishes to converse with him.   He desires

ardently to vindicate his innocence, to avenge himself on his enemies, and to be reunited to his beloved wife. He invokes the aid of heaven, and puts entire confidence in its aid.

Alfieri arrives, he perceives *Vivaldi* whilst he is earnestly engaged in prayer, and agitated by the most tender emotions with which *Rosamond* inspires him. He feels confused at being surprised, afraid of having committed an imprudent action, but his agitated feelings are soon calmed by discovering, in the supposed intruder, his ancient friend; *Alfieri* feigns not to perceive his uneasiness; *Vivaldi* runs to meet him and is about to embrace him, at which *Alfieri* appears surprised; *Vivaldi*, confused, asks him if he has forgotten him? *Alfieri* replies that he is addressing the *General Fernando*, but is undeceived by *Vivaldi*, who entreats him to examine his features, with which request *Alfieri* complies, but is unable satisfactorily to trace the lineaments of his friend. *Vivaldi* takes his hand, clasps it within his, throws off his disguise, and discovers in himself the son of the unfortunate family to which he had testified the most devoted attachment; they both burst into tears and throw themselves into each other's arms. After this ebullition of feeling, *Alfieri* testifies his fears for the safety of his young friend, since a reward is offered for his apprehension. *Vivaldi* tells him, that he hopes by his disguise, his exploits, and entire conduct, to procure the annulment of the unjust decree by which he, as well as his unhappy father, have been proscribed. *Alfieri* admires his nobleness of soul as well as his courage ; but the fear lest his friend may, by his proceedings, be discovered, strikes the soul of *Alfieri* with dismay. *Vivaldi* bids him take courage, and enjoins him to profound secrecy; *Alfieri* offers him his services. *Vivaldi* inter-

rogates him respecting *Rosamond*, the object of his attachment ; requests to know whether she mourns his absence ;
he is informed that she is a prey to the most poignant
sorrow, and that her affections remain unaltered. This
consoles *Vivaldi;* he gives his friend a letter, beseeching
him to deliver it to *Rosamond* with the utmost secrecy
(the purport of the epistle is to inform her that he has
returned to Venice) ; after embracing *Vivaldi, Alfieri*
retires.

An officer enters to announce that *Vivaldi's* guards
have arrested a stranger, whose appearance and intentions have appeared suspicious to them, and that they
have found on him a letter and a ring, which the officer
delivers into *Vivaldi's* hands ; he discovers, on perusing
the letter, that it is *Orsano's* hand-writing, and that it
discloses the proceedings of a conspiracy against the
state ; the ring is intended to extricate the bearer from
every difficulty.

An opportunity now presents itself to *Vivaldi* to declare his sentiments and to perform a noble action ; he
orders the stranger who has been arrested to be conducted to him, and that no mention is to be made of
what passes in this interview with him ; *Abelino*, es-
corted by guards, enters ; his terrific aspect and singular
dress fill *Vivaldi* with surprise. He interrogates him as
to himself, *Abelino* hesitates to reply, but on *Vivaldi's*
threatening him with death, he, terrified, consents to satisfy *Vivaldi's* inquiries on condition of his life being
spared. To this *Vivaldi*, prompted by personal interest,
agrees ; *Abelino* acknowledges that he is a bandit, that
he is come to Venice, on *Orsano's* invitation, to assassinate the Doge and the principal persons of the state.
The soul of *Vivaldi* is moved with indignation ; he pauses
a moment, smiles at an idea which arises in his mind, and

which he resolves to put into execution; *Vivaldi* orders *Abelino* and his associates to be conducted to a place of safety, till he shall determine on their dismissal.

Vivaldi determines to assume the disguise of *Orsano's* assistant, and to personate his character. He reperuses the letter, and promises to effect the deliverance of his country by the destruction of its enemies. He directs his officer to take away *Abelino's* arms and clothes, gives him some papers, and hastens joyfully to execute his plan.

SCENE.—*Pavilion in the garden of the Palace.*

Rosamond appears pensive; her desire of solitude has made her seek this retired spot; the exile of her beloved husband is the source of her uneasiness; she draws from her pocket the portrait of *Vivaldi,* devours it with kisses, and swears eternal fidelity to its original.

Alfieri enters; *Rosamond* expresses the pleasure that she feels at the sight of the confidant of her troubles, and her only consolation; *Alfieri* informs her that she may, probably, in a short time embrace *Vivaldi.* She is overcome with amazement, but cannot believe that such joyful intelligence bears the stamp of truth; *Alfieri* presents her husband's letter. She asks her friend where *Vivaldi* is to be found, and when she shall be allowed to see him; *Alfieri* requests her to be patient and cautious, since *Vivaldi's* safety depends on secrecy; *Rosamond* consents; after fresh injunctions, *Alfieri* retires. *Rosamond,* animated by the future happiness, is only afraid that the dangers to which her husband is exposed may frustrate her expectations; but her terrors vanish on reading the letter again, and she retires under the impression that she shall soon embrace the object of her affections.

ACT III.

A handsome artificial grotto is seen at the end of a garden; the entrance to it is by a grove of trees; a secret door is observed on the right hand.

ORSANO arrives, he appears plunged in a deep reverie; a thousand different thoughts seem to agitate his mind. His design to destroy the Doge and senate, to avenge himself for the refusal of *Rosamond,* and to place himself at the head of the state, engross his whole thoughts. His mind is a prey to conflicting emotions. He cannot, however, forget his passion. The features of the haughty fair are too deeply imprinted on his heart, and love still asserts its power. But suddenly the remembrance of his hated rival rises in his imagination, and his passion yields to the ideas of gloomy vengeance by which he is agitated. He swears to avenge the slights which he has received by the death of their authors. He has already disposed of *Vivaldi,* as he imagines. He now feels a mixture of disappointment and anxiety at not yet seeing his companions arrive. He begins to suspect some treachery, but his suspicions give way to joy on seeing *Anselmo* appear with the other conspirators. He rushes to embrace them. Several of them go to the avenues of the grotto to avoid surprise. *Anselmo* tells him that every thing is in readiness for action ; that their forces are augmented, and that the populace, aided by the care of *Orsano,* is now murmuring against the Doge. *Orsano* exults in his success. All the conspirators swear to destroy the chief men of the state, and to overthrow the republic itself, as also to assassinate the Spanish general, whose power and valour fill their minds with alarm.

They, however, hesitate to strike; their instrument, *Abelino*, is wanted to assist these nefarious villains. This obstacle is a thunder-stroke to them, and they remain silent for some time, when suddenly a knock is heard at the secret door. They are filled with dismay and astonishment. A second knock is heard. *Orsano* orders them all to be silent, and goes himself to the door. Three knocks, one after the other, are now distinguished. All recognize the signal of *Abelino*, who, on *Orsano's* opening the door, appears, to the satisfaction of all the conspirators. *Abelino* demands to speak with their chief. *Orsano* is pointed out to him. The bandit refers to the ring and the letter as testimonials of their engagement with him. The conspirators are satisfied. *Orsano* bids *Abelino* prepare to do his duty, and deserve the reward allotted him. The Doge and chief Magistrates are to be the first victims. The pretended *Abelino* wishes to know all the conspirators personally, that no mistake may arise, for he sees but a part of them. *Orsano* gives him the list of them. *Vivaldi* feels a secret joy. When the distrustful *Anselmo* shows *Orsano* his imprudence, he acknowledges his fault, and, under a false pretext, takes back the paper which he has given *Vivaldi*. *Vivaldi* pretends to be unmoved at this proceding. *Orsano* tells him that he must, above all, insure the death of *Rosamond*, as she is one of the principal obstacles to their design. *Vivaldi* shudders with horror. He, however, feigns to be unmoved by it, and coolly argues that the death of a woman will be a useless circumstance in so great a conspiracy. *Orsano* is enraged at his irresolution; and *Anselmo* takes the deed on himself. *Vivaldi* wishes to retract, but *Anselmo*, desiring to please his chief, opposes him, and adds, that *Abelino*, not knowing the person of *Rosamond*, may commit some error. *Orsano* tells all the conspirators to be in readiness when he shall deem it a proper time to give the signal. All swear on their swords to be faithful. At this moment a conspirator, placed in one of the avenues, gives the rest notice that *Rosamond* is directing her steps this way. *Orsano* orders all the conspirators to withdraw, and *Abelino* to go out the same way by which he entered. *Anselmo* is placing himself in ambuscade, when *Vivaldi* wishes to turn him from his purpose by pointing out the danger of his situation, but *Anselmo* affirms that there is no danger to be apprehended. *Vivaldi* is obliged to submit, and withdraws, stung with grief and regret for having given *Anselmo* such an opportunity.

Rosamond enters pensive, takes the letter of *Vivaldi* from her bosom, reads it, imagines that she sees him before her, addresses him, embraces him, and cannot refrain from giving vent to her passionate feelings. She then goes to a seat in an arbour, and muses on future events. *Anselmo* comes from his concealment, and, after having cautiously examined that all is safe, goes behind *Rosamond,* and is preparing to stab her, when *Vivaldi,* who has concealed himself behind the door, rushes out, arrests his arm, plunges the dagger into his heart, and conveys him behind some trees. *Rosamond,* at the noise which this occasions, turns and perceives *Vivaldi ;* struck with terror, she is preparing to fly. Her husband begs her to be silent, and shows her the body of *Anselmo.* He tells her to quit this spot ; to say nothing of what has happened, and that he watches continually over her preservation. *Rosamond* hurries to the palace, leaving her letter behind. *Vivaldi* withdraws by the secret door of a subterranean cavern, which conducts also to the palace.

PART THE SECOND.

ACT I.

The Doge's apartment.

ORSANO enters, joy sparkles in his eyes, he holds a letter in his hand, which appears by its contents to add to the success of the enterprize. It is the letter of *Vivaldi* which he has found. He hopes to make the treasonous designs of *Vivaldi* more apparent.

The Doge enters thoughtful ; *Orsano* accosts him, gives him the letter, and tells him that it will inform him who is the underminer of the state. The Doge is surprised ; *Orsano* retires, expecting the result of this step. The Doge reads the letter, by which he learns the return of *Vivaldi*, as also his amorous transports and expectations of future success.

The Doge concludes from these things that *Vivaldi* is the chief of the conspiracy forming against the state. He is enraged at his passion for his daughter. He sends for her. She enters ; he orders her to disclose to him the designs of her lover. She perceives the agitation of her father, and is alarmed for what may be the cause of it. He shows her *Vivaldi's* letter, at which she is confused. He asks her who delivered it to her ? She hesitates to answer. He asks if *Vivaldi* is in Venice ? She replies in the affirmative, and that she has not seen him. Her father upbraids her with her fondness for an exile, a traitor. She weeps. He is enraged at her unworthy attachment. She replies with firmness to his reproaches, that her husband is no traitor, that he is traduced, and that she never would have united herself with one capable of such actions. The Doge is filled with astonishment on learning that his daughter is married. He is informed that his deceased wife had *Vivaldi* secretly united to his daughter. He is enraged. *Rosamond* invokes the spirit of her mother, and informs her father that *Orsano* is the author of the condemnation of her husband, and that *Vivaldi's* innocence will soon appear. The Doge orders her to renounce her attachment. She refuses. He threatens *Vivaldi's* destruction. She begs him to revoke his decision, but he refuses, becomes enraged, and execrates his daughter, who falls into a swoon. The Doge sends for the Spanish general—he appears, and sees his wife on the ground, he runs to her, raises her, and places her on a chair. The Doge tells him that he must perform a great service for the state, by bringing the culprit *Vivaldi* to justice; that he is returned to Venice, and is preparing to subvert the government. He shows him the letter. *Vivaldi (Fernando)* promises obedience. *Rosamond* recovers her senses, and shudders with horror. The Doge exacts an oath from *Fernando*. *Rosamond* attempts to oppose this. *Fernando* swears coolly to give up the culprit. *Rosamond* testifies her abhorrence. The Doge is satisfied, and retires, repulsing *Rosamond*, who endeavours to address him. *Fernando* prepares to depart, he is brought back by *Rosamond*. This action fills *Fernando* with dismay, lest he should be discovered. *Rosamond* informs him that to be the accessary to the destruction of an unfortunate accused person is unworthy a hero. *Fernando* tries to avoid the gaze of his wife. He says that he must serve the state, and that *Vivaldi* has betrayed it. *Rosamond* replies that his assertion is false, and wishes destruction to the accusers of her husband. He pretends to laugh at her anger. She wrings her hands with vexation, reflecting on her own inability to avenge herself. *Fernando* advises her to forget *Vivaldi*, as he is the cause of her trouble, but she vows never to cease loving him. She then, recovering from her emotions, begs *Fernando* not to obey the orders of the Doge, by acceding to the death of an innocent person, but rather to ennoble himself by a glorious action. She throws herself at his knees ; her tears, her entreaties, her grief, are too much for the resolution of *Vivaldi*. He discovers himself. She is struck motionless with amazement. She runs to him, embraces him, and is about to give vent to her agitated feelings by her voice, but is restrained by the significant order of *Vivaldi*, to be silent. *Alfieri* surprises them. This is a joyful moment for all three. *Alfieri* tells them that the fête given in honour of *Rosamond's* birth is about to commence, and nothing is wanting but the presence of *Rosamond*. *Vivaldi* hastens to execute his projects, from which he anticipates a favourable result. He bids her tenderly adieu. An attendant from the Doge comes to conduct *Rosamond* to the fête; and all retire.

ACT II.

Delightful gardens of the Doge; grand illumination; every thing is prepared for a magnificent fete; a canal appears in the distance.

GONDOLAS are seen arriving on the canal elegantly decorated and filled with masks of every kind, who land and execute various dances. The *Doge, Rosamond,* and train, *Alfieri,* Senators, Venetian ladies, Venetian noblemen, &c., arrive to preside over and enjoy the festival. Grand *Divertissement,* executed by the noblemen of the court, the masks, gondoliers and moors. During the feast a man in a domino approaches the Doge with a mysterious air, and informs him that some one, unobserved, demands a private interview with him. He then disappears in the crowd. The Doge, after the dancing has continued for a short time longer, makes signs for all to retire. Every one withdraws, and he remains alone. He ruminates on the recent occurrence, and considers whether it may not be some advice for the good of the state. He is wrapped in deep meditation. *Orsano* appears in the distance, disguised as a Spanish soldier, accompanied by one of his guards. Both watch whether any one is observing them. The masked stranger presents himself to the Doge, who asks him what he has to communicate to him. He gives him a paper and disappears. The Doge opens the paper and reads the names of *Fernando* and *Vivaldi* impeached as the chief conspirators. Every thing seems to justify this accusation. Terror renders him motionless. When he recovers himself he sees that every thing confirms this intimation. He is preparing to give his orders, when on a sudden, as he is going out, the agent of *Orsano* darts upon him, and is about to assassinate him, but *Orsano* rushes forward, and, turning the blow aside, pretends to save his life. He then begs him to mark the Spanish dress of the assassin, who retreats with precipitation. The Doge thanks *Orsano*, and shows him the letter which he has just received; *Orsano*, exulting, enters into the Doge's sentiments, that *Vivaldi* is the chief conspirator against the state. The Doge sends for *Fernando*. His absence, as he is employed in executing his plans, confirms the suspicions of the Doge. He gives his orders to *Orsano*. Some noblemen and conspirators enter. The Doge summons them to the grand council called upon the occasion of the present danger.

ACT III.

Grand Council Hall; a throne on the left of the spectators.

ORSANO arrives, he meditates on the decisive moment to effect his projects. The Doge and *Alfieri* appear. *Alfieri* informs the Doge that *Fernando* wishes to vindicate himself from the charge brought against him. *Orsano* opposes it. At length, after some debate, in which the disposition of *Orsano* is plainly manifested, as well as that of *Alfieri*, the Doge agrees to hear *Fernando* in open senate.

Vivaldi enters. Just as he is about to commence his defence *Rosamond* enters. A movement of general surprise is excited. *Rosamond* undertakes *Vivaldi's* defence, proves his innocence, shows the injustice of his judges, and declares that she is the wife of the exiled unfortunate.

The whole court is seized with amazement. The situation of *Vivaldi* and *Alfieri* now becomes critical. The Doge and *Orsano* are enraged. *Vivaldi* displays a noble pride against his accusers. *Rosamond* has recourse to entreaties. *Orsano* storms, and the Doge causes *Vivaldi* to be arrested. *Vivaldi* and *Rosamond* bid each other adieu. *Vivaldi* is hurried away by the guards, but as he is departing a ray of hope beams across his soul, which rekindles his courage. *Rosamond* wishes to follow him, but her father orders her to be conducted to another spot. She refuses to quit the hall, and desires to be heard by the senate. During this scene *Alfieri* departs unperceived, and prepares to put in execution his project for saving the life of his friend. The Doge and *Orsano* try to persuade *Rosamond* to quit the spot, but she declares her determination to remain till death, or till she has procured the pardon of her husband.

The door of the hall is opened, the senators, among whom are some conspirators, enter in gradation, and place themselves on their respective seats. *Orsano*, at the head of the conspirators, occupies all the right hand side of the stage. The Doge places himself on the throne. *Rosamond* stands in the midst, with a firm countenance and a tranquil air. Two senators are at a table below the throne of the Doge.

The Doge informs the senate that *Vivaldi*, under the name of *General Fernando* is at Venice, that he has discovered the secrets of the state, and that he is even chief of the conspiracy with which they are threatened.

He adds, that the culprit is arrested, and that he is waiting the decision of the council. *Orsano* and several other senators condemn him to death. *Rosamond* affirms that there is another criminal to punish, which is herself, who is the accomplice of her husband. General surprise! She contradicts her statement of the cause of *Vivaldi's* return, and owns her share in all his projects, and that she entertains the same sentiments. Her father endeavours to excuse her to the senators. An officer runs in and informs the senate that *Vivaldi* has just been forcibly rescued by a senator. *Rosamond* throws herself on her knees and expresses her joy. A general murmur is excited through the assembly to know the chief of the faction. *Alfieri* appears. Another movement of surprise is excited. The friend of *Vivaldi* justifies himself by stating the virtues of the latter, the injustice of his arrest, and his wish to avoid committing a crime in the senate. *Rosamond* returns him her acknowledgments. The Doge threatens *Alfieri* with his anger, orders him to be seized ; and obliges them both to retire. A loud noise is now heard, and *Vivaldi*, in the dress of *Abelino*, and followed by soldiers dressed as bandits, appears. He revives the courage of his wife and friend. All testify their surprise, each in his own particular manner. Several senators on the side of the Doge go to oppose *Vivaldi*, who takes possession of his pistols, and threatens death to the first who moves. He declares his intention to bestow a new chief on the republic, and throws a glance at *Orsano*, who supports this resolve. The Doge is amazed and alarmed. *Vivaldi* names the conspirators, to the indignation of the Doge. The senators on the side of *Orsano* proclaim him Doge, a choice to which those who favour the cause of the Doge refuse to accede. *Orsano* draws his dagger, the rest of the conspirators follow his example, and dart forward against the Doge, who presents his body to receive their blows with the greatest courage. *Alfieri* and *Rosamond* protect him by throwing themselves before him. *Vivaldi* stops the proceedings of the conspirators by placing himself between them. *Group.* *Vivaldi* having made the Doge feel his situation, retires to his soldiers, applauds the conduct of the conspirators, which he declares to be worthy of reward. He turns to his men and gives them a seeming sign to seize the Doge, but all on a sudden, changing his design and attitude, he points to the conspirators with a majestic air, throws off his cap, his cloak, and beard, and appears as *Vivaldi*, in the dress which he was supposed to wear before his exile. A feeling of general surprise is excited. *Group.* The conspirators, being seized and disarmed by the soldiers of *Vivaldi*, are in the greatest consternation. The Doge and the rest of the senate testify the utmost astonishment. *Rosamond* embraces her husband. *Vivaldi* is calm, and seems to derive the most heartfelt satisfaction from the action which he has just performed. *Rosamond* recapitulates the virtuous actions of *Vivaldi* to the senate. A general satisfaction is expressed by all parties. *Vivaldi* promises *Orsano* his life if he will establish the innocence of his father; but on his darting a contemptuous look on him, as well as *Rosamond*, he orders him to be conducted to execution; and *Orsano* and the conspirators are led out. The Doge and the senators are lavish in their professions of gratitude to *Vivaldi*, and appear to be stung with deep regret for their past injustice. *Vivaldi* begs that all may be buried in profound oblivion, and requests that *Rosamond* may be indissolubly united to him, and that he may be deemed the friend of the republic. He extends his hand to *Alfieri* in token of gratitude. The Doge holds out his arms to him as a signal of embrace ; *Vivaldi* rushes into them, then turning to *Rosamond*, he presses her to his bosom. All the senators rising participate in their joy, and form around them a *General Group.*

NOCTURNAL ADVENTURES.

A COMIC BALLET, IN TWO ACTS.

CHARACTERS.

ALVAREZ.
ROSALBA and ANTONINA, *daughters of Alvarez.*
DON PEDRO, *in love with Rosalba.*
IGNATIO, *in love with Antonina.*
MARIQUETTE, *lady's maid to Alvarez' daughters.*
PASCAL, *the gardener, loves Mariquette.*
FRANCISCO.
DON FLOREZ, *master of the Bolero.*　*Villagers.*

The scene is laid at a village in Spain.

ACT I.

SCENE I.—*An apartment in Alvarez' house.*

FRANCISCO and *Mariquette* are discovered preparing for the departure of *D. Alvarez; Francisco* makes several attempts to engage the attention of *Mariquette,* whose affection he endeavours to conciliate ; the latter ridicules his silly pretentions, and rejects his advances. The feelings of *Francisco* seem hurt, and he complains of such cruel treatment ; and, having finished his work, he hastens to his master.

SCENE II.—*Antonina* enters ; she comes to tell *Mariquette* a secret, provided she will keep it so, and at the same time assist her in certain projects ; *Mariquette* pledges her word and honour to serve *Antonina* to the utmost. The latter then informs *Mariquette,* that her father being about to leave home upon some important business, she intends to take the advantage of his absence, in order to procure an interview with her lover, and to arrange their marriage. *Mariquette* approves of the plot, and promises every assistance in her power. *Antonina* blushes and delivers a letter to the maid, addressed to *Ignatio,* directing him to be in the garden at dusk. *Mariquette* smiles at her young mistress, and readily undertakes the commission ; the latter charging her to say nothing to *Rosalba,* her sister.

SCENE III.—*Rosalba* appears, and soon evinces a wish to be alone ; not knowing how, otherwise, to get rid of *Antonina,* she informs her that *Alvarez,* her father, desires to speak with her in private ; *Antonina* retires, and as she is going casts a significant glance at *Mariquette,* reminding the latter of her promise.

SCENE IV.—*Rosalba,* after a short reflection, determines to meet her lover that evening in the garden, during the absence of her father. She then gives *Mariquette* a note addressed to *Don Pedro,* appointing the hour ; *Mariquette* appears surprised, but instantly recovering, she promises to procure the meeting. The maid seems to admire the double rendezvous, and appears prepared to play a merry part in the affair. *Rosalba* withdraws.

SCENE V.—*Pascal*, having watched for an opportunity to speak to his *Mariquette*, appears at the door, and finding her alone, he advances towards her ; gestures of mutual regard are immediately exchanged. The wily maid informs him, that as their master is leaving home for a time, no restraint will then be placed upon their courtship. *Pascal* hears this with delight ; and *Mariquette* directs him to be in the garden at evening, but desires him to withdraw immediately, lest he should be discovered.

SCENE VI.—*Alvarez* enters, accompanied by his two daughters ; they seem discoursing upon the approaching departure, *Alvarez* intimating that he shall speedily return. *Francisco* enters and announces the Bolero-master.

SCENE VII.—*Don Florez* enters with his guittar ; and *Alvarez* gives leave to his daughters to take their lessons, intimating a wish to be present during the performance. *Florez* then gives *Rosalba* and *Antonina* instructions in the national dances, executing a Bolero alternately with each, and terminating the lesson with a *pas de trois*. *Francisco* now enters and informs his master that every thing is ready for departure; on hearing this, certain signs of satisfaction are visible on the countenances of the two young ladies. The dancing-master withdraws, and *Don Alvarez*, taking leave of his daughters, follows *Francisco*. *Rosalba* and *Antonina*, by turns, remind *Mariquette* of the commission with which she is charged, and retire.

ACT II.

A view of the front of Don Alvarez' *house, beyond which appears an arbour on the right and another on the left; in the centre stands a tree; the whole representing a handsome garden, surrounded by a high wall, in which appears a gate.*

SCENE I.—The gate is gently unclosed, and *Pascal* enters, looking cautiously about; he comes by appointment; his adored, however, does not appear, and he waits with anxiety. A slight noise is heard; fearing to be discovered, *Pascal* conceals himself behind the tree.

SCENE II.—*Mariquette* leaves the house, and hastens to the garden gate, expecting *Ignatio*. *Pascal* observes her, and prepares to play off a trick upon her; she appears anxious at the delay of *Antonina's* lover; upon remarking this *Pascal* supposes his mistress is inconstant, and soon betrays signs of jealousy. He waits, however, to witness the sequel, and climbing the tree, puts himself entirely out of a probability of being observed.

SCENE III.—*Ignatio* enters, and seems in some fear; but *Mariquette,* hastening to meet him, encourages him and brings him forward, expressing her joy at his arrival; *Ignatio* recovers himself, and acknowledges the civilities of *Mariquette,* at which *Pascal,* in the tree, is observed to be greatly agitated. The maid now flies to inform her mistress, and to conduct her to this extraordinary interview, while the enamoured youth exhibits all the signs of joy and gratitude. *Pascal* now perceives the real state of the intrigue, becomes cool, and laughs at his error.

Scene IV.—*Mariquette* and *Antonina* appear, upon which the enamoured pair express their delight at meeting each other, and the merry maid congratulates both.

Time growing short, however, for other business, *Mariquette* reminds them that, to avoid being discovered, they had better conceal themselves; upon this *Antonina* directs her lover to secrete himself in the arbour on the left, telling him she will return shortly. *Mariquette* having thus interrupted their discourse, hastens away to prepare for the arrival of *Don Pedro,* which she is to keep secret also. *Pascal* appears to enjoy this unusual scene, and seems impatient to play his part in it.

Scene V.—*Don Pedro* arrives. *Pascal* is once more in surprise; *Mariquette* is again on the spot, and runs to meet *Don Pedro*; she informs him that he may expect soon to see his *Rosalba;* the youth promises to reward her handsomely, and conjures her not to keep him in suspense, for that he dies with impatience to behold his beloved.

Scene VI.—*Pedro* exhibits all the transports of warm affection; he takes a small portrait of *Rosalba* from his bosom and presses it to his lips, then drawing his sword, swears an eternal fidelity, and threatens with death him who should dare to offend her. *Ignatio,* wishing to know the cause of *Antonina's* delay, gently uncloses the door of the arbour in which he is waiting, and soon perceives the infuriated lover; struck with fear at his menacing gestures, he immediately draws back and closes the door.

Scene VII.—*Rosalba* enters and flies into the arms of her lover, who receives her on his knees, while gestures and looks of the most ardent and romantic passion are exchanged.

Scene VIII.—*Mariquette* appears and interrupts these expressions of love, by informing *Rosalba* that she must return into the house to prevent discovery ; the amorous pair lament the shortness of their interview ; but *Mariquette* promises them soon to see each other again. She then tells *Don Pedro* that he must conceal himself in the arbour to the left. *Night approaching, the stage becomes more obscure.*

SCENE IX.—A slight noise is heard from the farther part of the stage ; it draws the attention of *Don Pedro ;* he searches to know whence it proceeded, and fearing to be observed, he hastens to the arbour, but finds the door closed ; after having made several useless efforts to enter, he turns to the one opposite, and immediately shuts himself in. *Pascal,* seated in his leafy concealment, laughs at the adventure ; he now descends the tree, and seems waiting with great impatience for his mistress. *Ignatio,* supposing the coast to be clear, again gently uncloses the door of his bower, and looks about narrowly for *Antonina ;* he seems prepared to go and seek her, while *Pascal* once more climbs his tree. *Pedro,* supposing he hears his mistress, opens the door of his retreat ; he perceives *Ignatio,* and mistakes him for a rival ; while the latter, struck with a sort of panic, dares not stir, and *Pedro* immediately desires to know his name and business ; but the unfortunate *Ignatio* has lost the power of speech, and prepares for flight ; *Pedro* becomes impatient, and begins to make use of threats, at which *Ignatio* takes to his heels ; *Pedro* draws his sword and follows, while *Ignatio,* unable to proceed further, takes refuge in the arbour where *Pedro* had been hidden, and shuts the door in the face of the latter ; *Pedro* trembles with wrath, but recollecting the cowardice of his antagonist, he despises him and becomes cool. Obliged in turn to hide himself, he enters the arbour in which *Ignatio* was concealed.

SCENE X.—*Antonina* enters, and seems agitated by

fear ; she holds a taper in her hand, and hastens to give
liberty to her lover ; she approaches the arbour, calls,
and knocks at the door ; *Don Pedro* appears, when the
affrighted girl, seeing a stranger, flies away, lets fall
the taper, and rings the house-bell with all her strength.

SCENE XI.—*Rosalba* and *Mariquette* enter at the noise,
the latter searches on all sides with her candle, to discover the cause of this disturbance, and at length informs
the young ladies she has seen a thief concealed in the
garden. *Rosalba* guesses the real state of the adventure, and attributes the fright of *Antonina* to her own
imagination ; in short, each finding herself not in a situation that will bear explanation, takes no further notice
of the affair, and they are about to retire, when the noise
of people approaching attracts their attention. They become affrighted, and having listened a short time, soon
distinguish the voices of *Don Alvarez* and *Francisco ;* they
are astonished at their unexpected return. The enamoured
youths appear half discovered in their respective retreats,
and seem greatly displeased with this new disappointment. *Rosalba, Antonina,* and their maid hasten into
the house.

SCENE XII.—*Alvarez* and his servant enter ; they appear greatly disordered, their features exhibiting marks
of terror ; their first care seems to be to secure the door ;
they then falter and fall upon a bank in the garden.
Having somewhat recovered, they examine every part to
discover if there are any traces of the thieves by whom
they fancy they have been attacked. It is fear that has
induced them to return without completing the journey.
They dare not knock at the house, dreading lest the
noise might again attract the robbers, and therefore prepare to await the opportunity of entering unheard. They
evince great terror, and start at every noise. *Pascal* is

observed scarcely able to contain himself, and turning from time to time in his nest, a slight noise follows, at which the valiant master and his man are horror-struck, staring at each other, yet endeavouring to take courage ; not daring, however, to cast a glance about them, though a deep silence now prevails. *Pedro* and *Ignatio,* believing that now at length all is quiet, advance slowly from their concealment ; they, however, soon perceive that the father of their mistresses has not left his position. At this moment *Francisco* discovers *Ignatio,* he cannot credit his eyes, and his terror becomes redoubled ; he informs his master, who dares not behold the object that creates the alarm, and turning away his eyes, he fixes them involuntarily upon the arbour from whence *Don Pedro,* sword in hand, is just issuing to make his escape ; *Alvarez* is nearly sinking with dread, while both the lovers are hastening away together. *Pascal,* having placed himself upon a branch too weak to bear him, it breaks and he falls near *Alvarez,* with a tremendous crash ; this completes the scene of confusion, and master and man fall one upon the other. The trio of lovers, taking advantage of this tumult, get clearly away, without fear of being called to account, and they are finally seen scaling the garden wall.

Scene XIII.—The two young ladies and their maid, alarmed at the noise, arrive at the scene with candles in their hands ; upon seeing *Alvarez* and *Francisco,* they pretend the greatest astonishment ; the latter is stretched on the ground in an ecstacy of dread. They, however, exert themselves to restore *Alvarez,* who still fancies he is surrounded by robbers. The two daughters now express their fears for *Pedro* and *Ignatio.* A knock is heard at the garden gate, and soon after *Don Pedro* and *Don Ignatio* appear at the head of a troop villagers.

They may be supposed to have been brought to assist at the extraordinary events passing at the house of *Alvarez;* and having been informed of the particulars, they pretend that it is themselves who have put to flight the robbers, and so saved the life and property of *Alvarez.* The stratagem succeeds, and *Alvarez* expresses sentiments of the liveliest gratitude, and the cunning villagers receive universal thanks. *Alvarez,* recovering from his state of alarm, recognizes, in *Pedro* and *Ignatio,* the sons of two old friends, which augments his joy, and he is at a loss how to reward their important services in his defence ; they inform him that he has only to bestow on them the hands of his two daughters, for whom they avow the warmest affection. *Alvarez* appears somewhat disconcerted at their demand, and seems meditating on his reply, and while he hesitates, every one gathering round him, beseech him to return a favourable answer. He then asks his daughters if they will consent; they reply, that it is no more than their duty to submit to his will in uniting themselves to those who have been his liberators. Upon this, *Alvarez* presents *Rosalba* to *Pedro,* and *Antonina* to *Ignatio;* ordering, at the same time, that the ceremony should take place immediately. The joy of the lovers is now complete. *Pascal* then advances, leading *Mariquette ;* he asks of *Alvarez* permission to form a third couple, by marrying that very efficient personage ; *Alvarez* readily gives his consent. A *Divertissement* follows, in which characteristic dances express the unusual gaiety prevailing at a triple union.

ZARA.

A ROMANTIC BALLET, IN FIVE ACTS.

CHARACTERS.

ALPHONSO VIII, *King of Castile and Leon.*
ERMANGERE, *his Queen.*
ZARA, *a beautiful Moorish woman.*
FERNANDO GARCIAS DE CASTRO, *the venerable tutor of Alphonso.*
MORICO, *a Moor, the friend and confident of Zara.*
ALVAREZ FANES, *Chancellor of Castile.*

Nobles; Officers of State, and ladies of the Court; people of Toledo; Knights and Castilian soldiers; Moors of both sexes; Balliadères; Spanish and Moorish young men and maidens.

SCENE,—*Toledo, in the time of Godefroi de Boulogne.*

ACT I.

*The theatre represents a hall in the ancient castle of Fanès,
at some distance from the centre of the town.*

FANÈS introduces *Ermangère,* and his old friend *Garcias :*
he shows them their new abode, and promises them his
most devoted services. The Queen and *Garcias* express
their gratitude and perfect reliance on his care. *Fanès*
quits them, in order to advance his friendly projects, and
to endeavour to bring back *Alphonso,* who has abandoned
his bride for a Moorish concubine, to a sense of duty and
the path of honour and propriety.

Ermangère gazes at, and thinks of, the distant palace
of which she was once the life and ornament; where she
shone as a Queen, the happy, beloved bride of her still
adored *Alphonso.* He has now deserted her for a low-
born Moorish damsel; driven her from his presence, and
compelled her to retire to Oveja. Overpowered by
these agonizing reflections, she gives way to the most
violent grief; *Garcias* endeavours to console her with a
prospect of future happiness; *Ermangère* expresses how
deeply sensible she feels at his attachment and solicitude,
and that she hopes, before long, to recompense him for
the kindness he displays towards her, and his devotion
to her service. This ancient friend and servant of the
Queen, who, like his mistress, has been compelled to
quit the court, is resolved to share in her destiny, and
swears to sacrifice every thing for her welfare. *Ermangère*
sheds tears of mingled tenderness and sorrow.

Fanès arrives; he informs them that the people, long op-

pressed by the despotism of the detested Moorish concubine of *Alphonso*, who has contrived to take the sovereign
power into her own hands, begin to murmur, and are on
the brink of breaking out into open tumult; that they are
desirous of expelling *Zara* and her attendant Moors from
the palace of *Alphonso's* ancestors, and of reinstating
Ermangère in her proper place—the throne of the Two
Spains.

Ermangère and her two faithful friends augur the most
happy results from this welcome event, which seems to
further their plans, and to hasten the execution of them.
Fanès conducts the Queen into one of the rooms conti-
guous to the hall, returns, and goes out, accompanied by
Garcias, to ripen the enterprise which they have undertaken.

*The scene changes to a magnificent apartment in the
King's Palace.*

Zara, splendidly attired, is seated near a table; she
appears occupied with the affairs of the state; a number
of courtiers and nobles are around her; among whom are
also many Moors. *Morico* is in immediate attendance on
her person, to receive her commands. *Zara* gives papers
and documents to the principal officers of state, enjoin-
ing them to attend to their contents with scrupulous
exactitude. They receive them with the most profound
respect, and severally depart.

The ambitious Moorish woman hands a decree to
Morico, which contains ordinances in favour of her own
people; and commands that they may be carried into
effect without delay. *Morico* makes a sign of strict
obedience, and retires.

The sound of horns now announces the return of

Alphonso from the chase; *Zara* prepares to receive him.

The King, accompanied by young Moors of both sexes, appears. He throws himself into the arms of the fascinating *Zara*, and expresses the raptures he feels at once more clasping her to his bosom. *Zara* receives him in the most tender and bewitching manner. *Alphonso* appears to be at the summit of felicity. *Zara*, proud of her conquest, enjoys the triumph of her charms: she commands her suite to follow them to a delicious retreat, which she has prepared for the reception of the King. They retire, followed by the Moors, &c.

ACT II.

Splendid gardens of the Royal Palace.

SEVERAL young Moors, in the most brilliant oriental habits, appear and make preparations for a magnificent festival.

Alphonso and his mistress enter, preceded by a troop of *Balliadères*, who make the air resound with their instruments, and scatter flowers in the path. Nobles and ladies of the court follow; numerous Moors are mingled in the group.

Alphonso seats himself to partake of the banquet, with *Zara* by his side; they are served with the most delicious refreshments, and exquisite wines. *Morico* is their *Ganymede*. The air is enriched with perfumes, and the loves of *Alphonso* and his mistress are celebrated by voluptuous music and dances. *Zara* and the infatuated lover express their mutual passion, and luxury and joy reign all around.

A sudden noise from without interrupts the fête.
General surprise! " Who," imperatively demands *Zara*,
" can have penetrated into this retreat ?"—*Garcias* boldly
presents himself to her astonished view. *Zara* recovers
sufficiently from her surprise to interrogate *Morico* as to
the appearance of the banished Castilian in the gardens
of the palace. *Morico* appears almost petrified, and is
unable to make any reply. The presence of his old and
faithful subject afflicts the King and overwhelms him
with confusion. His venerable tutor solicits pardon for
his boldness, and attributes this breach of obedience
to devotion for his sovereign's fame and happiness. *Zara*
can scarcely contain herself—she burns to revenge this
ominous intrusion of her detested enemy. The noble
Castilian, inspired with the love of his country and its
King, and braving the dangers which evidently menace
him, forcibly depicts to *Alphonso* his fallen, inglorious
situation—the neglect of his Royal duties—his injustice to
a virtuous and suffering wife—and the misery of his once
beloved and loving subjects. The freedom of his
language irritates the impetuous young monarch. *Alphonso* expresses his anger, and enjoins silence on the part
of *Garcias*. *Zara*, foreseeing the perils with which fate
threatens her, peremptorily orders *Garcias* to retire ;
the old noble looks upon her with disdain. *Alphonso*,
enraged at this insult to his mistress, commands that
Garcias be instantly seized. *Zara* and *Morico* urge
him on to a signal and immediate retribution for the
offence.

Garcias remains unmoved ; his venerable appearance
and bold deportment impress universal respect for his
person. His age, his rank, his virtues, the services he
has rendered the King, as well as the personal attachment he feels towards him, endow the old Castilian with

the privilege of speaking freely, of drawing a picture of the blighted glory of his sovereign—of his Queen languishing in enforced retirement, apart from the lord of her heart—and of the fast-coming ruin of his whole kingdom.

Alphonso is moved; he seems to waver. *Zara* perceiving this, and fearful of danger, meditates a scheme to save herself from falling from her "high and palmy state."

Garcias, encouraged by the emotion which *Alphonso* betrays, conjures him to abandon a woman who has dishonoured and disgraced him by plunging him into the lowest abyss of disgraceful voluptuousness and luxurious pleasures. *Alphonso* is dreadfully agitated; the veil is half removed from his "mind's eye;" but—he still loves—he still adores, and is still the slave of his triumphant mistress.

Morico attempts to encourage him, but is quelled into motionless silence by a single glance from the eye of *Garcias*, who now informs the King, as a last resource, that the people have revolted, and will only be appeased by the death of *Zara!*—This intelligence falls like a thunderbolt on the lovers' hearts! *Garcias* adds, that, with the aid of a few chosen and influential friends, he has hitherto succeeded in curbing the popular tumult; but that, if *Alphonso* is desirous of insuring his own safety, he must again become a hero and a king, and remove *Zara* and her Moors from his society and his presence. He points to a troop of armed Citizens, who have already forced admittance to the palace and are tumultuously rushing onward. By a single mandatory gesture he checks their further approach.

The amazed *Alphonso* knows not how to act; he is agitated, undecided, and indignant. The Moors betray their fears. *Zara* perceiving herself powerless, at this

moment, ponders on plans of present safety and future
vengeance; her wily imagination suggests to her a mode
of rescuing herself from the wrath of the people, by feign-
ing resignation to her fate, and abandoning her state and
hopes for the welfare of the King and the satisfaction of
his subjects. She implores the people's clemency, and
submits to a voluntary exile.

Alphonso, after having for some time struggled with
himself, promises to dismiss *Zara* and her Moors, and to
give himself wholly up to the wishes of his subjects.
Garcias is supremely blest. *Alphonso* looks toward
Zara; his eyes express, at once, the agony he feels in
tearing himself from her bosom, and his solicitude to
obtain her pardon for the course he has adopted. She
conjures him to cast her from his memory, and hereafter
to think only of burying their loves in oblivion in the
minds of his people, by noble and magnanimous actions.
The resignation and courage of *Zara* touch the monarch's
heart. By her countenance and gestures, she expresses
all that a passionately-adoring woman feels, who sacrifices herself to the happiness of her lover. She retires,
consoling herself, for her present disgrace, with the hope
that her glory will not be long obscured. *Morico* accompanies her, followed by the Moors and several guards.
Alphonso endeavours to conquer his feelings, and to conceal, from those who behold him, the grief that this unexpected separation has created in his heart.

Garcias makes a sign, and his noble Castilian friends
appear, with *Fanès* at the head. They express their
wishes to *Alphonso*. *Garcias* acquaints them that their
monarch is willing to satisfy their desires. A general
expression of loyalty and exultation! All throw themselves on their knees before *Alphonso*, who, affected
by this interesting sight, swears to sacrifice every thing

to satisfy his faithful subjects. He retires, accompanied by *Garcias*, amid the blessings of his people, who rejoice at his return to the path of honour, and look with confidence for happy days to come.

ACT III.

The King's presence chamber.

ALPHONSO, in his royal robes, enters, followed by his court. He seats himself on the throne, and all around wait for his commands. He prepares to seize the occasion of having an interview with *Ermangère*, when *Morico* appears and solicits permission to communicate to the monarch a secret of importance. *Garcias* exhibits some suspicions as to the proceedings of the perfidious follower of *Zara*. The image of the Moorish woman is too powerful in the King's heart to prevent him from listening to *Morico's* communication; he consents to hear what the Moor has to say, and dismisses his courtiers and attendants.

Morico now acquaints him that *Zara* supplicates permission to see him before her departure, as the last favour she shall ever ask him. *Alphonso* hesitates, wavers, and would fain refuse, but cannot. He yields; his passion so blinding him that he does not foresee the probable result of so dangerous an interview. *Morico* is overjoyed at his success, and flies to his mistress, whom, in a few moments, he brings back with him.

Zara, negligently attired and with her hair in disorder, appears; she advances slowly towards the King. Her countenance and manner evince the most bitter affliction.

Alphonso receives her without moving from his place, and affects an indifference which he does not feel. The wily *Zara* is not deceived by his assumed looks of cold dignity, although she feigns to believe that they are real. Tears stream down her cheeks, she confesses that she is guilty, but to Love alone is her crime to be imputed, and she implores him to pardon her. She expresses her remorse at having brought her King into difficulties, and her sorrow and despair at being abandoned by him.

Alphonso becomes agitated; he would fain draw a veil over the past; their final separation is the first step imposed on him by duty towards rendering his people happy; the public welfare imperatively demands the sacrifice of their mutual passion. *Zara* complains to heaven of the rigour of her fate; she expresses what grief the loss of her lover's heart occasions her; she is rejected and almost banished by him who so lately raised her to the honours of a diadem. She assails him with the most tender reproaches, reminds him of his love and his vows of constancy. *Alphonso*, with difficulty, bears up against her touching expressions, and tears escape from his eye-lids. His emotion does not pass unperceived by *Zara* and *Morico*, who now see that their triumph is almost certain. They mutually assail him— the one by expressing the most violent grief, and the other by her tears and her prayers. Thus the defeat of *Alphonso's* virtuous resolution is hastened. *Zara* threatens to put herself to death; he shudders at the thought; she seizes a poniard; he wrests it from her, and, unable longer to resist the impulse of his heart, he says that he still loves her. *Zara*, unobserved by the King, expresses her joy at the prospect of once again commanding as a Queen; she throws herself at *Alphonso's* feet, and covers his hand with kisses. He endeavours to avoid her caresses; but he, nevertheless, feels all his former affection for her returning, and is on the brink of becoming a victim to the magic influence of her charms. *Zara* grows more energetic and passionate in her appeal; she reproaches him with his cruelty, which is about to drive her to despair and death. She affects to retire, but the King stops her for a moment by an affectionate gesture. She appears resolved to die, and will not listen to his entreaties to live; she makes another motion to rush out, when the King hastens towards her, and almost on his knees conjures her not to fly from him. Joy returns to the bosom of *Zara* at this sight, and *Morico* expresses his rapture at the smiling prospect of a re-union between *Alphonso* and his mistress. The fascinated King at length expresses his determination that *Zara* shall be united to and reign with him! He gives orders to *Morico*, who hurries to execute them. *Zara* expresses the excess of her happiness, and vows to live and, if necessary, to die for her King. *Alphonso* informs her that his friends have calmed the irritated people, and they have now nothing to fear from popular clamour. He places the ambitious *Zara* on the throne, and shares it with her.

Morico, at the head of a troop of his friends and a few courtiers, appears, and all render homage to *Zara*. The re-union of the lovers is celebrated by a splendid fête, in the progress of which, *Zara* orders *Morico* to keep a strict watch upon their enemies, and to take all necessary precautions for her future safety. She instructs him also to compel *Fanès* to quit the court, and to secure the person of their greatest foe, the venerable *Garcias*. *Morico* testifies his satisfaction at the idea of revenging himself, and departs unperceived.

At the conclusion of the *Divertissement*, *Alphonso* and *Zara* retire, followed by their suite.

ACT IV.

*The theatre represents an armoury in the castle of
Fanès.*

ERMANGERE is discovered seated near a table, and appears to be pondering on her destiny. *Fanès* enters
hastily, and his agitation is a new source of alarm to the
unfortunate wife of *Alphonso.* She interrogates, and
earnestly presses him to answer her questions. He at
length acquaints her that the King has again taken the
Moorish woman to his arms; that he has placed her on
the throne, and once more become her vassal—the slave
of her caprice. He adds, that he himself is banished,
and that *Garcias* is groaning in fetters ; that the people,
however, enraged at this sudden revolution in the King's
sentiments, have again risen; and, led by several high-
spirited Castilians, have determined on putting an end to
the odious tyranny of the Moorish concubine.

This last intelligence inspires *Ermangère* with hope,
and her depressed spirits become a little elevated ; *Fanès*
now acquaints her that her valiant friends will soon appear at his castle, in order to make the necessary arrange-
ments for marching against those enemies which the state
fosters in its bosom—the Moorish followers and friends
of *Zara.*

Arms of different descriptions are brought in and arranged in *fasceaux ;* soon after the discontented troop
and their noble leaders arrive. Some of them are disguised as peasants, others as pilgrims, and the remainder,
in order more effectually to deceive their enemies, have
assumed the costume of the Moors. They all seem anxi-

ous for the fray. *Fanès* presents their chiefs to *Erman-gère;* they show her every possible token of respect, loy-alty, and devotion, and pledge themselves to shed their blood, if necessary, for her and their country.

Ermangère exhibits the most lively gratitude for their devotion to her cause, and blesses the banner which is to lead them against her enemies. The signal of depar-ture from the tocsin is heard, and the whole troop dis-appears, while *Ermangère,* confidently reposing on the justice of heaven, retires, attended by her faithful *Fanès.*

ACT V.

The theatre represents a magnificent pavilion; a garden is seen through the back entrance, adorned with statues, fountains, grottoes, &c.

ALPHONSO is discovered by the side of *Zara,* who is de-licately touching a lyre, and seems to be describing her passion for the King. Intoxicated with the charms of this seducing syren, the monarch expresses his love and the happiness he feels in her society. *Zara* smiles com-placently upon her royal slave. A troop of *Balliadères,* by their exquisite dances, contribute to the voluptuous-ness of the scene.

A distant noise of arms is heard, accompanied with cries of alarm from all sides, which fill the breasts of those in attendance with such terror that each thinks only of insuring his own personal safety. *Alphonso* and *Zara* dread some serious calamity. *Morico* rushes in, in evident dismay, to announce the revolt of the people and the army. All the citizens have taken up arms. The chief Castilians have assumed absolute authority, routed the Moors, and imperatively demand the appearance of *Alphonso* and the death of *Zara*. Consternation and despair of the two lovers!

Time presses, and compels them to adopt some resolution without delay. *Alphonso* seizes a sword, and seems to hope that his presence will be sufficient to calm the tumult. *Zara* foresees that her ruin is certain—terror seizes upon her soul—hope abandons her heart. *Alphonso* is dreadfully troubled to behold her in this state, but every moment is precious ; he presses her with transport to his bosom, and flies to stem the torrent of rebellion, and to save the object of his love. *Morico* also departs, to assemble the Moors again, and, with them and the other dependants of *Zara*, to oppose the revolted Spaniards. *Zara*, after imploring the succour of those who surround her, hastens, accompanied by her suite, to a place of shelter from the popular rage.

The scene changes to one of the courts of the Palace ; the city is seen in the distance.

Several Moors, pursued by Castilians, cross the scene ; a general combat between the people and the partisans of *Zara* ensues, in which the latter are defeated and driven off ; the theatre is left for a moment unoccupied, until the noise of the unequal conflict between the pursued and the pursuing dies away.

Zara enters alone ; her whole appearance is indicative of terror and despair. She hastily traverses the scene without knowing where to direct her steps. Her very dependants have now abandoned her ; she is deserted " by those her former bounty fed ;" she has become the object of general execration, and all accuse her of the

evils they have endured. The utter solitude and horrid
silence which reign around are more dreadful to her
than the noise of arms, the shouts of the victor and the
cries of the vanquished. She dreads the fury of the
Castilians, and works herself to the brink of madness at
the idea of falling by their hands, without revenge.
She calls upon heaven for immediate death; and exclaims
against fate, for having raised her from a lowly state to
the summit of glory, only to precipitate her in an instant
to the abyss of woe and wretchedness. In her fury she
becomes odious to herself. The shouts of approaching
citizens and a confused noise of arms announces to her
that her last hour is arrived. She awaits the coming of
her enemies with an intrepidity which is the consequence
of despair. A small number of Castilians who are in
search of *Zara* appear; they seize her, and, raising their
swords, are about to put an end to her hated existence;
but suddenly withholding their arms, they seem reluctant
to stain their swords with the blood of a woman, even
though guilty as *Zara*. *Fanès* arrives; he approves of
their forbearance, and orders *Zara* to be seized and led
to her fate. *Zara* for a moment eludes her enemies,
snatches a poniard from the hand of one of them, stabs
herself to the heart, and is borne off expiring.

Morico, with a number of Moors who have been made
prisoners, follow *Fanès* in expectation of having their fates
decided. They are condemned to banishment, and guards
lead them off after the body of *Zara* has been removed.

Alphonso appears, accompanied by his friends, the chiefs
of the army and people; he leads *Ermangère* forward, and
the Castilian knights do homage to the Queen. The
people crowd in, and testify their joy at this happy re-
union. *Alphonso* throws himself at the feet of *Ermangère*;
he expresses his repentance, and the excess of his grief

at having given himself up to a fatal passion which must soon have brought down ruin on his head.   Tears of tenderness flow from the eyes of *Ermangère;* she forgets the past in the present scene of happiness.   *Alphonso* vows the most constant attachment to her, and promises his people to devote his life to their welfare.   *Garcias*, the victim of *Zara*, is brought in fettered.   His appearance produces a general movement of indignation; *Alphonso* presses him to his bosom, and testifies the gratitude he feels to his old friend for his devotion to the Queen. General acclamations : joy reigns in every heart, and the curtain falls upon a brilliant and interesting *Tableau.*

CYRUS.

AN ENCYCLICAL OR HISTORICAL BALLET.

REMARKS.

AMONG the ancients those poems were called *cyclical* or *encyclical* which contained the general history of a man or a country. Wishing to make an attempt to preserve this species of composition in the Ballet, we have given the following argument. It will, accordingly, be seen, that we do not pretend to relate the entire history of the life of *Cyrus* in a single representation, but only the principal and most remarkable passages, and in such a manner as not to be subjected to observe strictly the laws of unity. In the mean time, such a natural succession may be preserved in describing the events of many years, that any appearance of interval will be imperceptible. Our Ballets of *Aphrodita, Vivaldi,* and *Dudley* may be regarded as compositions of this class. In the following specimen it has not been thought necessary to embody the idea any farther than the argument.

CHARACTERS.

CYRUS, *son of Cambyses, King of Persia, assuming the name of Artamenes.*

CYAXARES, *King of Cappadocia and Galatia.*

MANDANE, *daughter of Cyaxares.*

ARIBES, *confidant of Cyrus.*

MARTICIA, *Mandane's waiting-maid.*

THE KING OF PONTUS and BYTHINIA.

THE SON OF NITOCRIS, *Queen of Assyria.*

PHILODASPES, *a Prince.*

MAGI.

The scene lies at Synope.

EPITOME.

CYRUS is obliged to quit the court of Cambyses to avoid the cruelty of his grandfather, *Astyages.* The latter has been warned by an oracle that the above prince will become the most powerful monarch on earth. *Cyrus,* travelling in disguise, arrives at the court of his uncle, *Cyaxares,* with the daughter of whom, *Mandane,* he becomes enamoured. *Cyaxares* is about to undertake a war, and, in order to render his arms victorious, he proclaims a sacrifice to the God Mars, and upon the day of the ceremony, *Cyrus* tenders his services. The offer is accepted, and the young prince is appointed to a military command. *Cyrus* displays the most exalted valour, saves the King's life, and is loaded with honours and gratitude. *Mandane* pays particular attention to her father's preserver, and *Cyrus* is in expectation of the happiest result. The King now desires to know who he is, but the prince entreats to be excused a declaration of his birth. A rival prince, named *Philodaspes,* appears, and challenges *Cyrus* to single combat. *Cyrus* vanquishes his antagonist, but nobly refuses to take his life. *Mandane* beholds the young hero with such visible marks of delight, that the latter makes a confession of his passion, and is most favourably received. *Cyrus* having departed to serve in the wars of *Cyaxares,* a report is soon spread that he has met with his death, and *Mandane* is plunged into the deepest despair. At the very instant that funeral rites are about to be performed in honour of *Cyrus,* he returns, and mourning is changed into joy. Shortly after this, the young prince discovers a plot of *Philodaspes* to carry off *Mandane.* He rescues that princess, and is again rewarded and honoured. He at length discovers his real rank to *Mandane,* and unrestrained proofs of affection are exchanged. *Cyaxares,* understanding the connexion that subsists between his daughter and *Cyrus,* becomes highly incensed at her, and commands *Cyrus* to be arrested. The chiefs of the army immediately beg for the life of the young hero, but in vain, he is condemned to suffer death. Upon this, *Aribes* declares the name and birth of *Cyrus.* The latter then displays the greatness of his soul in pardoning his enemies. Finally, the marriage of *Cyrus* and *Mandane* is celebrated without interruption, and due homage is paid to the exalted character of the Persian prince. Having defeated the enemies of *Cyaxares,* he is regarded as his liberator; and being afterwards put in possession of a universal monarchy, the predictions of the oracle are completely fulfilled.

THE SORCERESS AND THE TROUBADOUR.

A FAIRY BALLET, IN FOUR ACTS.

CHARACTERS.

ALDEGONDE, *a wicked Sorceress.*
ALIDOR, *a young Troubadour.*
SILVIA, *a young Shepherdess.*
EUFROSINE, *a benignant Fairy.*
ARIDEL, *a Spirit attending on Eufrosine.*
Shepherds and Shepherdesses; Hunters and Huntresses;
a Villager; Sylphs attending Eufrosine; Demons un-
der the command of Aldegonde.

ACT I.

A wild uncultivated scene ; on the right appears a cavern, forming the entrance to the subterranean domains of Aldegonde. *Near the portal stands a tripod ornamented with magic devices.*

Scene I.—As the curtain rises *Aldegonde* is discovered surrounded by her court; in her hand she bears a mystic rod, and seems lately to have completed an act of enchantment; upon the tripod burns a magic flame. Before the enchantress, *Silvia* and a troop from the surrounding country are bending in adoration; they appear to pay her the most servile homage ; while *Aldegonde* boasts the ascendancy she has obtained over their minds. Satisfied with this proof of her power, she retires below to pursue her mystic and malignant occupations.

Scene II.—*Silvia*, a reigning queen of the rustic troop, leads off the dance to the sound of village minstrelsy. Flowery coronets are next suspended from the branches, and the young swains and shepherdesses exercise themselves in darting lances at them. *Silvia* alone gains the prize, and her conquest is publicly proclaimed. She is then placed at the head of the trooping nymphs holding the prize, a laurel crown. A trophy of reversed coronets is borne before her. She is then crowned, while the whole company, grouping around her, pay homage to their rural queen. Various dances are executed in her honour; after which the assembly disperses.

Scene III.—*Alidor* enters; he has seen *Silvia*, the nymph for whom he burns, but he has been unable to approach her ; she is indeed insensible to his looks of love, and always seeks to avoid him. He is, therefore, dejected, and knows not what course to pursue. Recovering himself, *Alidor* resolves still to follow the footsteps of the unfeeling *Silvia ;* it may chance that he will succeed in procuring a short interview. Thus decided, he departs.

SCENE IV.—*Eufrosine,* accompanied by her benignant spirit, *Aridel,* appears ; she is borne in a chariot drawn by eagles ; they alight, and *Aridel* shows her mistress the abode of her rival, where she practises her malignant enchantments, and holds dominion over the minds of men, satisfying her most wicked and inordinate desires. *Eufrosine* rejoices at this discovery ; she will now be enabled to punish her enemy, and rescue the enslaved people of these parts. Her attendant urges her to take revenge, and offers her most devoted services. Both appear meditating on the means to be employed to secure success to their designs.

SCENE V.—*Alidor* returns ; *Eufrosine* and her attendant go aside. The enamoured youth has not succeeded, and *Silvia,* the insensible *Silvia,* avoids his company. Dejected and despairing, *Alidor* sinks upon a swelling bank, and remains absorbed in thought. The benignant *Eufrosine* already knows his pain. *Alidor* recovers, but abandons himself to fate, and conjures the immortal powers to put an end to his sufferings. *Eufrosine* has already formed her project, and is determined to bring about the union of the young Troubadour and *Silvia,* at the same time resolving to punish *Aldegonde,* by inspiring her with a hopeless passion for *Alidor.* The attending Fairy applauds the plan, and both proceed immediately to put it in execution. Disguising themselves as shepherdesses, they approach *Alidor,* and offer to relieve his grief. The youth, supposing them to be some of *Silvia's* companions, asks of her welfare ; he then wishes to know their opinion, and expresses the force of his affection for the cruel damsel. The two young shepherdesses, sympathizing in his pain, beg of him to place his hopes in *Aldegonde.* They even advise him to seek out that Sorceress, whose dominion is as great as it is powerful. *Alidor* revives at this intelligence, he returns thanks to the kind-hearted shepherdesses, and resolves to seek the aid of the sorceress. The two pretended shepherdesses, foreseeing a happy result to their designs, withdraw. *Eufrosine's* attendant, on retiring, places a dart near the entrance to the dwelling of *Aldegonde,* and then hastens away to entice *Silvia* to the spot.

SCENE VI.—*Alidor* reflects upon the course he is about to pursue, and seems delighted by his illusory hopes. He prepares to enter the subterranean way, but his progress is suddenly arrested by the noise of footsteps, and a moment after he perceives *Silvia* approaching, and is charmed at this opportunity of addressing her.

SCENE VII.—*Silvia* enters hastily and in disorder; she has just escaped the pursuit of a young villager, who endeavours to get possession of the nymph, and to carry her off. The latter arrives and seizes his prey ; *Silvia* struggles in his grasp, and is nearly exhausted, when *Alidor,* springing upon the rustic, rescues *Silvia* from the ravisher and puts him to flight; while *Silvia* swoons upon the green bank.

SCENE VIII.—*Alidor* now seems to have obtained his most ardent wishes; fate at last grants him the means of addressing her he adores. He advances towards her, but as yet she has not regained her senses ; he supports her in his arms, yet trembles for the result, expecting a repulse when reason again resumes her sway—he speaks—

the nymph recognizes the voice and attempts to fly—the enamoured Troubadour endeavours to stop her—she screams, and escapes towards the subterranean entry—the Troubadour again arrests her flight. At this instant, perceiving the mystic dart, she seizes it and attacks *Alidor*. During this scene *Eufrosine* and her attendant have arrived at a distance, and witness the effects of their deep laid scheme. *Alidor* defends himself against every attack, and, influenced by the gestures of the Fairy, he turns the dart against *Silvia*, and she is wounded. A devouring fire instantly seizes upon the nymph, and seems to flame along her veins ; its power becomes irresistible, she falters, sinks, and swoons away. *Alidor*, suspecting that he has unintentionally wounded his love, flies to her assistance, and then hastens away in search of remedies.

Scene IX.—*Eufrosine* with her attendant, *Aridel*, advance ; they get possession of *Silvia* and vanish away into the air.

Scene X.—*Alidor* re-enters hastily, bringing medicinal plants, but he finds not *Silvia ;* he searches in every part, but *Silvia* is no where to be seen ; he calls her name, but echo alone replies. Grief again takes possession of his breast, and the only hope remaining, is to implore the help of the Sorceress. He retires, and in his absence *Silvia* is conveyed upon a cloud between *Eufrosine* and her spirit to the palace of *Aldegonde*.

ACT II.

A representation of the place where Aldegonde *holds her court. On the right appears a colonnade leading to the palace. Every circumstance is calculated to inspire sentiments of enchanting pleasure. In the foreground a fountain sends forth its glittering waters, and at a distance is discovered a gentle stream meandering along.*

Scene I.—*Eufrosine* and her attending spirit, *Aridel*, together with *Silvia*, descend from the skies, reclining upon a golden cloud. *Silvia* continues in the same insensibility into which she had been cast, until recalled by the Fairy. Opening her eyes, her heart also at the same instant opens to the impression of love. "How," she inquires, "have I been conveyed to the palace of *Aldegonde*, and why does my heart beat for *Alidor*?" This two-fold miracle she cannot comprehend. She next recognizes the two pretended shepherdesses, and their presence tranquillizes her fears—but where is *Alidor*—what is become of him? Perhaps, dejected and forlorn, he thinks no more of scornful *Silvia*—he has, perhaps, transported his love to some more favouring fair. *Eufrosine*, drawing near, bids her be calm, for that ere long she shall again behold the tender Troubadour, but while remaining at the court of *Aldegonde*, she must not unveil her sentiments of love for *Alidor*. *Silvia* meditates on what all this may mean. Harmonious sounds are heard; they announce the approach of *Alidor*; but *Eufrosine* and *Aridel* draw *Silvia* away, and hide her in a distant wood.

Scene II.—The court of *Aldegonde* advance, and prepare to meet the unexpected stranger, *Alidor;* he enters and entreats to be presented to the magic queen, to ask protection and solicit aid.

Scene III.—*Aldegonde* herself appears, and beholding the beauteous youth, demands to speak with him in private. The court retire, leaving their queen alone with *Alidor.*

Scene IV.—*Alidor* now relates how deeply he is enamoured of *Silvia,* how much he has endured for her sake, while she rejects his suit, and shuns his very presence. He entreats *Aldegonde* to soften, by her power, the heart of the cruel nymph, and rescue him from sufferings worse than death. While the youthful petitioner addresses *Aldegonde,* a soft emotion steals into her breast—she loves—she burns, and *Alidor* inspires the flame ; but he redoubles his entreaties for *Silvia.* Jealousy now begins to pain the Enchantress ; but she dissimulates, telling *Alidor* she will employ her power to serve him, yet secretly swears to destroy her rival, *Silvia.* She wishes to divert the thoughts of *Alidor* from his beloved ; she, therefore, commands a banquet to be instantly prepared, attended by amusing sports, purposing thus to inspire an idea of her person and her power.

Scene V.—The subjects of *Aldegonde* assemble, amongst them are intermingled *Eufrosine, Aridel* and *Silvia.* They have seen and heard all in their retreat. *Aldegonde,* taking *Alidor* by the hand, entreats him to partake the joys of the feast. Three damsels present to him the prizes about to be contended for—first a golden apple for the fleetest runner ; a bow for the best archer ; and a coronet for her who excels in the dance. A youthful troop immediately advance, and begin to dispute the prizes. *Silvia* gains the first ; upon which

Eufrosine and *Aridel* present her to *Alidor*, who thinking still upon the object of his love, seems to take but little interest in the scene ; but who shall paint his expression of surprise when he suddenly beholds that object ! He is about to throw himself at her feet ; but *Eufrosine*, by a look full of expression and intelligence, intimates to him, that to make such a discovery before the Enchantress would be imminently dangerous for both; in the mean time, *Aridel*, advancing towards *Aldegonde*, contrives to divert her attention. She presents to her a quiver, containing poisoned arrows, which, as by accident, she drops upon the Sorceress, who is struck by the descending darts. *Group.* *Alidor* hands over to *Silvia* the golden apple, and the latter rejoins her companions. *Silvia* soon wins the remaining prizes, which she receives in the same manner. All this time *Alidor* does not dream of the happy change that has taken place in the breast of *Silvia*. The two disguised fairies now invite *Alidor* and *Aldegonde* to partake in the sports. A noble dance begins, and during the formation of a certain group, *Alidor* understands that his love is requited; while, by the grace and agility of his motions, he, himself, charms every beholder.

SCENE VI.—The chase now succeeds to the pleasures of dancing; each person is presented with a lance by hunters, while *Aldegonde* orders and appropriates a costume for *Alidor*. The whole company now hastens away to the sound of the horn; *Aldegonde* seems confident of success in her design ; while the two lovers take this opportunity of whispering each other aside.

ACT III.

The scenery represents a deep and gloomy forest; at some distance a rugged road is discovered crossing the wood.

Scene I.—The chase; the sound of horns is heard mingled with the barking of hounds and the neighing of horses. Hunters and huntresses are divided over the scene in various groups.

Scene II.—*Aldegonde* makes choice of the opportunity afforded by the chase to make the declaration of her passion to *Alidor*. The umbrageous retreats in the forest, and the dispersion of the hunters, are circumstances extremely favourable to her intentions. The mistress of the magic art is now seeking *Alidor* on every side; he at length enters amidst a troop of hunters, and she immediately draws him aside, while the troop hastens away. The discourse soon becomes painful to *Alidor;* suddenly the sound of a horn announces that some inhabitant of the wood has been aroused from his lair.

Scene III.—*Silvia* passes by, conducting a group of her companions; she appears in the heat of pursuit, and prepared to lanch her dart at the flying stag. *Alidor* instantly perceives his beloved maid, and rushes out after her, leaving the Sorceress immoveable with astonishment.

Scene IV.—*Aldegonde* knows not what to conclude from the rude and abrupt departure of *Alidor;* she questions herself, but remains unsatisfied, and plunged in obscurity. In a few minutes, however, she beholds *Alidor* returning, accompanied by his *Silvia.*

Now is she fully convinced, and an unwelcome light

illumines the darkness of her illusory passion ; a super-
human fury takes possession of her soul, and she plunges
into the gloomiest depths of the forest to mature malignant designs of revenge, her sole delight.

SCENE V.—*Alidor* has informed *Silvia* of the ungovernable passion with which the Sorceress burns for him. The
gentle pair, dreading the effects of her infuriated jealousy,
determine to save themselves by flight, and conjure heaven to assist and protect them. As they are about to
escape, *Aldegonde* presents herself, and prevents their
progress. Struck with terror, they fall at her feet. She
raises them, and assures them of her friendship, and, embracing *Silvia* gently, blames them for their intended
flight. She informs them that the love she had expressed
for *Alidor*, while alone in the wood, was merely a friendly
stratagem to prove the truth of their affection ; in short,
she offers to unite them in her palace. Deceived by the
allurements of the Enchantress, blinded by love, and de-
luded by hope, *Alidor* and *Silvia* surrender themselves to
the direction of their most implacable enemy.

SCENE VI.—*Aldegonde* waves her wand, and the hunters and huntresses, as by instinct, immediately begin to
arrive. Impatient of delay, and fearing the escape of her
prey, the Sorceress commands that the unhappy pair be
conducted in state to her palace, where the hymeneal
ceremony is to be performed with suitable pomp. A slow
march is played, when all withdraw but *Aldegonde*.

SCENE VII.—The Sorceress finding herself alone, gives
vent to all the jealous ire with which she is filled. At
length, to soothe and satisfy her rage, she has recourse to
the aid of her art. *Invocation.* Raising her wand, it
changes to the shape of a circle ; she then indicates with
it the four points of the horizon, and striking the earth,
the rod resumes its former shape. A thick cloud now wraps

the skies in gloom ; lightnings flame along the air, and the savages of the forest send forth horrible howlings ; the ground appears in motion with earthquake—it opens, a black vapour ascends, and the demons of darkness arise. They remain motionless before her who has summoned them, awaiting her commands.

SCENE VIII.—*Aldegonde* informs them that she has called them up to execute her schemes of revenge, which have become lawful from the provocation she has received. The infernal spirits devote themselves to her service, with horrible imprecations; the Sorceress is satisfied. She then, with her bodkin, traces upon a tablet the figure of *Silvia*, and binds a riband round the picture. Having done this, she is presented with a vase of gold, into which she throws the portrait; the demons, who are ranged in a circle around her, now advance one by one, and cast into the vase the juice of certain poisonous herbs. *Aldegonde* then takes the head of a serpent, and pressing it between her hands, the venom flows in amongst the other charms ; at this moment the moon appears ; the silvery face of the queen of night is stained with faintish crimson, as if affected by the charm. The Sorceress seizes a torch from one of the demons ; she shakes the sparks from it into the vase, and a universal tremor, observable in all the surrounding objects, follows, and announces that the charm has succeeded. *Aldegonde*, by the power of her art, instantly transports herself and the infernal spirits to her palace ; they depart in a fiery cloud, and hasten to execute their dire and revengeful designs.

ACT IV.

The scenery is the same as that of the second act.

Scene I.—*Aldegonde* and her spirits appear in the air; they alight, and the gloomy twilight is illumined by their torches. *Aldegonde* places herself upon the tripod, and repeats her commands of revenge. Seated upon the mystic throne, the demons convey her to the fountain, into which she pours the contents of the vase amidst the most terrible imprecations. She makes a sign, and the spirits of darkness descend into the earth; nature resumes her wonted aspect, and all becomes tranquil.

Scene II.—The sound of the horn announces the approach of the hunter troop that are conducting *Silvia* and *Alidor* to the palace of the Enchantress, who, having whispered a secret command to one of her attendants, retires.

Scene III.—*Silvia* and *Alidor*, entering with their attendants, are invited to repose themselves; fruits are presented to them; a female slave, according to the orders she has received, offers them a cup of water from the charmed fountain; but scarcely has *Silvia* carried the cup to her lips, when a cloud of flame descends and envelops her, and the next moment she becomes a hideous monster. Every one immediately avoids her and escape for their lives, while she herself seems unconscious of this horrible change.

Scene IV.—*Silvia* perceives *Alidor*, who has returned to seek for her, dreading lest she may have been devoured by the beast. All-ignorant of her disgusting shape, *Silvia* hastens to throw herself into his arms, but *Alidor* seizes his hunter's javelin and aims a blow at her.

Scene V.—*Aldegonde* enters, and, arresting his arm, asks him if he would thus barbarously destroy his beautiful mistress? At this exclamation *Alidor* appears horror-struck. The detestable Sorceress, now smiling, presents *Silvia* with a glass. The nymph, amazed at the meta-morphose, abhors herself and flies towards the fountain, into which she is about to cast herself, when she is prevented by the demons, but she has again beheld her fearful form.

Scene VI.—At length, by the assistance of *Eufrosine* and *Aridel*, who are observed hovering in the air, she escapes the grasp of her enemies, and plunges into the stream. *Alidor* is about to follow her, but he also is prevented by the malignant demons ; aided, however, by the good Fairy, he eludes their hold, and flies to join his mistress in the flood. *Aldegonde* now perceives that a superior power defeats her intentions. Beholding the object of her love fled, and the victim of her vengeance escaped, she trembles with the fury of her wrath. *Aridel* now advances towards her, and threatens her with punishment ; she rushes upon this seeming shepherdess, who easily eludes her attack, leaving her vest in the hands of the Sorceress, and smiling at her impotent anger. *Aldegonde* instantly recognizes the spirit of her powerful rival, and, raging with disappointment, she fore-sees the inevitable consequences, and submits.

The scene changes, and represents a magnificent interior view of the palace of *Eufrosine*, the benignant Fairy ; she is seated on her throne and surrounded by sylphs. Near the Fairy appears *Alidor* holding *Silvia*, who has regained her natural form, and exhibits all the beauty and vigour of youth. *Aldegonde*, unable to endure the sight of the triumph of her rivals, makes a sign with her wand, when the earth yawns into a hideous gulf, and, surrounded by her demons, she precipitates herself into the regions of darkness, there to dwell for ever. *Eufrosine*, exulting in the just punishment of the cruel *Aldegonde*, unites the gentle *Silvia* to the constant *Alidor*, and prophecies their future uninterrupted happiness.

General rejoicings, sports and Divertissement.

DUDLEY*.

A GRAND HISTORIC BALLET, IN FIVE ACTS.

ARGUMENT.

THE troubles and wars caused by the dissention between the houses of York and Lancaster, are rendered celebrated by the accounts given of them in English History.

These two families aspired with equal ardour to the crown, for which they disputed with unexampled fury, frequently drenching that country with blood which they should have protected †.   *Henry* VI, of the house of Lancaster, at length attained to the crown, and his rival was obliged to submit.   During his reign the Yorkists, though they had missed their aim, yet they had not lost their intrepidity; they still entertained a hope of revenge, and flattered themselves they should be one day able to place upon the throne young *Edward*, son of the Duke of York, on whom *Dudley, Earl of Warwick* ‡, a man renowned in these wars, bestowed the most careful attention.   In the mean time, *Henry* VI continued to reign, but the weakness of his character rendered him ever insecure; *Margaret of Anjou*, his consort, perceived it, and, uniting talent with courage, she frequently preserved him from ruin.   Yet, notwishstanding the éfforts

---

* The History of England, and the tragedy of Warwick, have been my guides in composing this Ballet; a subject never before treated on by any other composer.

† The faction of Lancaster chose for their device, a red rose; that of York, a white rose.

‡ History relates that, in the latter part of his life, he became Duke of Northumberland.

of this illustrious Queen, the valour, policy, and conduct of *Dudley* rapidly advanced the interest of the Yorkists. They at length dethroned the reigning prince; and *Henry*, his Queen, and their son became the prisoners of *Edward*, who now ascended the throne. (Immediately after this epoch, the action of the following piece begins.) No sooner had *Edward*, with the aid of *Warwick*, effected his purpose, than the Earl departed for France, to conclude a treaty with the French King, *Louis* XI, and to obtain the hand of his sister* for *Edward*, who had consented to the match. This marriage was designed to establish firmly the English throne, and to procure a lasting and advantageous peace. During the absence of *Dudley*, *Edward* became enamoured of the *Lady Elizabeth*, who was beloved by the Earl, and so warm was the King's passion that he promised to espouse her immediately. Thus love incited him to commit an act of ingratitude against his greatest benefactor. Upon the point of the celebration of this marriage, the Earl arrived, bearing declarations of peace, with a promise from the French King of bestowing his sister on *Edward*. The latter having otherwise engaged himself, rejected the proposal, and *Dudley* felt the injury deeply. He perceived himself scorned by the King and despised by the people, both of France and England. He instantly searched for the cause of this sudden change in the King's conduct, and chance, aided by friends, instructed him in the whole proceeding. Upon this information the fury of the Earl became boundless, and he determined on means of the most terrible revenge. *Edward*, however, caused him to be arrested and thrown into prison; but the strength of his party, and the influence he had over the people, together with the advantage now taken by *Margaret* to recover the throne, effected the deliverance of *Dudley*, and exposed the false prince. Every circumstance seemed now to tend to the ruin of *Edward*; but the generous and exalted soul of *Warwick*, unwilling to take advantage of the weakness and ill-success of *Edward's* cause, induced him to rescue his prince from the hands of his enemies, and to confound their designs, thus adding another trait of generosity to immortalize his name. By his valour the Lancasterian party again sinks, and the former state of affairs is restored; while the people quietly submit to the heroic chief they admire. *Edward* is abashed by this act of magnanimity; he confesses

---

* Bona of Savoy, sister of the Queen of Louis XI.

the injustice his ungovernable passion urged him to commit. He now resigns himself to the direction of *Warwick,* who evinces a grateful joy at the change. *Dudley* becomes triumphant at court, with the people, and with his intended wife He only requires, as the reward of all his services, public respect for himself, and universal submission to *Edward's* lawful sway.

CHARACTERS.

DUDLEY, EARL OF WARWICK.

EDWARD OF YORK, *King of England, Son of the Duke of York, and descended from Edward* III.

MARGARET OF ANJOU*, *wife of Henry* VI, *who is descended from the house of Lancaster.*

ELIZABETH, *widow of Sir John Grey, in love with Dudley.*

SIR WILLIAM SOMMERS, *a friend of Dudley.*

THE DUKE OF SUFFOLK, *a confidential friend of the King.*

NEVIL, *an Officer attached to Margaret.*

Court of the King, Princes, Princesses, &c.; Officers; Soldiers; People ; Guards ; Sailors ; Scotch Chiefs ; attendants on Margaret ; Chiefs of the Queen's party ; attendants on Elizabeth.

The scene is laid in London, about the year, 1465.

---

* Daughter of Réné d'Anjou, King of Naples.

ACT I.

An apartment of Elizabeth's *in the royal Palace.*

SCENE I.—-*Edward* is discovered on his knees before *Elizabeth,* he is expressing to the beautiful young widow the passion she has inspired; subdued by the power of her attractions, he swears an eternal fidelity. *Elizabeth* blushes and appears embarrassed. The King conjures her to give a favourable reply to his wishes. At the ardent expressions of *Edward, Elizabeth* becomes still more disturbed. The image of the beloved chief is present to her mind; and feeling her heart devoted to to him, her situation is rendered distressing. *Edward* renews his solicitations, while the *Lady Elizabeth* dares not avow her real sentiments, and evinces evident confusion; the King, interpreting this fear and agitation as marks of her affection, flatters himself that he is about to obtain the acomplishment of his desires; but the lady implores the Prince to forbear awhile, to allow her time to reflect on such proposals. *Edward's* transporting passion will not admit of delay; *Elizabeth* rejects his solicitations. Jealous suspicions now inspire him; he would know her most secret feelings. The manner in which the *Earl of Warwick* has conducted himself induces him to suspect a mutual flame; he acquaints *Elizabeth* with his surmises; but she dissimulates, and endeavours to remove his fears by assuring him, that *Dudley* has inspired her with no other sentiment than that of admiration for his deeds; *Edward* consequently perceives no further obstacle to the accomplishment of his will; *Elizabeth,* by her own confession, is free, and his personal vanity flatters him that conquest is sure.   In short, he at last makes the youthful widow an offer of his crown; upon this *Elizabeth* is reduced to a situation of peculiar distress.

SCENE II.—*Edward* gives a signal, when *Suffolk* appears, and the latter is immediately commanded to make preparations for the nuptial ceremony; while a kind of consent is drawn from *Elizabeth*.   The latter, unable longer to resist the power of her feelings, appears on the point swooning, when an officer, entering hastily, announces the arrival of *Dudley;* the King is struck motionless by this news; but *Elizabeth* gradually revives, and becomes animated by hope.   *Edward* instantly countermands his orders, and prepares for an interview with *Warwick;* he takes leave of the object of his affection, promising a speedy union.   He retires, gazing on her to the last with an air of disappointed affection. The mistress of *Warwick* now laments her unhappy fate, but places all her hope in the protection of the hero she adores.

SCENE III.—*The Port of London with the Quay.*

The Thames is covered with vessels, whose streamers are floating in the air.   The Earl appears upon one of the most splendid of these; while strains of military music celebrate the arrival of the English warrior.   The people hasten in crowds to welcome him; warlike chiefs, his companions, surround the hero, but he alone is the object of universal attention and applause.   The King, attended by his court and followed by part of his army, arrives, and advances even to the water side, to receive the Earl, to whom this reception is a kind of triumph, and he appears fully to enjoy his glorious pre-eminence.   Each is anxious to show marks of devotion, and all receive a grateful acknowledgment of their zeal.   *Edward,* however, salutes *Warwick* with coldness, which, notwithstanding the surrounding multitude, does not pass unnoticed by the Earl.   *Dudley* bears peace to England, accompanied by terms of the approaching marriage with the sister of Louis.   Universal expressions of joy follow the declaration.   *Edward* alone appears inwardly agitated, and does not partake in the public sentiments.   *Dudley* now prepares to address him; but the King, fearing he might be called on to perjure himself, avoids an explanation, and defers the audience to some future opportunity; but in the meantime, commands the day to be celebrated by a public rejoicing.   *General fete and Divertissement.*

ACT II.

The stage represents sumptuous apartments in the royal Palace.

SCENE I.—*Dudley* enters, accompanied by his favourite, *Sommers;* the former expresses to his friend the joy he felt at the reception his countrymen honoured him with; *Sommers* shares in the satisfaction of the Earl, congratulating him on the glory and renown he has acquired. The latter now inquires for *Elizabeth,* and expresses the joy he shall feel at again beholding that lady; desiring *Sommers* to hasten and prepare her for the interview. *Sommers* is going, but *Dudley* recalls him, to communicate the observations he has made upon the deportment of the King, who had received him so coolly, and had even appeared so disconcerted at his presence, as to be almost regardless of the honours bestowed upon himself. *Sommers*, however, being entirely unacquainted with the peculiar circumstances in which *Edward* is placed, cannot divine the motives for such a conduct; but appeases *Warwick*, by representing that outward appearances cannot always be depended on; and that they ought not for an instant to disturb the mind of that man who has nothing to reproach himself with. The Earl repeats his message, and *Sommers* departs.

Scene II.—*Edward* enters, followed by his guards; *Warwick* hastens to meet him, proving his attachment and respect; but the monarch, unwilling to betray his real sentiments, affects a quiet indifference. The Earl now reminds him of the object of his embassy, and counsels him to prepare for his union with the French Princess, who will shortly arrive, for that such an alliance would be the seal of peace between the two nations. *Edward* acknowledges the care of *Dudley*, but gives him to understand that he cannot accept the hand of the French Princess; *Warwick* is astonished! He demands what has caused so sudden a change; but the King is unwilling to explain, yet appears determined to continue in his resolution. *Dudley* reminds him of the oath he has taken; but *Edward* replies, that he is prepared to defend his conduct before Louis; that his heart is already disposed of, and that even on that very day he is to be united to the object of his affection. The Earl expresses a wish to be made acquainted with the person on whom his choice is fixed; *Edward* replies, that a short time will discover every circumstance. The Earl, however, represents to him the error and danger of such conduct, and even reproaches him with weakness; *Edward* upon this appears greatly agitated; while the Earl entreats him to have some regard for his own honour, for the

advice of his ancient friend, and to avoid staining his
character. *Edward* appears deeply affected; he informs
Warwick that he has not yet disgraced his high rank,
but that he must be allowed to entertain those sentiments
of esteem and love which the best of women has inspired,
and even requests the assistance of *Warwick* in the affair; but the latter does not yet clearly conceive what
are the intentions of the young monarch. He accordingly entreats for an explanation, but *Edward* is too deeply
agitated to return an answer; and finding himself unable
longer to support the presence of his injured friend,
he promises to make him acquainted with his designs,
and withdraws.

SCENE III.—*Warwick* remains in the greatest astonishment; the remarks he had made upon the monarch's
behaviour at his arrival were founded on truth. Is it
possible that *Edward* can so have belied himself? And
what must be the allurements of the fair one who could
so have prevailed upon his resolution! The unhappy
and unexpected change causes in the Earl the deepest
concern, and he falls into a reverie of meditation.

SCENE IV.—*Margaret* enters, she appears occupied in
forming designs of revenge; she exhibits a melancholy
air, grief has cast a gloom over her features, yet they
have lost nothing of their natural loftiness. She remarks
the abstracted air of the Earl; the latter at length seems
resolved to seek satisfactory information respecting the
situation of the King. As he is about to depart, he is
prevented by *Margaret; Warwick* appears greatly surprised. She then acquaints him that, since his arrival,
she has learned the happy news of a peace being established between France and England, and that, therefore,
she hopes again, with her husband and son, soon to enjoy liberty. *Dudley* replies, that all as yet remains in

uncertainty, awaiting the determination of *Edward* with regard to his marriage. Upon this, *Margaret* replies, that if such are the conditions, the peace can never take place, since *Edward's* affections are fixed on another. *Warwick* appears astonished at how *Margaret* can have arrived at such information, and presses her to unveil this mystery. *Margaret* seizes this opportunity to sow discord, and immediately tells him that *Elizabeth* is to be united to *Edward*. *Warwick* is struck motionless with astonishment at this intelligence! Having recovered, he cannot yet persuade himself that what he has heard is possible; he cannot believe *Edward* capable of so base an action. *Margaret* replies, that time will discover the truth. *Dudley*, however, accuses *Margaret* of having invented the whole through hatred. The latter, wounded at such an imputation, expresses a hope that in a very short time she will be revenged, and even threatens the Earl with the consequences of her wrath, and retires.

SCENE V.—*Dudley*, deeply affected with what he has just heard, sinks into a chair, and, resting his head on his hand, meditates on the perfidy of *Edward* and recent unexpected events.

SCENE VI.—*Sommers* enters, evincing in his features some gloomy event; he fears to address *Warwick;* but the latter guesses the cause of his grief, unable himself to conceal his inward feelings. His friend at length assures him that *Elizabeth* is about to become the bride of *Edward; Warwick*, upon this, gives full liberty to his wounded and indignant feelings. *Sommers* endeavours to calm the incensed Earl, but in vain. *Warwick* will listen to nothing but the dictates of his own wrath, and, amidst the transports of anger, threatens the ravisher of his lady with terrible revenge. In vain does *Sommers* try by prayers and entreaties to soften and appease the anger of the infuriated nobleman; he swears that his former friend shall now become his most inveterate enemy; and *Sommers* seems to tremble for the consequences.

SCENE VII.—*Elizabeth* enters, and beholds the anger of her lover; her face is immediately suffused with tears. *Warwick* perceiving her, flies towards her, describing, by the most lively expressions, his love, his unhappiness, the perfidy of *Edward*, and his own wrath. Mutual marks of unalterable affection are then exchanged, and each takes an oath of eternal fidelity. *Dudley* swears that no power shall force *Elizabeth* from his protection; and that the traitor who would totally destroy his happiness, shall not escape the effects of his fury. *Elizabeth* shudders at these declarations of revenge. *Sommers* endeavours to console the unfortunate lady, and essays to deter his noble friend from executing his sanguinary intentions. *Elizabeth* also employs all her influence to calm his anger; she represents what will be the terrible consequences for both, if he persists. *Warwick* replies with a look of contempt and a smile of disdain, and remains unmoved in his resolution. *Elizabeth* appears in the deepest distress. *Dudley*, perceiving her situation, begs her not to afflict herself on his account, to console herself and allow him to act freely. *Elizabeth*, however, redoubles her entreaties, and conjures the hero to yield to her prayers for his own safety. She would persuade him to another interview with *Edward*, who, recollecting himself, might nobly return to a sense of honour, restore him to his rights, and ever treat that hero with respect to whom he owes all. *Warwick* still resists, but the gentle lady, throwing herself at his feet, obtains of him a promise to pardon for the present the unwarrantable conduct of *Edward*, and he even consents to see him, but will not give up his intention of some future revenge.   Hope reanimates the breasts of *Elizabeth* and *Sommers,* and each takes leave of *Dudley.*

ACT III.

A court-yard belonging to that part of the Palace allotted to Margaret of Anjou.

SCENE I.—-In this place, at some distance from the court, appears *Margaret;* she is accompanied by *Nevil,* her confident, together with the principal generals and officers of her party, both English and Scots.   In these she places her entire confidence.   *Margaret* acquaints them with the discord existing between *Edward* and *Warwick;* and consequently intimates the war likely to take place, of which it will become their duty to take advantage, in order that she may recover her throne and triumph over her oppressors.   The intrepid Queen then selects certain persons to spy upon the movements of both King and people.   She herself undertakes, by policy, to gain over *Warwick* to her interests, being determined to get possession of the great talent of that warrior. Her partisans applaud her courage and address.   *Margaret* commands them to be armed and ready to take advantage of the first tumult that may arise; her valiant followers swear to be faithful and ever prepared.   Joy again gleams on the countenance of *Margaret,* and she appears confident of success.   Her followers retire to forward the designs, and insure the triumph of the heroine.

Scene II.—*A sumptuous apartment in the Palace.*

Guards are attending at the further end. *Edward* appears absorbed in meditation ; his unfortunate passion and general conduct inspire him with dread for the future. The affront he has put upon his illustrious friend, and the anger of the latter, present to him the most fearful consequences.

Scene III.—*Suffolk* enters, and announces the approach of *Dudley,* who advances hastily. *Edward* is confused at the sudden and unexpected appearance of the Earl ; he endeavours to conceal his agitation, but *Warwick* instantly perceives it, and trembles with rage ; scarcely can he restrain his fury at the sight of one who has so deeply injured him. He informs the King of his dissatisfaction at the reception given him, and his conduct since. *Edward* seems desirous to make him sensible of his rank and power ; but the Earl, regardless of these, recounts the services he had done him, the battles he had fought, and the enemies he had vanquished in supporting his cause, and tells him, in short, that he owes the very throne to his valour and unalterable attachment. On the other hand, he represents to him the effects of his contempt and his ingratitude ; he tells him that his honour is lost, through the misplaced passion for a woman who had belonged to himself. *Edward,* offended at the freedom and reproaches of *Warwick,* commands him to abstain, and to pay a due respect to his authority ; informing him also, that if he persists, he shall find that punishment is in his power. The King continues, that he has not forgotten the services done for him, and that the high offices and employments of *Warwick* are a sufficient reward. As to *Elizabeth,* he declares that he finds it impossible not to love her ; that in this case he knows no other law than the dictates of his heart, and that he thinks himself fully at liberty to love a woman who is wife to no man. *Dudley* informs him that there is an oath of fidelity between him and *Elizabeth,* and that no power shall tear her from him ; adding, that it would be better for *Edward* to take his life than commit this act of injustice against him. *Edward,* feeling himself insulted, threatens to punish *Dudley* for his outrageous conduct, and commands him to obey; the Earl appears somewhat surprised at the bold and haughty tone assumed by the King, yet he trembles with internal anger, and makes a certain gesture, which seems to indicate contempt on the royal power. *Edward,* unable to support this last insult, calls for his guards, and commands them to take the Earl into custody, threatening an exemplary punishment for the outrages he has committed.

The Earl, beholding himself thus ignominiously treated, becomes furious ; with one terrible look he keeps off the guards who are about to disarm him ; he then advances towards *Edward,* and reproaches him with increased energy for thus rewarding all his services, and, throwing down his sword at *Edward's* feet, conjures him rather to sacrifice him upon the spot. As the guards are about to drag off *Warwick*—

SCENE IV.—*Elizabeth* appears, and beholds the last action of *Warwick's;* she seems overpowered by grief and astonishment. She kneels at the feet of *Edward,* and entreats him to sacrifice her alone, since her love for *Warwick* is the cause of the present misfortune. *Edward* is deeply wounded at this avowal of *Elizabeth;* jealousy takes possession of his breast, and he is deaf to her prayers. *Warwick* desires her to forbear entreating a monarch whose barbarous mind is incapable of any thing noble. *Edward* commands *Dudley* to be instantly imprisoned. The Earl departs in custody, yet though a prisoner, still menaces *Edward* with revenge. The distress of *Elizabeth* is now extreme. Tears and prayers find no attention from *Edward,* who reproaches her with having concealed her real sentiments. She again supplicates, and is again disregarded. *Edward* appears by turns tormented with the remembrance of the insults he has endured by jealousy and by love, and is on the point of devoting *Dudley* to destruction in his rage, but some remaining sense of gratitude restrains him, and he curbs his fury.

Elizabeth intercedes for the offender, and begs the King to do an action worthy of his rank ; but he declares that his resolution is unchangeable.

SCENE V.—*Suffolk* enters, and informs the King that his orders are strictly obeyed with regard to *Warwick,* but that the people murmur at his arrest; that the hero is greatly beloved in London, and that *Edward* may have just cause shortly to fear the consequences of this measure. He appears surprised at this news, but after a moment's reflection, he resumes all the haughtiness peculiar to his station, and, like an absolute prince, tells his confident that it will be a very easy matter to tame and keep down the people. He commands him to make preparations for quelling the tumult, and, approaching *Suffolk,* whispers him, and seems to communicate a secret of importance. The Duke shows a ready submission to the wishes of the King, and departs. *Edward* now accuses *Elizabeth* of all that has happened, and reproaches her with indifference, at the same time allowing some marks of affection to escape him; he then retires, threatening all who shall dare to oppose his authority.

SCENE VI.—The situation of *Elizabeth* still appears deplorable ; hope itself has abandoned her. Her attendants having entered, employ every means of consoling

her, but in vain, her grief refuses alleviation. *Warwick*
being mentioned, and the necessity of aiding that
hero, love soon reanimates her breast; she regains her
fortitude, and hastens away to contribute all in her
power for the preservation of the intrepid Earl.

ACT IV.

An apartment appropriated to Margaret.   *Night.*

MARGAGET OF ANJOU is discovered in complete armour ;
she is seated near a table, and reading a letter with the
deepest attention, after which she displays marks of
entire satisfaction in what she has read. She is surrounded by *Nevil,* her attendants, the leaders of her party,
and some Scottish warriors, all of whom appear to await
her orders. The heroine rises; her partisans advance
towards her, and she communicates the contents of the
letter, as follows :—That *Edward* and *Warwick* are become declared enemies ; that the latter is arrested, while
the people complain loudly of the King's conduct, and are
ready to rebel.—This information is received with marks of
satisfaction and joy; every one appearing prepared to profit
of an event entirely calculaled to advance the interests of
Margaret, who incites them to lose no time in their endeavour to effect the fall of *Edward ;* all declare their
zeal and readiness to serve her, and take an oath of allegiance. She then gives commands that all her followers
assemble, and hold themselves prepared for the intended attack ; proposing that an attempt be made to
liberate *Warwick,* who will become the principal support
of their party ; declaring also, that, with the addition of so
much talent and valour, success must be certain. This
counsel is received with universal approbation. *Dudley*

is the instrument with which they propose to satisfy their ambition and revenge, and to re-establish *Margaret* upon the throne of England. This measure seems to fill every breast with hope and courage ; so great, indeed, is their confidence in it, that already do they fancy the attempt is completed. In the mean time, the warrior-queen recommends the deepest circumspection, joined to an indefatigable activity, promising suitable rewards to all, and then departs at the head of one party, while *Nevil* conducts the other.

Scene II.—*A prison.*

Warwick is discovered ; he laments his captivity, and meditates upon the vicissitudes of fortune—he, who a few hours ago was the foremost man in England, is now plunged into a loathsome dungeon, like the vilest of criminals ! Notwithstanding his heroism, he feels deeply the pangs of disappointed love and royal perfidy, and appears lost in meditation on his wretched fate.

Scene III.—*Elizabeth,* followed by her suite, enters this gloomy abode ; she presents herself before her beloved *Dudley ;* mutual endearments are instantly exchanged, and the latter finds a momentary relief from his sufferings. He expresses to *Elizabeth* the surprise he feels at her unexpected visit. She then informs him that she is come from *Edward,* to entreat him to calm his anger, return to his allegiance, and endeavour to regain the royal favour. Scarcely has she delivered her commission, when *Warwick,* in the most decisive manner, refuses to listen to such conditions ; he admits himself somewhat in the wrong, but treats such a degrading submission with a haughty contempt. His mind broods rather on the means of revenge. *Elizabeth* employs the force of affection to dissuade him from his purpose, but he is immovable. He grieves to be denied the opportunity of revenging his affront in the field of battle. The trembling *Elizabeth* implores him to consider her unhappy situation. *Warwick* is affected at her distress, and promises soon to rescue her from the abyss of grief into which she is plunged. She, however, reproaches him with being the cause of the present revolt, and of the sanguinary combats that are about to deluge the country with blood ; but this representation does but increase the desire he feels to sacrifice his enemy. *Elizabeth* appears to dread the evil consequences; but *Dudley* recalls to her mind the guilty conduct of the King, his unprincipled designs, his own insults and ignominious chains ; the unhappy lady supplicates him on her knees, and bathes his hand with tears, but the Earl is immoveable. *Elizabeth* then reproaches him bitterly with the barbarity of his behaviour, and threatens to terminate her own woes by a speedy death. This determination appears deeply to affect *Warwick*, and he tries to recall the affection of *Elizabeth*, being prepared to make any sacrifice to regain her love. *Elizabeth*, unable to resist the united power of grief and tenderness, falls into the arms of *Dudley*.

Scene IV.—An officer, followed by a company of soldiers, enters and announces to *Elizabeth*, that the King commands her to leave this place, and to attend him immediately. The Earl desires to enjoy the company of *Elizabeth* a few minutes longer, but the officer repeats his order, and demands obedience. *Elizabeth* prepares to depart, conjuring *Warwick*, by a timely submission, to preserve his country from destruction, and herself from additional woe. She then bids him adieu, and retires.

Scene V.—*Warwick* appears dejected ; he accuses heaven of injustice, then implores death to put a period to his degrading punishment. Sinking upon a seat, he meditates on the wretchedness of his fate. He is aroused from his abstraction by a certain noise, like the clash of arms ; a momentary terror seizes *Warwick* for the first time ; the noise approaches, he suspects assassins, and prepares himself to meet the mortal blow.

SCENE VI.—Warriors bearing torches enter ; *Dudley* is astonished ; *Sommers* advances at the head of his men, and informs *Dudley* that he is the bearer of liberty, and then presents him with a suit of armour ; the Earl, in an ecstacy of joy, seizes first the sword, and then arms himself from head to foot ; he embraces his faithful friend, and returns thanks for his zeal in serving him. All his wonted valour and intrepidity appear now to have returned, and he burns for combat. *Sommers* informs him that the people have revolted against *Edward*, and that the latter is already a prisoner in his own palace ; and that *Margaret*, the warrior-queen, at the head of her party, is making gigantic strides towards the throne. The pleasure and surprise of *Warwick* upon this are unbounded ; *Sommers* counsels that not a moment may be lost, and commands all to depart instantly. As they are on the point of leaving the prison, *Warwick* suddenly stops ; every one appears astonished, while the Earl seems reflecting on some new thought that has seized him. The warriors gaze on each other, as if inquiring what has caused this extraordinary pause. *Warwick* has conceived a new project, that of a seasonable visit to the King, and he decides on pursuing this measure. He exhibits marks of self-satisfaction at this new plan of conduct, and requires of his chiefs an oath of fidelity in pursuing his measures ; they readily consent. " Well then," says *Warwick*, " let us act like heroes ; and to wage war against a defenceless King, confined as a prisoner, is an action unworthy of heroism.   Let us vanquish our enemies by a noble generosity.   Let us deliver *Edward*, but oppose *Margaret* and her partisans, and thus your character and mine will be placed in a proper light."   Having communicated his sentiments to all those who surround him, this exalted trait meets with universal approbation.   Honour and virtue seem to have found a support in every breast, while *Dudley*, impatient to add new lustre to his fame, gives the signal of departure, and marches out sword in hand at the head of his warriors.

ACT V.

Scene.—*A public square in London.   The Thames appears in the distance ; on one side part of the Royal Palace is discovered.*

A Combat takes place between *Edward's* soldiers, the people, and *Margaret's* party.   The latter, accompanied by *Nevil*, takes part against the King, and makes great efforts to get possession of the palace.   *Warwick* appears at the head of his warriors ; *Margaret* expresses the greatest joy ; her valour appears to increase, and she seems now confident of victory ; but she is deceived, the sentiments of the Earl are entirely changed, and instead of reinforcing the heroic Queen, he commands his troops and the people to fly to the relief of their King, and to oppose his enemies.   *Margaret* stands for a moment motionless and astonished at this change ; she beholds her hopes again cast down, yet she instantly regains her fortitude, and fights with redoubled fury.   *Dudley*, however, soon puts her party to flight, and then hastens to the palace.

Sommers continues still on the field, and succeeds in routing and taking prisoners that part of *Margaret's* followers composed of Scottish recruits. *Edward* and *Warwick* now appear together, and their public embrace gives general information that an act of oblivion has passed. In a few minutes a cessation of arms takes place; general joy is diffused around, and *Warwick* becomes an object of universal admiration. *Elizabeth* arrives, attended by her suite; when *Edward*, yielding up all claim to that lady, takes her by the hand and presents her to *Warwick*. The gallant prince still appears at a loss how adequately to reward the noble actions of the Earl; but the latter declares that the friendship and confidence of his King are a sufficient reward for all past services; *Edward* exhibits marks of a complete satisfaction. *Warwick* engages the army and people to be faithful and obedient to their sovereign, and prays for the happiness and prosperity of his country.

Universal applause follows these events. *Margaret*, having been taken, is now led in a prisoner; the haughty Queen appears to load the whole multitude with execrations, exposing and accusing *Warwick* in the most marked terms for his former treasonous conduct. The Earl disdains to reply, and the King commands her to be conducted out of his presence. No sooner does *Margaret* hear this, than, snatching a poniard from her girdle, she rushes upon *Warwick* to stab him; but the guards, perceiving her intention, seize her arm, and preserve the hero's life. This last act of *Margaret's* inspires every one with horror, and the King commands her to instant punishment. *Warwick*, however, implores pardon for the guilty Queen, and counsels to send her back into France; *Edward* does not attempt to reject this advice, and the guards prepare to conduct her away; she retires, loading her rival with imprecations, notwithstanding his generosity.

Edward signifies his wish that all animosity should now be forgotten and every gloomy recollection effaced, and that feast and friendly revelry be introduced to celebrate the triumph of the great *Earl of Warwick*. Himself unites *Elizabeth* to the hero, and appears to enjoy happiness in becoming the cause of theirs. *Dudley* expresses his deep gratitude and entire satisfaction, while the whole multitude salute *Edward* with a shout of applause; the young monarch gracefully acknowledges these marks of affection, and the curtain descends on a *General Group*.

ALCIDES,

OR,

THE TRIAL OF YOUTH.

AN ALLEGORICAL BALLET, IN THREE ACTS.

ARGUMENT.

THE ancient Philosophers feigned that the young *Alcides*, having attained the age of manhood and of reason, found himself doubtfully and dangerously situated where two roads met and took each an opposite course. He was at once invited by *Virtue* and *Pleasure* to proceed in those two ways. After having hesitated a short time, the hero decided on taking the road pointed out by *Virtue.—Xen. Mem.*, 1. 2, c. 1. Upon this ingenious fiction the present Ballet is founded. The same subject has been treated as an Opera, by Metastasio, entitled *Alcide al Bivio.* Maurin the performer has made a French Opera of this Allegory, set to music by M. Blasis, Sen.

CHARACTERS.

ALCIDES.

PHRONIME, *Alcides' Mentorial Governor, representing the Judgment.*

EDONIDE, *the Goddess of Pleasure.*

ARETIS, *the Goddess of Virtue.*

Nymphs, Genii, and Cupids, attending Edonide; Heroes, Heroines, and Genii, following Aretis; Monsters and Spectres.

The scene passes in the country about Thebes.

ACT I.

SCENE.—*Ancient and gloomy forest; in which may be distinguished two roads; the first on the right is planted with roses and other odoriferous shrubs, and leads to the abode of Pleasure. The other, running a parallel course on the left, presents a wild appearance, being overrun with thorns and briars, interspersed with rocks and flints, and conducts to the dwelling of Virtue.*

SCENE I.—*Alcides* and *Phronime* appear; the former, being surprised at finding himself in such a situation, inquires the meaning of his governor, *Phronime;* the latter replies, that it is by order of the Gods, and to

prove his constancy that he is now exposed to danger, but
that having resolutely conquered, happiness would ensue.
The courage of *Alcides* being excited by these expressions,
he burns to enter this unknown desert; *Phronime* extols
this ardour and promptitude; the former, notwithstanding, desires to know the nature of the hazardous trial to
which he is about to be exposed. *Phronime* then points
out the two roads, affirming that by the will of Fate and
the Gods, every mortal must make the momentous choice of
one of these two ways;—one which is easy and agreeable,
leading to Pleasure without a hope of return; while the
other, which is dangerous and difficult, conducting to the
abode of Virtue. He then describes the charming but
deceitful appearances of the first, whose end is misery;
afterwards the danger and difficulty attending a passage
through the second, which are however rewarded by glory
and happiness. The sanguine youth, inflamed by this
discourse, advances, under the guidance of his wise governor, to undertake this attempt; the old man informs
him that the choice depends upon himself alone, but that
he will still watch over his actions; that honour or disgrace is the unalterable consequence of this event, and
that, therefore, it is obvious which to choose. *Alcides*
promises to do honour to himself, and to select the
way to Virtue; upon this *Phronime* withdraws.

Scene II.—*Alcides*, now finding himself alone, begins
to mistrust himself; his fortitude appears sinking at the
absence of his Mentor. He meditates on his singular situation, then examines the two portentous paths of this
desert. He appears delighted with the lovely and flattering prospect of that leading to Pleasure; the approach
seems easy; every thing is calculated to excite agreeable
sensations. The beauty and variety of the flowers, whose
perfume is wafted through the air upon the wings of

zephyrs; the gentle whispering of the umbrageous foliage; the murmuring of crystal rivulets, and the warblings of the birds, all tend to perplex him in making the proper selection, notwithstanding the young hero recalls to his mind the advice he has received, and summons all his resolution to repel those deceitful delights. He now approaches the path of Virtue; it presents a view rugged, rude, and bare. The sight of this frightful wilderness, apparently deserted by nature, raises in the breast of *Alcides* a desire of proving his valour by braving its danger; his inward sensations direct him to this road, as his proper choice; but before he attempts to enter, he addresses himself to the immortal powers, imploring their counsel and protection, and that they would put an end to that anxious uncertainty by which he is tormented. He again takes a view of the way upon which he is about to proceed; he approaches, but is withheld by a secret dread; he once more summons his valour to aid him, and prepares for the trial. On the instant he is about to enter, he is struck by the sounds of melodious music; he stops to listen; when—

SCENE III.—*Edonide,* the Goddess of Pleasure, appears; she is accompanied by troops of those who are devoted to her service. *Alcides* is motionless with astonishment and admiration at the grace and beauty of this power. He is, however, soon on the point of hastening away; but is allured to stay awhile, by the surprise that *Edonide* exhibits at his flight. Can he, she inquires, be so insensible as to prefer yonder horrible wilderness to that abode of delights to which she would invite him? *Alcides* demands to know what are her designs, showing at the same time, by the severity of his countenance, that he is prepared to listen to nothing contrary to honour. She informs him that her palace is in the grove, which he may perceive in the distance, and that she bestows happiness on whomsoever is pleased to follow her. She adds, that every one confesses the power of her charms, and that, therefore, he ought to surrender his heart to her, obey her laws, and live in her dominions. *Alcides* appears fascinated as if by a delightful vision; the allurement overpowers him; but he asks for a further and more explicit account. *Edonide* replies, that she is the Goddess of Pleasure, the consolation of the unfortunate, and the joy of mankind. She offers to share with him the wealth of which she is possessed, reproaches his delay, and presses him to follow her immediately into the leafy recesses of the woods. The youth refusing, she complains of his ingratitude; he at length seems moved by the winning graces of the Goddess; her promises have charmed him, and he is reduced to doubt and indecision; still reason forbids him to yield. *Edonide* is offended at his resistance, and astonished at his temerity. She declares to him that reason and virtue destroy every agreeable sentiment, deprive life of every pleasure; that they present nothing but labour and pain, and are enemies to nature. " In me," continues she, " you will find the chief good is placed." She then earnestly entreats him to enter her dwelling of delight. *Alcides* is sensible of the offered enjoyment, but fears he is falling for ever into a snare. *Edonide* assures him of safety, and prepares to conduct him into her enchanting abode. *Alcides*, determined to avoid inglorious repose, withdraws himself from her; arms and fame are the objects of his desire, and he turns to the path of Virtue. *Edonide* pretends to warn him from a terrible fate which will there attend him. *Alcides* persists, representing that happiness will reward undaunted resolution. *Edonide* continues to press him to follow her, and in order to prevail, and at length in bringing him to submit to her empire, she makes a sign to her followers, and they immediately appear.

The scene changes, and represents the palace of the Goddess of Pleasure. Through a colonnade, at a distance, a beautiful grove is discovered. In the centre is seen a throne constructed with flowers, upon which Edonide *placing herself, causes* Alcides *to sit by her side.*

The youth, astonished at all he beholds, complies with the request of *Edonide,* and gives himself up to her powerful illusions, while nymphs, genii, and little loves, try, by sports and dances, to seduce him from all thought of Virtue. He expresses the delight he feels at the calm repose of the scene, disturbed only by the gaiety of amiable amusements. *Edonide,* with her companions, counsel him to leave every thing for such enjoyment, representing the danger and folly of pursuing glory, by which human life is deprived of every pleasure. To these persuasions *Alcides* yields a willing ear. He is surrounded by nymphs, and crowned with flowers ; while *Edonide* promises to make him the dearest of her companions ; *Alcides* expresses his gratitude, and gives himself up entirely to her direction. The troops of Pleasure envelop the youth in wreaths of flowers, and conduct him to a bower, to which they are directed by *Edonide,* who follows, triumphing in her conquest.

ACT II.

SCENE I.—*The stage represents the first scene of the first act.*

PHRONIME enters from the path of pleasure, conducting *Alcides,* whom he reproaches for having allowed himself to be enticed into so much danger, and expresses his concern at seeing his advice so soon forgotten. *Alcides* attempts to describe those delights which he found himself incapable of avoiding; but *Phronime,* seeing that he is disposed to give himself up to pleasure, and to suffer his fortitude to languish, will not listen to his discourse ; the young man conjures him not to suppose that he is entirely lost to a sense of his duty, but to believe that, overpowered by his feelings, he had strayed from the right path.   He professes his love and esteem for his prudent guide, whose counsel would conduct him to glory, and inquires what he shall do.   *Phronime* replies, he must strive against his inclinations, curb his passions, and so become master of himself ; that he must shun the dangerous path that leads to unlawful pleasures, and render himself immortal by a noble course of labours.   *Phronime* now makes a sign to him to enter the way that conducts to Virtue, and, representing the danger of hesitation and delay, retires.

SCENE II.—*Alcides* blushes at the rebuke of *Phronime,* rouses himself from the state of weakness into which he had fallen, regains his courage, and determines to enter the way of Virtue.   At this moment *Edonide* enters with her train, and arrests his progress.

SCENE III.—*Alcides* repulses and avoids her, but the

power clings to him, and essays to force him to his doom ; he strives to disengage himself, turning his head away from her importunities. She tells him not to confide in *Phronime*, who, jealous of her acknowledged power, would persuade him from her side, and expose him to danger which he vainly tries to conceal. She only seeks to lead him back to those bowers where true happiness resides ; but he still refuses to follow. She then upbraids him with the folly of disdaining the delights she offers, to pursue a fatal road. *Alcides*, knowing the dreadful consequences of such pleasures, informs her that he seeks for honour alone, by which he is inspired. The power repeats her flattering promises, and tries again to allure him to her bright abode ; but he again resists, resuming his own fortitude and recalling the good counsel of *Phronime* to oppose the charms of *Edonide*, whose power over his soul is not yet entirely overcome ; and notwithstanding her tender remonstrances, he breaks from her. Warlike music is suddenly heard, as if proceeding from the dwelling of Virtue ; *Alcides* listens in astonishment, and feels himself animated by the sound. *Edonide* recognizes the approach of her enemy, *Aretis*. She prepares to retire, and endeavours to draw the hero with her, but he bids her stay, declaring himself her protector.

Scene IV.—*Aretis* appears ; *Alcides* is struck with the majesty of her movement and the grandeur of her deportment ; the power of Virtue addressing herself to him exposes the deceitfulness of the chimera he is about to follow, and the offences he has already committed against herself. She explains the perfidious illusions of her rival, whose offered kindness is unworthy of his notice, and describes the certain destruction to which she would draw him, upon receding from the way of virtue and honour.

Alcides is deeply affected by this severe but elevated language ; he is sensible of its truth, and becomes inspired by the penetrating aspect of *Aretis*. *Edonide*, fearing to lose her victim, dares again to persuade him away. *Aretis* motions him from the power of Pleasure, who complains of his unkind resistance, and entreats him to avoid the severities and dangers of Virtue, who now represents to him the certain benefits she can bestow upon him, if he continues in her way. *Edonide*, regarding her rival with contempt, turns to *Alcides*, displaying all her winning charms, and, pointing to her blissful bowers, entreats him to follow her. The hero knows not on what to resolve ; his heart is divided between the powerful rivals, and he remains a prey to indecision.

Aretis informs him that she it is who guides and inspires heroic souls in the pursuit of honour and glory ; that by her instructions man rises superior to misfortune, and finds true felicity is placed in wisdom ; that she teaches him to despise sloth and encounter pains and perils, and in the end to immortalize himself by valiant deeds, while truth, humanity, honour and renown, will adorn his latter days. *Edonide* replies, that these are but flattering promises. " Come *Alcides*," continues the Goddess of Virtue, "immediately to my palace, where true enjoyment awaits your arrival." *Alcides* seems anxious to accompany her, and she again encourages him firmly to pursue his choice. *Edonide*, defeated and offended, retires, menacing the hero with revenge. *Alcides* beholds her departure with regret, and even essays to summon her back.

Scene V.—*Aretis* continues to caution the hero against the alluring flatteries of the power of Pleasure, counselling him to preserve his mind free from the thraldom of her charms. She endeavours to induce him to contemplate the benefits resulting from attaching himself to her principles.   Upon a sign being made by the Goddess of Virtue, the scene changes; a palace appears, the architecture of which is both noble and majestic.   All the worshippers and followers of Virtue are here displayed, each following appropriate avocation.   Heroes are exercising themselves in the ancient games; combats with sword and shield, warlike evolutions, wrestling, Pyrrhic dances, and every species of athletic sports are going on.

SCENE VI.—All hasten to do homage to the Goddess, and congratulate each other on living beneath her happy sway.   The power expresses to *Alcides* the noble manner in which her votaries pass their days, whence arise generous sentiment and undaunted valour.   The spectacle fills the young hero with delight, and he burns to prove his prowess among them and to live so gloriously; he is hastening to mix with the busy groups, but *Aretis* prevents him; the youth conjures her to permit him to join himself to the warrior bands.   She replies, they are but visionary shadows, fabricated to inspire the breast with enterprise, fortitude, and valour.   *Alcides,* turning to the power, implores her counsel and protection.   She replies, that all depends upon his own exertion, and then vanishes away.   The palace, with all the noble company of combatants, disappear, and the scene changes to the first of the first act, representing the two roads.

SCENE VII.—*Alcides* seems as if awakening from a dream; all that he has seen and heard causes the greatest agitation within him; he grieves for the loss of *Aretis,* and fears that the whole is no more than illusion.   Thus deserted, he invokes the aid of his dear *Phronime,* promising to yield himself up entirely into his hands, and to follow his prudent advice, which would lead him to glory and happiness. The hero then hastens away to throw himself at the feet of his beloved Mentor.

ACT III.

Scene I.—*The same as the last.*

Alcides is discovered, he appears in doubt and distress; he now fears to show himself to *Phronime*, having yet done nothing for his glory, nothing to accomplish that for which he was destined; he is oppressed by such recollections as these. At length, taking courage, he resolves upon a noble course of action, and prepares himself for honourable achievements.

The path of Pleasure again appears before him, but he is no longer affected by its deceitful charms; he despises the guilty repose that prevails there, and is now, at last, resolved to enter the way of Virtue. At this moment harmonious sounds are heard; the hasty march of *Alcides* is awhile arrested, and he listens with eagerness and delight.

Scene II.—The followers of Pleasure, and the votaries of Virtue enter in two groups, each advancing from their peculiar domain. Those of Virtue, proceeding on their own side, bear warlike instruments : a helmet, a sword, a shield, and a crown of laurel. Those on the side of Pleasure carry a coronet of roses, garlands, perfumes, and rich habiliments. *Alcides* expresses great astonishment at this exhibition. On one hand he beholds the perfidious troop of Pleasure ; on the other, the favoured worshippers of Virtue. The whole pageant produces in him agreeable yet conflicting sensations. Having ex-

amined the gifts borne by the train of Pleasure with indifference, he approaches those presented by the troop
of Virtue ; he beholds them with delight, and breaks out
into a transport of joy at the sight of the shining armour ;
he immediately takes possession of them, places the
helmet on his head, grasps the shield, and seizes the
sword, while his countenance betrays marks of impatience
to signalize himself in the field.   He returns thanks to
the Gods, and implores a continuation of their protection.   He appears confident and resolved; no longer
labouring under doubt and perplexity.

SCENE III.—The train of Virtue now retire ; *Alcides*
wishes to follow them, when the troop of Pleasure instantly take the place of the others, and, presenting an
obstruction to the path of Virtue by seductive blandish-
ments and persuasive flatteries, try to prevent the hero
from entering ; they envelop him in the entwinings of
their wreaths, and display measures and attitudes of the
most voluptuous description.   Every artifice is put in
practice to divert *Alcides* from his purpose ; he essays to
break from them, menacing and despising their effeminate
snares.   The subjects of *Edonide* redouble their endeavours, daring even to imprison him in their wreathed
bands, and so attempt to draw him to their retreats,
smiling at his threats.   *Alcides*, enraged at being thus
ensnared, and fully resolved to enter the way of Virtue,
hews himself a passage with his sword ; he then disperses and puts them to flight, and they again seek their
own abode.

SCENE IV.—Monsters, fairies, and demons, armed with
torches and serpents, appear, and take possession of the
entrance to the path of Virtue, presenting a complete
barrier to the progress of *Alcides*.   These horrible
spectres essay, by their menacing gesture, to deter the

hero from proceeding ; they indicate to him that destruction awaits his entrance into the road of Virtue. *Alcides* now perceives that this is all the work of the perfidious *Edonide;* not at all dismayed by this spectacle, but, on the contrary, resolved on conquest, he prepares to combat his opponents. After a desperate struggle, during which his life appears frequently in danger, *Alcides* rushes at once into the path of Virtue, and the monsters instantly disperse.

The scene now changes to the glorious palace of Aretis, *in which are seen statues of the most renowned heroes, together with allegorical representations of the arts and sciences.*

SCENE V.—*Alcides* is placed between *Aretis* and *Phronime*, and surrounded by heroes, heroines, and the genii of Virtue. He evinces feelings of triumph and delight, addressing expressions of the warmest gratitude to his prudent friend, and to the power of Virtue.

The valour and victory of *Alcides* is proclaimed and celebrated, while *Phronime*, advancing to the hero, presents him with a laurel crown. *Aretis* joins in the general expressions of felicitation, and promises *Alcides* a continuation of those enjoyments which are earned by undaunted perseverance in the path of Virtue. *Alcides* replies with expressions of reverence and gratitude. Success has crowned his efforts, and his name is numbered with the great and renowned. Noble dances and heroic sports immediately ensue, and the happy event is concluded by universal congratulations on the triumph of Virtue.

PART THE SIXTH.

PART THE SIXTH.

====

PRIVATE DANCING.

> " Que vos grâces soient naturelles ;
> Ne les contrefaites jamais :
> Dès que l'on veut courir après,
> On commence à s'éloigner d'elles."

DEMOUSTIER.

SEVERAL persons have employed themselves in writing systems for teaching Private Dancing, but their works contain the universal fault of every performance that has appeared upon the subject of dancing in general, namely, a want of principles, positively and clearly stated : such works are read, but almost nothing can be learned from them.

In giving theoretical laws for the formation of any art, and presenting means to bring that art to perfection, not only ought the laws to be clear, but the means should be practised. Never can we demonstrate so plainly to others, as when we ourselves have seen and experienced that upon which we discourse. In the mean time, we dare flatter ourselves that our treatise will not be found to deserve those severe criticisms which we, from a regard to the interest of the rising generation, have been obliged to pass upon other performances of the same nature. As in the second part of this work, so also in this, we have been particularly careful, in the lessons to pupils, upon the grace of their position, and the elegance of *contour* in their attitudes while dancing; attainments in our art which are both delightful and essential, but, at the same time, extremely difficult to acquire. To arrive at this desirable object, we shall more clearly explain ourselves by the aid of engraved figures, representing every position of which this species of dancing is capable. In designing these figures, we have been careful to adhere to the dictates of taste and art. Any dancer may be capable of executing a *chassé*, a *pas de bourrée*, a *contre-tems*, &c.; but that genteel air, those graceful manners, and that picturesque action, which are expected from those who have learned the art of dancing, are not to be acquired from all dancing-masters, many of whom are usually unwilling, or unable, so profoundly to study their art, as to produce on their pupils this important effect.

Although the system of private dancing does not require, of those who practise it, either extraordinary abilities or an intense application, in order to arrive at perfection, there must, however, be inherent in them certain physical qualifications, and some capacity, to insure success. Without these, a person would appear awkward and ridiculous in dancing; and it is far preferable to be a passive spectator than a clumsy performer. It may be observed also, that while a knowledge of dancing adds to the attractions of a figure, naturally symmetrical and agile, it serves but to render still more conspicuous, those who are incurably ill-shaped, unconquerably heavy, or insensible to any graceful motion.

The admirers of dancing will have conceived, it is hoped, a just notion of the art from the preceding parts of this work. They will, at the same time, have had an opportunity of observing, clearly pourtrayed, all the materials of which it is composed. Now, as the private dancing derives its origin from the theatrical dancing, there are many particulars in it which may be serviceable to the Amateur, as well as the Professors of the Art; such as, for instance, *the common mode of carrying oneself— the gait—some of the practical movements—some of the postures—a certain number of the steps and footings,* and, in short, *the gracefulness, the lightness, the liveliness, the elegance,* which are qualifications almost indispensable to every genteel person.

Having already, in *the First Part* of my work, explained the utility and advantages to be derived from it, even by those who do not practise this attractive art, excepting simply for their amusement, or as a kind of finish to an accomplished education, I shall now, more particularly, treat of the mechanical part, and theory of that species of dancing which is practised in polite society, and studied by well-bred and fashionable persons.

As soon as the dancing-master shall have ascertained the natural qualifications and abilities of the learner, it will be his business to begin by showing him the *five positions,* in each of which he must make him bend, and then raise himself upon the point of the toe. He will then teach him to make *petits battemens tendus* upon the instep, and, also, even *petits rond-de-jambes à terre,* inwards and outwards. The learner must, at first, practise with holding, and then afterwards without, in order to acquire the proper balance. (See plate XI, fig. 5.)

The master ought to place the body and arms of the learner in a right position, so as to render all the attitudes commanding and graceful. (See plate I, fig. 3, and plate XI, fig. 2.) The art of stepping with grace, of making a bow, of introducing oneself, and of carrying oneself in company, are essential points, and such as ought to be rendered as natural as possible to the learner.

To execute the bow properly, the following rules must be observed :—When walking, stop in such a manner that the weight of the body may rest upon that leg which is advanced. Then, moving the one behind, cause it to assume the *fourth hinder position*, the *third*, and the *second*. Having arrived at the latter, shift the stress of the body upon the leg forming it, and bring the other leg round into the *first position*, the heels being placed against each other, and the toes turned outwardly. (See plate XV, fig. 4.) After having bent the knees properly, incline the body according as it is represented in the same figure. Let your arms fall easily and naturally, and let your head assume an unaffected inclination ; for every movement must be executed with an easy air. Having made the salute, slowly raise your body to its usual perpendicular attitude, regain your customary deportment, disengage the leg which had been placed in the first position behind, changing it into the fourth behind, and shift the weight of the body upon that leg. Whether you intend to renew the salute, or to continue your walk, always finish upon the advanced leg. Usually, and in society where it is not absolutely necessary to observe a strict *étiquette*, the salute is generally executed in the *third position*, but the feet must be always turned outwardly. (See plate XV, fig. 3.)

Ladies, when performing their courtesy, must proceed in the same manner as gentlemen, excepting that they should incline, after the foot has assumed the *first position*, in order to stop on the *fourth position* behind, when the knees must bend, and the head and body incline, to complete the courtesy. (See plate XV, fig. 2.)

The method of presenting the hand while dancing is represented in plate XVI, figs. 1 and 2. The remaining positions and attitudes of ladies and gentlemen in Quadrilles will appear plainly from plate XVI, fig. 3, and plate XV, fig. 1 and 3.

After these introductory studies and exercises, which constitute the ground-work of dancing, and which lead the way to the perfection of every thing that is connected with it, the master ought next to give his pupil an insight into the knowledge of steps, the observance of time, Quadrilles, or Country-dances, Waltzing, and every other description of dancing which is in request in good society.

Let the master be very cautious how he suffers the pupil to proceed to the study of the above named dances, until after he has practised for some time upon the inceptive principles; for his good or bad success entirely depends upon the first lessons, and upon his assiduity in the rudimental task. Care must be continually taken to draw a line of distinction between private dancing and theatrical dancing. It would be improper to introduce certain scientific steps and elevated capering into a ball-room, where every circumstance shows, that movements of this description would be out of their place, and, consequently, would produce an improper effect.

Private dancing requires steps *terre-à-terre*, and the most simply natural postures possible. The ladies, in particular, ought to dance with a sort of amiable circumspection and a becoming grace, which, indeed, add to their charms, and heighten their attractions. Gentlemen ought always be attentive to their partners; and they should all of them move in unison in every step and attitude. They ought also to be careful in paying attention to the air of the music, and in showing that they feel all the harmony and expression of it. For a more detailed account of which, refer to what is said respecting the Music for Dancing, in the Second Part of the work, entitled the *Theory of Theatrical Dancing*.

The learner must preserve his arms placed in the position which we term *demi-bras*. (See plate XI, fig. 2.) Their contra-positions should be those described in plate I, fig. 3. For the position of the wrists and fingers, see plate I, fig. 1. For the position of the chest, head, and limbs, refer to plates I, III, and IV.

With respect to the collocation of the joints, and the inflexions of the body, it will be necessary for the learner to subject himself to the same practice as the theatrical dancer, in order that his dancing may produce a pleasing effect.

I shall here observe, that even amateurs, both in the preparation during the performance, and at the conclusion of their steps and *enchaînemens*, ought always to stand in the *fifth position*, and not in the *third*, as the generality of teachers of private dancing pretend; for the more the feet are crossed, the more precipitate the footing is, and the more showy the dancing: it is a natural consequence, and it cannot be obtained, except by accustoming the learners not to cross their feet but in the *third position*. Besides, this method assists the dancers in turning, and enables them to acquire that pleasing quality, turning, with facility. He who has not his feet well turned out, loses all the beauty of his steps. As to the movements of the body, they are nearly the same as those practised by stage dancers, with this difference only, that they should not be carried to that grandeur and elevation, should have less impulse, and be modified, and adapted to the circles of Private Dancing. The legs ought to be raised from the ground but very little above the method of the second position; however, gentlemen may raise them something higher: the peculiar style of their dancing being more powerful and unrestrained, will admit of more elevated steps. It is not necessary that the arms and bust should be kept in violent motion, they may rather remain in a graceful repose. Let the head be held erect, and the chin in a very slight degree elevated; gracefully incline the head to the motion of the body and arms. Let your countenance be expressive of cheerfulness and gaiety, and let an agreeable smile ever play about your mouth. Keep your shoulders down, bring your chest forward, let your waist be compressed, and sustain yourself firmly upon your loins. Let your bosom project a little, for this confers gracefulness on the dancer's attitude. Let the shoulders move with elegance and naturally. Let your elbows be curved, never squared, your fingers so grouped together as to correspond with the contour of the arms. (See plate I, fig. 2.) Ladies must hold their dresses with the tips of their fingers; their arms must be placed similar to the gentlemen's. The arms serve for an ornament to the body, and they ought to follow its movements with easy elegance. Let your body recline, as it were, upon the hips, and let the latter expand themselves, in order to facilitate the motions of the legs. Turn out your knees, and strive to give them pliancy, and to curve them well. By this means they will aid all the movements of the time and the steps. Let your feet be always turned out, and let your insteps acquire a degree of suppleness, and at the same time of strength, a circumstance which will give you a facility in curving the feet, in rising upon the toes, and in shifting the legs. The toes ought to be kept firm to the ground, and they should assist in giving effect to the steps, and in marking the time. In short, let each succeeding step be well connected with the other, and let all be executed with an easy elegance, and a steady grace.

QUADRILLES.

Changement de jambe, assemblé, jeté, sissone, pas de bourrée, echappé, glissade, tems de cuisse, coupé dessus, coupé dessous, entrechat à quatre, à cinq, brisé, sissone battue, entrechat à quatre sur une jambe.

FIGURES.

1. *Chassé en avant et en arrière.* 2. *Chassé de côté,* or *Chassé croisé,* or *chassé-déchassé.* 3. *Traverser, demi-contretems.* 4. *Balancé.* 5. *Tour de deux mains.* 6. *Dos-à-dos.* 7. *Chaîne Anglaise.* 8. *Chaîne des dames.* 9. *Demi-queue du chat.* 10. *Chassé huit.* 11. *Chassé sur les côtés.* 12. *En avant quatre.* 13. *Solo.* 14. *Le grand rond.* 15. *Le moulinet.* 16. *Balancé huit.*

THE MOST GENERALLY KNOWN FIGURES OF QUADRILLES*.

THE FIGURE CALLED LE PANTALON.

CHAINE ANGLAISE.

1.—The *chaîne Anglaise* is performed by two gentlemen and two ladies, opposite; they advance to change places, and, in passing each other, they present the right hand; each gentleman, after giving his right hand to his partner, who faces him, leaving her hand, he turns behind her, then gives his left to that of his partner, who is taking the place of the other lady; and all are again placed beside each other; each leaving hands, upon resuming their places. This figure, which is but the *demi-chaîne*, or half *chaîne Anglaise,* when repeated immediately on each resuming their places, is then called the *chaîne entière,* or, whole *chaîne Anglaise,* as here performed: it requires the time of eight bars.

BALANCE.

2.—Each gentleman turning and facing his partner, they set during four bars.

UN TOUR DE DEUX MAINS.

3.—Immediately after having set, each couple take

---

*The description of these dances was written by M. Gourdoux.

both hands, and turn round at their places ; in regaining which, they leave go hands : this is performed in four bars.

LA CHAINE DES DAMES.

4.—The two opposite ladies change places, and in passing give the right hand; afterwards, they give the left hand to the two gentlemen who are remaining in their places. Each gentleman, immediately upon his partner's moving off to perform the *chaîne,* must go off to the right, at the same time presenting his left hand to the lady, who is entering the place of her partner; he must then turn upon his left to regain his place, where, having arrived, he leaves the hand of his partner. This figure, which is done during the time of four bars, is repeated also, to form the whole *chaîne Anglaise,* which then requires eight bars, before each lady resumes her place.

LA DEMI-QUEUE DU CHAT.

5.—Each person of two couple presents the left hand, and goes off obliquely to the right, in order to change places; on arriving at each other's place, they leave go hands : this requires four bars.

6.—To regain their places, the two gentlemen and their partners perform the *demi-chaîne Anglaise.*—(See No. 1.) The remaining couple do the same.

THE FIGURE CALLED L' ETE.

1.—A gentleman and opposite lady advance and retire backwards, or *en avant deux,* during four bars.

2.—The same lady and gentleman cross and change places, passing from the right to the right, during four bars.

3.—The gentleman and lady go off each on the right

side, and immediately return on the left, during four bars.

4.—The gentleman and lady re-crossing, regain their places, during the time of four bars.

5.—The gentleman then sets to his partner, and his partner to him. (See the Pantalon, No. 2.)

6.—Each couple makes the *tour de main*, as at No. 3 of the Pantalon, the remaining six doing the same.

In this figure called *l' Eté*, after having performed the *en avant deux*, and gone off right and left, there is no more setting at the end. Custom alone has introduced the setting, which is intended only for that couple who have danced the figure among the rest; they then begin setting at the same time that the ladies of one couple, and the gentlemen of the other, commence crossing to regain their places, finishing equally at the same time, during four bars, after which follows the *tour de main*.

THE FIGURE CALLED LA POULE.

1.—The opposite lady and gentleman cross and give the right hand, during four bars.

2. The same couple cross again, presenting then the left hand, which they continue to hold across the dance, remaining at the side during four bars.

3.—The gentleman and lady still holding the left hand, now present each other the right, and set four in a-line, during four bars.

4.—The *demi-queue du chat* (see the Pantalon.)

5.—The opposite gentleman and lady advance and retire backwards, during four bars.

6.—The same gentleman and lady then perform the *dos-a-dos*, turning round each other until they arrive at the place from which they set out: this requires four bars.

7.—Four advance and retire, similar to the *en avant deux*.

8.—The same four dance the *demi-chaîne Anglaise*, to regain their places. (See the Pantalon). The remaining couple do the same.

THE FIGURE CALLED TRENIS.

1.—A gentleman and his partner present hands, then advance and retire twice, leaving hands at the second time; the lady going off, places herself to the left of the gentleman opposite, returns or retires backward: this requires eight bars.

2.—A gentleman crosses between two ladies, being then in a line, and crossing at the same time right before them, they change with each other at the extremity, to make a repetition of the crossing, together with the gentleman, and thus all three regain their places: this requires the space of eight bars.

3.—Set four. (See Pantalon.)

4.—Two gentlemen with their partners perform the *tour de main*. (See Pantalon.) The remaining couples do the same.

THE FIGURE CALLED PASTOURELLE.

1.—A gentleman and his partner present hands and advance twice, as in the Trénis; the lady then goes and places herself on the left of the opposite gentleman; which requires eight bars.

2.—The opposite gentleman, who is then between two ladies, gives a hand to each of them, and all three advance twice and retire, during eight bars.

3.—The remaining gentleman, who is left alone, then advances in his turn twice also, during eight bars.

4.—The same gentleman with the one opposite, and

the two ladies by their side, advance and present hands to perform the hands half-round, until each is opposite to his own place, with his partner beside him : this is done in four bars.

5.—The same four do the half or *demi-chaîne Anglaise*, to regain their places. (See Pantalon.) The remaining couple do the same.

THE FINALE.

1.—The two opposite gentlemen, each with his partner, perform a *chassé-croisé;* the gentleman dances a *chassé* while passing to the right, behind the lady; who at the same time performs a *chassé* on the left, while passing before him ; afterwards they do the *demi-balancé*, or, half-setting, in the space of four bars.

2.—The same two gentlemen and their partners perform the *chassé-croisé* back again; the gentleman on the left while repassing behind his lady; and the lady on the right while repassing before the gentleman; when regaining their places, they perform the *demi-balancé*, or, half-setting ; during four bars.

3.—*En avant deux*, or, opposite gentleman and lady. (See figure of l'Eté.)

4.—The same couple cross.

5.—They then go off to the right and left.

6.—The gentleman and lady re-cross to their places.

7.—The two opposite gentlemen set to their partners. (See Pantalon).

8.—They then execute the *tour de main*.

9.—The two ladies execute the *chaîne*.

10.—The *demi-queue du chat*. (See the above figure.)

11.—The *half*, or *demi-chaîne Anglaise*. The remaining six do the same ; and to conclude, the whole eight dance the *chassé*, similar to the *chassé-croisé* of four. (See preceding).

REMARKS ON THE FINALE.

The ladies frequently, in this figure, substituted the *moulinet* for the *chaîne des dames;* presenting their right hand, they went round in the middle of the dance during four bars; then relinquishing the right hand, they gave the left, and performed the *moulinet* back again. The ladies then, without disengaging the left, gave each the right hand to her partner, and all set during four bars. Each gentleman and his partner then executed the *tour de main,* while re-entering their places.

The *tems figuré* was formerly executed on the right, or at the side, when each gentleman and lady present went off, to place themselves before the couple who were on the right, in order to do the half-setting, or, *demi-balancé;* they then formed what is called the open *chassé,* until they appeared in two lines, each gentleman finding himself then opposite his partner; the whole eight then advanced and retired, each gentleman met his partner and performed the *tour de main,* until arrived at his place. This figure is no longer practised, in consequence of the confusion which dancers experience, who now perform Quadrilles or *Contre-dances* with numbers exceeding eight.

THE FIGURE CALLED DES GRACES.

1.—A gentleman with his partner present right hands, at the same time the gentleman gives his left to the lady who dances on his left, and the two ladies present each her hand to the other behind the gentleman at the waist, all three then advance, and retire twice during eight bars.

2.—The gentleman retires behind, stooping to pass under the ladies' arms, who are holding hands; the gentleman then, immediately rising, causes the two ladies to pass and turn under each of his arms, at the same time giving a salute, while the two ladies courtesy upon the *point d' orgue*, or at the pause, during four bars.

3.—A gentleman and two ladies dance hands three round and back again, returning to the same position from which they began: this requires four bars.

It is against the principles of dancing when persons perform this figure with two gentlemen and one lady. For since it is derived from the allemand of three, there should be two ladies and one gentleman; first, because it is more elegant, and secondly, because in executing the *passe*, (going under arms) ladies, who are generally not so tall as gentlemen, find it difficult to lift their arms to a sufficient height.

THE WALTZ.

THIS dance, which, as we have already said, came to us from Switzerland, has been modified and embellished by *passes* and groupings, in order to introduce variety to its monotony. The waltzes which we term *La Russe* and *La Sauteuse* are derived from it. It is composed of two steps, each of three beats to a bar, which also contains three *tems*, according to musical principles. Each of these two steps performs the *demi-tour*, or half-turn of the waltz, which lasts during one bar; the two steps united form, therefore, the whole waltz, executed in two bars. These steps differ one from the other, yet so as to fit one into the other, if it may be so expressed, during their performance, and in such a manner as to prevent the feet of one from touching and endangering those of the other; thus while the gentleman performs one step, the lady dances the other, so that both are executed with uninterrupted exactness, as will be clearly demonstrated.

In order to perform one of these waltz steps, place your feet in the third position, the right foot forward, then advancing the right foot in the natural way, not turning it out, to place it in the fourth position (first time), then immediately bring forward the left foot, turning the toe inward, and placing it crossways before the other foot, to form the fourth position, that foot being raised immediately, and the body is, at the same time, turned half-round; in placing the foot for the fourth position (second time), that foot which you have raised, while placing the last mentioned, must then be placed before the other in the third position, and outwardly, resuming its ordinary posture, and to perform the third bar. The step being thus executed while turning half round, will bring the face where the back was.

In order to execute the second step, and to perform at the same time the other half-turn, *demi-tour*, which completes the waltz, turn out the side of your left foot, the toe being inward, and moving the body round at the same time, place it in the second position (first beat), put the right foot behind the left, always continuing to turn the body (second beat), then bring the left foot before you, turning the toe inwards, the body turning also, to come half-round, at the moment you are placing the left foot in the second position, to execute the third beat of the second step, and the second half-turn, which completes the waltz.

By this example, it may be seen that a waltz is composed of two steps, each of which contains three *tems*, or beats, making six for both, and for the entire figure of the waltz, which is performed during two bars ; also, that when either of the two persons waltzing advances the right foot to begin the first step described above, the opposite person draws back the left foot at the same time to begin the other step, allowing his partner an opportunity of advancing her foot, both performing then the *demi-tour ;* when one repeats the step the other has just executed in the second *demi-tour*, to complete the waltz. When the position for waltzing is taken, in order that the step may be properly commenced, and that both persons may be in unison, the lady being on the right of the gentleman, he must go off on the left foot, turning himself before his partner, as if that had been his first position ;

and with respect to the second step described before, it is always performed by that person who has his back towards the side on which the waltz begins, as the person who faces that side always executes the first step.

To waltz properly, all the beats, or *tems*, should be clearly marked, being attentive not to turn upon *les pointes*, or toes, in the same beats, such a system not being convenient for the turning of two persons at once; every turn in a waltz should be clearly and fully performed, so that on finishing, the waltzers should come always opposite to the same side as they were on setting out; without which, the course of the waltzes cannot be followed, and the waltzer would, in consequence, fall upon those who are coming behind him, or who are in the middle of the room, which is very frequently the case.

Care should be taken not to make use of those vicious attitudes, the second of which is ever more indecent than the first, and which, indeed, have their origin in loose society.

The gentleman should hold the lady by the right hand, and above the waist, or by both hands, if waltzing be difficult to her; or otherwise, it would be better for the gentleman to support the right hand of the lady by his left. The arms should be kept in a rounded position, which is the most graceful, preserving them without motion; and in this position one person should keep as far from the other as the arms will permit, so that neither may be incommoded.

A NEW SET OF QUADRILLES,

BY C. BLASIS.

In composing the following Quadrilles we have departed from the usual course, by introducing more variety into their figures, and by endeavouring, in the disposition of those figures, to convey an idea corresponding to their titles, so that the latter may not appear either arbitrary or unmeaning.

ORIGINAL FIGURES.

L' AURORE.

1st fig.—A lady and gentleman *chassé sur les côtés*. *Demi-balancé* with the opposite lady and gentleman.

2d.—*Tour de deux mains* and return to your places. The same to be done by the remaining six.

3d.—Lady *solo* during eight bars.

4th.—The same lady crosses with the opposite gentleman, then back again and *balancé*, presenting hands right and left, then the *tour de deux mains*.

5th.—The *grand rond*.

LA FOLATRE.

1st fig.—*Demi-chaíne Anglaise.*

2d.—*Balancé.*

3d.—*Demi-chaíne Anglaise.*

4th.—*Balancé.*

5th.—Four gentlemen *en avant.*

6th.—Four ladies *en avant.*

7th.—The whole eight *chassé-croisé.*

8th.—*Chaíne des dames.*

9th.—*Chassé quatre* on your own side; *balancé; tour de deux mains.*

10th.—Then the two couple back again, *chassé en avant quatre,* and return to their places, repeating the *chassé.*

11th.—*Balancé* all; *tour de deux mains,* and the same for the remaining six.

LE CALIFE.

1st fig.—Gentleman *en avant* and *en arrière.*

2d.—Opposite lady *en avant* and *en arrière.*

3d.—Same figure for the three remaining ladies. They must finish the *chassé* with *en avant,* opposite the gentleman, then return to their places.

4th.—The same gentleman and the three ladies *en avant, tour de deux mains,* and return to their places.

5th.—The gentleman *balancé* with his lady, then both *tour de main.*

6th.—The gentleman *chassé* upon his own side, *balancé* and *tour de main* with his lady; then repeat the same figure with the three remaining ladies.

7th.—The same gentleman *balancé* with his lady, then gives both hands for the *grand rond.* Remaining six do the same.

LES BACCHANTES.

1st.—The whole eight *chassé, balancé,* and return to their places.

2d.—Ladies and gentlemen hands across and *grand rond.*

3rd.—Four *en avant.*

4th.—*Chaíne Anglaise.*

5th.—*Balancé.*

6th.—*Tour de deux mains.*

7th.—Four ladies by turns dance *solo,* four bars each.

8th.—The same figure for the gentlemen.

9th.—The whole eight *chassé en avant* and *en arrière.*

10th.—The whole eight *chassé croisé.*

LA TRIOMPHANTE.

1st fig.—*Chaíne Anglaise* for four.

2d.—The same for the other four.

3d.—Three gentlemen by turns *en avant deux, demi-balancé* and *tour de main.* But the lady dances the *tour de main* during two bars only, she then leaves the gentleman, and, advancing into the middle of the dance, executes four bars more, and then returns to her place.

4th.—The latter and her partner *balancé,* and *tour de deux mains.*

5th.—She then leaves the gentleman, advances into the middle of the dance, and executes a *solo* during eight bars.

6th.—All the gentlemen *en avant* take hands and enclose the lady, then set and go round her; she then liberates herself, and all return to their places. The same for the remaining couples.

LE PETIT MAITRE.

1st fig.—Gentleman *solo ; grand rond.*

2d.—Same gentleman *solo* during eight bars.

3d.—*En avant deux* with the opposite lady, then *dos-à-dos.*

4th.—The gentleman the same figure with the other three ladies.

5th.—*Chassé-croisé* all.

6th.—The same gentleman *en avant* and *en arriére* with the two ladies on his own side ; they set and return to their places.

7th.—*Tour de deux mains* for all.

LA COQUETTE.

1st fig.—*Chassé en avant* for all.

2d.—*Demi-balancé.*

3d.—*Tour de deux mains,* and return to your places.

4th.—Lady *solo.   Chassé* on your own side ; lady and gentleman *demi-balancé ; tour de deux mains* with the gentleman.   The lady then repeats the figure with the two other couple, and returns to her place.

5th.—The same lady *solo* during eight bars.

6th.—She presents both her hands to her partner, and they perform the *grand rond,* the *balancé,* and the *tour de main.*

7th.—*Chassé,* repeated by the remaining couples.

LA JALOUSE.

1st fig.—A gentleman and lady *en avant* and *en arrière.*

2d.—The same for the remaining couples.

3d.—Two opposite gentlemen and ladies, *en avant.*

4th.—They *moulinet.*

5th.—The same two ladies *en avant* and *demi-balancé ; tour de deux mains,* and return to their places.

6th.—A gentleman *chassé* on his own side, and *balancé* with his lady. He then performs the *tour de deux mains ;* but his lady having rejoined him by a *chassé en avant,* which she completes when he has finished his figure, presents both her hands to her partner, and takes him from the other lady.   Both then return to their places.

7th.—The same gentleman repeats the same figure with the other three ladies.

8th.—The latter gentleman's partner then uniting herself to him, she takes hands and performs the *grand rond ;* they then regain their places, set, and execute the *tour de main.*

9th.—*Chaîne Anglaise.*

10th.—The same for the other four.

11th.—The whole party *moulinet.*

LA VIRGINIE.

1st fig.—*Balancé* the entire party.

2d.—*Tour de main.*

3d.—Cavalier *solo double.*

4th.—Lady *solo double.*

5th.—*Demi-queue du chat.*

6th.—*Grand rond* after having presented hands.

7th.—The whole party *en avant* and *en arrière.*

8th.—*Chassé dé chassé* all.

EXPLANATION OF PLATES XV AND XVI.

PLATE XV.

Fig. 1. Attitudes and positions of ladies and gentlemen in country dancing or quadrilles.

2. The courtesy.

3. Other positions of ladies and gentlemen in quadrilles.

4. The bow.

PLATE XVI.

Fig. 1. Group, with the method of holding the hands while dancing.

2. Another group.

3. Other positions in quadrille dancing.

CONCLUSION.

—————

*In the following remarks, among other things, the rela-
tion subsisting between Dancing and the Fine Arts
is further considered.*

—————

" Les Arts sont frères et vivaux."

La Harpe.

The Ballet-master, like the prism, should unite in himself those rays of light which a general knowledge of the
fine arts spreads over the mind, and his productions will
then be tinged with those beautiful hues, which such a
knowledge must ever impart; embellishing them with an
interesting and unfading charm.   In poetry, painting,
sculpture, and music, he will discover a treasure of materials; great art, taste, and fancy, however, are necessary to employ such advantages successfully.

Pantomime may assume any shape, and imitate every
passion; it is a mighty Protean power, which may be
compared to the extraordinary genius of the great
Shakspeare.   The exalted style of dancing should present us with the attitudes and *contours* of Correggio,
Albano, and Guido ; every movement, every step should
convey a sentiment.

In the productions of the fine arts, we expect to see the beauties, not the defects, of their great model—Nature, imitated. The more fervid and active the fancy is, the more likely is she to carry us beyond the limits prescribed by reason ; hence arise the defects observable in the performances of men endowed with great genius. Reason should be the inseparable companion of the imagination. The desire of producing something new or uncommon frequently begets extravagance and improbability ; and it is this desire that allures artists from the imitation of what is fine in nature, and which has brought on a decline in the fine arts. Good taste is thus injured, and requires some time to recover itself. Even men of genius, fearing to pass for servile imitators, and confiding too much in their own powers, often forget the models of perfection, and produce things monstrous and absurd, which the public applaud because they are novel. Other artists of less talent, following the footsteps of their mistaken predecessors, out-do them in absurdity ; such is the pernicious consequence of a bad precedent ; and thus fantastic follies gradually increase, until every thing is distorted, and he who produces the greatest and most surprising deformity, is rewarded with that palm which is due to true merit alone : hence taste is destroyed, and truth, beauty, and sublimity are excluded from works of art.

In order to produce any thing excellent, that is to say, a work in which art and genius united have done their best, the instructions of great masters must be strictly observed : study their principles with the mind of a philosopher ; judge for yourself, but do not lose sight of truth and beauty—" *decor, splendor boni ;*" and strive to merit the praise of men of true taste and sound judgment. In this manner works are produced capable of enduring the hand of time.

We are indebted to the age of the Medici for the opera. Of all the species of the drama, this approaches the nearest to the ancient Greek tragedy. It possesses, indeed, all the theatrical splendour of the latter, with the additional advantage of uniting poetry and music more uniformly and closely. The celebrated Quinault modelled himself upon the Italians, and was the first who advanced the opera towards perfection; he produced regular and interesting works, and made them peculiarly susceptible of being united to music. La Motte, Fontenelle, Roy, Bernard, Marmontel, Du Roullet, Guillard, &c., imitated him, and enriched the lyric drama with their delightful productions. In Italy it was somewhat later that the opera arrived at excellence. Apostolo Zeno, a man of extensive learning, and a respectable poet, first began this glorious undertaking; and Metastasio, whose genius was far superior to that of Zeno, following his example, almost attained perfection. Several men of talent, such as Pariati, Calsabigi, Pallavicini, Coltellini, and some others, after the two great men above mentioned, produced some very valuable works, but they were very few in number. This circumstance, together with the mediocrity of their successors, caused the decline of that art, which soon after revived in France under more happy auspices.

According to the definition of a celebrated writer, French opera is epic poetry, dramatized and adorned with theatrical decorations. What the epic poet presents to the imagination only, the lyric poet in France undertakes to exhibit to the eyes; and the same thing must be effected by the Ballet-master in compositions of the elevated and heroic class. As the marvellous made visible is the very soul of French opera, so is it the essence of the mythological, fairy, and allegorical Ballet.

The Italians give the preference to subjects purely historical, consequently the Ballet-master can model himself upon the Italian lyric tragedy only, when he would treat on natural events. Those qualities which characterize pure tragedy and comedy are expected to be exactly preserved in the *grand* and the comic opera : these are the two principal species of which the rest are all more or less composed. Upon these the Ballet is modelled. Serious subjects must be stately and exalted, susceptible of magnificent scenery, and requiring the united powers of painting, machinery and costume. A series of interesting incidents, and pathetic situations must be displayed ; we must be struck and astonished by a train of varied and picturesque passion. Of all theatrical productions, the *grand* opera and the Ballet take the most complete possession of our senses; and be it remarked, that if the poet is expected to supply the musician with forcible contrasts, upon which music, avoiding monotony, may display its power and effect, the Balletmaster, also, should so arrange and dispose of his scenes and dramatic action, that the performance in the pantomimic department may always be striking, and expressive; delighting the sight by its grace, and interesting the mind by its energy.

Comic opera draws its origin from the *Farsa* of the Italians ; it first appeared at the ancient theatre of Naples. In France, Le Sage was the founder of it ; he caused a great number of amusing pieces of this character to be represented, and the regularity prevailing in them, procured him a complete success; he was most ably supported by Fuselier and d' Orneval. In Italy these were imitated by Lorenzi, Nelli, and Casti. The comic opera, or *opera buffa*, requires a gay and amusing style, lively dialogue, laughable situations, spirited action, and vivid characters. The progress of the comic opera, and of the Ballet of the same species, must be more rapid than that of a spoken comedy. Music and pantomime cease to please when they are wanting in quick dramatic action. The composers of Naples excel in comic music: Cimarosa is a perfect model.

Characters should be as clearly depicted and distinguished as one species of composition is from another. Some performers frequently speak and act the parts of kings, private individuals, and rustics, whose manners are so widely different from each other, in the same style and tone. But they should pay the closest attention to that interesting variety which, in nature, always distinguishes one rank from another. It may be difficult exactly to copy these peculiarities, but they are truth itself, and it is the first duty of actors to represent nature with fidelity; this, among the ancients, constituted their principal merit. The poet and the musician speak to the soul through the ear; the dancer and mime, like the sculptor and painter, do the same, through the eye, by charming it with grace and perfection of attitude, expression, and the other beauties of which the arts they profess are susceptible.

There is a close relation subsisting between all the fine arts; there is a similarity of character between the Iliad and the Hercules Farnese; between the works of Virgil and Raphael; David and Canova; Corneille and Michael Angelo; Carracci, Guido and Tasso; Delille and Dominichino; between those of Tintoretto and Lopez de Vega; Handel and Klopstock; Valentin and Cérbillon; Walter Scott and Paul Veronese; Guercino and Moore; Byron and Salvator Rosa; between some of the compositions of Mozart and the Dying Gladiator. Haydn may be termed the Phidias of music, and Boccherini its Correggio.

In comic and pastoral compositions, I have many times remarked affectation in the place of naiveté, and gaudy decoration instead of pure simplicity. Of compositions which are thus offensive to good taste, we may say what Cazotte said of Fontenelle : "The shepherd's pipe is bedecked with lace, and his sheep stray about adorned with collars of rose-coloured riband *." Authors of every description, when copying nature, frequently attempt to improve, or actually injure, her features, according to their own manner of looking at her, or to attain some particular object which they have in view ; thus, as it has been well remarked, Corneille represents his heroes such as they should have been ; Racine, such as they really are ; Crébillon, such as they should not have been ; and Voltaire, such as they would have wished to be. The productions, however, of these great men are models, which, together with those of England, Italy, and Germany, we should study in such a manner as to enable us to select with taste, so as to ameliorate the art we profess.

Shakspeare †, in the representation of characters, is a great master ; he gives us nature as he found her—simple or mixed, base or sublime, odious or charming. Here he thunders like Homer ; there he paints like Molière ; sometimes he is a Caravaggio, sometimes a Tiziano ; here we are lifted to the skies by his magic powers ; there he

---

* La musette du berger est garnie de dentelles, et ses moutons ont des colliers faits de rubans de couleur de rose.

† Always let it be remembered the author speaks of our immortal bard only from translations, and yet we see he displays a very proper idea ; could he read him in the original, we can easily imagine he would soon present us with his inimitable pieces in all the expressive majesty of the gestic art.　　　　R. B.

bears us to the deepest abyss of woe by the same art. The prodigious fecundity of this extraordinary poet supplies a treasure for selection; in this particular, he is, in fact, without an equal.

It is true that Eschylus composed ninety-seven pieces; Sophocles one hundred and twenty, and Euripides seventy-five; but the plan, characters and execution of one of the good plays of Shakspeare appear to me, to have required more labour than three entire tragedies of ancient Greece.

Music being an imitative art, she should never lose her propriety : nature is her guide, and sentiment her judge. Music, without expression, and in which we cannot in a moment recognize character, cannot be esteemed good. Of what use is it for a musician to display his ability in certain mathematical calculations and harmonic combinations, if his music wants melody and expression?—The drama offers the finest field for the composer of music. It presents opportunities of producing the most astonishing effects of which the art is capable. It is in the opera that the enchanting powers of music are felt most perfectly. Here it is that music should *paint* every circumstance; that those sensations produced in us by its sweet sounds should be perfectly analogous to the objects before our eyes, which are thus imitated by the musical art. And in order that such imitations be perfect, and produce a true effect, the poet and the musician should understand each other completely; so that what was formed in the imagination of one, may, by the art of the other, be exactly rendered to us in melody. They are dependant one upon the other, and the same feeling should guide both. When the poetry is weak and inexpressive, the accompanying music also must be wanting in meaning and energy. It is very difficult to obtain this most desirable union of talent; consequently, when the composer is yoked with a mediocre poet, to avoid the disgrace that awaits the latter, he endeavours to shine unaided by that which alone should inspire him. The musician cannot be blamed for not reducing himself to the level of a wretched rhymer; but he would have merited praise, had he avoided a connexion, the united productions of which must ever remain imperfect and unequal. How frequently may this remark be heard, " The music is good, but the words are indifferent." Music should be "*married to immortal verse;*" but unhappy are the consequences for both, when the match is unequal: the merit of the worthy party is thrown into the shade by the vulgarity of the other. When verse, intrincically good, is united to music almost faultless, then must they become " a blessed pair." If the musician ought to be cautious in his choice of poetry, the Ballet-master should act in the same manner, if he would avoid a fall. The musician must continually subject his talent to express the sense of the words or action for which he is composing; they will always impart an interesting character to his productions. There should be between him and the poet a kind of amicable contest, as to who shall best delineate feeling, sentiment and passion; and the happy result will be a production purely dramatic, instead of a concert composition. When the Ballet composer gives his instructions to the musician, the latter must consider him as his poet, and proceed accordingly. In the works of the great original Italian masters may be found models of what is truly beautiful: to prove this, study Jomelli, Sarti, Buranello, Sacchini, Guglielmi, Piccini, Paesiello, and Cimarosa; they have ever preserved the appropriate distinction between the comic and the elevated styles; they have strictly observed the rank, characters, and names of the persons whom they have caused to act and sing;

they delineate the dramatic action, and convey an idea of the locality of the scene. Such productions as these do honour to the art, and have procured for their authors deserved celebrity. Music has its Sophocles, its Euripides, its Mænanders, and its Molières. The style of the above-named composers is so pure, sweet, and expressive, that though a considerable length of time should elapse without having heard their works performed, their airs are recollected with ease and delight ; so difficult is it to efface the impression they have once made : than this, no greater proof of musical excellence can be given. If the pictures of Correggio, Tiziano, Raphael, and Dominichino had been executed to interest the eye only, would these masters have been considered almost as divinities in their art ? The man of genius ever addresses himself to the heart ; and to attain this end, he copies and adores nature—she is his tutelar deity—she cannot deceive him, and even her apparent wanderings are admirable.

Madame de Stael, speaking of Italian music, says, upon the subject of the comic operas of Cimarosa and his contemporaries , " La gaîté même que la musique bouffe sait si bien exciter, n' est point une gaîté vulgaire qui ne dise rien à l'imagination. Au fond de la joie qu' elle donne, il y a des sensations poétiques, une rêverie agréable, que les plaisanteries parlées ne sauraient inspirer *." This music is the language of elegant nature, in her gayest humour. That comic spirit which prevails throughout the best Italian operas of this class is the same as that which is to be found in Molière and Goldoni ; not that which

---

* The sensation produced by listening to comic music is no low enjoyment, incapable of affording pleasure to the fancy ; there are certain poetic feelings at the bottom of the joy it excites ; a dreamy delight that spoken pleasantries can never inspire.

prevails in the very indifferent productions of the herd of scribblers, who are ambitious of adorning their pieces with all sorts of low and wearisome jokes, peculiarly adapted to the audience of a fair. The true value of music may be judged of from the sensations with which it inspires persons of good sense and delicate feeling. Such alone have a right to give an opinion upon the art.

The music of the *grand ballet*, like that of the *grand opera*, should be energetic, majestic, and exalted; its style must be sustained throughout, and well adapted to express the meaning of the subject. Here is no need of noise or false colouring; it is only necessary to express the passions with that strength and simplicity in which they naturally appear. We might suppose that the same soul inhabited the bodies of Virgil, Raphael, and Pergolèse; for the samestyle of genius prevails through the Æneid, the Transfiguration, and the Stabat. Perhaps the art of music never produced a more perfect piece than the last named *chef-d'œuvre*. Let the professors of the other arts endeavour to imitate Pergolèse, whose compositions are simple, regular, elegant, exalted, and sublime. This great master has succeeded in every species of composition, and given to each its appropriate character and expression. He adored the beauties of nature, and his copies of them are inimitable.

On no occasion can an able musician display so fully the imitative powers of his art as in the composition of an overture. Then it is that melody and harmony present to him a treasure of sounds, which he may turn to the greatest advantage. The sounds of which musical expression is composed may be compared to the pallet of a painter which presents a store of bright colours, from the disposition of which, the genius of the artist is to be estimated. Overtures are well adapted for the dance, which is best sustained by instrumental music. An overture to an opera or a Ballet is most essential; it should be an introduction; in it should be sketched the principal subjects of the piece for which it is composed; and when it is ably executed, it may even serve as a sort of programme to the audience, putting them into that state of mind best calculated to feel and understand the succeeding representation. " An overture," says F. A. Blasis, " should be the subject of an extensive musical picture, composed, by gradations or transitions, of the principal incidents that form the picture, and which ought to emanate from the action of the poem." One of the best overtures which I have heard, and which perhaps gives the most perfect idea of what is requisite to this species of composition, is that of the *Jeune Henri*, by Méhul. This admirable piece is characterized by the exactest truth of expression, the most brilliant effect, and the truest local description. From the first bar to the last note, the composer is occupied in giving a masterly sketch of the approaching opera. In describing the chase, nothing is omitted, from the moment the hunters assemble and set out, to that in which they seize their prey; nothing can be clearer or more energetic than the manner in which every thing is expressed. When I am listening to the music of Méhul, I can fancy I am beholding the pictures of Giulio Romano; the style is learned and correct; the colouring somewhat gloomy, but full of energy. His manner is noble and majestic, and better adapted to express subjects of a severe character than those of a light and elegant nature.

I have seen a Ballet, founded upon his overture to the *Jeune Henri*, and which produced an excellent effect. It served as a programme to the Ballet-master; he followed it strictly, and the success attending his production proved that he perfectly understood the language of harmony.

From this we may perceive that the arts mutually assist each other. The same subject that has served the composer of an opera, and the Ballet-master, may, also, be adopted by the painter.

The overture of the *Délire* of Berton supplied a certain pantomimic actor with the idea of a very beautiful monologue, the subject of which he expressed by gestures arising from sensations inspired by the music alone. Hence it may be seen, the greater our share of sensibility and understanding, the more easily do we seize those analogous relations subsisting between certain objects. Frequently the performance of the admirable overture of *La Gazza Ladra* sets the feet of the dancer in motion, and inspires the gestures of the mime. Haydn's cantata of *Ariana* has served as interpreter to one of the most striking pantomimic scenes ever exhibited at any theatre. Grétry's overture of *Elisca*, a composition that will be ever new, suggested to me the idea of a grand movement of warriors and amazons. In my Ballet of *Pygmalion*, certain airs of Mozart supplied me with thoughts suitable to that work. The opera of *Camille*, by D'Aleyrac, so far superior to that by Paer upon the same subject, presents us with passages of an energy and brilliance well adapted to pantomimic expression. The works of Boyeldieu and N. Isouard contain music very applicable to the Ballet. But Cherubini, Catel, and Le Sueur, being totally void of imagination, are quite useless to the dancer. The musician of Pesaro offers us a rich mine, but it requires some judgment to work it. The airs ought to be better disposed than they have been by the composer, who did not set about his work like a philosopher as well as a musician.

When the Ballet-master makes choice of a passage which he may judge suitable to convey his pantomime, let him not be always governed by the method in which it is made use of, for very frequently an air which is pla nly intended to express serious emotions has been joined to words of a comic character, and merry music attached to tragedy. I knew an artist who involuntarily produced a most biting satire on those confounders of style. He took some of the finest parts of a comic opera, and prefixed them to a serious Ballet; while to a comic Ballet, he attached an infinity of airs from a tragic opera, by the same author. The choreographer was deservedly applauded for this display of judgment in adaptation.

The ancients were particularly careful in preserving the concord between music and dancing ; they required that the most perfect analogy should continually prevail between the two arts. Rythmical music ruled their attitudes while dancing; and hyper-criticisms directed every gesture of the pantomime. The style and expression of the music was exactly adapted to the character of the piece represented. Consequently their good taste was clearly displayed in the most perfect imitations of nature. The music of dancing should always be spirited, full of cadence, and susceptible of inspiring motion; that of Pantomime, proceeding more directly from intense feeling, ought to possess an infinite variety of colouring ; its changes of style and expression should answer exactly to the changes of internal feeling. Such was the nature of the musical system established amongst the ancient Greeks and Romans. When melody and harmony, preserving each its proper sphere, become true organs of the feelings of the heart, music must exercise a dominion over us, at once powerful and delightful.

The object of the Ballet-master, like that of the painter, should be to give perfect represensations of nature; he should consider himself as her mirror, and thus reflect the images which she presents with the greatest truth. The illusion of the scene ought to be so perfect, as to cause what is merely artificial to appear real, during the time of its representation. Neither a picture nor a ballet can be deemed excellent, unless the art used in producing it is so far kept down, that nature only is admired in it; art should do its work unseen; its greatest triumph is to conceal itself.

When the artists of the latter end of the seventeenth and the beginning of the eighteenth century, in their various compositions, substituted a false and studied affectation for simplicity; confusion for clearness; mannerism for grace; the monstrous for the grand; the ridiculous for true sublimity, art lost her attractions, and men of pure taste could no longer imitate her. These artists spared no pains to render their pictures pleasing, by their vivacity and the splendour and variety of their colours. For this purpose, they decked their designs with gold and silver, precious stones, gorgeous drapery, and "luxury's most costly chattels." They sought to dazzle and astonish the multitude. Persons they looked upon as mere accessary objects in their compositions. They did not trouble themselves to inquire if they had to represent Romans or Egyptians, ancients or moderns—whether the same or a different costume ought to be adopted, or if different, in what the variations consisted—whether the action which they were about to paint occurred in Constantinople or Paris, in Mexico or Madrid; if nature, manners and customs were the same in all countries; if they ought to display gods or men, heroes or peasants, virtue or vice.

To this ignorant system, we are indebted for Cæsars in "the turbans of the Moslems," the heroes of ancient romance clad in the Spanish costume, and a number of anachronisms and errors of all kinds. They have depicted matrons, each looking like a Lais; and placed the head of an Adonis on the brawny shoulders of a Hercules. They have given the attitude of a Virginius at the moment of sacrificing his daughter, to the wisest of men when receiving the poisoned cup. They have expressed the calm courage of a martyr by the despair of an ordinary man surrounded by tortures. As the Ballet-master should copy the beauties of painting, so he ought to avoid its defects; more particularly those that we have just noticed, which are in such bad taste as to render them unpardonable.

We should know how to select and imitate our models with propriety; especially if they are not productions of the art which we profess. The Campi, the Gatti, the Procaccini, and almost all the painters of Lombardy of the last age, and also their imitators in France, seem to have modelled themselves upon the poetry of Lucan. The manner of this poet, his descriptions, and his images appear to have contributed to the formation of their talent, and the perfection of the style which they adopt. They must first have studied the principles of their art in the works of Michael Angelo and Tintoretto, and the manner of these great artists led them by degrees to the imitation of the poet we have mentioned, and such other authors as were the most mannered and gigantic in their compositions. Michael Angelo frequently exaggerates, and those who attempt to follow his path, without possessing his genius and bold execution, must frequently fail. This has been the case with several of the painters of whom I have just spoken; they carried the mannerism of Michael Angelo further than he did himself; they exaggerated his faults without equalling him in his good qualities. They abandoned themselves to the inspirations of the poet of Cordova; hence they exhibited outrageous

action for energy; bombast for grandeur; the gigantic
for the mighty; the incredible for the sublime; contortions for classical attitudes; confusion and disparity of
objects for genius.   Their works are, however, to be
admired for bold and fine touches, good colouring and
vigorous design.   Like the author of *Pharsalia*, they
have flashes of genius and points worthy of the most classic artist; they seem to have taken up the brush after
having read the Latin poem, and, like it, their works are
not without fire, poetic feeling and occasional depth ; but
these good qualities are overbalanced by inequalities and
imperfections.   Spontini, it may here be permitted to remark, is the Lucan, if not the Seneca of music.   De
Momigny makes the following remarks on him: " The Melpomene of the opera, still in her weeds, for Gluck, Piccini
and Sacchini, had not espoused any of the men of talent
to whom she had given a temporary reception at her court;
she thought for an instant, that, in the author of the music of *La Vestale*, she had found a successor to her three
husbands; two airs, the style and expression of which
were beautiful, a duet, and the finale of the second act of
that opera, had almost decided the royal muse on sharing
her throne with Spontini : but on examining his partitions,
and on sounding his powers and the fecundity of his genius, she felt the imprudence of such a step, and once
more, but not without regret, she resumed her widow's
weeds."

A few observations on a passage in Montesquieu may
be of some utility to the actor, as to the expression which
he ought to throw into certain characters, and to the
Ballet-master, on putting them in such action as may be
most suitable to their condition.

" Michael Angelo," says Montesquieu, " is the master
who imparts nobility to all his subjects.   In his celebrated

Bacchus, he differs from the Flemish painters, who exhibit a falling figure, which is, if we may so express it, in the air. This would be unworthy of the majesty of a God; he paints him firm on his legs; but the gaiety of intoxication, and the delight felt at seeing the liquor which he pours into his goblet, are so well expressed, that nothing can be more admirable. In the *Passion*, in the gallery of Florence, he has painted the Virgin Mary standing up, and looking at her crucified son without grief—without pity—without regret—without tears. He supposes that to her the grand mystery has been imparted, and that she is enabled to support, with grandeur, that spectacle of death.

" There is no work of Michael Angelo in which he has not thrown something noble; his roughest sketches, like the verses which Virgil has left unfinished, are grand. Giulio Romano, in his *Chamber of the Giants*, at Mantua, where he has represented Jupiter hurling his thunder at them, exhibits all the Gods in a state of terror. But Juno is near Jupiter; she indicates to him, with a calm air, a giant on whom he ought to lanch the thunderbolt; thus he imparts to her an air of grandeur which none of the other figures possess. Those who are nearest to Jupiter are the most collected, and this is very natural; in a battle, terror ceases in the bosoms of those who are near the party that has the advantage."

This, I should call painting philosophically, rather than nobly. The great writer who makes the preceding observations, appears to lay more stress on the moral than the physical part of the works of painters and sculptors. The artist who gives more grace and regularity of features to a face than it naturally possesses—who improves the elegance of a form—who agreeably softens all the contours —who throws more harmony and *d' ensemble* into a groupe—who imparts a greater charm to an attitude—who renders a motion more graceful—who diminishes the horror of an act, and avoids representing what is merely low and trivial—such an artist, it appears to me, ought to be regarded as one who embellishes all that he touches, and endows all his subjects with nobility, rather than such a one as the illustrious Montesquieu describes. He will compose and excute philosophically, and with a perfect knowledge of facts, and the characters of the persons he is about to represent ; he will not begin his work until he has learnt the causes and effects, the history of the time, and all else that is relative to, or in any way bears upon, the subject of the picture he is about to paint. He will not give Cæsar the body of a Goliath, but rather paint him with the look and deportment which, in an instant, will show him to be a man of extraordinary mind, whose occupation is universal command. He will not simply draw a mere old man for a Regulus, but endeavour to adorn him with an appearance of that gravity and heroic grandeur of soul for which, in life, he was so remarkable. He will neither give Scipio the air and attitude of a poltroon, nor exhibit Socrates despairing at the approach of the poisoned cup, nor make a young Vestal look like a Bacchante.

Objects may be represented with the greatest possible nobility, and, at the same time, they may be placed out of their centre, and be altogether contrary to truth and history. It is also possible to be true and natural, and still to want nobility in a painting: as the greatest example of this, Rubens may be instanced ; numberless other proofs of the assertion may be found in the works of the Flemish, Dutch, and German schools. In painting and in sculpture, we are inclined to understand, that an artist, who is said to work with nobility, is one who embellishes nature, who makes her more lovely than she is in parts, and who adroitly, and with excellent taste, avoids tracing all that is common and imperfect in her works. Taking the word in its moral sense, Montesquieu is right. It is more noble to show courage and firmness in one's last moments than cowardice and trepidation; but an artist ought to paint only what has been, what is, or what could have been, especially in an historical subject. The apparent tranquillity of the features of a stoic in the midst of tortures is doubtless to be admired; but this moral and physical power must not be given to all; it would be untrue and improper to paint all the characters on the canvas as unmoved by the greatest calamities.

The examples given by Montesquieu do not seem to me to bear out his assertion. By deceiving himself, he has probably led others into error. Raphael is the painter who, of all others, throws most true nobility into his subjects; the expression of his characters also is ever true and beautiful, and often sublime.

If the painter, like the poet, wishes to convey a moral lesson or a fact in the garb of allegory, he may then join truth and fiction, and represent things that are the mere creatures of imagination. He may be noble in his manner, although the different portions of the picture, taken separately, would not be approved by philosophy.

All our gestures are purely automatal, and signify nothing if the face is dumb in expression instead of animating and vivifying them. An actor who only moves his body and limbs is like a painter, who, while he carefully finishes the other parts of his picture, totally neglects the countenance, and thus produces the resemblance of a being deprived of all emotions, or like a poet who "builds the lofty rhyme" with words of majestic and harmonious sound, symmetrically placed, but totally devoid of idea.

At the first glance the man of taste turns from such productions with contempt. The musician will meet with
the same reception, if he attempt to compensate for the
energetic expression of nature by a superfluity of modulations, a mob of far-fetched prettinesses, and by that musical trifling *(papillotage)* which disgusts and fatigues.
"Di tanti palpiti" is worth the whole labyrinth of harmonic
combinations of Beethoven; a single air of Paesiello is
preferable to all the insignificant rhapsodies of Morlacchi;
and the musical accent with which Madame Pasta sings
" Ah! quante lagrime" is of more value than all the false
brilliancy of Pisaroni; one of her eloquent and heart-
touching gestures in *Desdemona,* when she is about to
fall a victim to the Moor's blind jealousy, or in *Medea,*
when going to bathe herself in the blood of her children,
is worth all the multiplied action of Bassi and Belloc in
the same characters. A singer for the stage should be
an actor, and not a mere automaton; he should play his
part, and not simply come forward and prove that he is
able to execute a difficult air. Without picturesque expression, the stage loses half of its interest and its charms.

The mime who wishes to represent the character he
undertakes, with credit to himself, ought to imitate the
composer of music, who, previous to sitting down to his
piano to produce his airs, attentively reads the poem
which he has to embellish, penetrates into the ideas of its
author, reflects upon the sense of the words, studies the
character and situation of the persons represented, and
particularly remarks the class to which the work belongs,
whether serious or comic, pastoral, heroic or otherwise.
The mime should do all this before he plays his part; he
should make himself well acquainted with the subject of
the Ballet, the action and the characters, and impress
upon his mind all that the author is desirous of represent-

ing. Without this preliminary study, he cannot reasonably hope for success, and his performance will be blemished by discord of action, anachronisms, improbabilities, and faults of every possible description. The musician is the interpreter of the poet, and the mime of the Ballet-master.

Nevertheless, however talented the mime may be, he can never be truly expressive or interesting, if the Ballet-master do not give him parts suitable to his powers, and such as will excite in him that enthusiasm without which every thing, in the fine arts, is weak and languishing.

At the theatre, nothing should be neglected; every thing should be made to contribute to the charm of the illusion. Ignorance and foolish indulgence are really detrimental to talent. Those artists who deem any infringement on old customs derogatory to good taste, and thus, by following bad examples, give them a current credit, are most reprehensible. They seem to have a religious respect for those monuments which still exist of a corrupted style; and thus, through their influence, art is fettered and advances slowly toward perfection. The same observation is applicable to those actors who, exaggerating expression and costume, render every subject unnatural. There was a time when, while authors endeavoured to imitate the language, and to depict the manners and passions of the heroes of Greece and Rome, some of them either tolerated, or do not seem to have been aware of, the follies of ridiculous actors, who presented to their spectators an Augustus or Germanicus, an Achilles or an Alexander, in the court-dress of Louis XIV, or Louis XV. The singers and dancers at the same time represented the Heathen divinities, and the heroes of chivalry, in the most extravagant dresses. This and the tasteless declamation of the tragedians were equally applauded; these absurdities were perfectly analogous, and seem to have upheld one another. Clairon was the first who strove to banish from the stage this ridiculous mode of costume, by dressing in habits suitable to the characters she played. Le Kain and Chassé advanced the cause of correct theatrical costume, and Talma brought it to perfection. Garrick, Kemble, and Mrs. Siddons did for the English what Clairon, Le Kain, Chassé, and Talma did for the French stage. Maximilian Gardel was the first who danced on the stage without a mask, and threw off the trammels with which ignorance and prejudice had long enslaved his art; Dauberval and P. Gardel followed in his steps, and adopted a proper and natural costume.

It has been conceived by a great number of actors that, in representing heroes, and in fact any characters that had rendered themselves illustrious by their talents, their virtues, or their exploits, it was necessary to strain the voice, and to gesticulate vehemently, in order to give a proper idea of the greatness of the persons they represented. They seemed to imagine that because those persons were above mankind in general, on account of their genius, or their great deeds, they also ought to go beyond them in their manner of acting and speaking. Many performers of pantomime hold a similar outrageous opinion; and it is the imperative duty of the Ballet-master, if he can, to correct such an error in conception, wherever he discovers it.

It is impossible that any hero of tradition or history may, by means of exaggerated action, be made known to the spectators. The young mime should beware of imitatating those artists who seem to have modelled themselves upon that ancient actor who played *Agamemnon* mounted upon stilts, in order to impart an idea of the king of the assembled Kings of Greece; being unable to depict the grandeur of *Agamemnon's* character otherwise than by representing him as being endowed with extraordinary height.

Kings and heroes are but men; they are subject to the same passions as their fellow mortals; education and rank only render them a little different from others in their manner of speaking and acting; nature is the same in them as in us; she may vary, but she never changes. Talma and the best English tragedians have felt the truth of this assertion. It is not forced and exaggerated action that is required on the stage, but sufficient energy of gesticulation, to express the passion of the moment to the distant spectators; it must at the same time be so restrained by good taste, that those who are near may not take offence at its extravagance. The actor should possess the qualities of receiving and conveying impressions. There are some performers who, while they rouse the feelings of those who behold them, are perfectly cold and void of passion themselves; art enables them to express, by outward signs, what they do not feel, but nevertheless well understand. There are others, who are in a considerable degree affected by the sentiments which they wish to express, but they are totally unable to manifest them. For the stage, of course, the former sort of persons, although objectionable, are to be preferred by far to the latter.

Nature furnishes us with abundant means of interesting an audience. An actor should profoundly study the human heart, and the various pictures of life which the different classes of society present. The art of imitating nature does not consist in merely moving and speaking like such or such an actor, or in dressing a character like one who is celebrated for his performance of it; this is copying a copy, the vice of mediocre artists and men of little mind or originality. We should go to the fountain head of truth, and found ourselves on nature, and not on her imitators, however excellent they may be; they may improve, but they cannot perfect us. The master may teach his pupil much, but from nature, when the master has done with him, he will learn more; and, what is most important, he will acquire sufficient knowledge to correct the errors which he has been taught by one whom he once thought perfect in his art. There are some masters who do not scruple to set themselves up as models for their scholars; this is ignorance and folly. A good master points out what is good and corrects what is faulty, to the best of his power; but he does not insist on his pupil forming himself entirely on his manner—no individual being endowed with perfection in every department of the art he professes. Such a constraint would also tend to strangle in their birth all the emotions of a heart capable of feeling the beauties of nature, and the effects of a mind possessed of the power of devising means to express them.

Violent and excessive gesticulation is most frequently accompanied by want of sensibility. It is unnatural, and consequently obnoxious to good taste. A multitude of gestures is not necessary to express even the deepest passion of which the human heart is susceptible; the eye, aided by the slightest movement, will often make it as manifest as possible.

The time has been (and some performers in our own days are guilty of similar absurdities) when actors, whether the dialogue of the piece required it or not, assumed the most solemn and emphatic tone; they "split the ears of the groundlings" when saying or relating the most simple and indifferent things; some of them imposed on the multitude by an inflexible tragic deportment, which was, in most cases, ridiculous, because out of character;

while others, when playing an enraged hero, howled and shrieked like furies. The greater part of those actors invariably assumed the look of conspirators; on the first appearance of one of them, a spectator of taste would be led to believe that he had to murder three or four people in the course of the piece ; whereas, when the curtain fell, it turned out that he had murdered nobody but the author. The most monotonous and psalmodic declamation accompanied these mysterious looks. The actresses thought that when they laid aside the comic sock to assume the Greek or Roman mantle, it was improper to act naturally. They assumed the most lugubrious aspect, and their deportment and walk were those of a criminal going toward the scaffold. They spoke in that lamentable tone, the continuation of which is enough to distress the most insensible being ; they studied to give their voice a convulsive trembling, and to make each verse " drag its slow length along" in the most insufferable manner ; and finally, in order to produce great effects, they called to their aid deep, protracted or (if we may use the expression with impunity) wire-drawn sighs, tears, groans, sobs, and shrieks, when there was not the least occasion, or even excuse, for either. The mime should shun the imitation of these vices; denied, as he is, the use of words, in him they would become, if possible, more reprehensible and ridiculous than in a mock tragedian.

Why should we not act like those who are really under the influence of the passion which we are desirous of representing ? Must *Zayre*, in order to move and affect us, never for an instant drop the tone of bitter lamentation ? Is it necessary for *Hermione* to stun us unceasingly, in order to depict the rage which devours her ?— or, to render *Achilles* more outrageous than he is in the Iliad, in order to give the spectators a true idea of his impetuous character ?—" From the sublime to the ridiculous there is but a step."

The theatrical art is an union of all the others—poetry, music, painting, dancing, pantomime, architecture, &c.; well-informed persons, therefore, only can be good judges of the merits or demerits of dramatic productions. People in general, however, think otherwise ; the facility afforded of going to a theatre, and there enjoying a perfect liberty of thought and action, as it were, makes all men critics. Dramatic works have not the same advantages as other productions of art. In a theatre, all who pay at the door criticise the piece, and every body pronounces boldly and definitively on its value. If the same mob of judges were taken to a gallery of paintings and statues, two thirds, at the least, of them would frankly and modestly avow, that they were not connoisseurs enough to decide on what was presented for their opinions. And is it less difficult to pronounce judgment on the poet, the composer, or the performer, than the sculptor and the painter? We do not think so. A picture or a statue, expressing but a single action—the simple movement of a passion, makes an impression on our senses, which lasts as long as the object remains before our eyes, and gives us time to analyze our ideas, and to pronounce a just opinion upon it. But it is a different case with the talent of an actor, who, in a single hour, depicts many passions, and different combinations of them; during this brief space, he presents a multitude of pictures, each of which makes only a fugitive impression upon the mind, impatient all the time to arrive at the denouement. It is necessary to possess a fine tact, and considerable experience, to follow this moral painter in his rapid but powerful pictures, each of which disappears before its successor is exhibited. Mere literary knowledge is not a sufficient qualification for a man to become a judge of acting. A superior writer on philosophy, morals, or history, may not have the least idea of the picturesque of those same passions, with whose influence in society he is well acquainted. To be qualified to judge discreetly of the children of Thespis, it is necessary to have seen the world, to have examined with attention the physical expression and modulation of the passions in different physiognomies, and in the different stations of life, to have studied this expression in the tones of the voice, and to have a natural penchant for imitation.

The composer of Ballets, as well as the poet, the musician, and the painter, ought to consult the taste of the public for whom he works. All the civilized nations of Europe admire beautiful imitations of nature, and unanimously reject whatever is grossly at variance with her; nevertheless, the genius, the characters, and the manners of different nations, give each of them a particular idea of taste on certain matters. The artist who, without forgetting that " one touch of nature makes all mankind kin," submits to this difference of natural taste will thereby give an additional proof of his talent. In fact, if we call to mind the most illustrious men of England, France, Italy, Germany, Spain, and other countries, we shall find, that although they are admired for beauties which are not merely national, that they are not, in some instances " of an age, but for all time," they, nevertheless, have other merits which are not, and indeed cannot be, sufficiently felt and appreciated by readers of a different age or nation. The most ardent admirer of Shakspeare in France, even if treating the same subject, would never do so in a similar manner to the immortal bard of England; an Italian may passionately admire Klopstock, but he will not take him for a model; the

poems of Ossian may be applauded on the banks of the
Tagus, but they will find no imitators among the Portu-
guese. While we endeavour, so far as we can, to attain
perfection, we should not lose sight of the taste of the
people for whom we compose. (An attempt has been
made to carry this idea into effect, in the preceding programmes of different styles of Ballets.) The man of genius
belongs to every nation; happy is he, who, charmed with
the works of the authors of *Othello*, of *Britannicus*, of
Orlando, of *Telemachus*, of the *Lusiad*, of *Faust*, of the
Hero of La Mancha, &c. &c., may, by availing himself of
their example, and profiting by their exertions in the mine
of thought, one day attain a name equal to that of the
least of them!

We have already detailed the different dramatic styles
and opinions of the most celebrated critics on each of them,
and the ideas which a study of the best authors and practical observation have suggested to us on the subject.
The styles which are pre-eminent over all others are the
classic and the romantic. These offer us a thousand
means of succeeding : both have their charms and their
defects. If one may often be accused of tameness, the
other is frequently to blame for running into the opposite
fault. Each is supported by such splendid talent, that it
is difficult for the young author or artist to decide which
he shall make his model. If one attract by powerful
charms, he is soon after exposed to the seductive beauties displayed by the other, of which its rival is utterly
ignorant. A fine philosophy, a pure taste, and an un-
prejudiced mind, can alone endow him with the means of
steering an advantageous middle course between them,
adopting the beauties of both, without falling into the
faults of either. The artist cannot act thus without entirely laying aside his national prejudices. He should not

only respect the altars which have been raised to Thalia and Melpomene in his own country, but also reverence those which have been erected to their honour in other nations,—on the banks of the Thames and the Seine, beyond the Alps, and wherever else homage is done to the Muses. There are schools of actors as well as of authors; while we cannot help feeling discontented with the cold follower of the classic, and the extravagant votary of the romantic style, we applaud with transport those who are wise enough to be at once classic and imaginative, or romantic without becoming unreasonable. The actor should not lose his time in the study of those lengthened, and frequently useless, discussions of such critics as carry their views so far as to lose sight of the principal objects of criticism ; who, when they ought to have been discussing the merit of styles, have disputed upon authors, and when they should have treated upon authors, have merely babbled about style; authors have been thus decried on account of the style which they followed, and a species of composition censured and attacked through writers who adopted it. The author, or the artist, who pleases and interests the judicious and the feeling, must needs be a follower of nature, and, therefore, admirable whatever may be the style or school which he has adopted. The grand aim of the Ballet-master, the mime, and the dancer, should be the embellishment and improvement of the art; to grace it with all the nobleness, the splendour, and beauty of which it is susceptible; to render it worthy of the place it occupies among the other fine arts, and to make them all contribute as much as possible to so laudable—so desirable an object.

CONTENTS.

———

PART THE THIRD.

PART THE FOURTH.

546 CONTENTS.

PART THE SIXTH.

THE MOST GENERALLY KNOWN FIGURES IN QUADRILLES.

CONCLUSION.

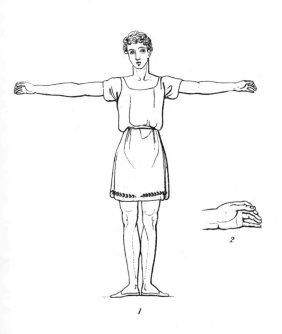

PLATE I.

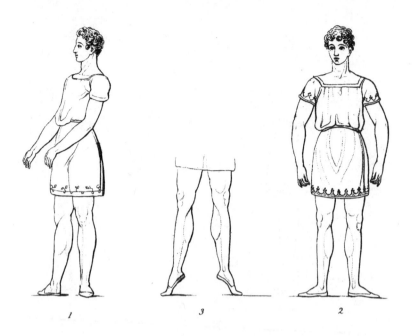

PLATE II.

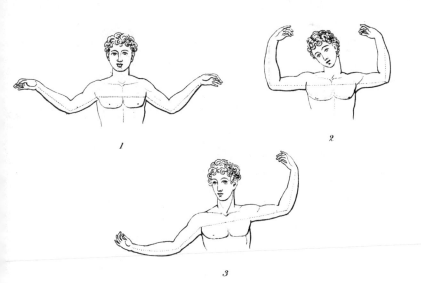

1

2

3

PLATE III.

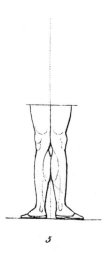

4

5

PLATE IV.

1

2

PLATE V.

3

5

4

PLATE VI.

1   2

PLATE VII.

3   4

PLATE VIII.

1

2

3

4

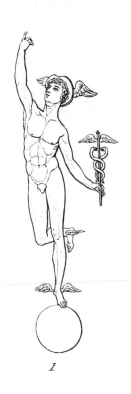

1

2

PLATE IX.

3

4

PLATE X.

1   2   3   4

PLATE XI.

1

2

PLATE XII.

3

4

PLATE XIII.

1

PLATE XIV.

4

2   3

PLATE XIVA.

5

PLATE XV.

1

2

3

4

1   2

PLATE XVI.

3

Quadrilles. by Mr. Blasis.

L'Aurore.

Fine.

La Fantasque.

Fine.

La Coquette.

La Jalouse.

Fine.

La Virginie.

Fine.

L'Irma.

La Léon .

Fine.

Two Original Waltzes by M.elle Blasis.
N.o 1. La Gracieuse.

La Bizarre.

22